Frank Roney, 1906

FRANK RONEY

IRISH REBEL

AND

CALIFORNIA LABOR LEADER

FRANK RONEY

IRISH REBEL
AND
CALIFORNIA LABOR LEADER

AN AUTOBIOGRAPHY

EDITED BY

IRA B. CROSS

UNIVERSITY OF CALIFORNIA PRESS
BERKELEY, CALIFORNIA
1931

UNIVERSITY OF CALIFORNIA PRESS
BERKELEY, CALIFORNIA

CAMBRIDGE UNIVERSITY PRESS
LONDON, ENGLAND

CONTENTS

LIST OF ILLUSTRATIONS

EDITOR'S INTRODUCTION

The labor movement of California has been unique in many ways, due largely to the fact that it developed out of conditions unlike those which prevailed in other communities. To the east of the Rocky Mountains, Organized Labor was from the first compelled to battle for higher wages, shorter hours, and improved working conditions. In California the reverse was true. The scarcity of population during the early period enabled the workers to start with a high rate of wages and with considerable control over working conditions. Until about 1870, they were concerned primarily with meeting the attacks of employers who were desirous of lowering the prevailing standards. With the completion of the transcontinental railroad in 1869, however, large amounts of eastern goods and great numbers of eastern laborers came into the California markets, and in the resulting competition old standards were brushed aside. The contest henceforth assumed a different character, and the labor movement became more closely allied in practices and in ideals with that of eastern communities.

Particularly unique to the labor movement in California was the ever-present competition of Oriental labor, first the Chinese, and then in succession the Japanese, the Hindu, and the Filipino.

EDITOR'S INTRODUCTION

It did not take long for an organized movement to develop among the members of the working class of California. Led by men who rose from the ranks and who were sent out from the East to champion their Cause, they blazed new trails in the field of Labor and in many instances established standards and practices later to be adopted by organized workers elsewhere. Kenaday, Winn, Kearney, Roney, Haskell, Fuhrman, are names that recall brilliant leaders during that early period.

I came to California in the fall of 1906 primarily to study at first hand this unique economic development and to write its history. I had been engaged at the task for only a few months when I realized that each successive wave of organization that had swept over the workers of the state from the days of the gold rush down into the early nineties, had been dominated more or less completely by some one personality. After 1893, however, the California labor movement became so complex that it was no longer possible for any one person, no matter how rarely equipped with outstanding qualities of leadership, to hope to dominate completely a situation so exacting in its demands.

During the "Uncertain Fifties" a number of unions had been organized, for the most part in a sort of "hit and miss" fashion, each union being interested only in its immediate demands, and usually disbanding when the occasion for its existence had passed. Early in the "Prosperous Sixties,'' however, success crowned the efforts of the few men interested in the formation of a central labor body, and in 1863 ''The San Francisco Trades Union'' was organized. During the next three years the local labor movement revolved around Alexander M. Kenaday, a union printer. Kenaday had assisted in organizing the typographical union of San Francisco in 1854, had served as its president, and had been instrumental in bringing about its affiliation with the national union of that craft. He was secretary, and later the third president, of the San Francisco Trades Union, and in the latter capacity originated the campaign, which was unsuccessful, for the eight-hour day in California. Kenaday also established the first labor paper on the Pacific Coast, *The Journal of Trades and Workingmen,* which survived for but a few issues. He further attempted, again unsuccessfully, to link the California unions more closely with the national movement by urging the establishment of local branches of the National Labor Union, of which he was at that time a vice-president.

During 1867–1873, the outstanding local labor leader was General A. M. Winn, a retired carpenter. In November 1867 he organized the first state federation of labor, ''The Mechanics State Council,'' and brought life and enthusiasm to the local movement. He also successfully carried on the agitation for the shorter workday, which resulted in the passage of the eight-hour-day law by the State Legislature in

1868. For some years thereafter, practically all craftsmen in the larger cities of California worked only eight hours a day. Winn, like Kenaday, entered the field of labor journalism by establishing a weekly paper, *The Shop and Senate,* which succumbed after a feeble existence of about a year.

Hard times and the anti-Chinese agitation during the seventies destroyed the union movement as such, and in consequence, the elements of discontent found an outlet in the campaign of the Workingmen's Party of California against the Mongolians. Although this movement was not trade union in character, nevertheless it enlisted the support and cooperation of those men who otherwise would have been active in the ranks of Organized Labor. Its leader, Dennis Kearney, an employing drayman, knew nothing about the ideals or history of unionism. In fact, at no time did he show any evidence of being even remotely concerned with the efforts of the workers to better their condition by means of that economic weapon.

Following Kearney, came Frank Roney, a molder, the man around whose life and activities is woven the tale told in the following pages. He dominated the labor movement of San Francisco during 1881–1886, and was capably assisted by a brilliant group of forward-looking men, such as Burgman, Hagerty, Wilson, Haskell, and others.

Succeeding Roney came Alfred Fuhrman, a sailor, whose greatest work was the organization of the brewery employees, but who visioned and created a Pacific Coast federation of unions, which was destined to be short-lived, but which it was hoped would be to the western labor group what the American Federation of Labor later became to the labor movement of the nation. In his work he was also assisted by certain lesser lights, but Fuhrman was the dominating figure from 1886 to 1893.

By the time that I arrived in California, both Kenaday and Winn were dead and forgotton. None of the local labor leaders had any knowledge of either of these two pioneers or of the work which they had done for the working class of the State. Kearney, a more spectacular personality, was remembered, but no one appeared to know whether or not he was still alive. I finally located an "old timer" who told me where I could find him, but my disappointment was great when I called at the address given only to find that he had died but a few weeks prior to my visit.

Only a handful of those active in the ranks of Labor in San Francisco remembered Roney and Fuhrman. It is indeed true that "Men close their doors to the setting sun." I found Fuhrman easily, for he was an attorney in San Francisco, having taken up the practice of law upon his retirement from the labor movement in 1893. Roney was more difficult to locate. I think that it was Burnette G. Haskell who told me that he had last heard of Roney as an employee in the foundry at the Mare Island

Navy Yard. Several letters passed between us and finally the long-anticipated conference was arranged.

I met Roney at his rooms in Vallejo just as he came from work. He was living alone, his first wife having died in 1904, and he was not at that time living with his second wife, whom he had married in 1906. Here was a big, broad-shouldered molder in dirty clothes, with rough, powerful hands hardened by working in the sand and with carrying the ladle. His hair was gray and shaggy; his moustache, large, bushy, and gray. His eyes looked out from under heavy eyebrows. I cannot remember their color, but I think that they were dark gray. I know that they were kindly, and just a little dulled with age, for Roney at that time was in his sixty-third year. His face carried a tired, but sympathetic expression. I felt myself in the presence of one who had found the world filled with misery, poverty, and selfishness, and had tried unsuccessfully to shape it more nearly to his ideals of what it ought to be. Although well along in years, and at a time when most men are willing to cry "Enough," he impressed me as still possessing vitality and energy sufficient to wage, if necessary, a good battle for the things in which he believed.

Roney was unlike the usual type of present-day labor leader. He had poise, deliberateness, culture of a self-obtained sort, a love and appreciation of the better things of life, a marvelous vocabulary of well chosen words, a strong but quietly controlled voice—in a word, a refinement seldom met with among those who at present lead the forces of Labor. His was an unusual personality, but the sort that I have met several times in the persons of the "grand old men," east and west, who participated in the working-class agitation of the eighties.

After changing from his working clothes, he consented to accompany me to a near-by restaurant where we sat for hours conversing about "the days of long ago." Back at his rooms, more hours were spent recalling the events of the past. Many other conferences followed, each as fruitful of information as the first, for Roney was a veritable mine of data concerning the labor movement of San Francisco during the period 1876–1886 in which he had played a part, usually a leading part. By nature he was a leader in all the movements with which he had been connected. He knew men, their ideas and activities. He placed dates of events accurately. He explained many things to me that I had misunderstood, and told me many others of which I had been ignorant. While we conversed he also recounted his experiences as a rebel in Ireland, where he had been a member of the inner group of the Fenian organization.

I was amazed at his remarkable memory, unclouded by the events of passing years. I marveled that one so long removed from the happenings of the past and without notes or data to guide him could recall so many events so accurately, and especially place dates with such uncanny exactness.

As little by little he unfolded his life's story I began to urge him, and then to insist, that he write his story for me so that it might be read by future generations. I felt that here was a man whose biography was worth recording, not alone for its historical value, but because of the inspiration it would hold for others. I wanted the rank and file of the California labor movement to know something of the trials and troubles, the failures and successes, of one of their group who had taken such a prominent part in laying the foundation of the present status of Labor in this State. I felt strongly in accord with one who wrote, "Not the great historical events, but the personal incidents that call up single, sharp pictures of some human in his pang or struggle, reach us more nearly." I remembered in 1903 having read with keen interest and profit *The Story of a Labor Agitator,* by Joseph R. Buchanan, in which he related many incidents that had occurred in connection with his efforts to better the condition of the workers of the Rocky Mountain region. I remembered Henry George's statement that "The history of the struggle for human rights will never be complete without the personal records of the men who occupied important positions on the firing line in that crucial period between 1880 and 1890."

Here was a man who had played on the western rim of the United States a far more constructive part than had many better known figures in the eastern labor movement, yet whose name was unknown to the writers of labor histories and to the present leaders of the working class, both east and west. Here was a man who had taken a vital part in one of the many attempts to free Ireland from the domination and oppression of England, and because the part that he had played was to a great extent secret in character, none of the historians of Ireland or of the revolutionary movements of that country had mentioned his name and work.

Consequently I urged with all my power of persuasion that Roney write his autobiography for me. But, modest as such men usually are, he took my urgings lightly. In fact for some years he scoffed at the idea that any person other than myself could or would be interested in what he had attempted to do for the poor and oppressed of Ireland and of the United States. In a letter addressed to me, dated October 28, 1907, he wrote,

> I really do not see the use of placing my biography before the world. If I had accomplished something of value to the people or had written or spoken in a manner out of the common, there might be some excuse for inflicting such a biography on the world. As I have done nothing to merit distinction more than hundreds of well intentioned men have done, it would be a mistake to deprive me of my obscurity. I have no vain-glorious ambitions to serve, and am supremely satisfied to believe that I contributed a little towards planting the seed that in time will fructify and give to poor suffering mankind the full fruit of their industry. That self-consciousness is enough for me.

I continued to insist, although with no apparent effect upon his attitude of refusing to listen to my pleas and arguments.

In January, 1909, Roney was taken seriously ill. He gave up his employment at the Mare Island Navy Yard, and went to Watts near Los Angeles to be with a son. On February 28, 1909, he wrote:

> After New Year's Day I became so unwell I believed I was going to die. There was a continuous downpour which added to the depression, and as I had a son here I proposed to die where he was rather than among strangers, however kind and considerate they might be, if I could only make the trip in all that storm. So I quit the Navy Yard and arrived here more dead than alive. Since coming here, I have bought a little place and otherwise have recruited so that I believe myself good for a long time.

My insistence now began to take effect, for a few months later he informed me that he would soon start writing the story of his life. In his next letter, however, he advised me that the State Legislature had authorized the taking of a census of the Japanese and that he was to be one of the enumerators; consequently, the autobiography was to be postponed. Roney obtained this employment with the State Bureau of Labor Statistics as one of the census-takers through the influence of one of its deputies, who was the son of the elderly woman whom he had married in 1906. For reasons known only to themselves, Roney and his second wife wished to keep their marriage "quiet," as he wrote me, and up to the time of her death in San Francisco in September,

1912, they had never lived together as man and wife, although constantly planning to do so.

Roney returned to Watts after serving for about fourteen months on the staff of the State Bureau of Labor Statistics. He did not long remain there, but again returned to San Francisco. His affairs seemed to go from bad to worse, and on January 23, 1912, I received a most pathetic note telling me of his failure to obtain employment of any sort in that city. He concluded with the following statement:

I am so disturbed mentally that I am unable to write as you wish. I think, however, I will be able to do something in the line you suggested very soon. I am fixing up such trifling affairs as I am concerned in, preparatory to entering the Home for the Aged and Infirm, a county institution, where I may bury myself, or at any rate be removed, while I live, from contact with the outer world. I am thinking of going to the Home on Thursday to be no longer a trouble to any one and to be forgotten.

His old pride, however, got the better of him, and on February 18, 1912, he informed me that,

When it came to put my resolution into effect I balked. I could not by any reasoning I attempted bring myself to do this thing, and yet I did not know what to do or which way to turn. Conditions have not improved a bit since then and still I am averse to taking this final leap into obscurity. I am obscure enough as it is but that would mean total obliteration.

Roney continued tramping the streets of San Francisco, unsuccessful at finding employment. I have never learned how he subsisted in the meantime. At last on January 8, 1913, word came from him that he was leaving for Los Angeles permanently to reside in that city. He added,

> The invitation comes from a son with whom I corresponded very rarely. Had he known I was so used up he would have asked me long ago. But to my relatives and most of my friends I have never made complaint, bearing in silence the afflictions it has pleased God to visit upon me. These are mainly due to a proper discretion as to the want of looking ahead and making hay in the right season. However, I don't kick at anyone but myself, and I do that in a cheerful mood.

Apparently he was for a time thereafter happily situated. He had no "bread and butter worries," and at last started to write his life's story. On August 3, 1915, I received a letter from him which in part was as follows:

> I am getting along slowly and not very satisfactorily with the writing. Only 520 pages are written. A good deal of it will have to be rewritten and some of it will have to be cut out. I write at intervals and not for long at a time. I got as far as Vallejo with it. . . .
>
> You will think it a ridiculous production, I fear, and open both to criticism and censure. However, there is a bit of originality about it which, for its awkwardness, is its only commendable feature.

In October, 1915, he sent me the manuscript with the request that I make suggestions for its improvement. I read it with care, noting suggested changes here and there, rearranging sentences, checking spelling, removing occasional grammatical errors, and subsequently returned it to him with my comments. Roney replied as follows on February 16, 1916:

I would have been better satisfied if you had been harsh, knowing that your intentions were for the production of something decently readable and my own good. I may assure you that I am not at all charmed with this production. When I compare it with what I have read from others, it falls far below what it ought to be. But for the life of me I cannot amend my errors by my own criticism. . . . The fact is except here and there throughout the story, I wrote mechanically and not sympathetically with the work itself or those who might read it, if it ever will be read by others than you and me.

On December 16, 1916, Roney wrote that his son, with whom he had been living, had given up housekeeping in order to get rid of him and that he had been left "homeless as well as penniless and without employment. . . . I could hardly conceive this thing to be possible, that so much ingratitude and lack of regard for a parent, who has always been kind to him and generous, could exist. But one never can tell." I never knew how or with whom Roney lived thereafter. But although his heart was broken, his spirit and determination appeared to be indomitable. He would not permit himself to be crushed by any disappointment, no matter how great.

With some persons, youthful enthusiasms and early love for a Cause pass only with death. Burnette G. Haskell, that brilliant, erratic, and radical agitator in the San Francisco labor movement of the early eighties, wrote as follows to Roney in the spring of 1906: "Damn that old Cause that keeps our consciences working all the time and will not let us sleep and dream in peace. . . ." So, too, with Roney. Age and disappointment had not dimmed his love for the under-dog, nor weakened his desire to assist the working class wherever possible. Accordingly, we see him during 1915–16 becoming closely allied with the labor movement in Los Angeles. He writes articles for *The Citizen*, a labor paper of that city, describing how the workers of San Francisco won their battles during the formative period of the eighties and advising the Los Angeles workers to do likewise. He makes friends with those who are leading the local movement. He is elected secretary-treasurer of the Los Angeles Metal Trades Council and is again on the firing line of the forces of labor. He was then seventy-six years of age. I have often thought how fitting it might have been had he "died in the harness" as the secretary-treasurer of that labor body, which was one of many such organizations formed in accordance with a plan which he had formulated and published as early as 1869.

Time sped on. Our letters became less and less frequent. In the fall of 1923, in response to my inquiry as to how the manuscript was progressing, Roney wrote that,

> I wished to get it into better shape if I can, but the obstacles prevent speed. I am somewhat handicapped for lack of facilities to write and also physical disadvantages. The weather is as favorable for me to do the work as I need expect. Yet I can hardly do it.

I will send it along with its imperfections and omissions, trusting to your kind offer to whip into shape the subsequent additions I will send.

On February 7, 1924, he wrote that,

My facilities for working are anything but good and my physical disabilities are many and are often, too often, present inopportunely. I will get to the end of it, I hope, soon, and not a great while from now. Just favor me with your patience.

Each written message carried indications of increasing physical infirmities. The body would not respond to the urgings of the brain. His penmanship was not so strong nor so virile as before; the letters of each word were not so carefully formed; but the thought behind every sentence was as clear and as penetrating as always. The body might weaken, but the spirit refused to grow dulled with years.

Finally on November 10, 1924, came the last message, in which for the first time Roney acknowledged that the end was not far off. It was penned with an unsteady hand. He wrote as follows, consigning the manuscript to my care:

When I requested your forbearance some months ago, I was under the impression that with the coming of good weather I would be able to add something of value to the manuscript, but I find now that winter is coming and nothing done in the interim. I am unable to do what I then hoped to do. I give the job up and so send it to you with all its imperfections.

I regret that with procrastination has come physical weakness which prevents me from further effort in the matter.

It was my intention to write on the Japanese question in which I had been intimately concerned for fourteen months, and other matters. Now I can't do it. Pardon me.

Two months later Death stilled for all time the voice and pen of this friend of the poor and oppressed of two nations. On the morning of January 24, 1925, at the age of 84, Frank Roney, Irish rebel and California labor leader, expired suddenly while dressing. He was then living in Long Beach, California. He was survived by a wife, his third, whom he had married a few years prior to his death.

Thus passed a man who gave much of himself that others might enjoy better and fuller lives; who sacrificed family, fortune, and future to a faith in ideals; a leader who found human souls weak and faithless, but who in spite of endless disappointments continued to the last his efforts to better the condition of the oppressed.

Roney was an idealist forced by the nature of events to attempt to fit into this earthly scheme of things. His head was in the clouds although he made a serious effort to keep his feet on the ground. The ideals learned at his mother's knee and in the private school and the church of his youth remained with him throughout his life. As a lad and young man he took his Faith much to heart. One of his earliest disappointments, while engaged in organizing the Fenian movement, was to learn that the Catholic Church was interested in salvation after death rather than liberty for the masses while alive.

Thenceforth, the Church dropped completely out of his life, for his personal religion was concerned with securing economic and political freedom and happiness for the downtrodden of the earth.

Roney loved the ideals of Freedom. Throughout his life they dominated his ideas and his activities. Happiness in all walks of life would come if only the people might have Freedom. Poverty, misery, crime, all these would pass away with its attainment. He wanted the Irish people to be free; he wanted the American workingman to be free; and to obtain that Freedom, he for one was willing to sacrifice self, friends, and family.

As an unmarried man and leader of the Irish rebels, his earnings as a craftsman went to pay part of the costs of the Fenian uprising. As a political leader in Nebraska, his wages went to pay the costs of the campaign of the National Labor Reform Party. As a married man and a labor leader in San Francisco, he bore without complaint much of the expense of carrying on the agitation for the organization of the trade union movement in that city. In one of his many letters to me he wrote that, "The expenses of those early days of struggle [in San Francisco] were borne by each individual as best he could. This kept some of us in a constant condition of impecuniosity, not to say of absolute poverty." A strange contrast to present-day conditions when salaries, sometimes large sums, are paid to union officials, and costs of organization and management are borne by the rank and file of the movement!

Yet that was the life that Roney chose to lead. He had opportunities, many of them, to change his ways, to turn his back upon those for whose welfare he eagerly fought. Wealth could have been his, but he preferred to cast his lot with those whom he felt needed his assistance. His ideals would not let him accumulate wealth by questionable methods or at the sacrifice of the interests of others. In addition to the instances of such rejected opportunities cited by Roney in the following pages, he told me of still another, viz., of how Irving M. Scott, a prominent employer in the iron trades of San Francisco, urged him to establish himself in the foundry business. "You will find," said Scott, "that after your years of sacrifice for these workingmen, they will forget you and flout you. Nor will they consider that you have done anything for them. They will give to the fellow without honesty that due which is yours." And Roney, in telling me of the incident, added, "I have lived to see Scott's prophecy fulfilled completely. The ingratitude that I experience is the only thing in my career that causes me sometimes to think that I should have followed Scott's advice. But what's the use of regrets of that sort?"

But in spite of the shameless ingratitude which the workers have always shown toward those who have sacrificed their personal interests in order that the lot of the common people may be improved, with the memory of his disappointments, and they were many, and with the companionship of only poverty and friendlessness in his old age, Roney still had the courage, the faith in his ideals, frequently to say that "Under the same circumstances, I'd likely do the same thing again."

Roney was tolerant, tolerant of the opinions and ideals of others, tolerant of the shortcomings and weaknesses of those who failed him in his hours of need. He had learned the spirit of tolerance from the teachings of his mother and from the practices of his father. To him at all times men were of equal worth regardless of race and ancestry. He stood for men, not for race or creed. It was therefore difficult for him to modify his ideals and wage a campaign against the Chinese in California and against Chinese-made goods, as he did while a member of the Workingmen's Party of California and as secretary of the League of Deliverance. But he did so because he felt that he was not fighting the Chinese as Chinese, but as workers who were lowering the plane of living of the California people. He waged an equally vigorous campaign against the members of his own white race who were non-union men and who were working long hours and for low wages. Roney was not one of those weather-vane individuals who sacrifice principles in order to follow the crowd. If the crowd wanted to follow him, it had to follow where he led. His ideals meant too much to him to be quickly or easily cast aside for reasons of diplomacy.

Although Roney was tolerant of the ideas of others and of race and creed, he was nevertheless a hard man with whom to work. He had decided opinions as to how everything ought to be done and felt that he was correct. From his viewpoint, his ideas were the only ones for the group to accept and he fearlessly fought to uphold them, brooking no interference or opposition from his associates. Sooner or later he broke with practically all of the latter. In his own story that follows, he tells how he broke with Kearney, Devereux, Haskell, Fuhrman, and others. In all cases, naturally, he felt justified in doing so. But Roney did not believe himself to be without faults. He recognized many of his own shortcomings and criticized himself as severely as he did others. And, so far as I have been able to ascertain, he never attempted to condone his own actions, although at times he willingly and gladly did so in the case of others.

Roney was a leader, a born leader of powerful and dominating personality. As a young man in the Fenian movement he early became an outstanding figure because of his qualities of leadership. In Omaha, Salt Lake City, San Francisco, wherever he went, he was a leader. He was inherently an organizer. He had learned the necessity and benefits of organization in the Fenian uprising. He held constantly before him the memory of his father's action as secretary of the Belfast carpenters' union in not permitting a demand for the ten-hour day to be made until the men were completely organized. To organize thoroughly was one of Roney's fundamental principles, but he was never willing to use the power of organization brutally or uselessly. Strikes and labor disputes of all kinds were, in his opinion, costly and to be avoided wherever possible. Employers should be met with, talked with, arbitrated with—in fact, everything humanly possible should be done to prevent conflict and monetary loss to both sides. But if a strike proved necessary and unavoidable, then every means was to be employed to make its outcome favorable to the workers.

Roney was opposed to the policy of the closed shop. He felt that the task of organizing the workers should be carried on by the men themselves and that the employers should not be compelled to do it for them. He held to the idea that if a workingman is forced to join a labor organization, he cannot become a loyal member thereof. There might be occasional exceptions, but in his opinion that general rule prevailed. He wanted the workers to be informed concerning union ideals, principles, and history. He wanted the union movement to build for the future and to build intelligently. He considered the closed shop a step in the wrong direction, and was determined at all costs to oppose its becoming an integral part of the program of Organized Labor in San Francisco. His public denunciation of the brewery strike and the subsequent boycott, because they ran counter to his ideals of unionism, cost him dear, for it resulted in his being branded a traitor by old associates for whom he had sacrificed and struggled. But ideals were dearer to him than the plaudits of the crowd. He could not be happy unless he did those things that accorded with his fundamental principles.

Roney was original. He devised new schemes and methods, which were later made use of by the forces of Labor, both here and elsewhere. He had vision and foresight such as are seldom found in a labor leader. As early as 1869 he proposed the plan of organizing unions into trades councils and suggested that the union movement of the country would be much more effective in its demands if organized along those lines. He lived to see his plan adopted in part by the unionists of every large city, who have organized iron trades councils, building trades councils, printing trades councils, etc. He lived to see the American Federation of Labor adopt his ideal in part by establishing certain national trades departments within its organization. Yet for these things he received, and asked, no credit.

It was Roney who introduced the boycott in connection with the campaign against the use of Chinese-made goods. It was Roney who first attempted to establish an arbitration board in the iron trades of San Francisco. This plan was partially put into effect in 1910 and continued thereafter for some years. It was Roney, who, so far as I know, was the first to draft a bill and have it presented to Congress calling for the compensation of employees injured in the service of the federal government. These are but a few of the ideas that sprang from the fertile brain of this western labor leader of the eighties.

Roney's ideals as to labor organizations were largely those of the early English trade unionist. He was interested in the skilled craftsman; he was not concerned with what happened to the unskilled. Nor did he approve of political action by union men or by unions as representing Organized Labor. Throughout the following pages he continually refers to his opposition to the attempt, frequently made, to mix unionism and politics. It is difficult, however, to reconcile his stated principles in this regard with some of his actions. Early in his leadership among the unionists of San Francisco he takes part in a successful attempt to place a union man on the local Board of Supervisors. Later, as he finds it impossible to obtain employment at his trade because of the employers' blacklist, he accepts a political job in the City Hall, from which position of vantage he continues his activities as a labor organizer. Again, he obtains employment as an Immigration Inspector at the Port of San Francisco. Some years later he actively campaigns as "an old labor leader" for George C. Pardee, Republican candidate for the governorship of the State. But the human being who achieves consistency is rare, especially when the stake at times is bread and butter for a growing family, and when the absorbing ideal ever in mind is the desire to aid the working class in its progress toward better things, irrespective of personal gain or loss.

This volume tells the story of Roney's life, with its joys and disappointments, written in the twilight of his eventful career. It tells of his activities as an Irish rebel and as a labor leader. It is concerned with his philosophy, with his estimate of many of those with whom he came in contact, and with his own personal shortcomings.

The story is Roney's. As editor I have made changes in the manuscript only for the purpose of attaining clarity of statement and a more satisfactory and logical arrangement of the narrative. Corrections have been made of misspelled words; names of Irish towns and battles have been checked; sentence structure has at times been modified. But the story is Roney's. No statements have been modified in any manner that might change their meaning. Nothing has been eliminated for the purpose of conveying a thought different from that intended by the author. Several pages of material have been omitted as having no bearing upon the main thread of the narrative.

The reader may be surprised at the choice of words used by the author, but I wish to make it clear that the vocabulary is Roney's. The use of words and phrases in a quaint sense caused me many times to have recourse to the dictionary for the purpose of checking thereon, and in each case I found that they had been used correctly. In his writing as well as in his conversation Roney continually surprised me by the excellence of his diction.

Roney wrote the manuscript in long hand, with few paragraphs, and with no section headings or preface. I have broken the story into paragraphs and sections, have added section headings, and have separated several pages from the rest of the manuscript to form a preface. Roney wrote as the ideas came to him. He also wrote, as he said, "mechanically." He followed no logical outline in presenting his material. I have therefore taken the liberty of rearranging some of the pages and paragraphs of the manuscript so as to have the story progress in a more logical manner than it did when it left Roney's hands. I have added footnotes wherever deemed necessary to enable the reader to appreciate more clearly the part that Roney played in the Fenian uprising and in the labor movement of California.

Acknowledgment is gratefully made for financial assistance received from the Heller Committee for Research in Social Economics and for editorial suggestions made by my colleagues Professors Carl C. Plehn, Stuart Daggett, Jessica B. Peixotto, and Felix Flügel.

Ira B. Cross

FRANK RONEY

AN AUTOBIOGRAPHY

PREFACE

As the result of reciting a few episodes in my life, some of the friends who heard them gained the impression that they should be placed in continuous form, believing that even though they were not instructive they might at least be entertaining if fairly expressed. I have never thought that anything that I might choose to recount was worthy of such attention. There is scarcely a man of average intelligence, inclined to activity in the affairs of life, but has incidents to relate which are of as great intensity, if not greater, than those in my own life. Autobiographies are usually effusions of vain men, disposed to hand bouquets to themselves out of pure desire to extol ordinary events into the magnitude of being of stupendous interest to mankind. I have no such delusions. The chief reason why I now propose to oblige my friends is that I am otherwise unoccupied and feel that perhaps a review of my life will afford me some slight personal pleasure and remind me of occasions when, had I availed myself of the prevailing conditions, another and perhaps more luminous story could have been written.

All that I have written is from memory. I kept no letters or records to guide me or to boast of, for I never expected to write a line about any event or matter in which I was concerned. That habit contracted and so essential to safety when organizing in the Irish revolutionary movement clung to me most decidedly. Neither have I kept a record of my activities in San Francisco. I did keep, in a desultory way, a few clippings from newspapers which I put in a scrap-book and gave several years ago to Dr. Ira B. Cross, who at that time was connected with the Economics Department of Stanford University, but who subsequently went to the University of California. Professor Cross was then engaged in writing a *History of the Labor Movement in California.* They may have been of some value to him, but they fell far short of my actual trials and labors. Of these no individual knew much connectedly. My associations were too numerous and diversified to allow of any one person becoming in all particulars familiar with my actions.

FRANK RONEY

LONG BEACH, CALIFORNIA
1915

I

BOYHOOD AND YOUTH

I

BOYHOOD AND YOUTH

The family circle—

I was born in Belfast, Ireland, on the 13th of August, 1841, the eldest of a family of three girls and five boys. Two of the latter died when quite young. My father served an apprenticeship of seven years to the trade of carpenter at a time when apprentices were no longer domesticated in the house of the employer. The working hours were from sunrise to sunset with two intermissions for meals. Trade unionism was gradually forging its way ahead despite the conspiracy laws then in force in Great Britain and Ireland and the antagonism of the magistracy, who, being of the employing class, never failed to punish with severity every violation of those laws or any movement attempting to abridge the privileges of the employer.

My father became a member of the first carpenters' union formed in Belfast, and for a time was its secretary. He was careful to avoid, and advised against, all friction with the employers until almost all the carpenters in the town were members of the union. Then the demand was successfully made for the ten-hour day. This being secured so easily, other unions in the town adopted the same course, and soon the ten-hour day was generally acknowledged.

I remember the agitation for the reduction of the daily working hours to ten, because most of the leading carpenters of the town were in the habit of meeting at our house to discuss the situation. Secretaries of labor organizations in those days were their executive officers, as I believe they still are in England and Ireland. They were usually selected for their competency, and rarely received compensation. At a time when technical education was rare among working people and all forms of organization were banned by conspiracy laws,[1] the position of secretary of a labor union was one requiring skill and caution to guard himself and his organization from being embroiled in litigation and to keep out of prison for violating the conspiracy laws then in force. Education was an essential qualification, and where the secretary was of proved honesty, he was a person of distinction among his fellows, looked up to and consulted on all matters affecting the trade. Unless the union was a branch of a national organization, the

[1] Under the common law of England, organizations of workers were long classed as conspiracies in restraint of trade and their members were subject to arrest and punishment. In 1799 and 1800, two statutes were passed which further strengthened the common-law doctrine. But in 1824, as a result of the efforts of Francis Place, a statute was enacted by Parliament which legalized unions among the workers. The statute gave very liberal powers to combinations of the laboring class, in fact, too liberal for the times, and in 1825 another measure was passed by Parliament which restricted the activities of such organizations only to efforts at regulating the hours and wages of their members.—Ed.

secretary of a local union in those days received no compensation, nor was any ever expected. Every member did what he could to build it up and to strengthen it by increasing its membership.

My father, as well as I recollect, seemed to possess the confidence of his associates notwithstanding the undercurrent of sectarian hate and distrust that permeated the people of Belfast at that time. He proved that he could always be depended upon to do their work faithfully, no matter what the nature of the dispute or with whom the antagonism existed. His course had the effect of broadening the views of many of the best of his associates and of liberalizing them to a great extent. When he became an employer he persisted in the same course, the only discrimination he made being against non-union men. He always claimed that union labor was more reliable and efficient, and, as a matter of economy, in the long run the cheaper. A man who devoted seven years to an apprenticeship to a trade, endowed with the possession of a fair degree of brains, and had instilled into him by conscientious parents the principles of *meum et tuum,* was always a good, faithful, reliable, economical, and competent worker. My father inspired his workmen with confidence in his fairness, and they reciprocated fully by inviting his confidence.

My mother was the youngest daughter of John Thompson, a tobacconist. My grandfather when a young man became a United Irishman and at the time a Republican. Belfast, his home town, was then the hotbed of Republicanism as it is now the hotbed of Orangeism and intolerance. It was on Cave Hill, a short distance from Belfast, that Wolfe Tone, Henry Joy McCracken, and several others met, after the manner of Winkelried and other Swiss patriots, and swore to expel the English Government from Ireland and establish a republic, and for that purpose formed the Society of United Irishmen.[2] My grandfather took an active part in organizing that society, and when they took the field against the British at Saintfield and Ballynahinch and elsewhere, he became a captain under General Henry Munroe.

Upon the defeat of the insurgents at Ballynahinch, my grandfather made his way back to Belfast and remained in hiding until the effects of the uprising had measurably died down. Although there had been a price set for his capture, he escaped with the aid and connivance of the Masonic fraternity, of which he was a member. He later became associated with Mr. Phillip Johnson in the tobacco business.

[2] Theobald Wolfe Tone, a lawyer of 28, and his friend, Samuel Neilson, were chiefly responsible for the organization of the Society of United Irishmen in 1791. The stated object of the revolutionary society was to forward "a brotherhood of affection, a communion of rights, and a union of power amongst Irishmen of every religious persuasion, and thereby to obtain a complete reform of the Legislature, founded on the principles of civil, political and religious liberty." The society was suppressed by the Government in 1794, whereupon it became secret and more revolutionary in character. Plans were made for a revolt, and efforts were put forth to obtain assistance from the French Republic. The latter sent an expedition consisting of seventeen large warships, thirteen frigates, and 15,000 men, which left

He never voted for any officer under the British Crown, and believed that if the British Government could not be driven out of Ireland by force, he could at least to some extent cripple it in its finances. So he engaged in the smuggling of tobacco from the Isle of Man, thereby greatly profiting himself and his partner.

The Isle of Man is situated about equal distance from England, Scotland, and Ireland in the Irish Sea. Its three main ports were harbors of refuge for smugglers from all parts of the world and also for pirates. These freebooters had their agents in each of the three countries named and also on the Isle of Man. When a cargo was discharged free of duty, the agents on the mainland were notified. They had their regular customers, who were notified in turn. The fishermen engaged in this profitable business—who were the real smugglers with its attendant risks—were the last notified. Although coast guards patroled the coast at all points likely to be frequented by the smugglers, few captures

Brest on December 15, 1796. Severe storms and accidents at sea caused it to fail of its purpose. In March 1798, the Government actively set about to put down the rebellion. McCracken, a linen manufacturer, at the head of 4,000 men, was defeated in an attack upon Antrim. Munroe, a linen draper, with 5,000 followers, was defeated with great slaughter at Ballynahinch on June 13. McCracken was executed in Belfast, and Munroe was hanged before his own door in Lisburn. Wolfe Tone, who was then in France, succeeded in inducing the French to send two other expeditions to Ireland. Both failed, and Wolfe Tone, who accompanied the last, was captured and sentenced to be hanged; but he succeeded in committing suicide, dying on November 18, 1798.—Ed.

were ever made. Ardglass, in the County Down, and its vicinity were the favorite places where the contraband tobacco was received and carried to other parts of Ireland. Wagons were the only conveyances at the time. Loaded with hay or vegetables covering tobacco leaf for the market at Belfast, these wagons would make the twenty-eight-mile journey, timing their arrival when all was safe from discovery.

Thus the firm of Johnson & Thompson waxed rich and prosperous, one member of it deliberately glorying in defrauding the Government as the only means within his power to punish it for its atrocities upon his countrymen, while the other, smug and loyal, accepted his share of the smuggled profits far more eagerly than his partner, whose one aim in the smuggling business was revenge. In 1849, Queen Victoria visited Belfast after opening the Industrial Exposition in Dublin and, in appreciation of the loyalty (?) of Mr. Johnson, then Mayor of Belfast, made him a Knight and subsequently raised the title to that of Baronet, making it hereditary. The Johnsons are now members of the British aristocracy.

My grandfather's hatred of British rule in Ireland, or of anything aiding it, never weakened during his life. One of his sons became an Orangeman. That was the hardest blow ever struck him. He regarded that society as the foulest blot upon the country. A rigid Presbyterian and hereditary

Covenanter, he never acknowledged the right of the British Crown to Ireland, besides he was a thoroughgoing Republican. He viewed the Orange Society as an ultra British association, to which no decent Irishman could conscientiously belong. It was intolerant in deed and thought. It was opposed to liberty, favored oppression, denied free speech, and restricted the exercising of every noble impulse except the false ones emanating from an Orange Lodge.[3] To have a son join such an association was wormwood and gall to him. He called his remaining family together and with the air of an old-time patriarch told them that he had disowned this son. In the future they must also disown him; they must neither succor nor comfort him in life or in death; they must regard him as one dead and unforgiven.

I believe that every one of the family faithfully observed the injunction. When this son died, the news was brought to my mother. I remember well that she and I were the only members of the family who accompanied the remains to the grave. My mother had become a Catholic prior to her marriage, and with a heart overflowing with tenderness and compassion for her wayward brother, believed that she was not violating any pledge to her father by doing as she did. Her conduct made a deep impression upon the Orangemen in attendance at the funeral, who were aware of her father's proscrip-

[3] The Orange Society, an anti-Catholic organization, was founded in the County of Armagh in September 1795.—Ed.

tion, some of whom concluded that whatever might be said against the Catholics there were still a few good ones to be found in the land.

Youthful experiences—

My earliest recollections are of a visit made to my grandmother's at Saul in the County Down, about two miles from Downpatrick. I was less than three years old. My grandmother decided that I should spend a portion of time under her tutelage, though I fail to remember any special instructions I received other than how to deport myself, the saying of my prayers, and my conduct at table. These had already been given me by my mother, of whose capability for such duty my grandmother had serious doubts.

A journey of twenty miles by stage, the distance to Saul or Downpatrick from Belfast, was considered even by adults in those days to be quite an undertaking. My parents were unable at the time to accompany me to my grandmother's home. I was accordingly brought to the stagecoach's booking office, kept by a lady of advanced years, named Featherstone, and assigned by her to the care of the guard (or as termed in the United States, the conductor). The guard was a fascinating figure to my juvenile fancy. I had never seen a guard before. He wore a scarlet coat with large brass buttons. Over one shoulder he had slung a small leather box holding letters; from the other was suspended a bugle which he sounded as the coach started on its journey and also at every crossroad summoning the people for their letters or small packages, which he distributed. He knew all the people on his route. He was a Government official and our coach carried the mail.

At that time there were no railroads in that part of Ireland, so mail coaches were in universal use. In a few years after 1844, a railroad was built to Dublin, then one to the City of Derry, to be followed by one to Downpatrick. The building of these railroads created intense hostility among the people whose territory they traversed, as well as among the large number of men employed in hauling freight and the products of the farmers to market. The farmers did a large proportion of their own hauling. It was generally claimed that the railroads would sound the death-knell of all prosperity by creating universal unemployment, the abandonment of inns and roadhouses on the way, and the general demoralization of the economic system then prevalent. A few years of their operation demonstrated these predictions to be entirely fallacious, as had been the case with the introduction of the spinning jenny in England a few years before, followed by the steam loom, which instead of causing idleness led to general employment of all kinds of mechanics and laborers in machine-shops, foundries, and shipping.

The distance to Downpatrick was about twenty miles. A branch road to Saul began about two miles northward forming a V, beginning at what was known as Quiole Quay. At that point my Aunt Margaret, with a cousin, Alice, and others, were awaiting me. Much against my will I was handed down from the top of the stage into the arms of my aunt and was led by her to my grandmother's house. I hated to leave the lovely coach guard, his bugle and brass buttons.

My grandmother rigidly inspected me from head to foot, also the bundle containing my clothes, after which I was given something to eat and put to bed. My grandmother's appearance didn't inspire me. She looked austere and very solemn. She was dressed in black with white collar and cuffs, and spoke as she looked. One of her peculiarities was to wear her spectacles on her forehad, which at once diverted my attention from everything else. I had never seen people wear spectacles that way before and wondered how she could see out of her forehead. I never saw them once covering her eyes though she had the keenest sight imaginable, as I soon discovered.

In the morning at breakfast I had a seat at the table with the grown folks, my grandmother presiding sedately and solemnly. She brewed the tea in an urn with boiling water from a copper kettle, kept hot by an alcohol flame alongside. She knew just how much tea and water to use, but it seemed to me that she had forgotten me in her calculations, for after she had filled the cups for each of the grown-ups and handed them out, there was no tea in the urn for me. I had not been used to tea at home. Its introduction into Ireland as a breakfast beverage at that time, or a few years before, was slow. I never heard of coffee being used at that date. Instead of being served with tea, I was handed a cup of warm water and milk, the water having been passed through the tea urn. For about four days I took my cup grudgingly and without complaint, but finally I asked grandma whether it wouldn't be better for her to give me my "tea" directly out of the kettle instead of putting the water in the urn. She turned her eyes severely upon me, but said nothing, the elders trying to smother a laugh at my temerity. It was clearly rebellious talk that I had indulged in, as my aunt later told me, and merited correction, but nothing happened except that in the future I was given straight milk.

Traditional influences—

In Ulster, at that time, every phase of life, public and private, was tinctured with a sectarian bias. Before engaging in any enterprise however insignificant, or forming any acquaintance however necessary, the question of religious belief always took precedence. Doubt of the honesty of the person with whom you were obliged to do business almost always existed until association and experience proved your misgivings unfounded. As I have stated above, my mother had been a Presbyterian but became a Catholic prior to her marriage. My grandfather, Jack Thompson, had in his earlier manhood been a United Irishman and a rebel to the British Government. My mother inherited all of her father's hatred of the British Government, and without being conscious of it, early indoctrinated me with the same feeling. Henry Joy McCracken was her hero. His sufferings and his death upon the scaffold at Corn Market, and his sister Mary's courage in being present at the execution, dressed in green, and her cutting off a lock of his hair as a souvenir, were recited to me time and time again, and made such an impression on my young mind that I felt that if, when I became a man, I failed to avenge his death, I would be derelict in my duty to my God and my Country.

This feeling was intensified by our annual visit to his sisters, the Misses McCracken, who lived in a large house on Donegall Street. All the year round the blinds of the windows of their house were drawn, denoting their mourning for their hero brother, except on St. Patrick's day, the National holiday, when the light was admitted and the two antiquated ladies, dressed in green for that one day, would hold high and solemn festival. No others but my mother and I and the old servants were ever present on those solemn occasions. The impressions made upon me became permanent. With these ladies and the descendants of the old rebel stock that remained in Belfast, no sentiments of sectarian bias ever existed. My mother alone was a Catholic, the rest were Presbyterians, but that did not debar her from full participation in their confidences and hopes.

My father also regarded all with whom he had dealings solely from the standpoint of their individual merit without regard to whether they were Catholic or non-Catholic. I was too young to remember anything clearly of the agitation going on for the repeal of the Act of Union between Ireland and England. My father was a "Repealer" and attended the meetings of his club regularly. I remember his hostility to the Young Ireland Party, for he was then and always remained a firm believer in a government conducted by the "Queen, Lords and Commons of Ireland." Young as I was, and but little versed in the history of Ireland, I used to nauseate at the expression "Queen, Lords and Commons of Ireland," and preferred Smith O'Brien and John Mitchel to Daniel O'Connell and his galaxy of talent.[4]

[4] Although for centuries Ireland had been a part of England, it had an alleged Parliament of its own until 1800. The lovers of Irish freedom, however, claimed it to be a Parliament of, for, and by the British in Ireland. In 1800, a bill for the union of Ireland and England was adopted by the Irish Parliament, its passage being effected by means which need not concern us here, but which have been condemned by both English and Irish historians.

On January 1, 1801, the Act of the Union became effective and Irish liberties were further curtailed. An agitation immediately started for the repeal of the Act of the Union. Daniel O'Connell, born in 1775, was one of the outstanding leaders, if not the most outstanding, in that agitation. In fact Ireland's history for the first

O'Connell's repeal movement—

I was too young to understand the momentous events transpiring in Ireland up to and including the year 1848. O'Connell's repeal movement which had aroused all the people of Ireland to the importance of securing legislative independence as the primary means of restoring at least a part of their rights, of which they had been deprived during a long period of persecutions, reached its zenith and became largely overwhelmed by the Young Ireland Party. O'Connell's death[5] took place in the same decade, as did the Great Famine and pestilence. I knew nothing of these latter occurrences which left such indelible marks upon my unhappy country,

half of the nineteenth century is reflected in the activities of this idol of Irish Catholics.

During the thirties the O'Connell movement fell from its "earlier high aims," and the younger, more restive element broke away in 1847 and formed the Young Ireland Party, sometimes known as "The Confederation." John Mitchel, William Smith O'Brien, and Thomas Meagher were some of its more important leaders. These three men, however, pushed ahead of their more conservative associates and planned open rebellion against the mother country. Being arrested, tried, and convicted, Mitchel was sentenced to fourteen years' transportation beyond the seas, and Meagher, O'Brien, and some of their close associates were sentenced to be hanged, but were later transported to Van Diemen's Land for life exile.

O'Brien was given an unconditional pardon in 1854, returned to Ireland, and died ten years later. Mitchel and Meagher escaped from Van Diemen's Land in 1852 and fled to America. Mitchel fought for the Confederacy in the Civil War, while Meagher fought for the Northern States and rose to the rank of Brigadier General. He later became Governor of Montana Territory, dying in July, 1867.—Ed.

[5] O'Connell died in Genoa, Italy, on May 15, 1847.—Ed.

reducing the population from over eight millions to four millions within three years, from which, after the lapse of many years, it still bears the marks.[6]

School days—

In every neighborhood at the time there was at least one school usually conducted by a woman more or less qualified, to which the youngsters were sent to receive the elements of education. Such schools were in part fashioned after our kindergartens of today according to the whims and methods of the self-appointed teachers. The teachers were responsible only to the parents and imparted their knowledge, such as it was, in a slipshod way, without system, and as a result, without making much headway with their pupils. The main object was to keep the children off the streets, and if they acquired knowledge, well and good; if not, no especial harm was done.

I was sent to several of these primitive institutions, being changed from one to another by my discriminating parents, who promoted me when they thought fit, for each of the teachers enjoyed in a popular way a certain intellectual status, which enabled the parents to select the teacher next in order

[6] The Great Famine began in 1845 with the partial failure of the potato crop of that year. A worse failure occurred in 1846 and 1847. Mr. Roney is in error in his statement regarding the extent of decrease in the population of Ireland because of the famine. Authorities appear to agree that about a million people died either from starvation or from "famine fever," and that about another million emigrated to other lands between 1846 and 1850.—Ed.

as the person best qualified to train the budding intellect of the juvenile aspirant for scholastic honors. I believe my progress was decidedly slow and in keeping with the want of system and ignorance on the part of my instructors. The National School System had been recently established and was regarded by the people with sentiments of suppressed hostility. Tutelage cost but little, thus placing the National Schools upon the footing of pauper institutions which, to proud parents, was a brand they did not intend should be placed upon their offspring. In addition to the low cost of tuition—only a penny a week—books and other school accessories were free if demanded, and a regular system of graduation was observed under qualified instructors.

Of course, my parents could not think of sending me to a half-pauper school. Accordingly, I became a pupil of "Ellis' Academy." The principal was an austere but amiable man. He had been a curate of the Established Church, doing the work of the parish while starving on inadequate remuneration. Being poor and unfriended, he was unfrocked for some cause or other and deprived of his living, cast upon the world's charity to die or starve or go to perdition. He established this school with a bitter hatred in his heart of everything English, including their Church, of which, inconsistently enough, he remained a member. I shall always think of Mr. Ellis with the kindliest feelings of respect and admiration. He was supremely just in all his dealings with his pupils. The very soul of honor, he abhorred every trifling act from a pupil conveying the least expression of meanness or want of courage. He taught us self-reliance, and here and there in our curriculum he cautiously and carefully instilled into us boys a deep and lasting hatred of English law and government.

Beginning in the lower grades, I rose year by year until the proud distinction was gained of being the head boy in the school. I seemed to enjoy the confidence and esteem of my classmates whether I really merited it or not.

It was customary in our school at the time, and in imitation of the practices of more pretentious institutions of learning, for the elder boys to have attached to them a juvenile whom we termed a "fag." The "fag" was simply the servant of his principal. He performed every menial office too humiliating for the elder boy to perform, ran errands, carried messages, and had to be promptly on hand at the beck and call of his superior. In return the "fag" enjoyed all the reflected glory that enveloped the elder boy. If the elder boy stood well with the other pupils, the "fag" reveled in the popularity of his superior, for whom he acted in all things as a diminutive representative. Any slight or injustice put upon the "fag" was deemed a slight or injustice upon the elder, and it became his duty to vindicate the "fag" and to punish, if he could, every encroachment upon the latter's personal rights. An assault upon the "fag," of whatever nature, was an attack upon the elder boy.

We had a very turbulent, quarrelsome, and dominating boy in the school who was always involving himself and others in trouble. He had gained a reputation as a fighter and had thrashed every boy who attempted to thwart him or dispute his doings. I thoroughly disliked the boy for his arrogance and the meanness of which he was frequently guilty, and held no intercourse with him whatever. He felt the slight I put upon him, which was participated in by the whole school.

In a moment of resentment at this treatment, which he rightfully attributed to me, he asked my "fag" to do something, which was refused. Whereupon he hit my "fag," which meant a challenge to me. I was the only boy in the school with whom he had had no altercation. He believed that if he conquered me he would have the whole school at his feet and would ride roughshod over all of us. It was arranged that we should go to a quiet place after dismissal and there settle the issue as to which one of us was to dominate the school. The excitement was intense, and I need hardly say I had the entire school at my back. Upon reaching the battlefield, I at once divested myself of all superfluous apparel, in which I was assisted most dutifully by my supporters. My opponent showed no alacrity in putting himself in a fighting attitude, which gave me considerable courage, and I demanded that he give me the satisfaction required. He still hesitated, and finally turned and ran from the scene with all his speed. I won a bloodless victory because of his cowardice, and peace reigned thereafter in the school. Had this boy shown any courage, I believe that he would have licked me completely. He was a strong, chunky fellow and was used to boxing. I had had no experience in that line. I was a tall, slim chap, and thoroughly disliked all personal combat of that character.

I later attended the Government school of design two or three evenings in the week for about two years and acquired some knowledge of art through the instruction of very competent teachers. I also availed myself of the use of the school library and familiarized myself with the struggles and achievements of Raphael, Angelo, Cellini, and other great masters. I won a prize in the free-hand drawing of an angel, and was promoted to the modeling room where, under careful tuition, we were taught to model in clay.

I attracted the attention of an Italian frequenter of the modeling room named Pichioni, a painter and sculptor, and an expatriate. Signor Pichioni, as I afterwards learned, was the son of the physician to Bomba or Frances, the last king of Naples, and fled with him when Naples became an integral part of the Kingdom of Italy. It was with supreme delight that I hailed Mr. Pichioni's entrance as a member of St. Vincent de Paul's Society. He was equally well pleased when he found me a member, and we became the best of friends although he was old enough to be my father. His employment as an artist was rare and brief. His wife was a most excellent and very handsome Scotch lady, who treated me with great consideration and kindness. It was a long time before I learned the secret of how Mr. Pichioni maintained his family during his periods of intermittent employment. He had a workshop in the rear of his house where he made plaster casts of those figures and articles which Italian venders are in the habit of hawking about in large cities. He made those figures, and from their sale to his countrymen he eked out, with his wife's management, an apparently comfortable, even though precarious, livelihood.

Frequent visits to the shop soon made me an adept in making those casts. I could put the molds together, mix the alabaster to its proper consistence, and in all respects do the work as well as, if less speedily than, Mr. Pichioni. At length he got an order to paint several large pictures and the Stations of the Cross for a distant church. He needed the work for its revenue, but how his family was to subsist while he was engaged upon it perplexed him greatly. He was an exceedingly proud man, and excepting myself no one knew of his sad embarrassment. I promptly volunteered to keep up the supply of the plaster casts if he thought that that would relieve the situation, and after some deliberation he reluctantly agreed to my proposal. He knew I was expert enough to do the work, but to accept my labor without compensation was more than his pride could stand. I convinced him eventually that he would be under no obligation to me and that it would be a distinct pleasure for me to do the work. I believe he yielded because he saw no other way out of his difficulty and I did the work dutifully during his absence.

Charitable activities—

During my father's activities as a union man and after he became an employer, he always maintained his standing as a dutiful Catholic. Upon the introduction of the Society of St. Vincent de Paul into Belfast he became one of its earliest members. This Society was organized for the purpose of discovering those in abject need and, without relation to their sectarian alignment, of relieving their distress by dispensing weekly alms in the form of the necessaries of life. Sometimes, too, the rent was paid, and frequently donations of clothes were given. It was my father's desire that I keep aloof from vicious companions of my own age and, as far as he could accomplish it, be surrounded with an atmosphere of devotional practices. The St. Vincent de Paul Society presented to him the most expeditious means of effecting this, and accordingly, at the age of thirteen, I was formally inducted as a member of St. Patrick's Conference of that society. This led to my further enrollment as a member of the Christian Doctrine Society, of which, in a short time, I became secretary. The duties exacted from members of this society were to visit the houses of persons known to be Catholics whose children were never present at Sunday-school. I now often wonder at my temerity in visiting the houses of those delinquent parents and lecturing them upon their indifference and carelessness in the bringing up of their children. I did this with a zeal that in most cases brought results. The astonishment is that I was not bodily thrown out of the premises. As a junior member of the St. Vincent's Society, I was equally energetic and was often reprimanded for discovering cases of destitution far in excess of the society's means of relieving them. I believe that if the funds of the Bank of Ireland had been placed at my disposal to relieve the distress and penury I encountered, I would have depleted them in a short time and thought that I had done only part of my duty.

I remember discovering a case that caused a good deal of talk and which when described excited the risibilities of those who heard it, not in derision or for any humor to be found in it, but rather for the patience and grim stolidity or resignation of the sufferers. I visited an old barrack of a house that had been in its earlier existence a house of some consequence. It had fallen through neglect into a habitation for the very poorest and was then the worst kind of a shelter. The windows were nearly all broken and during winter nights were stuffed with rags to keep out the damp air and retain what heat was possible. In one of the rooms about twenty feet square I found five families, one in each corner and one in the middle. There was neither bed nor mattress in the room. How they slept or what comfort they obtained day or night in such crowded quarters was beyond my powers to discover. And yet, in all their distress, the poor creatures appeared measurably cheerful and hopeful. When I asked how it was possible for so many to crowd into so small a space I was told that they had got along well enough till the occupant in the middle had taken in a lodger. In my report to the conference, when I stated this fact, I was amazed at what I thought was the heartlessness of the members in laughing at the statement, and I felt badly offended. I could see nothing in the case warranting the least pleasantry, and indignantly told them so.

Somewhat later there was an outbreak of cholera in Belfast and a Relief Committee was appointed by the Mayor. The epidemic was apparently confined to those districts inhabited by the very poor, the sanitary conditions of which were as poor as the occupants. My father was a member of this committee and knowing my industry in finding the worst and most neglected cases and, being no doubt apprehensive of my spreading the disease by such irregular methods as I would be likely to adopt, gave me strict orders to keep away from the districts affected and under no circumstances to have anything whatever to do with a cholera patient. To restrict me at such a time was, I thought, a rank injustice to myself as well as to some poor unknown and forgotten creature, and I accepted the interdiction with very bad grace. At length I could stand the inactivity no longer and one afternoon went into the stricken district in which I had operated as a member of the St. Vincent's Society. The conditions were appalling. Coffins being carried out with dead bodies in them, thrown into wagons by the dozen, met me at every turn. Doctors rushed hither and thither. All was in confusion, and the situation was such as to intimidate any person of irresolute mind. The groans and cries of the tortured and helpless victims appealed to my desire to relieve and help.

Passing along I looked into a house, the door of which stood open, and saw a large man lying upon a poor bed, everything around him in disorder. He appeared to be in agony and was pathetically asking if some one in God's name wouldn't hand him something. I entered and promptly volunteered my assistance. He was conscious enough to know that he should have had the medicine given to him which an apothecary had left, but it was out of his reach and he was too weak to reach it. When he had been stricken his wife had fled in terror, leaving him unattended, to die alone. The horror and inhumanity of the situation came to me afterwards, but at the moment I was entirely unaffected. I gave him his medicine and proceeded to put the place in order. I made him as comfortable as I knew how and then left. A few hours later I returned and found that he again needed my help. I helped him as best I could, but feeling that a doctor should attend him I rushed to the nearest place where one could be found, and brought him to the stricken stranger. The doctor prescribed certain indispensable attentions which I volunteered to perform and I remained with my patient several hours longer. Next day and many days thereafter were spent with my patient and I was gratified and repaid for my efforts by seeing him become convalescent and eventually fully recovered. Neither my father nor my family knew anything of what I was doing. If they had I would either have been chained up or turned out of the house. Fortunately none of my family and none of our immediate neighbors were afflicted with the disease.

A long time afterwards I learned that my patient was not a Catholic. He had needed my help and it made no difference to me what his faith might be. I suppose I never would have known what his religious belief was had he not announced the fact himself. It came about several years afterwards during one of the internecine wars so prolific in Belfast at one time. I was then a young man and with my customary carelessness had wandered into one of the disturbed districts inhabited mostly by the Orange faction. Almost before I knew what was happening I was surrounded by a crowd which demanded that I curse the Pope as a preliminary to a beating which I was sure to get whether I complied or not. Suddenly a big powerful middle-aged man pushed himself into the mob shouting "No! No! No! You don't harm this chap without harming me. This is the chap that stayed with me and saved my life when everyone else abandoned me. You can't hurt him without hurting me." Needless to say, I was grateful to him for my rescue from the hands of the angry mob. He and I became fast friends, and when, sometime later, I was organizing for the establishment of an Irish Republic, he was one of my best aides and proved to be a true Irish Nationalist.

The first job—

My future occupation became a matter of some concern to my parents. A college career with a profession at the end of it was entirely too expensive for them to consider. My mother wished me placed in a mercantile or other clean, light occupation, believing as all fond mothers do, that her son would in the course of time make his mark. My father wanted me to become a mechanic but conceded my right to choose for myself. An opening, which pleased my mother, presented itself in the office of Connolly Sherard, a large real estate agent, with whom my father was well acquainted. Accordingly I was installed in Mr. Sherard's office to learn all the secrets and manipulations necessary to a full and efficient knowledge of the real estate business.

For a week I was detailed to accompany a junior clerk and learn from him how collections were made and whatever other preliminary points were necessary as a foundation to reach the top in the profession. In my second week's service I was considered sufficiently qualified to be given special territory and to go it alone. I was given fifty notices of ejectment to serve. The houses were situated in one of the poorest districts, where as a member of St. Vincent de Paul Society I had often dispensed relief to the residents. I served three notices out of the fifty. I was a supreme failure, but was as serene and happy upon returning to the office as if I had been successful. Every one of the tenants had hard luck stories to tell of sickness, being out of work, or some other disaster equally depressing, and I knew them to be in the main entirely true.

I returned to the office and mounted the stool at my desk, placing the unserved notices upon it. The clerk next to me asked why I had not served them. I told him that the people were too poor to pay the rent or to be thrown out. He gave me a look of consternation, which did not disturb me a particle. When Mr. Sherard returned from dinner, he called on me to give an account of the day's work. I at once jumped from my high stool, cheery and confident, noting as I did so a look of pity in the eyes of my fellow-clerk. "Well, Frank, how did you get along today?" was the first question asked. I manfully answered that I thought that I had got along very well. "How many ejectment notices did you have when you left the office?" I told him fifty. "How many did you serve?" When I said, "Three," he seemed for the moment bereft of speech. Then he echoed, "Three! Three! Why not all of them?" I told him that the people were too poor to pay, that they had sickness or were unemployed, and that they were altogether in a bad condition, so that I had decided not to serve them. He was choking with rage, while I stood before him perfectly calm and collected. "Who gave you the right to determine such a matter? Your business in this office is to do as you are ordered without equivocation or sentiment, and on tomorrow you will go to the same people and serve the notices or leave this office."

I at once informed him that I would not do so and was prepared to leave his office at that moment. He became furious, and unless it was my calmness that prevented him and the possible dread of a criminal prosecution, I do not know why he restrained himself from giving me a good licking. "Get out of here at once!" he roared, and with the utmost deliberation I took up my hat and left.

That ended my career as a land shark and evictor. My father was highly displeased with my conduct, but my mother was delighted and later told me so.

Then I knew that I was right. Where the poor have been concerned I have at no time in my life departed from that course.

Apprenticeship—

My father, as the general foreman for James Connor, with whom he had been a fellow-apprentice, had to do with ordering castings used in the construction of buildings. Visiting a foundry with him one day, I was enchanted to know that making castings in iron was merely an amplification of my work with Mr. Pichioni, the difference, as it appeared to me, being merely in the material used and a variation in method. I insisted against my mother's protests upon becoming a moulder, and was accordingly apprenticed to Traver Forbes of the Ulster Foundry for a period of seven years.

It did not take me long to discover my mistake. The associations in the foundry were repugnant to me. My fellow-apprentices were vulgar in the extreme and without the least refinement. They were given to lying on the least, or without any, provocation, and generally were disposed to viciousness. The impressions made were probably due as much to the manner in which I had been brought up and to my early associations as to any fault on their part. I had acquired a sedateness and perhaps a somberness from my intimacy with the poor and their pecuniary troubles that caused me to look at the frivolities and animal exuberances of these boys with contempt. I could not mingle with them without, as I thought, belittling myself. At the same time I was entirely free from all notions of superiority or pretentiousness. They were simply not congenial to me, and I felt that to be one of them would be to lose the identity of my real self. I had a light heart and could appreciate a good joke or anything of real fun when no hurt was given another, but fun to them meant annoyance to others.

The apprenticeship system, practiced by the guilds in preceding eras and continued into the then modern system of industry, which had been made inevitable by the invention of the steam engine and the development of machinery following the introduction of the spinning jenny, was changing very rapidly. The limitations requiring the oldest son to follow the occupation of the father had in most occupations entirely disappeared. Large factories had risen on the ruins of the small shop and the hand-loom weaver. The individual carder and spinner, except in some remote parts of the country, found their work done on a larger scale in the factory. Unless they followed their work to the big town adjacent, they were out of a job. To do work cheaply was then, as it always has been everywhere and at all times, the watchword and guide of all engaged in competitive manufacturing in this earliest period of its development. The free-trade shibboleth of John Cobden, that "Competition is the life of trade," intensified the industrial warfare.

Developments in manufacturing machinery, especially in that used in the production of textiles, increased the demand for cheap labor and led to the wholesale employment of women and young children in the mills and factories. To cheapen production still more, a division of labor was evolved destroying, except in special occupations, the traditional practice of those following a trade of being complete masters of it in all its branches and details. New methods of specialization in moulding castings for machinery by machines were in operation in Lancashire and in parts of Yorkshire in England and were a pronounced success. Strong boys and handy men were used as operators of the new moulding machines, dispensing largely with the ancient apprentice system. Many of the boys so placed acquired a degree of skill at their employment which gained promotion for them by slow degrees and ultimately qualified them as moulders. Only in very exceptional cases did these boys become competent mechanics and never did they attain the rank to be entitled to the highest current rate of wages. The union, or "The Friendly Society of Iron Moulders of England, Ireland, and Wales," at that time recognized two ratings in each foundry for its members, the minimum rating being the standard. A seven years' indentured apprentice to any trade became a very rare thing shortly after I started on my career as a moulder.

The employers still retained a remnant of the old system which required that they were conscientiously obligated to place every opportunity of learning all phases of the trade within the reach of the apprentice, enabling him thereby to become a proficient workman. As establishments increased in size this duty devolved upon the foremen, who generally were not at all conscientious in carrying on the old practices in that regard. Economy in production was exacted from the foremen, causing them to place apprentices upon jobs for which they had displayed an aptitude, thus preventing them forever from becoming first-class mechanics. Inducements in the form of a bonus or increased pay were frequently resorted to by foremen to get apprentices to continue for long periods on special jobs and thus forego the chance to become finished workmen. Where successfully applied, this practice at the same time relieved the foremen from the responsibility of instructing their apprentices in all aspects of the trade. Fortunately in my case, however, no such obstacles were placed in my way of becoming a good moulder. I was always put with first-class journeymen and invariably found them to be conscientiously disposed to perform their whole duty by me.

Pioneers in labor movement—

One of the men with whom I was placed was a very old loam moulder, named John McArdle. When very young McArdle had been taken to England by his parents and had there learned his trade. He had been a member of the Friendly Society of Iron Moulders from the day of its formation in Bolten-le-Moor and delighted in telling me of the struggles, persecutions, and adventures of his associates, who were among the earliest of the pioneers in the trade union movement in England. Conspiracy laws of an earlier period still remained on the English statute books and were relentlessly enforced. To be a member of a trade union in those days required the utmost courage, the most astute discretion, and the keenest discrimination as to what might be accomplished for the collective as well as for the individual benefit of the members. Precipitate action or illy matured plans often led to arrest, and repeated violations of the law usually resulted in the guilty being transported as felons to the colonies. Arrests, prosecutions, and imprisonment were frequent occurrences and were accepted by those pioneers in the labor movement as the inevitable consequence of trying to rescue future generations from the dire thraldom of which they and preceding generations had been the victims.

Education was slowly and painfully spreading its influence in quarters and among classes which hitherto had gone without it with entire ignorance of its loss. The Saxon's sturdy recognition of fair play, and the equity which should prevail between man and man irrespective of so-called hereditary social rights, were illuminated by rays of thought coming from the great writers of the eighteenth century in advocacy of man's inalienable right to life unfettered and undegraded. Agitation, comment, sympathy, and finally active interest and material support followed the arrest and persecution of the pioneers of trade unionism, especially when Parliamentary inquiry established the justness of their cause and in time brought about the abrogation of the old restrictive laws.

The individual and personal sufferings of those martyrs to the cause of economic emancipation made a permanent impression on my mind, already affected by the material sufferings of the poor whom I had met. The origin of these wrongs and sufferings was beyond my capacity to understand. How to obliterate them I had no conception. I had been taught that the virtue of charity was a wise and holy quality to cultivate and exercise. The poor and the suffering we always had with us, and it was a humane and Christian duty to relieve them to as great an extent as possible. I heard reports repeated throughout Ireland of victims and heartrending scenes at the ports of departure of the immigrant ships. I read of the poor on the coast of Donegal at Gweedore and Cloughanealy living for weeks on seaweed in a land of plenty. I read reports of the killing of rack-renting landlords and their agents, of strikes in England and the destruction of property, and sometimes of the assaulting of the starving wretches whom necessity compelled to take the places of the strikers. I heard of conflicts between the populace and the police and occasionally between the populace and the military, and felt, as a young man, that those evils and abuses could be regulated or abolished only by revolution or successful political action. I was inclined to favor the latter means.

Youthful reformer goes forth—

Disgusted with my trade and fired with the belief that I could do something to set matters right, I resolved to leave home, in fact, to run away. As a preliminary, I proposed to go to Dublin and visit the scenes where great men had in time long past made great sacrifices to emancipate the people. I hoped to gain enough inspiration by visiting their places, to equip myself without other effort as the future emancipator.

On the train I met a soldier, a corporal returning from a furlough, and made him the confidant of my hopes and ambition. He was entirely sympathetic. When we reached Dublin he took me to a respectable lodging. In a few days I had visited all the points of historic interest in the city and found myself one morning at the house of the parish priest of Clontarf, who was a distant relative of mine. Upon hearing my story the good old man left his house to show me over the ground that tradition attributes as the battlefield whereon Brian Boroimhe decimated the last of the Danish invaders. I was also shown the spot upon which was erected the platform from which O'Connell spoke to one of the greatest audiences he addressed during his agitation for the repeal of the Act of Union.

I had never before been in a place where intoxicating liquor was sold and I was then seventeen years of age. My mother, an ardent follower of Father Mathew, the temperance advocate, had long impressed me with the evils arising from an indulgence in strong drinks and I revered her admonitions and advice with sincere and pious regard. My soldier friend, however, prevailed upon me to enter a place of this kind where I found two ancient citizens, apparently his friends, regular habitués of the place, who proved to be perfect encyclopedias of the history of Dublin. They knew every event of importance that had taken place in Dublin during the preceding century, its participants, and all the incidents to the minutest detail. I was interested and delighted with their conversation. Their tales were not perhaps so accurate as they might have been, and were, I dare say, strongly colored according to the bias of their minds. But as the tales were well told and interesting, I devoted a large amount of my time to listening to them.

At these meetings I met a young fellow who professed to be a grandson of the celebrated John Philpot Curran, whose daughter Mary Curran was the sweetheart of Ireland's most pathetic, chivalrous, and picturesque hero and martyr.[7] Upon being informed of this fact I took very kindly to the young man, who excelled as a conversationalist and who was most agreeable in many ways. He professed to be a medical student at Trinity College with the right of entry to the city hospitals and clinical lecture rooms. He took me to many of the latter and acted the part of guide to perfection.

Among the places visited was a concert hall where light meals were served during the performance. It was a very old established place and had been, and in fact was then, the rendezvous of the college boys who often sallied forth on a political debauch, ending with a hand to hand conflict with the police, and sometimes with the military being called out to suppress the disorder. It was rather an historic concern and under the name of Jury's had undergone no changes internal or otherwise for nearly a century. Madam Picolomini, an Italian prima donna,

[7] The reference here made by Roney is to Robert Emmet, who led an unsuccessful revolt against England in 1802. It is probable that Emmet could have escaped from the country had he not delayed to bid farewell to his sweetheart Sarah (not Mary) Curran. He was but 25 years old at the time of his execution, September 20, 1802. In "the hearts of the men and women of Ireland his name has remained enshrined, more intimately, and with deeper love than that of many, who gave long lives of strenuous, self-sacrificing, faithful service to her cause."—Hayden and Moonan, *A Short History of the Irish People*, p. 458. His oration delivered before the court which sentenced him is still considered one of the classic utterances in the long history of the struggle of the Irish for freedom.—Ed.

was then paying her last visit to Dublin prior to her marriage and retirement from grand opera and the stage. Her last apearance was to be made on a Friday night, called "boxing night," when the élite of Dublin and the surrounding country were to be present in all their glory.

My newly made friend invited me to be one of a party of his student friends who had secured a box or stall for the performance. As we were of the some physical makeup, he asked me to accommodate him with the loan of a clean shirt and ten shillings as he was then temporarily out of cash, and he knew that his laundry would not be at his lodgings in time to permit him to make a proper appearance at the party. I readily complied. We were to meet at a cigar store near the College on Dame Street, and after the performance to adjourn to Jury's. I was promptly on time but my good friend failed to appear and I have not had the pleasure of casting eyes on him since. This was my first experience with a confidence man, and while it weakened my confidence in men it unfortunately did not destroy it, for I have had many experiences of the same sort since. But with it all I am still unreformed in this particular.

Newspaper writer—

Prior to going to Dublin, Mr. Denis Holland, an able newspaper man, had founded in Belfast a tri-weekly paper named *The Examiner.* In this enterprise he had associated with him the subsequently infamous Richard Pigott,[8] a son of Judge Baron Pigott. The paper was conducted on moderate Nationalist lines and was of strong Catholic tendencies. The establishment of juvenile reformatories then held a prominent place in the debates of the British Parliament. Imagining myself to be versed in the manner in which such establishments ought to be conducted, although having had no experience whatever except from my contact with the needy, I wrote an article, a most exhaustive and no doubt very prosy article, of about a yard's length upon the subject and dropped it into the editor's box in the office of the paper. I waited anxiously for its publication, but as the days passed and it did not appear, I came to the conclusion that if Mr. Holland were a great literary man he was decidedly deficient in discrimination, since he failed to discover in my effusion the superiority that I believed it possessed. My surprise was great and my pleasure supreme when after several weeks, about six inches of my article, containing the pith of my long-winded production, appeared in the editorial space of the paper above my initials.

[8] Richard Pigott subsequently got into financial difficulties and for years lived by writing begging letters and by similar means. In 1889, a Parliamentary Commisson found him guilty of having forged certain letters purporting to have been written by Charles Stewart Parnell, one of the leaders in the campaign for Irish freedom, in which the connection of the latter with the perpetration of certain outrages in Ireland was supposed to be admitted. Pigott confessed, fled to the continent and later committed suicide in a Madrid hotel.—Ed.

I imagined myself a writer and proceeded to pen a further equally long and, I now believe, incoherent treatise on some national topic. I did not trust this valuable production to the ignorant, prejudiced, and perhaps jealous manipulation, criticism, or mutilation of Mr. Denis Holland. I had a warm and faithful admirer in a boy of about my own age who accompanied me around on visits to his and my friends and when the opportunity appeared, which it invariably did, he would ask me as a special favor to read to our friends my poorly constructed production. I filled to his and my own delight and satisfaction the rôle of the Delhi editor, who read to his subscribers the manuscript that he had neither the means nor opportunity or desire to put in type.

My money began to give out and I had done nothing yet towards making the tour of the country preparatory to launching out as its regenerator. I had never felt the pinch of want, and I saw something must be done to replenish my exchequer if I proposed to live, not to speak of embarking on a vague and ill defined itinerary. Mr. Holland accompanied by the irrepressible Pigott had recently founded in Dublin *The Irishman* as the rival of the *Nation*,[9] and had brought along with him from Belfast as an important aid to his success in his new

[9] The *Nation* was founded in 1841 by the Young Irelanders. In addition to serving as the organ of those who favored the repeal of the Union between Ireland and England, it was employed as a means of preserving and cultivating the Gaelic language and literature.—Ed.

venture Mr. Shanley, his foreman printer. I knew Mr. Shanley very well as a friend of my father and believed that he would receive me cordially, which he did. He at once assumed my guardianship, installing me, with the approval of his admirable wife, in his house as a member of the family. He also secured me employment in the North Wall Foundry of which Mr. John Alhol, a Scotchman, was foreman and part owner.

Mr. Alhol looked like the pirates that I had read of in one or two hair-raising novels that I had come across earlier. There the resemblance ceased. He spoke loudly and with emphasis, and chewed tobacco like a goat; the odor of whiskey was always unpleasantly with him. He dressed in a pea-green jacket, and with the blackest of black hair covering his whole face he was a sight to inspire a timid boy, such as I was, with fear, if not with absolute dread. I found him to be everything but what his looks and appearance indicated. He was a man of superior education, of gentle manners, of a deeply sympathetic nature, prone to giving good advice both as a workman and as a man, gifted with great executive ability, and as a mechanic a highly finished product. He took a deep interest in me and had I continued with him, following his instructions inside and outside of the workshop, I believe that I would have been largely the gainer and that perhaps my subsequent career would have been much different. At this time, however, my father came to Dublin on business and prevailed upon me to return home, which in my secret heart I was in no way loath to do, but upon the stipulation that he would see that I should not be sent to jail by my employer as punishment for having run away.

Brief as were my experiences away from home, I had learned something which proved quite useful to me in later years. My opportunities to distinguish the difference between people or to note the variations in their character and conduct had previously been limited. I had formed the impression that those of my immediate family and friends were the best and most dependable of any in the world. The people of other counties in Ireland and of other countries were simply tolerable to me because they were necessary to population. I had in my absence from home met Dublin people and others from various parts of Ireland who actually compared favorably with my Belfast friends and relatives. More astonishing still, I was thrown into daily intercourse with Scotchmen and Englishmen who were the equals of my intimate friends. This surprising revelation came to me gradually, compelling the belief of a narrowness of observation on my part, which I had been unwilling to admit. In after years the lesson taught me in Dublin became more enlarged so that in the German, Frenchman, Spaniard, Italian, Indian, and Negro I found men as good and as bad, as sincere and as unreliable, as I had met in Ireland or among my friends. I set up a new standard of measurement for those with whom I had dealings, estimating them for their deeds and honest purposes, and not because of accident of birth or origin of race which was beyond their power to control.

Back in the foundry—

My father had much difficulty in making good his promise to keep me out of jail on my return home. He accomplished it, however, after a tedious lawsuit first in the Court of Quarter Sessions and later before the Seneschal in the Ecclesiastical or Bishop's Court. This latter court was a relic of olden times when the burden of administering the law in cases of slander and other acts involving moral turpitude devolved upon and was eagerly accepted by the clergy of the Established Church.

Instead of returning to the Ulster Foundry to complete my apprenticeship I went to work in Comb's Foundry. This was a place especially engaged in the manufacture of flax spinning and linen weaving machinery. Specialization in all lines of production had made considerable headway, and this was the largest and best equipped establishment of its kind in Ireland and one of the greatest in the British Isles. It was also one that the moulders' union of the period could not control. Nearly all the journeymen were members of the union, but the preponderance of boys in all stages of apprenticeship was so great that it was considered wisest to let the plant severely alone rather than attempt to unionize it.

Nearly all the employees, both men and boys, were employed upon special parts of the work and each excelled in the quality and quantity of the detail given him. A few were employed on jobbing work, and I was one of them. Even in this we were urged to the highest tension by the inducement of an extra shilling or two when the foreman considered it necessary to hurry us to complete a particular job.

A large outside job, not connected with flax spinning, was contracted for by the firm to be completed in a given time. The foreman proposed to sublet the contract to three of his best men with the privilege that they might select three apprentices to aid them on whatever terms might be agreed upon between them. I was one of the boys selected. The terms were that each of us, journeymen and boys, was to be paid regular wages and overtime at the rate of time and a half for every hour worked after six o'clock, and the balance, whatever it amounted to, was to be equally divided among the six of us.

We worked one week on this agreement, the most strenuous week I ever worked in my life. When it came to the settlement, after paying each his regular wages and overtime, there was only a paltry sixpence apiece coming to us. It was quite clear to me that our seniors were acting dishonestly with us, so on the following morning I refused to go on with them longer and my fellow-apprentices decided to do likewise. The journeymen did their best to talk us out of our resolution and promised better results next week, but we were immovable. The foreman knew that we had been defrauded and did not insist or even suggest the continuance of the partnership, which was at once dissolved. He gave each of us boys a big advance in wages, removed the older men, and we finished the job to his satisfaction. The increased wages stood to the end of our apprenticeship, long after the job had been completed. The foreman was an Englishman, who proved himself in this small matter to be a more honest and fair man than our Belfast and Irish leading men. My ideas of men and conditions were expanding and changing.

Social contacts and first romance—

I still maintained my standing as an ardent member of both the St. Vincent de Paul Society and the Christian Doctrine Society, and performed my obligations and duties to each with the same regularity as formerly. Joe Clark had gone and in his stead I began to associate with a middle-aged oddity named Jimmy Ferguson.

Ferguson was a tobacconist who lived with his aged mother and spent his leisure time in reading the *Spectator,* Goldsmith, and Johnson, and in reveling in the literary productions of that very literary period in English and Irish history. He was quite eccentric and affected being a philosopher. That he was profound in many things was admitted by all who met him. Some of his vagaries were absurd in the extreme, and whether he knew it or not he would deliver himself of the rarest and quaintest humor, his gravity lending zest to his humor. I learned a good deal from Jimmy Ferguson, who had the kindliest and softest heart a man could possess.

It soon appeared to me that I could lead him anywhere, and what I said was law to him. I never for a moment took advantage of that influence. What I did was to open a new field for him by introducing to his house a set of the best young men that could be gathered together. Ferguson had hitherto led an obscure life. He had no relatives but his mother, and his oddities precluded his having any friends. He was pleased beyond measure to receive my friends who became his regular nightly visitors. We formed a club, and as his house was a large one we had ample room for the modest festivities that we occasionally indulged in and enjoyed under his roof. Every member of the club, with the exception of myself, had some special talent. Discussions on every imaginable subject were indulged in without acrimony, and excursions into the country were of frequent occurrence.

Our club lasted about three years and only once during that time was its existence threatened or the least discord apparent. When a dearth of subjects for discussion occurred we resorted to card playing as an amusement and sometimes to checkers. We all looked upon gambling as a vice leading its followers by degrees down to a condition where dishonesty became master and where friendship in its truest sense was obliterated. Cheating, lying, treachery were the characteristics of its votaries, so far as we had observed, and drunkenness, loss of self-respect, debauchery, and destitution were its invariable results.

An Irish funeral—

Although my time was fairly well occupied with the club and the duties of long standing already mentioned, I still had some time to spend in the company of the sweetest girl I ever knew. Elishia Dobbin was my junior by two or three years. She had lived all her previous life in the country and had lately become our neighbor. My sisters and she became fast friends which naturally led to our intimacy. We became much attached and had she lived I have no doubt we would have been married. But death from tuberculosis claimed her before she was eighteen years of age. When that happened I thought that the world was a blank and believed that in a little while I too would take my departure for a better and happier existence. I was one of the chief mourners at her funeral, which took place near Toome Bridge.

The funeral cortégé left Belfast early on a beautiful spring morning and was met by a large number of sorrowing friends and relatives about a mile from the place of interment. The funeral party from Belfast left their carriages to make, as was the custom, the remainder of the journey on foot. My place was behind the hearse with the father and brother of my dead sweetheart. Preceding the hearse were a number of women whose heads were covered with scarfs or shawls. The morning was yet young and beautiful and the foliage of the trees was gently stirred by a soft light breeze coming from over the waters of Lough Neagh. The birds were caroling and twittering and all Nature looked glad, clothed in her resplendent verdure seen nowhere else but in Ireland. Suddenly there arose on the morning air the saddest and most mournful cadences, the most appealing and pathetic notes I have ever heard. It was from the women in front, the "keeners," as they are called, that the sounds came, and I was so overwhelmed with their penetrating effects and the consciousness of my loss that had I not clung to the arm of Henry Dobbin, I would surely have fallen to the ground.

So we buried her in the old churchyard at Toome Bridge, and there her fair form has decayed and been mingled with the dust of her fathers. The winds that blow across Lough Neagh, sighing among the trees, sing forever their memoriam to the purest and sweetest Irish maiden that God ever made and, in His inscrutable will, took to Himself so prematurely. *Requiescat in pace.*

II

A SOLDIER OF THE IRISH REPUBLIC

II

A SOLDIER OF THE IRISH REPUBLIC

The call to enlist—

It was several weeks after the funeral before I was fit to resume my customary routine. I had served my apprenticeship and was a full-fledged journeyman. I was most economical in my expenditures. Instead of banking my savings I converted them into gold and stored the money in my trunk. I was so intent upon saving that I felt that I was becoming a miser. I took delight in letting the gold coins slip through my fingers and would gaze upon them in the solitude of my room as the most important agent for good or bad that man had invented. My gold hoard simply ravished me. I was stingy in my almsgiving and in my donations to other worthy objects. I spent nothing except through downright pressure. I kept up my visits among the poor, was attentive at my work in the foundry, and frequented our club, but felt in it all that I was very much and sadly changed. There was no buoyancy in my actions and everything but the accumulation of money was distasteful to me.

About this time I was induced to attend the Sunday afternoon meetings of the Ulster Patriotic

Association. At first the addresses palled on me. I could see nothing in the proceedings but the opportunity for several poorly informed aspiring young fellows with limited brains to hurl their thunders, such as they were, at the hated British government. They proposed no practical measure for the advancement of the people of Ireland or for lifting them out of the slough into which they had been cast by the collapse of the Repeal Movement, the famine, and the failure of the Young Irelanders.

Little by little I became alive to the possibility that this society might be made to accomplish something of practical benefit. My ideas in this respect were all vague and were merely a revivifying of my earlier notions which I had when I had gone to Dublin. It came to me as a surprise when the chairman of the meeting on a Sunday when the attendance was unusually large, and I suspect because he was short of orators, called upon me for an impromptu speech. I was well-known among the young men, but as a talker I was not known at all. I felt that if I should embrace the opportunity and not be able to lay down a plan for future action, yet I could at least let the audience know what sort of Irishman I was, leaving it to them and the future to devise and mature a feasible course. I had in mind the example of Henry Joy McCracken, Robert Emmet, Wolfe Tone, and those patriots who went to their deaths for Ireland, rather than of Grattan and O'Connell. What I said I do not remember. I only know that my talk was loudly applauded, and it was agreed that steps should be taken to enlarge our sphere of action and to devise some method by which to extend and centralize our organization, its purpose being Ireland's separation from England.

I had noticed among the regular attendants a well dressed young man who paid marked attention to everything that passed. At the end of the meeting he was introduced to me as Mr. John Nolan. I knew that he was a stranger in the city but I knew nothing of his business,[1] character, or antecedents. He impressed me as an honest man and an enthusiastic Irishman. He explained to me the existence of an organization which was assuming national proportions, having for its object the establishment of a republic in Ireland.

I supposed from the early instructions of my old teacher, Mr. Ellis, that a republican form of government, such as that of the United States, was the true and only method of abolishing poverty, because in that country all were upon a level of equality. I rather imagined that this was not entirely the case in the American Republic, as a fierce struggle was then being waged for the abolition of slavery. Mrs. Harriet Beecher Stowe's *Uncle Tom's Cabin* had made me a warm advocate of the emancipation of the Negro. Where such injustices could be inflicted under protection and approval of law I believed that

[1] John Nolan was a draper employed by some of the large firms of Dublin as a traveling salesman.—Ed.

other inequalities were likely to prevail, but the exact form of their application was not quite clear to me at that time. However, a representative republican government was, I believed, much more preferable than a monarchical government, fostering, as it did, a landed aristocracy, maintained by grinding down the poor with exorbitant rents and taxation.

I accepted Nolan's program, however, and became a soldier of the Irish Republic.[2]

[2] James Stephens and John O'Mahony were the originators of the Fenian movement, or, as it was sometimes called, "The Irish Republican Brotherhood." These two Irish patriots had been active in the uprising of 1848 and had fled to Paris when the English Government succeeded in crushing that rebellion. They remained in Paris for some years planning and plotting for the freedom of Ireland. It is said that they agreed to establish an oath-bound organization for that purpose as soon as possible. O'Mahony went to the United States in 1852 or 1853, and Stephens returned to Ireland somewhat later. In 1857, a special messenger from New York arrived in Ireland, and searching out Stephens advised him that a group had been organized in the United States which would support a revolutionary movement with men and money if Stephens would take the initiative in its formation. O'Mahony, who was quite a Gaelic scholar, gave the name of "Fenian" to the organization which Stephens and his followers in Ireland called "The Irish Republican Brotherhood." The Fenians, or Finnia, were the mythical chivalrous companions of Fionn, the son of Coul, whose deeds play an important part in the traditions of Early Ireland.

O'Mahony established himself in New York as the "President of the Irish Republic," appointed a group of associates to his "cabinet," and collected funds for the support of the movement in Ireland and for the maintenance of his "sham government," but at no time did he visit Ireland to assist Stephens in the actual work of organizing the revolt.—Ed.

The stage setting—

At that time I was about 21 years of age, and during those few years great events had transpired in Europe. France had changed her rulers twice, and Napoleon the Little, as he was called by the great Hugo, was an exile on the Isle of Guernsey. The Crimean War had been fought in the interest of Turkey's stability in Europe. Cavour, aided by the arms of Garibaldi, had created a new and united Italy under Victor Emmanuel. Nearer home the great Chartist Movement in England had collapsed with the conviction of three great Welshmen, Frost, Williams, and Jones, who were sentenced to be hanged, drawn, and quartered for advocating the same measures and for expressing themselves in language no more emphatic than was used fifty or more years later by at least two Ministers of the British Government, Lloyd George and John Burns.[3]

[3] The Chartist movement, lasting approximately from 1837 to 1848, was based upon the demands of the lower classes of England for universal manhood suffrage, vote by ballot, division of the country into equal representative districts, annual Parliaments, abolition of property qualification for membership in Parliament, and payment of members of Parliament so that a poor man might serve therein.

John Frost, Zephaniah Williams, and William Jones, leaders of the Welsh Chartists, were arrested for participation in an armed attempt to release one of their comrades from the Newport Jail. They were sentenced to be hanged and quartered on January 16, 1840, but were subsequently deported to Van Diemen's Land. They were given conditional pardons in 1854, but not permitted to return to England, although Frost finally won an unconditional pardon and returned to England in 1856.

The Chartist movement did not collapse with the arrest and conviction of these three men, but continued until 1848 with no immediate results.—Ed.

Feargus O'Connor and Bronterre O'Brien, Englishmen of Irish parentage and name, were the leaders of this movement, which singularly enough never took a deep hold upon the Irish masses, owing to their hereditary attachment to clanship and the chieftain.

Early organization—

Nolan and I met frequently. I soon learned how far he had progressed locally in the work of organization. I also became acquainted with those whom he had enlisted in the new movement, among them Michael McGinn, Edward McGannon, and John Griffith. Griffith, as a boy, had been a Young Irelander, and only associated himself with the new movement to prove that he had yet some hope of Ireland's redemption. He lost no opportunity of making speeches on these lines, but declined to take an active part as an organizer in bringing about the desired goal. The others were new residents and strangers in Belfast and therefore could do comparatively nothing to forward the organization.

At the beginning of our organizing efforts in Belfast, John Nolan, Michael McGinn, Edward McGannon, and myself, in imitation of the example of Wolfe Tone and his companions when founding the society of United Irishmen, journeyed to McCarl's Fort, the most prominent point on Cave Hill, and there renewed our obligation to organize and fight for the establishment of the Irish Republic.

It was evident to me that an active, aggressive course had to be adopted if the organization was to be extended. James Stephens, the "Head Centre" of the organization,[4] came to Belfast and met our limited force, learning from each what he could do either as a recruiter or as a furnisher of arms. He installed me as the first "centre" in Ulster,[5] with the rank of colonel and commissioned me to have 5,000 men organized and, as far as possible, armed within three years. I had no difficulty in getting together my first thousand. Through them I hoped to extend the organization into the country. To do this required means. Nolan and I were each in steady employment at good wages, and as neither of us had dependents to support, we devoted our earnings to building up the organization. In about a year the gold in my trunk, which I had been so fond of handling, had almost disappeared, and I was thence afterwards cured of the inclination to become a miser. As a matter of fact, I went to the other extreme.

[4] The followers of Fenianism were grouped into "circles," which were analogous to regiments. A "centre" was considered as being equivalent to a colonel. He chose nine others who were known as captains, each of whom in his turn chose nine sergeants. Each of the latter then chose nine others who constituted the rank and file of the movement. The colonel was supposedly known only to his captains, each captain only to his sergeants, and each sergeant only to his immediate followers. But as John O'Leary, one of the historians of the agitation states, ". . . this rule was often violated." *Recollections of Fenians and Fenianism,* vol. 1, footnote p. 84.—Ed.

[5] Ulster, or North Ireland, is made up of the following counties: Antrim, Armagh, Cavan, Donegal, Down, Fermanagh, Londonderry, Monaghan, and Tyrone.—Ed.

From my men in the city I learned of men in various parts of the province who would willingly join and become organizers. Meantime, the organization was steadily growing in the city, and several centres were appointed to keep the growing organization in disciplinary form. Drilling became an active duty, each group of one hundred or less adopting whatever course was most expedient and safest in the acquisition of efficiency as future soldiers and also in procuring arms.

Nolan had enlisted William Harbinson, a color sergeant of the Antrim Militia, who also had charge of the armory of that regiment. This practically gave us control of over 1,000 rifles and a large quantity of ammunition. Nolan and I placed ourselves under Harbinson's tutelage in the study of Casey's *Tactics* and the manual of arms. Our instructor was most proficient. He was essentially a military man, a disciplinarian, quiet and undemonstrative, also well informed. He simply stipulated that for obvious reasons he was to be unknown in the organization. Only the most discreet and reliable members ever met Harbinson.

In Harbinson's neighborhood dwelt a man named Edward Smith, who had, as a seafaring man, traversed the globe. Mr. Smith was a high degree Mason and a non-Catholic, but an intensely implacable enemy of England. He became one of us, handing Nolan, who swore him in as a member, a handsome sum to facilitate organization. Mr. Joseph Biggar, a sturdy Presbyterian and a large pork packer and merchant, also contributed handsomely towards Nolan's expenses. Mr. Biggar afterwards became a member of Parliament and one of Parnell's staunchest and most unyielding supporters.[6] Neither of these men wished their connection with the organization known, and their wishes were duly respected. At a later date Smith, however, at my request placed his house at the disposal of Pagan O'Leary, when that eccentric gentleman came to Belfast to seduce the military from its allegiance to England.[7] Nolan also gained the adhesion of John Wesley Johnstone, and through him was given access to a magnificent set of young non-Catholics in Newtownards.[8] Every-

[6] Justin H. McCarthy, in *Ireland Since the Union*, p. 227, has the following to say regarding the support early given to Parnell by Joseph Biggar: "Any history of that wild and stormy period of obstruction would be incomplete which failed to do justice to the ability, the courage, and the loyalty of Mr. Biggar. When Mr. Parnell was still a young, almost unknown and untried member of the House of Commons, unsifted in the perilous enterprise of facing hostile and howling majorities, Mr. Biggar sat by his side, faithfully and undauntedly, through all the brunt of the battle."—Ed.

[7] Seamus MacManus, in *The Story of the Irish Race*, footnote p. 617, states that "The army in Ireland was honey-combed with Fenianism, and the police force likewise. The army was so Fenian that many regiments were entirely unreliable from the British point of view. Thousands of the men had taken the Fenian oath. The work was begun by O'Donovan Rossa, who swore in a soldier named Sullivan, a native of his own Roscarbery—and this soldier swore in another, and so on. But it was the remarkable character, Pagan O'Leary, who, tackling the work some months after Rossa had begun it, made a big success of it. John Devoy and William Rowantree stepped into the gap and continued the work, when O'Leary, betrayed by a soldier at Athlone, was sent into penal servitude."—Ed.

[8] Sometimes spelled "Newtown Ards."—Ed.

one of these men became organizers, extending the organization to Grey Abbey, Donaghadee, Bangor, and Comber, entirely or almost entirely non-Catholic territory. The Catholics in this territory were considered to be, with an isolated exception here and there, utterly worthless as Irishmen and were of the material from which informers are made. They were accordingly left alone.

As an evidence of the principles actuating the Newtownards men, the following personal experience may be of interest. I started out with one of them, one lovely Saturday afternoon, to visit the "Greenboys" of "Greba," as Grey Abbey was called in the Scotch dialect of that section. In front of us we noticed a man swinging his arms, waving his hat, and performing other antics of a peculiarly absurd character. He was evidently drunk and enjoying himself to his full bent in a solitary way and in keeping with his condition. When we came abreast of him and he noticed us, he belched forth most stentoriously the favorite malediction of the Orangeman, "To Hell with the Pope," expecting our approval. This was evidently the way he was enjoying himself from the time we had sighted him. No sooner had he uttered the exclamation than my Presbyterian friend, McBride, the blacksmith, left my side and with a powerful blow laid him out quite inert in the dust of the road. I ran to the poor fellow's relief and from appearances I concluded that he was dead. Blood was flowing freely from his nose, and he lay there utterly prone and motionless. I was in a dreadful state of trepidation and protested against such violence, but McBride stood there glaring at the unfortunate creature and said not a word. I secured some water from a house near by and bathed his face and otherwise relieved him, and at last he heaved a great sigh and opened his eyes. I raised him up and dragged him under the shade of the hedge at the side of the road.

During it all McBride stood there sternly looking at the man but never moving to give a helping hand. In a little while the poor Orangeman became perfectly conscious but remained dazed. Then my companion stepped forward and asked the man if he knew who was speaking to him. He said that he did. He was then asked if he knew what had happened to him and what was the cause of its happening. He said that he did not. "Well, I'll tell you," said McBride. "You were cursing the Pope. If you had cursed King William I would have struck you just the same. We are Irishmen in this country and not sectarian bigots; so, if you like you can have me arrested, for I knocked you down." Nothing in the shape of arrest or prosecution resulted from this occurrence. Having made the fellow as comfortable as I could, I proceeded with McBride to Grey Abbey.

The Greenboys—

The Greenboys were the relic of the United Irishmen of 1798. The organization had been preserved during the intervening time in the hope of ultimately realizing the expectations of its founders, i.e., separation from England. They were a sterling body of men and not one of them was a Catholic. It was from this section of County Down that the parents of Andrew Jackson emigrated. Many of his distant relatives were still residing there.

From one of the men in Belfast I learned of Mr. James Blaney Rice of Tyholland in the County of Monaghan. Upon visiting Mr. Rice I found it an easy matter to enlist him in the cause. For years he had been known as an enemy of England's domination in Ireland. He was a man of independent means, of fair education, and of most exemplary habits. He had improved his fine physique by a total abstinence from all alcoholic beverages, the use of tobacco, tea, or coffee and everything else that could be dispensed with upon which the British Government levied taxes. His reputation for probity was well established and known far and near. In a short time Monaghan and Cavan counties and the country around were well organized through the instrumentality of James Rice.

About the same time I heard of another man, equally as popular as Rice was in his section, who lived at Ballynahinch, and I called upon him. Mr. Gawn Dick was, I found, an hereditary rebel. Unlike

Rice, who was an ardent Catholic, Dick was an equally ardent Presbyterian. He owned a large farm and was also engaged in the occupation of a cattle dealer. He was likewise superintendent of the Sunday school attached to his church. In all his business transactions Dick's word was his bond, so that any movement that he became connected with was at once popular. I had no difficulty in enlisting him. Knowing of my projected visit he had assembled a large number of young Presbyterian farmers from the surrounding country, who received me most courteously and who all joined the organization.

I became aware of another influential man in the city of Armagh, Mr. George Gillen, and upon visiting him found him a ready recruit. The organization was growing apace in Belfast and was steadily spreading throughout Ulster extending into almost every village and hamlet. Wherever it was practical to engage in drilling it was done. At the same time, Nolan and I pursued the study of military tactics under the tutelage of Harbinson. Our Sundays and other available days were taken up either together or separately in making recruiting trips to distant parts of the province and invariably with success.

I tried to keep in touch with the drilling parties of my own immediate organization, but was not always successful as it was imperative that they should change their grounds so as to guard against exciting suspicion. I had cautioned them always to protect themselves by stationing guards in such positions that they might be warned against surprise—the police were becoming quite active at this time. Having a message to give to a company of recruits I set out to find them and learned from a member, whom I met coming from the drilling place, where they were. Instead of going the most direct and easiest way to the spot I chose another way, for the purpose, if I could, of surprising them. A small stream lined with tall trees was, they thought, enough of protection on that side without placing sentry or guard. Listening attentively I soon got range of their location from the almost whispered commands of the drill master. Without any trouble, I crossed the stream and was in the midst of them before they realized it. I was immediately set upon and would have been killed if one of the men in the obscure light had not recognized my voice. Not a man of them ran. It was a shock to them, however, and an experience to me, for I realized only after it was past, the danger of my experiment by the rough handling that I received. It taught them to be better guarded in the future, and it taught me not to repeat the trick.

My visits to Downpatrick and its neighborhood were more frequent than formerly. Now I was usually accompanied by Nolan. On the occasion of Nolan's first trip, we visited the grave of Thomas Russell, the intimate friend and companion of Robert Emmet, who had sent him north to rally, for the struggle of 1803, the remnants of the United Irishmen remaining after the failure of 1798. Like Emmet, Russell was captured and hanged, and his grave was almost unknown. Most of the people of Downpatrick were unaware that one of the ablest and best of Ireland's patriot martyrs was buried in their local churchyard. It may not have been in accordance with the precepts in which we two Catholics were instructed, but we knelt at the grave of this martyr of liberty and with devout fervor prayed that Almighty God would receive the soul of this Protestant hero with mercy and forgiveness.

A tragedy of patriotism—

My grandmother's sister, Alice Small, was, when Nolan and I became frequent visitors to her place, about eighty-four years of age. She had always been a silent person, never interesting herself in ordinary family matters or appearing to be concerned with anything beyond carding wool, spinning yarn, and knitting stockings. She always had two pairs of woolen stockings for me at every Christmas, handing them to me without a word and without waiting for a word of thanks. It seemed to be a self-imposed formal duty which she performed with annual regularity. I often tried to have her tell me the story of her young womanhood and to know why she had lived the silent unobtrusive life which she had for so many years, but she never responded to my requests. I had heard her story from others but never a word from her. It ran thus:

When she was a girl of about eighteen she had for a sweetheart a young farmer named Cotter to whom she was to be married when either Ireland was a free country or the turbulence of the times had moderated. Cotter was a United Irishman and took an active part in adding to its membership and in other ways making it as formidable as possible. When the demand was made for men to meet the British troops at Saintfield and thence afterwards under Henry Munroe to take their stand at Ballynahinch where they met disaster, young Cotter responded with a heart high with hope for victory. He was the only son of a widowed mother, but when the call came, fired with the justness of the cause that he espoused, he bade her and his sweetheart Alice farewell with the prayers and blessing of both for his safe return and with victory as his reward.

During his absence his sweetheart resolved to remain with his mother for mutual encouragement and consolation. Occasional and vague rumors of skirmishes would reach them, but nothing definite or decisive. At length after several anxious weeks the news came of the defeat at Ballynahinch and the scattering of Munroe's brave little army. A few nights after the news of the defeat had reached them Cotter came to his mother's house exhausted from his efforts and in want of food. When he had eaten he retired to his room in the rear of the house to sleep. The two women remained awake in anxious trepidation to warn their loved one of approaching danger. Martial law prevailed and as a consequence all lights were extinguished after a certain hour each night. So the women sat conversing in whispers in the dark with their hearing bent to catch the faintest sound of approaching danger. Soon there was borne to them the sound of the tramping of horses' feet and they knew by bitter experience that it was a troop of Welsh cavalry on one of their nightly raids to harass and persecute and, if need be, to punish some recalcitrant. Nearer the sounds came, yet the poor women were hopeful that their house would be passed. They were unwilling to disturb the sleeper. Such good fortune was not theirs, for the tramp of horses ceased at their house and the order was given by the officer in command to open the door.

Alice ran to his room and awakened her sweetheart while the mother delayed all she could in unbarring the door. In his bare feet, without hat, and in his night dress, Cotter jumped out of the window and fled in the gray of the morning, hoping to reach friendly succor several miles away. The soldiers, discovering the bed upon which Cotter lay to be still warm, knew instantly that a rebel had just left it and as the sun was rising noticed the fleeing man racing through the fields in the distance and began his pursuit. Cotter knew every short cut through the country in the direction toward the haven he was aiming at, and he knew that the cavalrymen had to limit themselves to the roads. He was soon beyond their reach. The River Quoile had to be crossed to assure him of undoubted security. He plunged in and crossed it successfully and felt himself free. But he was fatigued; the sun was at the horizon; and he was almost nude. He sought a secluded grassy spot and there resolved to recuperate and remain until friendly darkness would permit him to proceed to his destination.

While he slept a professional beggar woman passed and noticing a man in his scanty attire knew that he must be a hunted rebel for whose capture a neat sum was sure to be given. Proceeding on her way she met the troop of Welsh horsemen, and being questioned by the officer in command, gave the information as to where the hunted rebel lay. Being assured that she would receive a reward, she conducted them to the spot where Cotter lay oblivious to the approaching danger. He was arrested, and mounted behind one of the troopers was brought back in the afternoon to his mother's house, where on a tree in front of it and in the presence of his broken-hearted mother and sweetheart, without indictment or trial, he was strangled to death.

It was a sad and pitiful story, brutal and inhuman. The atrocity of the murder of her Irish patriot lover broke the heart of my poor grand-aunt whose long life afterwards was spent between praying for his soul and in heaping maledictions upon his murderers. When she came to understand the cause of my frequent visits to Saul and Downpatrick, she opened the floodgates of her heart and bade me with her blessing to go on, and expressed the hope that she should live to see the day when every redcoated minion of the British Government would be driven out of Ireland.

The Church and the revolt—

The ill-advised conduct of members of our organization in many parts of Ireland made clear to the Government that a widespread, active, and intelligently conducted conspiracy existed. It was impossible to suppress the foolish burst of patriotism displayed by these indiscreet, light-hearted members.

The *Irish People,* a newspaper, was established in Dublin by James Stephens with two objects in view, first to expound the doctrine of militant patriotism as well as to control its exuberance; and second, to make manifest those who were the covert enemies of Irish liberty while claiming to be its sincere friends.[9] Word had gone forth that the Sacraments were to be denied all members of our organization desiring them and that nothing less than the total abandonment of the Cause would entitle a

9 The *Irish People* was founded in November, 1863, as the mouthpiece of the Fenian movement. Its editors and writers preached open rebellion against the English Government, holding that constitutional methods had led only to dismal failure. The journal was published under the direction of three able, fearless, and brilliant writers, Charles Kickham, Thomas Clarke Luby, and John O'Leary. The strength and vigor of its articles did much to spread Fenianism throughout Ireland. On September 14, 1865, its office was raided by

religiously disposed man to receive them. As many of the priests, upon whom devolved the enforcement of this order, had been educated at Maynooth, which received annually the sum of £30,000 from the British Government, Stephens printed on the editorial page of each issue of the *Irish People* what purported to be the oath that every priest took upon his ordination. The Presbyterian Church had also been in receipt of a large annual sum from the Government, which was judiciously distributed among the pastorates, especially in Ulster. These endowments were looked upon as bribes given by the English Government to wean the rising generations of Irishmen from their disloyalty and make them more docile slaves to the misrule imposed upon their predecessors and themselves.

Thus, in addition to conspiring against the Government, the young men of Ireland were confronted with the stern antagonism of their clergymen. To offset this, however, many priests and some ministers were active propagandists of rebellion, and this convinced the young men that they were not offending against dogma, and that the fulminators of anathema were simply ecclesiastical police faithfully earning their bribe money. The *Irish People* was

the police, the plant confiscated, and the editors and some of their associates arrested, subsequently to be found guilty of treasonable activities and sentenced to imprisonment.

Most authorities on Irish history give September 15, 1865, as the date of the Government raid, but John O'Leary in his *Recollections of Fenians and Fenianism,* vol. 2, p. 205, states that it occurred on the evening of September 14, 1865.—Ed.

careful to foster this idea with the result that no heed whatever, or at least very little, was paid to denunciations, warnings, or fulminations by the clergy.

If the Dublin Castle and police authorities had their spies in every quarter, as we were told they had, so also had we. While their spies were venal and their information usually exaggerated and nearly always unreliable, the information given us was invariably accurate. Information was received that Cardinal Cullen's forthcoming Lenten pastoral (1864) would contain many distasteful expressions which it would be advisable for our men to hear and mark their disapproval of at the right moment. Marlborough Street Church, the cathedral, was jammed with interested worshipers on that eventful Sunday morning preceding Lent. The Cardinal sat on his throne in full pontificals. After the first gospel, as is usual in Catholic churches on Sundays, the celebrant made the customary announcements for the ensuing week and then proceeded to read the pastoral by His Eminence. The most profound silence prevailed as he described the duties to be observed during the penitential season by all Catholics. But when he began to describe the dangers to be encountered and the calamities to be invited by disobedience to the mandates of the Church which forbade rebellion and resistance to lawful authority, he was unable to proceed farther. Fits of coughing began toward the altar and spread over every part of the church. Everyone present seemed to be afflicted with a most distressing cold. At length the occupants of the front seats arose endeavoring to reach the entrance, and in a little while the great church was comparatively empty. The Cardinal was amazed and the priests at the altar were dumbfounded at the demonstration.

Bishop Moriarty, at the same season, announced that "Hell was not hot enough, nor eternity long enough to punish those guilty of participation in the conspiracy." Several other bishops expressed themselves in terms of condemnation, but in milder form. One high ecclesiastic, John McHale, Archbishop of Tuam, had nothing of an expostulatory or reprimanding character to offer. On the contrary, he denounced eviction and its consequent suffering, misgovernment and its evils, and many of the visible wrongs under which the poor were laboring. His pastoral we construed as an approval of our plans and actions.

The damage wrought by the bitter hostility of most of the hierarchy and priesthood of Ireland at this juncture of our movement was incalculable and I regret in many instances became permanent. Individual controversies between priests and youthful enthusiasts, and alienation of the latter from the Church, were of everyday occurrence. The point was even discussed at the time that if Rome was at the back of English domination in Ireland, then Rome should be abandoned and an Irish Church established that would be true to the heroic traditions of the country and its suffering people. Nothing came of this proposition as we were all more anxious to push our organization forward to supreme excellence than to waste time in polemics. That the annihilation of British power was sure to follow was devotedly believed by all of us.

The controversy changed me as well as many another young Irishman. From being a devout communicant I became careless and indifferent. A successful revolution seemed of greater moment to me than all the spiritual benefits to be derived from religion. My membership in the Christian Doctrine Society had lapsed a long time before, so also had my connection as an active worker in the St. Vincent de Paul Society. I still retained a lively desire to help the poor and hoped that a revolution would place them in a position independent of temporary relief where all would be free and equal.

Dr. Denver, Bishop of Down, was, I understood, a distant relative of my father. He was a scientist more than a churchman, and also a mechanic of established reputation. When my father told me that the Bishop wished to consult me about making a pattern for castings to be used in the production of a new and powerful light, I readily consented to meet him. The invitation was simply a decoy. When the Bishop entered the room where I was waiting with my father, he began at once to berate me for my connection with a treasonable conspiracy and demanded that I at once cease my membership in it. Regarding the Bishop as the political servant of England and therefore an enemy to Ireland, and forgetting that he had never till that time said a word to indicate on which side he was, I replied right boldly that, although I regarded and respected him as my spiritual director and superior, I refused to allow him to dictate to me my course in politics. I refused also to address him as "My Lord," the ecclesiastical title given bishops the world over. I felt that I was too loyal and sincere a Republican to acknowledge any aristocratic title.

The venerable Bishop pointed out to me the dangers and ruin awaiting the individual who participated in such enterprises, such as imprisonment, possible death on the scaffold, and disgrace. His arguments and appeals touched me not at all, but rather confirmed me in the belief that I was right. Nothing could be more acceptable to God and man than to suffer for one's oppressed country, and if need be to die the death of a patriot and martyr. Failing to impress me along these lines he turned to the Church's censures and endeavored most forcibly to show the punishments in the other world awaiting those who disobeyed the commands of its pastors. The terrors of excommunication did not weigh with me. I felt that it was a God-given privilege and a sacred duty to work and suffer and die that others might be blessed and happy, and no Church censures could change or controvert, stultify or deny what God had so firmly planted in my mind and soul. I told the Bishop that he could, if he chose, publicly excommunicate me, but that if he did he was doing the work of England by singling me out for arrest. He never did so.

I then left him and my father together, and knowing that a number of our leading men were holding a meeting I went there and gave them a detailed account of my interview with the Bishop. Had I yielded to the arguments and appeals of the Bishop at that time, our organization in Belfast and in Ulster would have been destroyed. I had been its most active, primary builder. My reputation among the young men was considered good, and I was quite popular with them. I was conscious of all this and felt how much depended upon my decision in the matter. Failing to prevail upon me to abandon the cause, the Bishop made no further attempts to influence anyone else.

O'Donovan Rossa—

The organization grew wonderfully stronger. Samuel Kerr, the Mormon leader in Belfast, became an active organizer. Tom Russell also became a member. Both were fellow-workers with me in the foundry and were non-Catholics. These men with John Waters, who was related to Francis Davis, the poet of the revolt of '48, began vigorous work among the local non-Catholic element of the population.

About this time our local organization was in prime condition. Drilling was going on every night in every available spot in the vicinity and was done so systematically and carefully as to attract no attention from those outside the organization. Arms were steadily being smuggled into the city and were safely distributed. Nolan and I could enter or depart at any hour of the night from the military barracks on Queen Street. Several ordnance sergeants were commissioned officers in our service, and they had control of all arms, ammunition, and other supplies stored there. The armory of the Antrim Militia was practically in our keeping, and with the aid of the Irish soldiers stationed at Belfast, Carickfergus, and other adjacent points most of whom were members of our organization, the arms and supplies stored there were at our disposal. Belfast was never in such condition for successful rebellion as it was at that period and up to 1865.

The laying of the foundation stone of the O'Connell monument on Sackville Street, Dublin, was considered a national enterprise, and was sure to attract thousands to the metropolis.[10] Jeremiah O'Donovan (Rossa),[11] who for several years had been the Chief National Organizer, availing himself of this opportunity, invited representative men from all over Ireland, England, and Scotland to meet him.

[10] The exercises held in connection with the laying of the corner stone of the O'Connell monument took place on August 8, 1864.—Ed.

[11] Commonly known as "O'Donovan Rossa" from the place Ross, where his family lived.—Ed.

I had met Rossa in Belfast and received his invitation with pleasure. At this time Rossa was a widower. He had been a merchant in the town of Skibbereen, County Cork, when he first connected himself with the organization. Through the indiscreet, swaggering folly of some of the members and the aid of the informer Sullivan ("Goulah"), he was arrested with others at the same time that arrests in Belfast were made of a number of what were then called "Ribbonmen," but are now known as Hibernians. There was no relation whatever between Rossa's group and the Hibernians. Rossa's organizations was Irish and National; the "Ribbon" society was sectarian and Catholic, and was banded to fight the Orangemen.[12]

Upon the death of Rossa's wife, he received, if I remember correctly, about £8,000 insurance. Stephens was serving as a tutor in the families of

[12] O'Donovan Rossa and some of his friends had organized the "Phoenix National and Literary Society" in the little town of Skibbereen. Stephens visited the place in May, 1858, and enthused the members of this local organization as to the possibilities of freeing Ireland by means of an armed rebellion. Recruits were added from neighboring districts, drilling was engaged in, and plans for the uprising went forward most vigorously until in December, 1858, when the Government arrested some twenty members of the society. Through the testimony of an informer, Sullivan, nicknamed "Goulah," the Government was able to convict Daniel O'Sullivan, who received a sentence of ten years' imprisonment. The others, including O'Donovan Rossa, after being held in jail for eight months, upon the suggestion of the court, pleaded guilty, and were released on a bail of £200. The Government thus crushed the "Phoenix Conspiracy," but the latter was only a part of the larger Fenian movement which was then developing most rapidly.—Ed.

some of the wealthy residents of Dublin and was sorely handicapped for the necessary means to enable him to extend the revolutionary organization. Rossa gave up his business, and placing his capital at the disposal of Stephens, became the Chief National Organizer of the movement, and later the business manager of the newspaper, the *Irish People.* To Rossa's money, generously and unostentatiously given, was due the extension of our organization in the southern and western portions of Ireland as well as in England and Scotland. The impression has long prevailed that this growth of our movement was accomplished by the contributions given so plentifully and generously by the Irish in America. To O'Donovan Rossa alone is due the credit for the fact that, in the places mentioned, the organization was in prime condition for effective work.[13]

Maria Shaw—

In Dublin, O'Donovan Rossa lived at the home of Maria Shaw. Miss Shaw was a young County Carlow woman of great mental and executive ability, who, when it was thrust upon her, became the ablest of managers in several of the venturesome enterprises connected with the organization. Her life was

[13] John O'Leary in his *Recollections of Fenians and Fenianism,* vol. 1, p. 135, footnote, states that, according to James Stephens the revolutionary movement received a little less than £1,500 from America during the period 1858–1864, and about £31,000 during the next two years, or a total of £32,500, of which £7,000 was seized by the Government.—Ed.

a daily, living sacrifice, and her subsequent poverty and neglect were the usual rewards which follow unostentatious, unselfish industry in every cause which aims to free mankind or any portion of it from the yoke of oppression, whether it be religious, political, or economic in character.

Maria Shaw was related to Andrew and John Nolan.[14] She resided with her widowed mother and brother William, who afterwards became a San Francisco policeman. Her home was in that district of Dublin formerly inhabited by the lesser luminaries of the aristocratic world, with which Dublin in its earlier history abounded. It still retained a few of the traits of its departed greatness, consisting mainly in the width, cleanliness, and silence of its streets and the height of its sparsely tenanted dwellings.

Maria Shaw ostensibly carried on the business of a *modiste,* and employed several women. Her real business was dressmaking, and this she conducted successfully, supporting her family with the proceeds. She was of medium height, dark complexioned, active, and decisive in all her movements. She was plain of feature except when her enthusiasm was appealed to, then she became luminous. She had a tender heart for the poor and those in sorrow and an equally strong and determined one when it came to combatting injustice. She was a good and con-

[14] The two Nolans were loyal and active organizers in the Fenian agitation.—Ed.

vincing talker, not a public or platform speaker, but a sensible and frequently brilliant conversationalist. Long prior to the suppression of the *Irish People,* she was known to all the prominent members of the organization who visited Rossa at her house, where he lived until his marriage to a Miss Irwin of Clonakilty.

It became necessary to raise a fund to assist the families of the men under arrest in Dublin and elsewhere in Ireland and awaiting trial. Miss Shaw proposed the holding of a fancy fair and directed it with the aid of Mrs. Michael Scanlon of Chicago and a few other ladies. She dispensed the money raised and otherwise contributed for that purpose judiciously and fairly, causing afterwards neither adverse comment nor reflection upon her management.

To the political prisoners confined in Mountjoy Prison she was a veritable angel. Her correspondence with many of them, all written with her own hand, must have taken up a large portion of her time. Every letter was optimistic, infusing courage and hope, and if the person favored were familiar with the affairs of the organization in Ireland and could read between the lines, her letters gave him a most encouraging insight into conditions. Her letters were censored, so that to convey news of importance in plain language was a difficult matter. She was so well informed regarding the men in all parts of Ireland and the strength of the organization that when Edward Duffy assumed temporary charge[15] she became invaluable as the only reliable person he for a time could depend upon for the information necessary in order to fill up the places of the men arrested or whose flight to avoid arrest had created the vacancies.

After the collapse of the Fenian movement, with her mother and brother she emigrated to the United States. The last I heard of her, she was living in St. Louis, Missouri, pursuing her vocation of dressmaking, unknown as the brightest, most energetic, fearless, and cautious of the many good and intrepid women identified with the effort to establish a republic in Ireland.

Pagan O'Leary—

In carrying on the work of organization Rossa adopted the plan of inviting his visitors to dinner. Among the large number present I was particularly taken with John Ryan, of Liverpool, and Michael McLaughlin, of Glasgow. The proximity of the place of meeting (Dublin) and the easy access from Belfast, unattended with danger, made it a pleasant and practical duty. I also made the acquaintance of Jim O'Connor, later a member of Parliament and one of the earliest members of the Home Rule Party. O'Connor was at that time acting as bookeeper for

[15] Colonel Thomas J. Kelly assumed charge of the Fenian movement in Ireland after Stephens had escaped to France. Kelly later went to England and Edward Duffy succeeded him as Acting Head Centre. Duffy was known as the "Fenian Emmet."—Ed.

the *Irish People* and was its real business manager. I also became acquainted with Pierce Nagle,[16] the notorious informer who went under the name of "John Cooper."

At the same time I became almost instantly the friend of "Pagan" O'Leary. The "Pagan" was certainly a curiosity. His real name was Murphy. His parents had designed him for the Church, as is the case with so many Irish families who pinch and torture themselves in order that a member of the family may become a gentleman as well as a servitor of the Lord. I believe that young Murphy was placed in St. Jarlath's College at Tuam. By all accounts he progressed fairly enough in his studies, but being under no special discipline as regards hours, he, with others of his fellow-students, was in the habit of frequenting the dinner table of the leading hotel on Sunday afternoons. The Repeal Movement was in full swing, and politics and discussions as to the merits of the Young Ireland movement that was superseding O'Connell's peace policy frequently held sway at public dinner tables as well as at private ones.

On one of those occasions several junior officers of the British Army were present, one of whom was a member of the Waterford or Beresford family. The Beresfords for years, in one way and another,

[16] Our author is referring to Pierce Nagle, the Government spy, through whose testimony the leaders of the Fenian movement were convicted, following the raid upon the office of the *Irish People* on September 14, 1865.—Ed.

had been extracting out of the blood and muscle of the manhood of the country thousands of pounds sterling annually. The common topic of the state of Ireland being as usual under discussion, all present took an unrestrained part in it. Hot words were hurled back and forth between the officers and the students, Beresford leading the officers while Murphy filled the same rôle for the students. Beresford became personally abusive of his opponent as well as contemptuous of everything Irish and exasperated Murphy, who in a moment of passion picked up a carving knife and plunged it into Beresford's body. A general mêlée followed, ending in a victory for the students. The wound was pronounced dangerous and possibly fatal. Murphy therefore fled to America as the safest place of refuge.

Upon arriving in America, having neither trade nor training whereby to subsist, and being limited in funds, Murphy enlisted in the United States Army and went to Mexico, to impose on that country what he had been fighting against in his own. A spent bullet from a Mexican rifle hit him squarely in the forehead, making an indentation large enough to admit the tip of one's forefinger, but otherwise leaving him apparently uninjured. His brain, however, was affected by the wound, for almost immediately afterwards he proclaimed himself a pagan and adopted the name "O'Leary" in admiration of the Ard-Righ or high King of Ireland who ruled when St. Patrick first preached the gospel, and who refused to abandon his pagan faith for the light of Christianity. The monarch's name was O'Leary.[17] The adoption of or return to paganism was in the opinion of O'Leary a proper and logical preliminary to Irish independence since, if adopted, it would abolish both Orangemen and Ribbonmen and all sectarianism. On all other questions he remained perfectly sane, although sometimes foolhardy in his conduct.

After our organization had acquired strength, Pagan O'Leary returned to Ireland believing that he could be of assistance by corrupting the British Army. He had become a carpenter in the meantime, but to follow that occupation was intensely irksome to his enthusiastic nature. The "Pagan" attached himself to me most closely because, I suppose, I was more tolerant of his idiosyncrasies than the majority whom he met. While I remained in Dublin, I found him every morning parading the corridor of the hotel before my bedroom to tell me of some of his adventures with the soldiers on the preceding day. I listened to him kindly and petted him, and as I learned to know him better, I admired him for his unflinching loyalty to the Cause, in the unlimited success of which his belief never wavered.

At the "Pagan's" own request Stephens later sent him to Belfast to work among the soldiers stationed there and specially committed him to my

17 The monarch referred to was Laoghaire, son of Niall of the Nine Hostages.—Ed.

care and protection, warning me under no circumstances to permit him to meet any of our men. The reason for this was that his wild talk about returning to paganism and his denunciations of Christianity would scare or intimidate those of our followers who were religiously disposed and who were sensitive on that subject. I found him desirable quarters to operate in and a suitable residence, and duly cautioned him as to his mode of procedure. He agreed to comply with all my instructions, but did not stick to his promise, for I was notified within a week that he was in danger of arrest. I had some difficulty in getting him out of town, but succeeded.

In a few weeks I heard of his arrest in Athlone, where he had gone on the same mission. He was tried at the Court of Assize, and convicted of debauching Her Majesty's loyal soldiers. He received a sentence of seven years' penal servitude. It is customary, in fact it is imperative, for each convict to declare what religious faith he professes when he becomes a convict, and as O'Leary persisted that he was a pagan without sympathy or love for Christianity in any form, and as paganism was not acknowledged by the prison authorities as being either popular or respectable, he was doomed to solitary confinement on bread and water for seven days. When asked again as to his religious adherence he still remained a pagan and was returned for further punishment. When questioned again his answer once more gained for him a repetition of his punishment. Upon being asked the fourth time he weakened in his declaration. It was not within the physical nature of the sturdiest adherent of paganism to withstand the wearying effects of such drastic treatment, so he resolved on compromising. "You have got two religions in this place, I believe," he said. "To one or the other I must profess to belong. One is the robber's church, the Protestant, and the other is the beggar's church, the Catholic. Put me down as a member of the beggar's church, but I will still be a pagan."

What became of the poor "Pagan" I never heard; for long before the expiration of his prison term I was far in the western part of the American Republic.

A clash with Orangemen—

On the return of the last trainload of excursionists from Dublin to Belfast, after the laying of the foundation stone of the O'Connell monument,[18] an attack was made upon the train by Orangemen, both at the entrance to the Ulster railroad station and from a bridge under which the train passed on its way to the station. Riots of this sort often occurred in Belfast, ending generally in the discomfiture of the Catholic party. They were usually of short duration, seldom lasting longer than a week. This utterly outrageous and unprovoked assault on a

18 The cornerstone of the O'Connell monument was laid August 8, 1864.—Ed.

number of inoffensive travelers aroused the indignation of the men of our organization, and we resolved to punish the Orangemen and if possible convince them by force, if we could not by reason, of their error. It was not a pleasant undertaking for men to embark upon, especially when we had been preaching the doctrine of national unity and the destruction of sectarian prejudice.

We realized that the Orangemen were not Irish and that nothing could ever make them such. Decent, intelligent Englishmen and Scotchmen refused to acknowledge any kinship with them. They had been nurtured by Tory landlords and speakers in the belief of their superiority, although most of the poor creatures were as poorly off, and many of them more so, than those to whom they claimed to be superior. It was the assertion of the old hereditary ascendancy idea passed down from the despoilers in the persecutions and murders of the penal days. Catholics, who claimed mere human rights, were looked upon by the ignorant Orangemen as preposterous aspirants for those things that were exclusively in the possession of themselves. The poorer the Orangemen were, the more rigid were their objections to all the reasonable demands or requests of the Catholics.

To us who were Nationalists, the Orangemen presented themselves as an obstacle to our success. We looked upon them as the pliant and ready tools in an emergency of the English Government's stability in Ireland. We recognized that while many Catholics entertained sentiments of bigotry and intolerance as bitter and as deep-seated as those held by the Orangemen, there was some justification for those sentiments because of past wrongs ruthlessly inflicted upon them or their ancestors because of their religion. We knew for the same reasons that in a fight with England we could depend upon Catholics when we could not depend upon a solitary Orangeman, however oppressed he might be.

We had a powerful organization locally and if need be we could add to it in plenty by issuing a call upon our friends in the surrounding country. We accordingly decided to give the Orangemen a good drubbing. The strife lasted for about two months. Business was generally suspended. Mills, factories, workshops, and stores were shut up and in many instances barricaded for fear of looting, which indeed was largely and frequently indulged in. Constabulary and troops were drafted into the city in great numbers. Martial law was proclaimed and an internecine war was waged such as Belfast has never experienced before or since.

At the end of the fight, brought about mainly by exhaustion and a limitation of supplies, it was learned that the casualties among the Orangemen in killed, wounded, and missing were much greater than on our side. There were also more Orangemen captured by the police, and when brought to trial, a greater number of convictions was secured among them. The Orangemen were aided and favored by their wealthier brethren, who did not fight, and by the magistracy, mostly Orange in sympathy. On the other hand non-Catholics actively led the Catholics, contributing in every way to their victory. The most active and prominent non-Catholic taking part in the conflict was John Wesley Johnson,[19] formerly of Newtownards, one of the most indefatigable workers in the Nationalist cause. It spoke immeasurably well for the Catholics to follow the lead of those not of their faith, for it showed their confidence and earnestness in following those who proved themselves to be enemies of the representatives of oppression.

During the hostilities Mr. Andrew Nolan, a brother of John Nolan, came to Belfast to view the situation. He asked me to take him through the principal disturbed districts in order that he might make his observations first hand. I escorted him all through the Orange district unmolested, and we had almost crossed the Boyne Bridge, which spans a dirty, lazy, filthy stream, and were nearing Dr. Drew's church, which was situated on the boundary line dividing the two districts, when I was recognized by one of the crowd gathered there, as an intruder. A rush was made for us and the customary demand made by the leader that we curse King William. Before we had time to say anything in protest or approval, a squad of policemen drew up across the end of the bridge and our would-be Orange assail-

[19] Spelled "Johnstone" on p. 59.—Ed.

ants fled precipitately. We were thus fortunately saved from a sound mauling or worse. Nolan was inclined to laugh at the affair when it was past, but had it not been for the timely arrival of the police it might have proved to be a most serious and disagreeable experience.

Trade union affiliation—

Prior to my patriotic enlistment, I had become a member of the Friendly Society of Iron Founders of England, Ireland and Wales. I was not impressed with the procedure of that society. It seemed to have no soul. It looked like a purely sordid affair. The ties binding its members were its benefits. Strike, out-of-work, sick, death, and superannuation benefits were the only links I could see holding it together. It was purely an English affair, carried on as a business enterprise without reference to any idealistic aims. English trade societies are mostly distinctive, unsentimental business partnerships, conducted with a rigid honesty as commendable as they are beneficial in a material way to their members. The education of trade unionists is carried on elsewhere in lyceums, reading rooms, and through the medium of libraries and free popular lectures. These were all numerously and diligently attended, but the union hall, club house, or meeting place was entirely free from such activities.

Beyond sending my weekly contributions to the Moulders' Union I took little interest in that organization. It was too sleepy, too inactive an organization to suit my temperament at the time. Politics and related matters were strictly prohibited, and I personally knew nothing or comparatively little about the economic conditions then prevalent. I had made an effort to stir things up and put life into the union, but was so severely sat upon for my temerity that I was diffident about attempting it again.

At one of the quarterly meetings of the union a letter was read from the executive officers in London informing us that we were entitled to send a delegate to an international convention to be held in Geneva, Switzerland. In ridicule of my former attempt to stir the union to action of some sort, one of those most opposed to my ideas suggested that I be selected as their representative and sent to Switzerland, as I would be likely to find it the best place to ventilate my foolish notions. As the scene of operations was far off no harm would result to any one but myself or those who heeded me. So I was chosen as their delegate, but I did not go.

International Affairs

It has been a matter of deep regret to me ever since that I did not attend that gathering. Garibaldi, with his crown of freshly worn laurels as the hero of a United Italy, presided. Proudhon, the Frenchman and author of works on Anarchism, and Bakounin, the Russian nihilist, were there. I believe that

Karl Marx, the father of scientific Socialism, was also present as well as several advanced thinkers from among the trade unionists of England and other countries, including one, I think, from the United States of America.[20] Subsequent familiarity with the works of these men and the influence they have exercised in forming opinions and beliefs on economic questions has caused me deep regret that I did not attend that convention. Socialists, anarchists, and nihilists, all able and all earnest propagandists of their special theories designed for the benefit of mankind, made up a gathering of which it was surely worth being even an obscure member, as I would have been. It is possible that at that time I would have been carried away by the advocates of the most extreme propositions, who could most plausibly appeal to my heart as having the surest, most reasonable, and quickest way to relieve the world of so much distress and misery. I now know that I was an undoubted visionary, ready to jump at once into any Utopian scheme likely to abolish poverty.

At the time of the Trent affair,[21] it looked as if England's neutrality between the warring sections of the United States was at an end, and that she was

[20] This was the first congress of the International Workingmen's Association, the "First International," held at Geneva in September, 1866.—Ed.

[21] On November 8, 1861, Mason and Slidell, representatives of the Confederate States, were taken off the British steamer Trent by the officers of the San Jacinto, a boat belonging to the Northern States. War with England over the affair was narrowly averted.—Ed.

resolved to declare openly her hostility to the Northern States. She had been covertly aiding the Confederacy all along by every means and subterfuge at her command. The arrest of Mason and Slidell on an English ship en route to Europe as envoys of the Confederacy was a bold step on the part of the Northern States, which our revolutionary organization applauded and which we believed would force England into war in support of the Confederacy.

In order to encourage the American Government in its course and to show the United States how we stood, a great meeting was held in the Rotunda in Dublin.[22] Delegations from all parts of Ireland attended the meeting at which resolutions were adopted declaring our willingness to aid the Northern States in case of a conflict between them and England. The resolutions were not idle vaporings, as many such expressions are, but were the utterances of determined men ready to fulfill every pledge made. The hall, the largest in the city, accommodated over 5,000 people. It was crammed to overflowing by representatives of at least 50,000 willing, loyal men, prepared to sacrifice themselves in vengeance against England.

I do not claim that this meeting prevented the English Government from declaring war against the United States, but I do claim that it did greatly intimidate England. It also demonstrated to the United States where our organization stood. Fifty

[22] This meeting took place on December 5, 1861.—Ed.

thousand determined men in England, Ireland, Scotland, and Wales were obviously quite capable of creating a ruinous diversion at home on behalf of the United States, and the British Government knew it. If we could have done nothing else we would have left her palaces, Parliament houses, and great cities in ruins, destroying her factories and arsenals, crippling her shipbuilding and ammunition plants, leaving all England a scene of destruction and devastation too horrible to contemplate. We were willing to do this even though we ourselves and our country went down in the ruin, leaving no hope of resurrection behind us. We had men everywhere, and all were eager for the day of vengeance and retribution. That was the condition in Ireland at the time of the great meeting in the Rotunda, and those were the intentions of the men of our organization had England declared war against the Northern States.

The Confederate cruiser "Alabama" put into Belfast Lough ostensibly to get provisions, but really to create sympathy for the Southern Cause. The aristocracy, Orange magistracy, and men of wealth, whom we classed as the natural enemies of the Irish people, hailed the coming of the vessel, knowing her mission, as an event by which to show, in the reception given her officers, how desirous they were to see the American Republic smashed to fragments. The town put on its gala garb and with a band playing and banners flying the enemies of Ireland boarded a tugboat decorated with bunting, visited the ship and escorted the officers of the cruiser to the city. Carpets were laid from the gangplank of the tug to the carriages, and the sworn enemies of the American Republic were escorted to all points of interest in the city and vicinity, and fêted at a banquet where every speaker delivered messages of comfort and encouragement to their Confederate guests. Bumpers were most heartily drunk to the destruction of their common enemy, the United States. No Irish Nationalist could complacently accept the compliments paid these officers as the expression of Irish opinion, and when in after years many of us were forced to leave our country, we naturally attached ourselves to the Republican Party, principally because the South, whose representatives were thus fêted by our enemies, was the dominating power in the Democratic Party.

The Ribbonmen—

Our organization was well advanced in Belfast and its immediate vicinity but lagged in the country, so when the opportunity was given I availed myself of a job in Gardiner's Foundry in the City of Armagh. Armagh was the center of a great flax-growing area extending from Newry in Down to Dungannon, Omagh, and Cookstown in Tyrone, and from Caveri to Portadown. The intermediate territory was studded with small groups of our men, but a thoroughly systematic organization had not yet been effected.

The backwardness in organization was largely due to the opposition of one of the branches of the Ribbonmen. This order had recently split upon the issue of aligning with non-Catholics. One faction called themselves the "old," the other the "new." The latter was headed by a man named Nolan, a resident of Manchester, England, who held that religion was no bar to Irish brotherhood and that all Catholics and non-Catholics should bury their differences and work as one man for the success of the common cause, namely, Irish liberty. The "old" were of the opinion that non-Catholics could not by that fact be Irish patriots and should therefore not be associated with. I regarded the "old" group in the same way that I did Orangemen, and classed them as such. The same motives actuated both of these latter groups, the difference being in their faiths and their colors and the mottoes of their insignia. The "old" group was quite strong in Armagh and contiguous counties.

The flax buyers of Armagh were a numerous, energetic, intelligent, and patriotic set of young men. They attended all the markets in the territory mentioned and knew the farmers, storekeepers, and artisans from long and close association. A very few of them had associated with the Ribbonmen, "old" or "new," and those few readily abandoned that organization when they were made familiar with the organization that I desired to propagate. I commissioned nearly all of them as organizers with magnificent results. It became my duty to visit the new men in their several localities and to appoint those whom I deemed best qualified as local "centres." Soon the organization was booming in every direction. Attention was paid to places in which it was suspected that arms were stored. Drilling proceeded with caution and regularity.

The nature of my activities began to be understood by others than those immediately interested, although I did my best to keep them secret. I was in the habit of meeting a few of the friends in the hotel facing the Mall (a small town park in the center of the city) and of remaining with them until about 11:00 P.M. On a particular Saturday I went out into the country to adjust a slight difference that had arisen between some of the men. The next morning the dead body of a man was found in the Mall with his skull crushed. In height and general appearance he was mistaken for me because I always passed through the Mall upon leaving the hotel, usually unaccompanied. What gave confirmation to the supposition that it was I who was to have been murdered was the fact that no rigid investigation was made of the murder. The victim was identified as an inoffensive Orangeman.

I was notified by James Rice that he had arranged a conference between the principal men in Monaghan County, representing respectively the "old" and the "new" factions of the Ribbonmen, and that he wished me to attend. Accompanied by three of my best Armagh men I drove to the town of Monaghan. As it was a secret society and I was not a member of either faction, I could not participate in the conference. By a system of relay messengers I was kept well informed of the proceedings, advising my friends as to the arguments and methods best calculated to bring about a union of the two on the broad basis of non-sectarianism. The conference lasted to a late hour Sunday night and ended in absolute failure. The "old" insisted throughout that unless non-Catholics were excluded they would not belong to our organization. When about a mile from Monaghan on our return to Armagh, we were assailed by a fusillade of ginger ale bottles which my companions charged to members of the "old" faction.

I was more successful in weakening and in ultimately destroying the "old" faction in Armagh County. Instead of soliciting them as a body I took them individually, convincing each one of the folly of his organization without assailing its purposes. The County Master fought against the encroachments as long as he could, and when he found himself almost alone came to me offering himself as a volunteer member. He also brought along his regalia, rule book, and other paraphernalia of the Order, and as an evidence of his good faith and total surrender gave them to me to do with as I pleased. To prove that I did not wish to know anything about the working of the Order, I placed the package in the fire as he handed it to me and both of us watched it being consumed to the last particle.

The parish priest of Armagh—the cathedral was then in course of construction—in addressing the congregation at the last mass on a Sunday toward the close of my residence in the city, warned those present against strangers who were inveigling young men into illegal associations, and like Wm. Carleton's "Roddy the Rover," betraying them to the Government. His remarks were so pointed that every one in the church, including the police present, knew that he was alluding to me. I was thus pointed out to the police as a dangerous and undesirable resident as plainly as if I had been mentioned by name. The priest's address, however, failed of its effect. The men had more confidence in me than they had in him. To mark their condemnation of his conduct it was resolved to close the church against him when he came to celebrate the last mass on the following Sunday. The church was enclosed on all sides by goodsized buildings and high walls, and the only entrance was through a tall iron gate. The people were gathering in numbers when his Reverence, approaching the gate, found it locked and the key gone. He shook the gate violently as if that would open it, but it was unyielding. He sent a boy to a blacksmith shop down the lane for a sledge hammer and chisel, determined to break the lock if necessary. All the hammers and chisels in the blacksmith shop had mysteriously disappeared. No one could tell him how or why this thing was done, so he returned to his house and the congregation dispersed.

Archbishop Dixon was much incensed at the scandal and wishing to know all about it, after having questioned the priest he sent for George Gillen, a leading Catholic and one of the earliest members of our organization. Gillen informed the Archbishop, without hesitancy, that the gate had been locked as a rebuke to the priest for acting as an agent of the British Government in designating men for arrest and in charging offenses against them of which they were not guilty. He told him further that if harmony was to be restored the priest must be removed and his zeal on behalf of the Government repressed. The people were not willing to accept the priest's version of politics or his style of expressing them. Within a week the priest was removed to a distant parish and harmony was restored.

The episode placed me in the limelight more than I desired and it became evident that more attention was paid to me by the police than I cared for. My future usefulness was handicapped by the priest's denunciation, and I realized that for the benefit of the organization I would have to move.

John Ryan—

Learning by correspondence with John Ryan, of Liverpool, that he was unusually busy in procuring arms and smuggling them into Ireland, I decided as

Frank Roney, 1883

a matter of immunity from arrest and good policy to join him. Ryan was purchasing all the arms he could get money for, and incidentally robbing members of an English regiment of all the arms that he could get away with. It was customary for the Lancastershire Militia to hold annual encampments followed by a review by a general designated by the War Office. Tents were erected and everything was carried on as if in actual service. The arms were stacked some distance in front of the tents. Ryan had strong boxes made in which to store the rifles and had them placed at convenient points contiguous to the encampment where wagons in charge of reliable teamsters were stationed, ready at a moment's notice to haul the plunder to the nearest railroad station and then to ship them to Holyhead for transmission to Kingstown near Dublin.

An abundance of liquor was supplied to make the soldiers, including the sentries, stupidly drunk. When all were in that condition the arms were quickly removed to the points designated and no time was wasted in boxing them and hurrying them away to Ireland. Over one thousand stands of arms were stolen in that manner and sent to Ireland without attracting the attention of the Government to the guilty parties. Ryan personally knew every man engaged in the enterprise. Remarkably enough the scheme with variations was repeated a number of times. The soldiers when aroused from their drunken debauch could give no account of how they had lost their arms or who took them or where they were. The arms had been lost, that was all that could be said, and no investigation could discover what had become of them.

Ryan was a prominent member of the "new" Hibernian or Ribbonmen faction and frequently urged me to join it, alleging that I could do more through its agency and associations than I was capable of doing otherwise. I failed to appreciate his representations and refused to belong to any association of a political character whose membership qualification was based on sectarian grounds. All Irishmen who were opposed to England's domination in Ireland, were alike to me. The better they served Ireland the nearer and better friends we were.

Newspaper confiscated—

It was while I was in Liverpool that the *Irish People* newspaper was seized and its plant confiscated by the Government.[23] John O'Leary, Kickham,[24] Luby, O'Donovan Rossa, and others were arrested. This event created consternation among many of our people. The excitement increased when Stephens was arrested a few weeks later.[25] The

23 This occurred on the evening of September 14, 1865.—Ed.

24 Kickham was not arrested until November 11, 1865, being taken in company with Stephens and others.—Ed.

25 Stephens was not arrested until November 11, 1865. As a "Mr. Herbert" he had been living quietly in the suburbs of Dublin, tending his garden entirely unsuspected by the police, who were eagerly searching for him. Kickham, Hugo Brophy, and Edward Duffy were with Stephens at the time, and were likewise arrested.—Ed.

arrests were made upon the testimony of Pierce Nagle, an attaché of the paper, who had been for some time acting as a spy. It would have been a difficult matter, however, for the Government to prove its case against any of those arrested had it not been for the evidence furnished by the documents found in Luby's possession when his house was searched.

Thomas Clarke Luby—

Thomas Clarke Luby was a literary man and an enthusiastic Irish Republican. He hoped, when the fight was won, of which he had no doubt, to write an authentic history of the organization that accomplished the victory. It was a foolish thing to do and a violation of a fundamental rule laid down by Stephens to "keep no incriminating documents on your person or where they can be traced and found, and to keep your mouth shut in case of arrest." Luby's transgression of the rule made it easier for the Government to convict him and his co-editors.

Luby was a talented, pure-souled man whose one desire from boyhood was to see Ireland a free nation. He was a graduate of Trinity College, of which his uncle, a wealthy man, was a Fellow. He was often urged to abandon his hopes and associations for Irish liberty and become the heir to his uncle's wealth, but he refused, preferring poverty and its attendant suffering to the surrender of his dearest and fondest aspirations. His degree acquired at college entitled him to the distinction of being called "Doctor." He ranked next to Stephens in the organization, possessing to a less limited degree the ability and astuteness of that very talented man.

John O'Leary—

John O'Leary, another of the contributors to the *Irish People,* was a literary man of well established reputation, whose life had been devoted to the redemption of his country by the propagation of ideas of true patriotism. He had been associated in the '48 movement with Smith O'Brien and Thomas F. Meagher, retaining through the intervening years all the ardor of his young manhood. He was not known as an active member of the organization. His ability and earnestness warranted his being frequently consulted on all important matters affecting our plans.

Charles J. Kickham—

Poor Charles J. Kickham, the poet of the movement, was almost blind and deaf.[26] Those defects did not gain for him the least mitigation of punishment or lighten the labors of the prosecution in securing his conviction.[27] He was the musical soul of the organization and its inspiration; crippled, but a

26 As a young man he had been an ardent sportsman. One day while drying some wet powder before a fire, an explosion occurred which permanently impaired both sight and hearing.—Ed.

27 Kickham, O'Leary, Luby, and others were sentenced to twenty years' penal servitude. O'Donovan Rossa, because it was his second conviction, the first having been in 1858 in connection with the sup-

rebel. He sang as the rebel he had always been and was relentlessly punished as a rebel, finally dying a rebel, in death as pure and as devoted to the Cause as he had lived.

Marking time—

I had not been in direct communication with Nolan during my residence in Liverpool, but hoped that upon my return to Dublin my previous acquaintance with many of our followers would open the way to meeting him or the sucessors of those who had been sent to prison. Nolan had been appointed temporarily to direct the organization. Regular, systematic correspondence was at no time maintained between organizers and the "Head Centre." Men like us were given every latitude in the way of appointing local organizers and adjusting differences when they arose, and reports were made when the opportunity presented itself. Generally speaking, approval was then given to all acts since the previous report. In fact every organizer, such as I, was a lesser chief limited to the territory with which he was familiar.

I returned to Dublin and for three days scoured the public and private haunts of men with whom I was familiar, hoping through them at least to reach

pression of the Phoenix Society, was given a life sentence. This was subsequently commuted to a shorter term. Rossa upon being freed, came to the United States where he was hailed as one of Ireland's outstanding patriots. He later returned to Ireland, dying in Dublin in August, 1915.—Ed.

Nolan. My search proved fruitless. All had gone under cover and nothing was known of them or whether they had ever existed. I expected to borrow enough money from Nolan to carry me to Newry, for considering the state of affairs I did not think it wise to go either to Belfast or to Armagh. I had spent my earnings in Liverpool and had very little money when I reached Dublin. A three days' quest satisfied me of the futility of pursuing it longer and on the evening of the third day I headed for Newry on foot. On my way I overtook a man and engaged him in conversation. I soon discovered that his sympathies were entirely with the men in prison and their Cause. I learned further that he was a farmer living between Swords and Balbriggan. His name was O'Brien. He invited me to his house for the night, which I promptly accepted, and was entertained by him most hospitably. On the following morning I had further conversation with him, which led to a perfect understanding and an intimate and agreeable friendship afterwards.

I reached Newry the second day, tired and footsore, and went to the house of James Taylor, foreman and part owner in a large foundry. Mr. Taylor welcomed me most heartily, offering me room and board in his house and also, when I was ready, a job in his foundry. Mr. Taylor had known me from infancy. He was a friend of my father, and had been an Orangeman in his youth, but had given it up as a piece of folly. For many years he had been secretary of the moulders' union in Belfast and foreman of Rowan's foundry. As secretary of the Masonic and Odd Fellows' lodges, he was frequently hard pressed to get up his quarterly reports, and in this I assisted him to his entire satisfaction.

I remained quietly with him in Newry for several weeks without attracting attention, getting into touch with my friends at Armagh and conducting correspondence cautiously and carefully with my friends in Belfast, while at the same time adding to the membership by enlisting every eligible man I could reach in the town and vicinity. I was biding my time for the chance to go to Dublin to restore the links in the chain of organization which had been broken by the Government's raid upon our head offices.

Stephens' escape—

One day I was surprised to receive a note from the telegraph operator notifying me that he held an important telegram for me which I must call for at once. When I reached the telegraph office I was met by James Loughry, a former school teacher at Larne in the County of Antrim, whom I knew. He informed me that I was wanted in Dublin and must be there on the following night as it was planned that Stephens was to be liberated from the Richmond Bridewell, and I was required to take part in the liberation. It was late in the afternoon when the message reached me. I had to be off on the fast morning train to Dublin if I hoped to participate in Stephens' escape. I told Mr. Taylor that the telegram was about my father's serious illness, which was about the most telling excuse I could give for my sudden departure. He had been holding back a portion of my wages which it was imperative that I should get at once. He did not have sufficient money and the bank holding it would not open until it was too late for me to get the train that I should take for Dublin. Having deceived him as to the cause of my going I was obliged to stick to my story to avoid suspicion and by taking the next train hoped that I might reach my destination in time to take part in the escape. It was late in the evening when I arrived in Dublin. I could find no one who could tell me where Nolan was, so I was obliged to content myself and hug my disappointment in regret.

The escape took place without a hitch, creating a profound sensation, for it was quite clear that the fugitive was aided by the guards inside the prison. A reward of £2,000 was immediately offered for the recapture of Stephens or for any information leading thereto, but it failed of its purpose. Stephens remained in the city for many months, conducting the affairs of the organization and being visited by many men from time to time from various parts of Ireland. He was securely housed in the suburbs of Dublin, in the house of an English Episcopal clergyman, a Rev. Smith, who had come to Ireland to improve his health. Rev. Smith had met Stephens, and after studying the conditions of the country and its people had become convinced that separation from England and the establishment of a republic was the only course left open to the masses.

It was commonly supposed that Stephens' escape was made by means of a ladder placed inside the prison walls. As a matter of fact Stephens left the prison by the front entrance. Nolan engineered the scheme, although the janitor, John Breslin, was the principal agent.[28] Breslin and several others were placed under arrest, and subsequently tried.[29]

[28] There has been some dispute as to the means employed to effect Stephens' escape. The most complete narrative appears to be that recorded by Major Henri Le Caron (T. M. Beach) in *Twenty-five Years in the Secret Service: The Recollections of a Spy,* pp. 164–166. Le Caron, who was not known to be a spy in the employ of the English Government, was sent by the American leaders of the Irish agitation to visit Paris in 1881 for the purpose of consulting with John O'Leary and Patrick Egan. He first met Stephens at that time and heard from him the details of his escape from the Richmond Prison.

Stephens, as reported by Le Caron, claimed that he owed his freedom to the bravery of J. J. Breslin and Daniel Byrne. Breslin by great cleverness obtained the key to Stephens' cell from the nail upon which it hung in the prison safe. He had an impression made of it and in company with Byrne freed Stephens. Two tables placed on top of each other and a ladder enabled Stephens to reach the top of the wall, from which he had to jump about twenty feet to the ground below. A storm was raging, and as Stephens is reported to have said to Le Baron, "It was no joke to jump twenty feet into the darkness."

Stephens jumped to the ground, landed safely, followed a gravel path as directed, reached another wall, threw a handful of gravel over it and thus attracted the attention of eleven armed men, his friends, who were awaiting the signal. They threw a rope over the wall, and by means of it Stephens escaped from the prison into the arms of his bodyguard.—Ed.

[29] Some authors state that Breslin and his associates escaped detection and fled to America.—Ed.

They were acquitted as no evidence was procurable with which to convict them. This same Breslin with Tom Desmond, the latter some years later serving as sheriff of San Francisco, were the men who led in the escape of the Irish political prisoners confined at Freemantle, Australia,[30] who later landed at San Francisco.

Stephens' escape shook the confidence of the British Government in the loyalty of its servants and officials. The extent to which disloyalty pervaded the ranks of the officials was unknown and was a new and very potent cause of serious concern to the Government. The Fenian organization had been looked upon as one of those spasmodic efforts at rebellion characteristic of Ireland for several centuries which, when the time came, would be ruthlessly crushed by England's brutal soldiery. But our movement appeared to be different from anything hitherto carried on in the cause of rebellion, thus necessitating the adoption of other methods in the hope of successfully throttling it. The spy system had failed to produce results. Terrorism was equally deficient in accomplishing the desires of the Government because of the facilities afforded by new and successful methods of heralding such deeds broadcast to the world, and England hoped to retain her prestige, falsely assumed, of being the defender of the oppressed and liberty-loving nation-

30 Six Fenian prisoners were thus rescued from the convict settlement at Freemantle in 1876.—Ed.

alities. To meet the situation, troops of all kinds were increased. Regiments composed chiefly of Irish were ordered abroad, and every preparation was made to suppress the least attempt at revolt.

The reward of £2,000 in gold coin for information leading to Stephens' whereabouts failed to produce an informer. This gives a fair idea of the sterling qualities of the men composing our organization. It also demonstrates the inefficiency of the detectives, who, of themselves and without the aid and cooperation of stool pigeons or informers, could accomplish nothing.

Nolan, whom I met the day after Stephens' escape, informed me that it was Stephens' desire that henceforth I should consider myself a member of his personal staff. This position was one of immediate danger, and placed me in a position of being liable to arrest at any time. As I was more familiar than any one else with conditions in the north, my connection with the "Head Centre" was deemed a necessity.

The American branch—

The members of the American branch of the organization had made themselves ridiculous by forming what they called a *de facto* Irish Government, with a President and Cabinet housed expensively in New York City. The funds contributed in America to aid in Ireland's liberation were wasted on this fantastic government[31] got up to flatter the vanity of an honest, but foolish and weak old man, crazed with the glories of a line of patriotic ancestors. Mr. John O'Mahony, "President of the Irish Republic" located in New York City, three thousand miles distant from the scene where it was hoped to establish one, actually committed a prodigious blunder when he assumed that title and called into existence his sham government. He did more than that when he permitted the frittering away of vast sums of money to uphold the pretentious dignity of his Lilliputian outfit. Money subscribed in all earnestness, and given so lavishly and freely for a specific object, should have been used more effectively for the Cause. However, the extravagances of this absurd pretense of government were the only stain upon the entire movement. To add to the waste, a number of men who had served in the army of the United States, being out of employment upon the termination of the Civil War,[32] were sent to Ireland, and received their pay in American currency as generals, colonels, and captains. These salaries, so much in excess of their legitimate expenses, enabled them to live sumptuously and extravagantly. Because of their style

31 O'Leary, *op. cit.*, vol. 1, p. 136, states that about $500,000 was collected from Irishmen and supporters of the Fenian agitation residing in Canada and the United States. About one-third of that sum found its way to Ireland.—Ed.

32 It is said that at the close of the Civil War there were over 200,000 disbanded Irish soldiers eager for any sort of adventure, but more particularly interested in the possibility of a contest with the British Government.—Ed.

of dress, their swaggering and open-handedness in bar-rooms and hotels, all of them became marked men. And besides, they were not at all backward in letting their mission in Ireland be known.

But little of the American money was spent upon the organization in Ireland. Large sums were transmitted to an agent in Paris and by him forwarded to a London banker, Henry Labouchère, who issued cheques payable by various banks which were his correspondents in Dublin. The failure to receive a large sum on time to pay off the American officers, who were ever clamorous for money, caused me to be sent to Paris to learn the cause of the delay.

Paris and the Carbonarii—

Paris was then a sort of rendezvous for revolutionaries. London was the headquarters. Cavour's treatment of Garibaldi in sending him to the Island of Capua, and the rigid enforcement of military rule in Italy, caused the dispersion of the restless spirits who had in large measure contributed to the success of Victor Emmanuel's arms. Cavour's diplomacy in bringing about a United Italy forced them to seek safer scenes for their continued operations. Some of them resided in Paris and were the friends of our financial agent from whom they learned of the progress of our struggle in Ireland. They were sincere in their wishes for our success and entirely willing to aid us in any way possible. I certainly admired these world's workers, whose labors were directed towards the establishment of free government everywhere. I was very much impressed with the few whose acquaintance I made.

On the evening of the third day of my arrival in Paris I happened to be in a quiet section of the city in the company of two of my new revolutionary friends with whom I had spent the afternoon. We had visited several cafés and everything between them and myself was most pleasant. We sauntered idly along, away from the crowded part of the city, discussing, as we went, various phases of revolutionary prospects, oblivious to all else. All at once my companions remembered an important appointment that had to be kept and it was then the hour. With profuse apologies for their oversight they took their leave directing me which way to go, and hurried off.

I was still speculating on the subjects of our conversation when a carriage drew up alongside the walk and two men jumped out. They saluted me in English, at which I was well pleased, and asked to be directed to a certain place. I assured them that I was a stranger in Paris and that I had never been in that part of the city before. In fact I knew nothing about the city. They invited me to a seat in their carriage, undertaking to drop me at my hotel, as there was no use of their proceeding further on indefinite directions. I entered the carriage and saw that it contained another occupant.

The cabman had no sooner turned his vehicle than I was seized, blindfolded, and tightly bound.

My struggles to free myself were of no use. I had read of *lettres de cachet* and of robberies by this means, and concluded that I was undoubtedly in the hands of banditti, but for what ultimate purpose it remained to be seen. Not a word was spoken by any one in the carriage. The driver evidently understood where to go without directions. I was decidedly uncomfortable. If I was being arrested by the police as a political prisoner I knew of no means to free myself, as all of my friends were in a dubious position themselves. To seek their aid would probably compromise them and make my position better defined as a political disturber. If robbery were the object I could congratulate myself upon the fact that they would get little in return for their efforts. My imagination was at a loss to figure satisfactorily what my position was or what treatment I might expect. All I could do was to keep my nerves rigid and await developments.

We traveled a great distance. At length the carriage stopped and I was led by a man on either side into a building, through a long passageway, and thence into a close stuffy room. The cords binding me were removed and I was told to lie down and stretch out my limbs, which were immediately fastened as were my hands. Then the bandage was removed and I found myself surrounded by a number of men clad in dark gowns which also covered their heads. Memories of the Inquisition and other continental devices for punishment or extorting confessions from refractory prisoners flashed upon me.

Presently one of them began questioning me. My name, birthplace, and age were the first questions asked. What was my business in Paris? Sightseeing and pleasure was my answer. Did I know a certain Irish political refugee, naming our agent? I did not. Did I know others, mentioning them? I did not. Did I not express myself thus and so to this, that, and the other person? Not that I remembered. Then I was told that I would be torn limb from limb or they would get the truth and a complete confession from me. When I refused to enlighten them the order was given to stretch me. Accordingly one of them began to use a lever and I felt the cords which bound me beginning to tighten. Without straining or hurting me but upon my refusing to answer the questions again put to me, the lever was moved another time.

I was kept in this position a short time when the bonds were relaxed. Then the hoods were thrown back, revealing several of my friends. I was told of the character of the organization and its objects, and asked to take the pledge of membership, which I did. Later I was informed that this was the famed Carbonarii which had done so much for Italy and was willing to do as much for Ireland, and that its members were prepared to do everything possible for any country seeking political freedom. I made no effort to establish this society in Ireland or elsewhere, holding no correspondence with its members and never met but one member of it afterwards. He was an Irishman and had become a member in Genoa in about the same way that I became one.

My visit to Paris gave speed to our agent, for money was plentiful upon my return.

Without a knowledge of our real strength and condition, the American officers began to rebel at inactivity, becoming clamorous for a fight. Many of our local leaders were of the same mind and were quite as insistent. Stephens was disappointed in his expectations as to what America should have done judging from the magnitude of the contributions given. Desirous of ascertaining the exact state of affairs for his own satisfaction and that of the officers, he resolved upon summoning representatives from all parts of Ireland for the purpose of questioning them as to their numbers, armament, and resources. An American general was to do the questioning in Stephens' presence. I visited the northern representatives notifying them when to be in Dublin.

The British organization—

In case the concensus of opinion should prove to be favorable for an immediate uprising, Stephens considered it advisable to ascertain beforehand the attitude of the British republicans toward the revolt. This was most essential. Already, we had powerfully strong organizations in all the great centers of population in Great Britain. To augment our forces by reinforcements not distinctively Irish would demonstrate the unanimity prevailing among all the people of the British Isles for a republican form of government in Ireland. The obvious effect of such a union was perfectly plain.

Rumor had it that the British Republican Association was very strong, especially in all the large manufacturing centers. Its exact strength no one knew outside of its members, and they were not all accurately informed. Charles Bradlaugh was its inspiration and head. As a radical thinker and publicist he was preeminent throughout England; as an honest and fearless man, he had no peer; as a man of benevolence and kindness to the poor, his reputation was well and long established. That I might see Mr. Bradlaugh, Stephens gave me a letter of introduction to the wealthy radical banker in London, already mentioned,[33] with whom he believed Bradlaugh was intimate, or if not, he was the person who would know the best means of bringing about the introduction. This banker had handled considerable American money for our organization and was well aware of the purpose of its use. His public utterances stamped him as a pronounced radical and his great wealth shielded him from the persecutions that a man of smaller means would have suffered. He received me courteously, assuring me of his

[33] Henry Labouchère.—Ed.

friendship for "Mr. Power,"[34] the name signed to the letter of introduction by Stephens, and agreed to bring about the desired interview.

Interview with Bradlaugh—

When I met Mr. Bradlaugh, I was instantly impressed with his ability as well as his sincerity and honesty. That he was a man of physical and moral courage showed in every lineament and beamed in every line of his rugged and expressive face. I felt perfectly at ease and was proud of the privilege of meeting this remarkably great man. His religious unbeliefs did not scare or intimidate me a particle. These were well known to me but they were never once alluded to by him. We had met for another purpose, to which he strictly limited himself. A three hours' conference satisfied me that Ireland had a substantial and able friend in Charles Bradlaugh. He assured me, so far as lay in his power, that we could rely upon the practical support of about 100,000 British republicans. He advised me to see another man of admitted ability and considerable wealth, who was just emerging into public life, a great speaker and one of vast influence with the republicans. He gave me a letter of introduction and wrote a direct letter to this gentleman, upon whom I called two days later.

34 Stephens quite frequently signed documents with the *nom de Plume* of "J. Power."—Ed.

Bradlaugh and Chamberlain—

The contrast between Bradlaugh and Joseph Chamberlain, the man referred to, was most pronounced. Bradlaugh was typical of the Saxon in every detail; Chamberlain was just as clearly representative of the Norman. I saw that he was a politician and doubted his sincerity. I was not so frank with him as I had been with Bradlaugh, adopting an almost entirely different course. He agreed that English republicans should support Irish republicans and, for that matter, all republicans, and that, so far as he was concerned, he would neither speak nor advise against such an alliance nor in any way impede it. I let him know that we were strong enough, active, and quite determined enough, to wreak vengeance upon England and the English Government for all her past cruelties and treacheries, unless assured beyond a doubt of the support of English republicans. This was the only way England could be saved from annihilation. This braggadocio floored him.

I at that time formed an unfavorable opinion of Joseph Chamberlain and have lived to see my opinion fully justified. Beginning his public career professedly as an ardent republican, he ran through the whole political gamut by degrees, dying disappointed that he had not reached the goal of his ambition, which was to become a member of the British peerage. England, and for that matter every other country, has too few such men as Bradlaugh and are cursed by too many of the other sort.

Three, or nearer four, hundred men saw Stephens during the few days that I was absent in England. A word from any one of them to a policeman would have put into the pocket of the informer the neat sum of £2,000, and no one else would have been a bit the wiser for it. But the hiding place of Stephens was not disclosed. This is something for Irishmen to boast about and be proud of, for the pecuniary inducement to be a traitor without fear of discovery was great.

Loyalty within the organization—

We have had our informers and traitors in the past and we may have others in the future. Hardly any great and good Cause anywhere in the world has been without them. But the traitors in our Cause, at that time, in proportion to the widespread character of the organization, its ramifications in quarters and among people least open to suspicion, its armaments, and its preparations for the conflict, were insignificant in the extreme. The loyalty and sterling honesty of the local leaders were unimpeachable and remained so to the last.

The backbone of the organization from the beginning was its intelligent young men, whose conditions in life in the majority of instances would have been better served had they never belonged to it. Few of them had ever been the victims of landlord oppression or felt the lash of the evictor. Almost all of them were in comparatively easy circumstances. They were conscious of England's oppression of the rural manhood of the country by its system of land tenure, and realized that only by independence could they hope to see their country assume her proper place as an industrial nation.

Stephens was well satisfied with my reports regarding the situation in England. Mr. O'Mahony's American Irish Republic vapored along and continued to rake in the coin from its members and to lavishly spend it in bluster and threats, but beyond this its supporters did not seem capable of going. The conscientious American officers were disgusted with the actions of their ridiculous baby government and asked for better things which, unfortunately, were not forthcoming. Stephens did not propose to order his men into the field to be slaughtered, notwithstanding the assurances which had been received from England. The "rising" was therefore postponed.[35]

Stephens' escape to France—

After Stephens' escape from the Richmond Bridewell, his efforts to keep in touch with the "centres" of the movement placed him continually in a precarious and dangerous position. The detec-

[35] By some members of the movement Stephens was severely criticized for not calling for the revolt at that time, it being held that the movement was then in its position of greatest strength.—Ed.

tives were unusually alert and eager to get trace of his whereabouts. Consequently, it was decided to get him to France, where he had many friends. He could speak the French language like a native. It devolved upon John Nolan to devise means of spiriting Stephens out of Ireland. This he did successfully without a hitch and without exciting suspicion. On a given day, a small sailing vessel cast anchor in Dublin Bay opposite Clontarf. About the same time a carriage with blinds drawn and containing two gentlemen was making its way through the streets of Dublin to the Drogheda Road. The carriage stopped at Clontarf and the two men got out. Spying the sailing boat in the Bay, they walked leisurely in the direction where it was lying off shore at anchor. At the same time a small row boat put off from the vessel and made for a fisherman's landing near-by. The shortest and stoutest of the two men stepped into the row boat, and was taken out to the vessel. He got aboard, the anchor was weighed, sails were unfurled, and the vessel departed for France bearing our leader, James Stephens. Stephens subsequently took up his residence at Brussels, Belgium, and was later joined by his wife. I believe that he died during the early nineties.[36]

[36] McManus, *op. cit.*, p. 617, and R. B. O'Brien, *Two Centuries of Irish History, 1691–1870*, p. 467, state that Stephens went to America from France, where he continued for a short time as the nominal head of the Irish movement. He then returned to Paris, where he lived in poverty for many years, returning to Ireland shortly before his death at Blackrock, County Dublin, in 1901. Cf. John Mitchel, *Jail Journal*, p. 449.—Ed.

Stephens was a learned, able, and indefatigable worker, devoting his life to Ireland's independence, and dying in comparative obscurity. Some of those who responded to his call to visit him after his escape from Ireland condemned him for not ordering the "rising" in 1865, and called him a coward. Stephens was a conscientious man and was possessed of complete knowledge regarding the strength of our movement. He knew that our inability to secure sufficient arms for the uprising would only result in the butchery of the revolutionary forces and retard for a hundred years the realization of our dream of an Irish Republic. Had the organization been as fully prepared as it was in Ulster, it is certain that an uprising would have been ordered regardless of the consequences.

Police and detectives—

It was necessary to keep up the *esprit de corps* of the men and for that purpose members of the staff were kept constantly moving from place to place. One of my excursions led me into County Donegal. One of our men, a school teacher named O'Donnell, for whose capture a reward of £200 was offered by the Government, had been on the "run," as it was called, for several months. The people gave him every protection and divided their scanty food with him. His own means had long since been exhausted. To encourage him and at the same time to aid him materially, Stephens commissioned me to deliver to him £50 and a pair of ivory-handled pistols.

I had never been in that county. I was told that the Irish language was commonly spoken in it as well as the English, that the people were suspicious of all strangers, and that I must exercise the utmost care to be successful. I was instructed to make myself and my mission known to the butler of the leading inn in Bundoran, I think it was, and to be guided by his suggestions and advice.

In due time I arrived at Enniskillen and put up at the house of one of our friends named Maguire. I was also given the names of several of our friends living in the vicinity of Lough Erne. I arrived the day before the boat sailed and through Maguire sent the message to two of the men to meet me. When they came we went into a consideration of how to meet as many of the men as possible without attracting the attention of the police, who were unusually vigilant. I made a rough sketch of both the upper and lower Lough Erne and made a mark at those points where our men were located, with their approximate numbers. Having made arrangements for the meeting on the night of my return from Bundoran and given some words of encouragement to those whom I met in Enniskillen, I took the boat early next morning.

Without making my observations pointed, I leisurely and carefully scanned my fellow-passengers to discover by their actions and appearance if any of them was unduly solicitous about me. A careful scrutiny assured me to my great relief that I was not being watched. It was market day when I arrived in Bundoran, and little stalls filled with all sorts of wares were distributed over what I took to be the market place. I carelessly asked one of the venders the way to the inn or hotel. I was amazed to find that he would not answer me. He pretended that he did not understand me. He spoke Irish but also understood English well enough to answer. Then glancing behind me I noticed two tall men handling some of the articles at a stall and the suspicion occurred to me that I was being followed.

To test the matter, I went carelessly around a booth enclosed on all but one side and through an alley-way where I again paused to inquire my way to the inn, with precisely the same result. I turned facing the direction from which I came, and sure enough there were my men still following me. I struck out for the main street of the town and finally landed at the hotel, which I think was named the Leitrim Arms.

I made myself and my mission known immediately to the butler, telling him that I was being followed. He had just finished telling me that when I was ready for bed to call for him and he would light me to my room, when my two gentlemen walked into the hotel. With great presence of mind the butler said, "All right, sir, you prefer it rare," as if I had been giving the order for dinner. I was equally quick when I said, "And butler, bring a small bottle of claret."

It was the winter season. The boat had been a long time making the trip and it was almost dark when I arrived. Candles were lit and the fire was made to blaze, while the butler took the order for the dinner of my two watchers.

To throw the policemen off their guard, and if possible to shake their suspicions, I made some remarks about the weather and the slowness of the boat. I then invited them to have a toddy, to which they agreed with great alacrity. About ten o'clock I pretended to be quite drowsy and calling the butler told him that I wished to retire. On the stairs going up to the room and in the room when we reached it, he told me to put my boots outside my door as is or was the custom, not to sleep, and at about midnight to leave the room, pick up my boots and come carefully downstairs in my stockings. After he left me, my policemen friends passed my door in about twenty minutes going to their rooms. Soon the house was perfectly silent.

At the hour agreed upon I carefully made my way down stairs. The butler instructed me to walk to the end of the street where a car awaited me which I was to get into without speaking, and that the driver would take me to the man whom I had come to see. I followed his instructions perfectly and before two o'clock met O'Donnell, who thankfully received the pistols and the money.

The butler was awaiting my return to the hotel, and soon thereafter I was in bed with my boots outside my room door as they had been when the sleuths passed the night before, and where they could be seen by my watchers in the morning on their way downstairs. My two shadowers were in the coffee room in the morning when I went downstairs, doubtless believing that I was a prodigious sleeper. Making pretense that I was a drummer for a Dublin hardware house, after a hurried breakfast I went forth to seek orders for my house and carelessly left one of my fake business cards on the table, which the butler, who was watching, informed me they picked up and pocketed. My friend Andrew Nolan was the manager of the firm which I claimed to represent, so, if inquiries were ever made concerning me, I knew that I would be properly vouched for.

The morning after my return to Enniskillen I had torn up and thrown into the fire the last scrap of incriminating paper on my person, just as two policemen entered the sitting room. They called for two bottles of porter and in a friendly way asked me to join them in a drink, a most unusual proceeding on their part. I readily agreed. Then they began to ply me with questions about the state of the country, how it affected business, my occupation, the name of the firm I represented, etc. In return I politely inquired why they desired this information, telling them that in my experience it was a very unusual proceeding.

One then produced a copy of the *Hue and Cry*, the official paper circulated by the heads of the police department to keep the police informed regarding those for whom rewards were offered and the nature of the offense they were alleged to be guilty of. He asked me if I was not John Morris of County Carlow, for whose capture the reward of £200 was offered. The description as to personal appearance, height, complexion, and clothes, even to the striped trousers which I wore, tallied with me very accurately. I agreed with them that the resemblance was striking, but assured them that I was not Morris, and to prove this offered to pay for telegrams to Dublin and Belfast to convince them of their error. They were positive, however, that I was the man they wanted and informed me that I could explain all to the Hon. Captain Butler, the stipendary magistrate before whom they proposed taking me, who was a relative of the Earl of Erne. The latter was, I believe, at that time the Grand Master of the Orangemen of Ireland. I vehemently protested and declined to go with them, but they insisted and said that they would use force to compel me if I did not comply.

I was searched in the Captain's presence and questioned by him at considerable length. Some gold and silver, a small prayer book, a few business cards, and my diagram of Lough Erne was all that they found upon my person. My handbag, containing a few additional business cards and some toilet articles, was also searched. The Captain sent me to a cell where I remained about three hours. While there I was entertained by a would-be "sympathetic" policeman, who in the fulness of his heart assured me that he detested his uniform and was longing for the day when he could throw it off and declare himself a true Irishman. He remarked upon my military appearance and supposed that I had seen service in the United States. I looked at the fellow and knew that he was there to coax from me some admissions of my complicity in the proposed rebellion, or at any rate to get me to say something of a compromising nature. I paralyzed him when I told him that I would report him to Captain Butler and have him not only dismissed from the police force but arrested as a traitor to his Queen. I stumped him completely. He then began a different tale, abjectly apologized, and confessed that he believed a mistake had been made in my arrest. He was let out of the cell, while I remained an hour longer.

I was again interrogated by the Captain, and asked to explain my possession of the diagram and the prayer book. The diagram was a rough estimate made of the population surrounding the upper and lower loughs, I said, to aid me in forming an opinion of the busines that I might do, and the prayer book was not an unseemly article to have in one's possession in a Christian country. The plausibility of the explanation was accepted, but did not entirely satisfy the Captain, who expressed regret that he could not hold me. To do so required an excuse of some sort for his justification, and I gave him none.

The news of my arrest went around the country like fire, obliging me to postpone the meeting previously arranged, for fear of the possibility of bringing others under suspicion. I left the town that night and reached the village of Lisnaskea at a late hour. I had walked the distance, about four miles. All was profoundly silent. I found the inn without difficulty and aroused the landlord, who was apparently glad of a stray guest. He showed me to a room containing an old-fashioned four-poster bed, curtained, and a fireplace with a grate. He kindled the fire, already prepared in anticipation of such a visitor, and at my suggestion joined me in a glass of punch which I thought I needed very much after my lonely journey. I instructed him to have me up in the morning in time to have breakfast before catching the train which was to carry me to the main line and thence to Dublin.

The next morning when I boarded the train there was only one passenger in the first-class compartment. He was muffled up beyond recognition, and I at once proceeded to do likewise. Passengers on trains in Ireland and England at that time kept themselves aloof from promiscuous intercourse with their fellow-travelers and austerely avoided every notice of them. I was pleased to do this, and be able to get myself together after my adventure of the few days previous. It was winter-time and very dark. I was quite well satisfied to be left to myself. I was therefore much surprised when my companion addressed me, remarking how cold and dark it was. I was reluctant to talk, but decided to be agreeable, not expecting anything startling from my fellow-traveler. He soon produced a flask of whiskey and invited me to take a drink as protection against the chilliness of the weather. I did so, after which he made himself known to me. He was a sub-inspector of police, but owing to the ferment in the country was kept unusually and disagreeably busy. He was now on his way to Dundalk, where he expected to hear something disadvantageous to the agitators and disturbers and hoped there would be good ground for arrests. I assured him that he had my utmost sympathy and that I further hoped for his success.

I believe that he must have been drinking the night before because the whiskey that he drank in my presence would not have made him so interestingly loquacious. I informed him that I was a commercial traveler, and deplored the state of the country because of injurious effects upon business. I actually impressed him with my sincerity. He again produced his flask and we had another "swig." I gained enough information from him to warn me that something serious was contemplated affecting the men in Dundalk, so that when we arrived there, learning that I would be detained at least fifteen minutes, I telegraphed Mr. Jack McCabe, of the

Drogheda *Argus,* to meet me at the railroad station as I had important news for him. When I met McCabe, I told him what to do, and he did it, as he was in touch with the situation and the men in Dundalk, and I was not.

I continued on to Dublin, where my first performance upon arriving was to have my beard and whiskers shaved off. It made so great a change in my appearance that when I met my friends in Casey's Hotel they did not know me. Nolan had a trip cut out for me to Belfast to begin at once and in the afternoon I was on my way to the North again. Nothing of importance happened on that occasion except that I did not go to my father's house, remaining, so far as my family was concerned, strictly *incognito.*

The so-called detectives were visiting every hotel and house in Dublin where suspicious strangers stopped, taking their names and occupations. The American officers had received little money of late because of the dearth of funds contributed to their "government" in New York. The wasteful expenditure of the money already contributed began to be understood by the contributors and it put a curb upon their liberality. A number of the officers abandoned their stylish quarters in Dublin and came to live in Casey's City Mansion Hotel, which was a commercial travelers' hostelry.

A traitor—

One of the Americans who came to live there was John Corydon. I never learned what his rank was but I knew he was a trusted messenger between the President of the Republic, O'Mahony, and Stephens, the Chief in Ireland. He had several times carried written communications most successfully both ways. Corydon was a native of New York City and could speak the Irish language fluently, which gave him high standing with several high officials of the Republic who were sentimentally inclined. He was a lithe, active, and mentally keen chap.

Over all those stopping at Casey's there hung a cloud of depression, owing to the lack of funds, that was irresistible and quite contagious. Everyone connected with or related to our organization felt it and showed it. It would grip me at times not as an insoluble financial problem, but as predicating the end and ruin of our hopes for the establishment of a real Irish Republic on Ireland's soil.

Mr. Peter Gill, proprietor and editor of the *Tipperary Advocate* and later a member of the British Parliament, a most excellent gentleman, with whom, during his residence at Casey's, I had become quite friendly, told me that a raid would soon be made on all noted places, and advised me to get lodgings elsewhere. The recent taking of the names of strangers in dwellings and hotels throughout the city was a preliminary step to that end. I did think of going to O'Brien's at Swords, but thought again that if I did so I would be partly beyond reach of my Chief when immediately wanted. So I decided to remain, whatever the outcome.

After dinner one night early in January, feeling the prevailing depression more acutely than usual, I went to the front of the hotel to smoke. It had just ceased raining when a woman passed displaying her white petticoat and seemingly a little the worse for drink. At that moment Corydon joined me, and being attracted by the woman's appearance, decided to follow her. Looking down the dimly lighted street I could see that he had overtaken and stopped her. He returned almost immediately and requested me to keep for him a gold watch of considerable value presented to him by admiring friends in New York, and a pocket-book which he said contained a large sum of money. The following afternoon I returned them to him just as he gave them to me, never once thinking about examining the contents of the pocket-book. That woman became his mistress. Corydon later turned informer in order to obtain the funds with which to maintain her in some degree of elegance.[37] After my arrest and during my confinement in Mountjoy Prison, Corydon appeared one day to identify some of the prisoners. He ignored

[37] Corydon betrayed to the Government the plans of the Fenians in England to capture Chester Castle, seize the arms stored therein, hasten to Holyhead, seize the steamers in port, cut the telegraph wires, and invade Ireland before the Government forces could act. He also disclosed the plans of the Fenians for a general revolt in Ireland to take place on March 5, 1867, thus enabling the Government to meet the uprising at every point and to crush it effectively.—Ed.

me absolutely. Each time that I came around making the circuit of our large exercising cage I stared at him as a challenge, but each time he utterly failed to notice me. I attributed the omission to my honesty in keeping and restoring to him unexamined the articles which on that rainy evening he had committed to my care at Casey's Hotel. However infamous a wretch may become, there seems to be left in him a spark of the virtue he has thrown aside if, as in this instance, the favor has been one of substantial benefit.

Imprisonment—

The days of January 1866 dragged along dully. All activity seemed ended. Nolan seldom came to Casey's. A number of the officers had returned to America. Those remaining were moneyless and bankrupt. Reports from the country indicated that the organization was in a healthy militant humor. Stephens considered a rising either premature or belated and, if resorted to, equal to a butchery.

Occasional arrests were made which kept interest keenly alive. O'Leary, Luby, Rossa, and the others were tried, convicted, and imprisoned at Pentonville. Early in February the British Parliament suspended the Habeas Corpus Act and wholesale arrests were made simultaneously the following day[38] in Dublin and throughout Ireland. I understood afterwards that about two thousand men were arrested in Dublin

[38] February 19, 1866.—Ed.

alone.[39] About twelve of us, including the proprietor, were arrested in the City Mansion Hotel (Casey's) and lodged in the Chancery Lane Police Station. At night, however, and with a policeman apiece for a guard and cavalry as the escort for the group, we were landed in the historic Kilmainham Jail. The crowd of prisoners and policemen gathered that night in Kilmainham Jail was immense. After being searched we were each placed in a cell.

While in the police station I noticed how poorly it was guarded and proposed to Captain Jim Murphy and Casey that we overpower the guard and escape. They thought such action inadvisable and, from their talk as it seemed to me, not in keeping with the dignity of a political prisoner. I was not at all impressed with the dignity thrust upon me, rather regarding it as a preliminary to wearing stripes for many years in the prison quarries at Portland, where dignity elicited little respect and no opportunity for its display.

I might here say that my arrest had been effected that morning while I was in bed. I protested vigorously against it and refused to get up and dress. The occupant of another bed in the same room, Captain Maurice Fitzmaurice, an American, accepted the order of arrest with complacency and proceeded to clothe himself. The policeman left the room for a

39 Our author's figure is too large. Various authorities state that during the first six months, under the suspension of the Habeas Corpus Act, 756 persons were arrested, many of whom were released after serving short terms of imprisonment.—Ed.

short time and while he was absent I stepped to the window to see what chance there was to escape by making a rope of the bed sheets. I could see none and returned to bed. Four stalwart policemen were called in to help me out of bed when I persisted in my refusal to get up. Each took a corner of the feather-bed—there were no mattresses in those days—and dumped me onto the floor. I reluctantly and protestingly put on my clothes.

Kilmainham Prison—

My jail cell in Kilmainham measured six feet by ten feet and was twelve feet high. A barred window was at one end. The iron door had a much smaller window in its center opening to the outside, through which the warden passed in the food or whatever else was needed, thus making it unnecessary to open the door. A hammock was fastened on one side, and when in use was attached by eyes fixed in the opposite wall. A small table and a stool fastened to the floor constituted the furniture. The gas jet was turned on or off from the outside.

I soon realized that I was a prisoner, and as far as I could make out very well secured. Then I began to think. I am of the opinion that the first thoughts of every prisoner, no matter for what cause he may be confined, are taken up with the idea of being freed. They were undoubtedly mine. Then came the thought of how to relieve the solitude by communication with my fellows. I found that I had a small knife which had been overlooked when I had been searched, and I began tapping upon the hammock fastenings in the wall. Imagine my delight upon hearing a response, although of course there was no code to make our tapping intelligent. I discovered that I also had a small piece of pencil which had been overlooked and a piece of tobacco given to me by my guardian policeman after the search.

Naturally, I asked myself what was to be the outcome of this most undesirable confinement. Was it to end in hanging, or in prolonged imprisonment, or merely in temporary detention? No matter in what way it was to end, I was resolved to keep an even temper and to be surprised at nothing that might happen. Neither would I be scared or intimidated. I was clearly in a hole of my own making, and although arrested through no cleverness on the part of the alleged detectives I was nevertheless very securely imprisoned without much prospect of being liberated. To accommodate myself to the conditions and to make the best of them, no matter what might turn up, was, I reasoned, the wisest and best course to adopt. To worry or fret or lament or seek sympathy or to believe myself a hero and a great patriot, the victim of a cruel conscienceless Government, was as far from my thoughts as I was at that time from freedom. I was at war with the British Government and it had got the best of me. Equanimity of thought brought to me an untroubled mind followed by resignation. I kept a light heart and a cheerful, hopeful mind during my imprisonment, never once being depressed or discouraged.

Fellow prisoners—

It was in Kilmainham that I learned to know John Morris, for whom I had been mistaken in Enniskillen. I recognized the resemblance as very striking, the difference being that he had an imperfection in one of his eyes, while I had none. I recognized Color Sergeant McCarthy and also Corporal Brennan, the man whose oath later convicted McCarthy of high treason, the sentence of death pronounced upon him subsequently being commuted to life imprisonment. McCarthy had been arrested at Aldershot in England in the act of administering the oath of the Irish Republic to a soldier. He was an intelligent man, fully conscious of what he was doing, believing that the establishment of a republic in Ireland was the true and only way to rid the country of rack-renting landlordism and to restore its long suppressed industries and commerce. Physically he was a splendid specimen of manhood. Brennan was short, stout and by no means so intelligent a man as McCarthy. He was an easy subject for English officials to work upon in the production of an informer. He had none of the high ideals of his country's future and was unable to make any sacrifices for any ideals. He sacrificed principle to save himself from imprisonment and aided in the conviction of his superior, who after a long term in prison was pardoned and returned to his relatives, an old, decrepit man.

I managed to communicate with both men, believing Brennan to be true blue, and also with others. Although every precaution was taken by the prison keepers to prevent it, we soon established a regular system of telegraphy all over the prison, leaving no one ignorant of anything of importance passing on the outside.

Plan for escape—

I conceived a plan for a general jail delivery, which, if it had been carried out, would have made Stephens' escape seem like the work of a baby. Unfortunately a large number of us were transferred to Mountjoy Prison a few days before we had decided to make the attempt. The feasibility of the plan commended itself to every man in the prison. Its execution and success depended solely upon the celerity displayed.

There were about four hundred prisoners in Kilmainham at the time. About a hundred exercised in the two prison yards at the same hour. The gate of one yard was secured from the inside and that of the other from the outside. No guards were stationed on the outside of either. A company of soldiers occupied rooms well in front of the prison and out of view of the passage between the two yards. When off duty the soldiers, divested of their jackets, lay carelessly around the room or engaged in card playing. At stated intervals the soldiers inside the yards, numbering five men, were relieved. There were also four policemen and one warden in each yard.

On the morning of the day agreed upon for the execution of the plan, a signal was to be given whereupon each prisoner would tear his bed sheets, make a gag of one piece and have the others ready as binders. Upon a signal and before the guard was relieved, the soldiers and policemen were to be seized and gagged, and deprived of their arms and uniforms. The prisoners were then to act as usual—as if nothing had happened. When the relief guard came on they were to be seized, gagged, stripped of their uniforms and arms, and guarded as prisoners. The prisoners dressed as soldiers would then proceed to the guard room, cover the soldiers with the guns, and take possession of the remaining rifles and ammunition. The officials of the prison would then be seized and locked up in the vacant cells, the keys taken, the remaining cells opened, and the prisoners liberated. When the officers of the prison and all the soldiers had been placed in the cells, the prison doors would be opened and all would disperse. Before doing that, however, whatever ready money was at hand would be equally distributed. Visitors or those having business with the prison, who might happen to be on hand, would be admitted and locked up. The scheme was entirely feasible. It required confidence, celerity, courage, and determination, and could have been effected without bloodshed. Hours would elapse before the discovery of the jail delivery, and most of the men by that time would have successfully escaped. To get out of Mountjoy Prison, to which some of us were soon sent, was quite another story, and I made no effort or proposal to that end.

Mountjoy Prison—

Conditions in Mountjoy Prison were superior to those in Kilmainham. The prison was under the immediate supervision of the Government, while the other was only partially so. The cells in both prisons were of the same dimensions, but those in Mountjoy were more sanitary. The wardens in the latter prison were more courteous and what was best of all, we were in almost immediate possession of every thing of importance on the outside affecting us. For example, we had the news of Stephens' departure from Ireland the day after it occurred. Along with the news of Stephens' escape, there came to us prisoners at Mountjoy the information that Colonel Kelly[40] of New York had been installed as the chief of our movement and that he had left Ireland for England. Kelly had been figuring to quite an extent in Stephens' place before our arrest, owing to the necessity of protecting the latter from the possibility of discovery and arrest.

[40] Colonel Thomas J. Kelly.—Ed.

McLaughlin and Kelly—

It seemed to some of us that Colonel Kelly's chief desire was to see that the American officers were as well cared for as the state of the finances would permit. A little while prior to my arrest, Mike McLaughlin, of Glasgow, came to Dublin, desirous of meeting someone with the ability to help him out of an awkward situation. He had been ordered to bring two hundred men from Glasgow to Sligo in anticipation of a fight, and, having done so, had them quartered in places where they attracted the least possible attention. He had been furnished money with which to pay their fare and expenses pending the "rising." But when the "rising" was delayed and the cash became scare he had these men upon his hands. No message was sent to him to have them return to their homes in Glasgow and the expenses kept mounting higher each day. In despair McLaughlin came to Dublin. No one could or would tell him where to get relief, as all familiar with Colonel Kelly's dwelling place had strict orders to keep it profoundly secret. McLaughlin had been in Dublin two days without making headway and was in a despondent way when he came to Casey's Hotel and met me. He unbosomed himself to me and asked to be advised. I felt that his men were as entitled to consideration as were the American officers, although his men were classed as privates. I knew Kelly was in receipt of money from America, ostensibly for the organization. These men were a part of the organization and were peculiarly situated.

I decided that McLaughlin should see Colonel Kelly notwithstanding the secrecy of his location and so I brought him to the house. The Colonel knew McLaughlin and the cause of his visit, and was dumbfounded. He protested that he had no money and that McLaughlin must do the best he could in settling the bills and in getting the men out of the country. McLaughlin, to emphasize his demand, produced a revolver and gave the Colonel ten minutes to produce enough money to pay a little over half of the indebtedness. The money was immediately forthcoming, and McLaughlin took his way west the following morning. The Colonel suspected me of informing McLaughlin of his residence, but was too discreet ever to mention it publicly.

For one who is blessed or cursed with a sanguine temperament and an irresistible desire to be doing something, it is not a pleasant thing to be doomed to rigid solitariness, without books, writing materials, or any of the accessories essential to the active and profitable occupation of the mind. To be thrown upon oneself in a long period of solitary confinement is a severe test upon the mental strength of anyone. When to this is added the belief that the hopes so buoyantly held have been destroyed and that all the labor of years has been swallowed in the maelstrom of annihilation, the situation becomes all the worse. Fits of melancholy would seize me at intervals when

I permitted my mind to review the past. But they were of short duration. Instinctively I would arouse myself and resume with greater vigor my endless tramping back and forth in my ten-foot cell. I never indulged in a spasm of misanthropy, never allowed moroseness the least footing. Still these feelings would unawares steal upon me, but I would shake them off by resorting to my seemingly eternal tramping in my narrow confines.

Maria Shaw—

The pleasantest and most encouraging oasis in this desolate desert was the weekly letter of Miss Maria Shaw. I was disinclined to communicate with friends, members of the organization then unsuspected, for fear of drawing the attention of the police to them and thus involving them in the situation that I was in. I received letters from my family regularly, which were always welcome, but those from Miss Shaw were sympathetic and hopeful, and often in an indirect way, gave me information very much desired and acceptable.

How this young woman found time to perform all the duties that she assumed on behalf of all the prisoners and to compose so many cheery weekly letters, each of them necessarily different, I never could understand. I have never seen her but once since I left prison, but I have heard of her and have thought of her gratefully as the guardian angel of our movement at its most supreme moment of trial.

Maria Shaw never received due recognition of, or substantial compensation for, her sweet, kindly, and arduous labor.

As a relief to the monotony of our prison life, new prisoners would arrive from distant county jails and others to whom we were accustomed as fellow-prisoners would depart for America. These trifling variations and changes always afforded me a momentary and mild excitement. It was hinted to me several times that I would find no difficulty in obtaining leave to go to America if I desired, but I never took any notice of those hints. I decided to remain in Ireland and believed that I would eventually be allowed my liberty. I knew that great disorganization had occurred in the ranks in Ulster, which I believed I could re-establish when once free, for I still had the belief that all was not yet lost. As it neared the end of the year I could see that most of the prisoners had gone to America. Also it was further believed by the Government that the spirit of hostility was completely dead. I was then set at liberty. James Irwin, a brother-in-law of O'Donovan Rossa, was set free at the same time.

During my stay in prison, great events had happened on the continent. France and Austria had been at war, as a result of which Savoy and Nice had been ceded to the former country. It is quite remarkable that I have no remembrance of that or any other event of importance occurring during my year in prison. It seems to me now as if I did not live during 1866, that I was perfectly and practically dead during that time. Stranger is the fact that the blank still remains with me for I have neither cared about nor read anything consecutively about the occurrences of that period.

Religious estrangement—

Another thing had happened to me. From being the regular communicant and attendant at church that I had been, I became utterly lax in that respect. Instead of being spiritually disposed, I imagined myself a thoroughgoing materialist. The unlimited and, as I believed, unmerited censures of Cardinal Cullen, Bishop Moriarty, and other ecclesiastics of lesser note had so estranged me from all church practices and observances that I believed that I was a deist or pantheist or something of that sort. To be orthodox was to be a simpleton. To believe otherwise than as Voltaire, Paine, and Rousseau taught was the height of folly and clear proof of unmitigated ignorance.

Like many of the young men of our movement I became a free-thinker on religious matters, but never a zealot in advocating my views. I was liberal enough not to condemn others for believing differently, insisting likewise upon that privilege being conceded to me by others. My favorite textbook was a pocket edition of Volney's *Ruins,* which I was seldom without. I certainly flattered myself that I was a high-class apostle of unbelief without preaching it as apostles do. During the period of my boasted unbelief I never lost hope in the ultimate rescue of the poor and lowly from the trials and sufferings of their harsh and torturing existence. To remove all hardship and distress was still my predominating idea. My young life had begun that way and it had been mainly with the hope of trying to abolish that distress that I became a republican soldier.

The thought sometimes came to me in prison that after the fight was over and the republic had been established, poverty, dire distressing poverty, would still remain. To have it otherwise was a problem that I could not solve. My confidence in politics as the means to that end was not so firm as it had been, but I could see no other way out of the difficulty and knew of no other method. I knew nothing of Political Economy.

New plans for revolt—

In an hour after my liberation, I was in the rooms of Ed. Duffy, Acting Head Centre, who had succeeded Colonel Kelly. Duffy was exceedingly anxious to have Ulster reorganized. He had made the attempt, but beyond or outside of Belfast he could not go. The fact of being under bond for my future good behavior did not deter me from agreeing to have Ulster in line in a short time.

After a week spent in Dublin following my release I returned to my father's house, which I had been away from for two years or more. He lost no time in procuring me a job in Moore's foundry, located, I think, on Mill street. This was the concern in which my father had wished me to become a partner at the time that I became a journeyman. But I had already become a soldier of the Irish Republic and, believing a revolution inevitable, thought it the utmost folly at that time to go into business. To have him invest his money in the foundry and to lose it through my actions would, I was sure, be criminal. So now I went to work in the place which I might have partly owned.

My next business was to become reinstated in the Moulders' Union. I had stopped my contributions for the same reason that I had refused to become a partner in the foundry. It was a question whether I had forfeited my right as a first-class member of the union by the non-payment of my dues. The secretary, Mr. Moneypenny, claimed that I had not. Mr. James Taylor, of Newry, the previous secretary of the union for eighteen years, agreed with Mr. Moneypenny, but a number of intensely loyal Orangemen, who were members of the union, claimed that I had, and that in consequence I must lose certain privileges because of my negligence. A special general meeting of the union was held to determine the matter, when it cropped out that the opposition was purely on account of my alleged disloyalty to the Government, which seemed to have been proved by the fact that I had been imprisoned.

My good, loyal non-Catholic friends, led by Sam Kerr, the Mormon elder, and Tom Russell, a stalwart Presbyterian, rallied to my support unanimously. I was defeated by four votes. I refused to accept the decision and insisted upon another meeting being held. Meantime, I was advised by Taylor that in case of being again defeated, I should appeal to the Executive Committee in London and that he would briefly give them a statement of the case. The result of the next meeting was the same as that of the first. I then appealed to the Executive Committee in London, which directed the Belfast branch to reinstate me forthwith or their charter would be forfeited. My politics, beliefs, or practices were to be no bar to my membership, and those holding different views were wrong. It was a bold, honest and clean decision, and coming from Englishmen staggered the bigoted loyalists of Belfast. The membership of the union at the time was nearly three hundred, of whom not more than fifty were Catholics, showing that my rebellious principles had made good headway among my fellow-workers. Only about six of the Catholics were of our organization, the others voted for me out of pure antagonism to the Orange opponents, and not in support of my republicanism.

I was certainly, so far as appearances went, on my good behavior, for I seldom left the house in the evenings. My sisters, however, had more parties than formerly. At those parties I met all the men whom I wished to see, and by means of letter writing, I soon had Ulster in an organized condition.

Captain Jim Murphy, one of those arrested with me in Casey's and who had gone from prison to America as soon as he was permitted, had returned and was in charge of the Glasgow section of the organization. Through Duffy I received a pressing invitation to visit Murphy. I met the Captain, who gave me what he considered an account of the correct state of the organization in Ireland and elsewhere. In order that I might communicate with him without fear of discovery, he gave me a bottle of invisible ink to be used with a quill pen on newspaper, and another bottle into which I dipped the feather end of the pen and drew it across the part written upon with the other liquid, thus revealing the matter written. I was ignorant of those substances at the time and considered the performance something wonderful. He informed me that it was the product of Edmund O'Donovan, the son of Professor O'Donovan. Edmund was, I believe, a very talented young man, who knew something of chemistry as well as many other matters. He afterwards, I heard, went to France, became an officer in the French Army, and later figured as a correspondent for a French newspaper in the Soudan while England was kept busy trying to subdue the people of that region.

The rescue of Colonel Kelly and Captain Tim Deasy from a prison van in Manchester and the killing of a policeman in connection therewith caused somewhat of a commotion in both England and Ireland. The arrest, conviction, and execution of Allen, Larkin, and O'Brien for complicity in the affair very greatly intensified the feeling in Ireland.[41]

About the time this feeling had died out a messenger came to me with the information that a conference was to be held in London where a few of the best informed men of the organization were to meet General Cluseret and General Vivquain of the French Army, who had consented to assume the command of the Irish Army provided the state of the organization and its armament warranted them in doing so. As I was best informed as to the condition of affairs in Ulster I was requested to be present. I consulted William Harbinson, and between the two of us, it was agreed that he should make the journey, for the reason that, being under surveillance, my absence for a week would surely attract attention and probably lead to some disastrous surprises for us. Besides, Harbinson was a military man and was well informed regarding our preparedness. He was also free from all suspicion.

[41] The revolt of March 5, 1867, having been a failure, Kelly, with his aide de camp, Captain Deasy, was in England making preparations for another revolt when they were arrested by the officers of the English Government and lodged in the Manchester jail. A number of the local Fenians attempted to rescue the two men as they were being taken to court in the prison van. In the mêlée which ensued, one of the police officers was killed. Kelly and Deasy escaped and were never recaptured, but five of those arrested for complicity in the affair were tried and sentenced to be hanged. Two of them were later released, but Michael Larkin, Michael O'Brien, and William P. Allen were executed on November 23, 1867.—Ed.

I was sorry to be obliged to forego this trip, but we were all, each of us, required to do what was reasonably best regardless of our individual preferences. As a result of the conference General Cluseret decided that a revolt with a reasonable hope of success was not visible to him and advised against such an attempt. He also refused the command, and both he and Vivquain returned to France. Harbinson believed that the General was correct as a military man and wise as an individual. The decision was distasteful to some of the men in the South, who insisted upon warfare with brief and disastrous results.

Harbinson—

At the conference there was an American officer, General Massey, who became an informer, causing the arrest of those present at the meeting, including Harbinson. Harbinson's arrest caused as much excitement and insecurity among the loyalists as did the arrest under the Habeas Corpus Suspension Act of the sixteen young non-Catholic men at Newtownards. That intelligent, well-to-do non-Catholics should be rebels was a thing unheard of and never expected. Here also was a confidential man, having charge of the armory of the Antrim Militia with its arms and stores, allied with the revolutionary party. The folly of allowing Harbinson to go upon that mission was now apparent. Yet it was done for the best and at his own request. None of us anticipated the presence of an informer at such a meeting. But he was there just the same and an American general at that. If I could have seen into the future I would certainly have gone, and willingly accepted the fourteen years' penal servitude that that infamous modern Norbury,[42] Judge Keogh, dealt out to all who were brought before him and his packed juries, whether convicted with or without evidence.

Harbinson died suddenly of heart disease in the Antrim County Jail. His loss was the most grievous blow sustained by us in Belfast. This was demonstrated by the attendance at the funeral. About two thousand men, four abreast, marched solemnly behind the hearse to Friar's Bush burying ground without a command and apparently without a commander. As we passed the point leading to Sandy Row, the Orangemen's quarters, a large crowd was gathered and I believed that I saw in the faces of many of them evidences of sympathy, which I took for a good omen. The procession marched along without molestation.

Toward the end of the year 1867, a gentleman called upon me to confer about the present and future of our organization. From the beginning and up to that time it had been autocratically governed by one man. So long as Stephens was that man, I was perfectly satisfied that it should be so governed. If Edward Duffy's health had permitted him to gov-

[42] Roney is referring to Judge Norbury who presided at the trial of Robert Emmet.—Ed.

ern I would have been equally well satisfied. But to be governed by a man like Colonel Tom Kelly, who could discriminate against poor men in favor of others better provided for and more capable of caring for themselves, was something to which I certainly was opposed.

New plan of organization—

Mr. John O'Connor, the gentleman who called upon me, submitted a plan of organization more democratic and in keeping with our pretensions as republicans. The plan called for the election of a director for each of the four provinces, two for England and one for Scotland. Each director was to be assisted by a deputy and a military secretary, who were also to be elected. The entire group of representatives was to constitute the Supreme Council. I readily agreed to the plan and immediately set about to call a provincial convention. The convention assembled at Whitehouse and I was chosen chairman. The plan of organization was concurred in without a dissenting vote. I was also elected Deputy Director and Ed. McAleese was chosen Military Secretary. As Ulster was credited with being largely non-Catholic and intensely loyal, I proposed that the Director be a non-Catholic whose disloyalty to England was unquestioned, and as I had in mind a man so qualified I asked to be authorized to offer him the position without mentioning his name because he might decline it, which would necessitate its being offered to another. Besides, I wished to give him the assurance that his selection was by vote entrusted to one man and not by the method usually adopted by conventions. This was agreed to and the convention dispersed.

The man whom I had in mind was Thomas Neilson Underwood, barrister-at-law of Strabane. He was an hereditary rebel, his grandfather, Rev. Neilson, having been hanged for his loyalty to the Irish Cause in 1798. He was a man of superior mental ability and possessed of independent means irrespective of his profession. He was also related to the Lieutenant Neilson who served under Garibaldi, whom a few of us entertained at a dinner presided over by Lieutenant Denis Hayes. Hayes had served under Major O'Reilley in the Pope's Army during the same war. It was a hopeful sight to see the two lieutenants representing opposing causes fraternizing on the common ground of loyalty to their native land. Mr. Underwood accepted the dangerous position without hesitation and took the obligation.

On the Saturday preceding the day when we had agreed to meet in Dublin to perfect the organization of the Supreme Council, and when hurrying home from work to get ready to catch the afternoon train, I was arrested by Head Constable Jaques, who immediately hurried me to the nearest police station. That night I slept in the County Jail.

Imprisoned again—

Solitary confinement in this prison had reached the highest degree of perfection. Nothing could be more so. I seldom saw and was never spoken to by a warden, unless it was to have him give an order of some sort. In chapel I was enclosed in a box and could see no one but the priest at the altar. For exercising I had a limited space where I could not even see the shadow of my neighbor exercising at the same time. The governor, a former army officer, was quite considerate, furnishing me with clean extra bedding and the use of his library. My meals were sent to me from home.

I never could learn how or why I was arrested on that particular day or at whose instance it was done. The deputy directors of the other provinces were also arrested on the same day, which indicated to me that someone, who was well informed, was at the bottom of it. I do know that the creation of a Supreme Council was obnoxious to those who had been conducting the organization on the one-man basis, and that the deputy directors were known to them. The directors of the other provinces were chosen in the same way as the one in Ulster so that only two persons knew their names, i.e., the man who made the selection and Mr. John O'Connor, to whom their names were given so that they might be better protected.

Edward McAleese, our Military Secretary, was arrested in a populous neighborhood at an hour when the streets were crowded, and since he was well-known, the mob which collected jostled the police in such a way that he broke from them, ran into a house, and was never recaptured.

Mountjoy again—

I remained in the Belfast Jail for about three months, when without warning I was removed to my old quarters in Mountjoy Prison in Dublin. I was awakened about four o'clock in the morning and told to get ready to leave. I was given a pint cup of hot coffee to fortify me for the journey. I knew not where I was to be taken. In due course I was brought to the Governor's office and the formality of transferring me to the six armed policemen was gone through with. I vigorously protested and resisted when the sergeant in charge offered to shackle me. I appealed to the Governor, who said that I was no longer in his charge and that if I were, he certainly would not handcuff me. It took several policemen after a fierce struggle to handcuff me to another young man, a telegraph operator whom I did not know. Both of us were seemingly bound for the same destination.

In passing my father's house I asked to see my mother. We had plenty of time for the short delay, but the brutal sergeant was too full of his responsibility and importance to grant my request. My mother's dream was thus fulfilled. On the morning of the day of my arrest she told me that she had

had a dream to the effect that that would be the last time that she would see me. I laughed at her fears by assuring her that there was no danger of that occurring. Having confined myself so closely to the house she apparently had confidence in my assurances. Instead of telling her that I was going to Dublin I had led her to believe that I was going to an aunt at Saul near Downpatrick for a few days' vacation. I had been keeping to the house at nights so long and so steadily that she had no apprehension that the mishap she dreamed of could be due to my activities as a revolutionist. I never saw her dear face again, now nearly fifty years ago. I am not a believer in dreams or in omens, yet this dream of my dear mother and its complete fulfillment is something to shake the faith of the most skeptical unbeliever.

On my way to Dublin the train stopped at Newry for passengers en route from Armagh. When my presence was discovered the car in which I was riding was surrounded by a mob of flax-buyers, all warm friends, who had just arrived for the market. I was overwhelmed with the kind expressions of the boys who, against my wishes, thrust handfuls of coin upon me insisting that I would need it and expressing the regret that they could do nothing more for me.

At Drogheda, John McCabe and his wife, formerly Isabella McMahon, were there to see me as if they knew that I was coming. When his wife saw me she began to cry as if her heart would break. We had belonged for several years to a musical society which I had rarely attended. She had a magnificent soprano voice and had toured the country singing Irish melodies illustrative of the scenes in Dr. Curry's splendid and instructive panorama of Ireland. We had always been the best of friends and now to part forever, as it proved to be, seemed so trying upon her fine sensitive nature that she could not restrain herself. John, her husband, invited me to the lunch room at the station and the dour sergeant to my astonishment consented. McCabe urged me to escape assuring me that every precaution would be taken against recapture. I had given my word to the policeman to return and was resolved to do so. Arriving at Amiens Street Station, the sergeant admitted that he did not know the direct way to the Mountjoy Prison and asked me to lead. I promptly refused unless he would remove the handcuffs from my companion and myself, which he did, I think, with trepidation.

Owing to the representations and insistence of Dr. McDonnell, the prison physician, an able as well as humane man, the rules, since my earlier release, had been relaxed in favor of political prisoners. Longer time was allowed for exercise, during which smoking was permitted provided the prisoners furnished their own smoking material. Prisoners could also select a companion to talk with. In addition, those whose previous habits required a stimulant were allowed one bottle of stout each day. With these improvements I decided to worry through my time as composedly as possible as I had done previously, unless I happened to be presented to Judge Keogh,[43] when that would end it all.

Freedom at a sacrifice—

Several months after my return to Mountjoy I was surprised one day to receive an unsolicited visit from Father Cody, the prison chaplin. As he was an officer of the prison he could admit himself at any time to our cells. The priest and I were excellent friends notwithstanding the views that I held. He hurriedly asked me if I knew a certain man in Belfast, giving his name and occupation. I said that I did. "Well," said he, "he has turned informer." Without another word he left my cell. I knew that this man could give Judge Keogh enough of an excuse to give me the customary sen-

[43] William Keogh, a staunch supporter of Catholic rights and an opponent of the Government, had been a leader in the Tenant Right League. In spite of his protestations of loyalty to the Irish Cause, he went over to the Government at the first opportunity, was appointed Solicitor-General and later a Judge, and became known as one of the severest men on the Bench in sentencing Irish rebels. McManus, *op. cit.*, footnote, p. 612, comments upon him in the following manner: "And he was soon comfortably seated upon the Judge's bench, grinning at the dupes whom he had betrayed, and glad of the opportunity to send into transportation, or on the gallows, the 'foolish' ones who preferred to give up their lives in preference to giving up Liberty and Ireland. This scoundrel's name became a by-word for rottenness. He lived long to enjoy the place and pelf for which he sold his soul, and to be the despised and the scorned of his countrymen."—Ed.

tence of fourteen years. I knew too that there was no use in sending for the priest to question him further. He, as an officer, had said all that he would say. I saw my dream of early liberation vanishing and knew no way to act but to remain as I was and await developments. In the afternoon of the same day I was notified that a visitor was below to see me. Mr. Joseph Keenan, the most intimate friend of my father, was the visitor. He stood several feet from a wire screen that divided the room and I stood about the same distance from it on the other side. Alongside each of us was a warden with paper and pencil taking notes of the conversation. Our talk was entirely about the family and our friends. At the close he said, "It's a wonder to me that you never think of going to America." Father Cody's intimation and Mr. Keenan's suggestion meant something. But what to do was not suggested.

At a late hour that night when all was as silent as the grave in the prison, a rattling of keys and the sound of voices speaking at my door awakened me. As the door opened a bullseye lantern was flashed upon me in my cot and in the uncertain light I distinguished a man in a court dress with cocked hat, knee breeches, and a sword. I concluded that this was the man who was about to order my removal to another prison preliminary to my trial or to badger me with questions. I decided that I would not answer any questions. Whatever the cause of the visit I was determined to take my medicine courageously. When he spoke I recognized him at once. Ascertaining that I was awake, he next asked me how I liked prison life. I told him in reply that there were worse things in the world although I did not like imprisonment. "Well," said he, "if you should think of leaving it and going to America I will take your application into consideration." And the cell door closed, leaving me in darkness with my aroused burning thoughts. The visitor was Mr. Murray, the Government prison director in charge of all the Government prisons in Ireland.

I slept none that night and in the morning applied for permission to go to America. Before noon the Governor came and informed me that my application had been granted. He also informed me that a vessel was leaving Queenstown in two days and that a passage ticket and some money besides what I had brought with me was in his office. I told him that I would start the next morning, which appeared to be satisfactory. I wondered at the celerity of the transaction and at how naturally I fell into the way that I was expected to go without advice or direction. I discovered later that my father was directing it all and had substantial reasons for the speed. And yet I knew nothing about it at the time. Next morning I left Mountjoy Prison with Daniel Liddy of Limerick and John Maguire of Ennis under an escort of six policemen in plain clothes. To my great surprise my father was there to greet me when I got free of the prison. He then told me how it had all come about, and why and how such expedition had been shown. My father's reputation for loyalty to the Government and his probity as a business man stood high in the community and with the officials. He had been notified that an informer had appeared, and also as to what the informer would testify to against me. He asked that publicity be withheld for four days, which the officials understood was to give him an opportunity to get me out of the country. They knew what my fate would be when the informer's statement was officially accepted and they did not wish to punish my father by having his son convicted. My father and Mr. Keenan had come to Dublin together, Keenan to see me and my father to see Mr. Murray. My father had been attending the annual conference of the St. Vincent de Paul Society for several years, and had formed the acquaintance of Mr. Murray, who took a deep interest in that organization. The acquaintance developed into friendship. It was in Murray's power to let me go to America so long as there was no specific charge against me. The night that he saw me in the prison he had been attending a levée at the Castle and had driven from there to the prison to give me a hint, if I would take it. My father knew of my application as soon as Murray received it and at once purchased my ticket, which, with £50, reached the Governor's office at about the same time as my permit to leave arrived.

My father was made the means of conveying to me a letter notifying me that Mr. Fitzgerald, otherwise J. J. O'Kelly, would follow me to New York in a month and asking me to prepare as many good men as I might meet for the news that he was coming as the envoy of the newly organized Supreme Council.

It was a deep disappointment to me to be obliged to leave Ireland, but it was preferable to being a prisoner at Pentonville or anywhere else. My imprisonment would contribute nothing to the advancement of the Cause, whereas in America I might be able to aid it to some extent. That was the only consoling thought that the situation afforded. I had the gratification of saying farewell to Henry Dobbin and a few other Belfast men at the Blackpool railroad station a little north of Cork City as our train passed it. Mr. O'Reilly, a flax mill manager, had gone there to operate the flax mill established by Mr. John Francis Maguire, member of Parliament and formerly Mayor of Cork City, and had taken Henry and the others along to assist him in making the enterprise a success.

Our last night in Ireland spent at Queenstown was a most boisterous one. I made the six policemen, in whose charge we had been placed, so hilariously drunk that they were singing rebel songs and making rebel speeches with as much abandon as if they were members of our organization, as possibly they were. Next day we were placed on board an Inman steamer, a receipt was given by the Captain or supercargo for our delivery, and in the evening we took our farewell look at the green hills of suffering and holy Ireland. I never was so utterly depressed. It was like breaking the ligaments of my heart, for we were never to return.

England and Ireland—

I was only one of the many young men whom the British Government in its mad injustice to the people had forced out of a land whose history and traditions, whose heroes and martyrs, were themes to arouse the most generous and noble thoughts in the bosoms of the most callous. Had England pursued a policy of ordinary friendship to Ireland she would not have been threatened periodically with rebellion. She would have possessed, instead, the love and loyalty of a warm, generous-hearted people. The young men of whom I was one would have been the best and truest of her people. The English working people were not much better off than the Irish. All were exploited to maintain an idle tyrannous gang of aristocrats. The Irish brand of the animal was the worse, for they had neither pity nor consideration for the poor.

I lay down my first night at sea with a heart loaded with misery, and with my fondest dream as far away as ever.

We were in mid-ocean when St. Patrick's Day came around, and we resolved to celebrate it in a sane and proper manner. To do so, the Captain's consent was necessary. I was chosen to interview the Captain, who gave his consent stipulating that all lights should be extinguished at ten o'clock. Captain Leach was a big-hearted, generous Scotchman, who understood the good as well as the weak points in the ordinary Irishman. He ordered that whatever was needed to contribute to the festivity that could be had aboard should cost no more than if bought in Cork. I was told that this was an unusual concession.

I believe that I tried to make a speech which was really not a speech but a string of abbreviated reminders of who we were, what we had left, and what we should do in the land to which we were going. Singing and dancing and more speeches, such as they were, and the day was pleasantly ended.

III

THE NEW WORLD

III

THE NEW WORLD

New York City—

On the morning of our arrival in New York harbor I was the very first on deck. The ship was at anchor and the sun had not yet dispersed the clouds that hung over the land. In my heart I hailed America as the land of Liberty where all were equal and where poverty was unknown—the land which my dear old teacher had taught me and the boys committed to his care, to look upon as their final home; the land of Lincoln, that one great towering human figure of all who had labored to make the United States a nation. No name in American history is in my opinion so great as that of Lincoln. No other name so commends itself to the downtrodden of the world as his. When other memories now esteemed great shall have perished, his will live and be loved by the generations to come. I was brimming with anticipation and delight to set foot on this land, so young and so great, where I thought human misery found neither voice nor echo.

Maguire and I were about the first to land. We secured lodgings in the house of an Englishman on Seventh Street. Most of the others were being looked after by the Immigration Board, waiting for directions to their future homes. Having nothing to do after being housed, we strolled down to Castle Garden to see some of our late fellow-passengers and bid them farewell and wish them success. We were known to them all, and as persons who had figured as political prisoners and been forcibly obliged to leave the country, we were regarded with confidence.

So this was America!—

On nearing the entrance to Castle Garden one of the female passengers, a rather handsome girl, was about to enter a carriage, but paused when she saw us to tell us of her good fortune in getting a fine situation at good wages which, as her money was not enough to carry her to her friends out West, would enable her to do in the way she wished, for evidently she had pride. She introduced us to a flashily dressed woman as her future mistress. I did not fancy the woman's appearance and instinctively took a dislike to her. She showed none of the exterior qualities of a lady and her facial appearance was against her. I began questioning her, when her hesitation and evasiveness and little contradictions satisfied me that she was not what she represented herself to be. I remembered reading stories of unsuspecting female immigrants being decoyed into houses of prostitution and believed that this was an attempt to capture another victim. My questioning was so pointed and insistent that the woman lost her temper and called me an obscene name. At this stage she was joined by a young man, also flashily dressed, who demanded what business it was of mine to interfere and prevent the girl's going to a good position. My reply to this challenge was to take the girl's bags out of the carriage and bring her back to Castle Garden. Maguire, a strong athletic young fellow, proposed thrashing the fellow, but I considered it indiscreet and that part was omitted.

And so that was America! I had never heard of so bold an attempt being made at home to waylay and ensnare a virtuous girl and fling her into the depths of an infamous life, as was made on that occasion. Such things may have been done and the same sort of people may live in England and Ireland, but they are not so unblushing in their pursuit.

Irish Republic—

To prepare the way for Jim O'Kelly as the envoy of the Supreme Council, I first called upon Mr. M. Scanlan, who with Rev. David Bell, an ex-Presbyterian minister, formerly of County Antrim, was publishing a paper called the *Irish Republic.* The American politics advocated by the paper was Republican.

Scanlan had been the most active member of the Fenian organization in Chicago and had also gained some reputation as a poet and writer. He was largely instrumental in getting up and making a financial success of a fancy fair in that city to raise funds for the organization in Ireland. His wife, also, when on a visit to Ireland, with Maria Shaw got up, with the assistance of other ladies, a fair in Dublin, to raise funds for the benefit of the families of the men arrested in Ireland and then suffering imprisonment. Scanlan was a staunch Republican and as sound on the Irish as he was on the American version of that political belief.

Rev. David Bell—

Rev. David Bell had been ejected from his pastorate because of his extreme views on Irish politics, and later, because of his opinions, had been deprived by the Synod of his church of the right to exercise his functions as a minister. I had often met him at our meetings in Belfast where with some Catholic priests, who were also members of our organization, they discussed our hopes and our work. Bell preceded me to America by about a year and was not yet an American citizen, but he was naturally a Republican and fitted well into the vocation of a newspaper man for he was an able writer and a good speaker.

The many friends, whom I had known in Ireland and again met in New York, received me very cordially and accepted my reasons justifying the necessity of a change in the form of the organization at home. To meet them and others whom I did not know, with little loss of time, I became a member of a secret organization which had just been formed, whose ostensible object was to carry out the original program at as early a date as possible. In this society I met O'Mahony, Murtagh, Moynahan, and many others, and mentioned the coming of O'Kelly. For about two months I busied myself exclusively with this task and then met O'Kelly, leaving to him the finishing of the work.

American friends—

Incidentally I met and was introduced to Mr. Horace Greely, Mayor Hoffman, later governor of New York, James O'Brien, Sheriff of New York, and others. Mr. Greely had always been recognized as the warm, consistent friend of Ireland and of Irishmen and at the time held the position of the foremost journalist in America. It was an honor and a pleasure to me to meet so famous a man and to be assured by him of his unalterable desire to see my stricken country invested with her natural rights. Mr. Hoffman was explicit in proclaiming his hostility to England's claim to the ownership of Ireland. Mr. O'Brien was a politician and, though Irish, had no views on the matter.

It was beginning to dawn upon me what an American politician really was. To make it illuminating I may tell this story:

American citizenship—

One of my Armagh friends, a printer who was employed on the *New York Tribune,* invited me to his room on a Sunday afternoon. Noticing an article neatly framed hanging on the wall, to my surprise I discovered it to be his certificate of naturalization. He had been in the country only a year. I asked if it was genuine and he said that it was. He further informed me that there was no difficulty in getting one's citizenship papers provided one got in with the right persons. I had made up my mind to declare my intentions of becoming a citizen, which he stated was folly and a waste of time. I must be a citizen at once. With this in view I was introduced to a deputy sheriff, who was also a saloon keeper, and proceeded to the office of Nathaniel Jarvis, clerk of the Court of Common Pleas in the City Hall. While waiting my turn to approach the desk and within hearing of the clerk, a perfect stranger came up to me and most effusively began asking me questions about my family in the most familiar way. I was dumbfounded and when speech came to me, before I could say a word another familiar and equally unknown friend started similar inquiries. At last it was my turn at the desk. The clerk, who had heard my new friends, asked in the most matter of fact way if I wished my citizenship paper and when I said that I had come to make my declaration of intention to become a citizen my two *quondam* friends left hurriedly. Mr. Jarvis proceeded to fill in my answers without being the least disturbed. The deputy sheriff was in the corridor waiting, and smilingly invited my printer friend and me to take a drink, but my friend said "No," alleging pressing business elsewhere. He informed me as we went up town on a street car that I had done an exceedingly dangerous thing and that if we had gone to the saloon there was no telling what would have happened to us.

Politicians who engaged in that sort of business had few opinions on any questions of importance regarding Ireland or anything else because their spare time was too much occupied in fabrications to allow them to be momentarily honest enough to have any opinions. This illegal admission to citizenship was so shamelessly possible because it was alleged that the records of declaration had been consumed by a fire in the clerk's office, whether intentionally or not could not be said, and all that was required by the person seeking his citizenship paper was to present himself to the clerk with two witnesses, and a little complaisant perjury completed the job. This and a few other trifling matters began disillusioning me. I began to perceive but little difference in the ordinary ways of life as practised in America and as practised by those among the same class in the large cities of England and Ireland. The impression made was rather in favor of the English and Irish cities.

Between visiting the leading men of the so-called American Irish Republic, which had practically collapsed, and impressing upon them the lesson of our failure in Ireland and its cause, and that our hopes for the future were centered in the Supreme Council, and meeting other persons in a social way, I spent about two months of time in New York. I believe that an election was near at hand and great interest was shown in it by prominent men identified with the cause of Ireland.

I had read of and heard stories told of how the immigrant was captured upon his arrival at Castle Garden and made a Democrat before he understood the difference between the political parties or what either stood for. No such attempt had been made to inveigle me, owing perhaps to the fact that I had expressed my preference for the Republican Party. An Irishman at that time professing allegiance to the Republican Party was looked upon by his countrymen classed as Democrats as being a renegade, and if a non-Catholic, he was by some sort of logic associated with the defunct "Know Nothings." At least he was a "nigger lover and a Black Republican." So far names of dubious character or implication had not deterred me from doing what I considered right, and I was resolved that they never should. I had in mind the reception given in Belfast to the Confederate officers by the Orange magistracy. I had seen how anxious the English aristocracy was to destroy the American Republic by covertly aiding the Confederacy. They were the natural enemies of my country and her Cause and were therefore my enemies. They and their allies and the upholders of the Confederacy were the backbone, as well as the brains, of the Democratic Party.

The young men coming from Ireland were all Republicans, and so at the suggestion of Mr. Scanlan, a Republican Club was formed, not that we could vote, but for the purpose of teaching our countrymen independence in politics and who were their real enemies in America. The club was organized in Armory Hall on the Bowery, and Tom Masterson was its first president. I was elected a member of its executive committee. I never served, however, for about that time I left New York for St. Louis.

Old world and new world labor—

After some months in New York, my funds began to get low, and it became necessary for me to get employment. Seeing a crowd around a low brick building, the windows of which were removed, leaving strong iron perpendicular bars allowing inlets for air, but providing barriers against unwelcome visitors, I peered into the semi-darkness and saw men, bare-headed and bare-footed, almost nude, racing back and forth, handling between trips, small wooden tools most dexterously. I asked a bystander what was going on inside, and was told that it was a foundry. The information made me gasp. I had never seen or heard of a foundry like it, and became interested. To see men half nude, exerting themselves as these were doing in a place imperfectly lighted, black and dirty, and perspiring on this hot morning, was a revelation to me. If this was moulding in America, then I decided it were better for me to return to Ireland and go to prison and remain there rather than degrade myself as these free American citizens were doing.

Mechanics, and for that matter all others in the old countries where I had had experience, never worked in so exhausting a way as those men did. The Europeans worked rationally, intelligently, and well, and had some of their work remaining for the next day. The American moulders seemed desirous of doing all the work required as if it were the last day of their lives. I learned that the men, whom I was watching, were stove-plate moulders and that they worked by the piece instead of by the day. The harder they worked the more they earned. This was also a new feature to me.

Competition among the employing stove-makers was so keen that, in order to get ready and speedy sale for their wares, prices, because of competition, were reduced as low as could be consistent with the cost of labor, price of iron, and other incidental expenses including cost of management, leaving a margin of profit sufficient to cover a good percentage upon the capital invested and add to the extension of the plant. The prices of the material used were regulated by a standard which gave all an equal chance, although in this respect, where unusually large quantities of fuel and iron were purchased rebates or reductions followed, giving a fortunate buyer advantages over his less financially favored competitor. Wages of the moulders were periodically reduced to meet the demands of competition between employers and the more this was done and the greater the reduction the harder the men worked. There seemed to be no conscience among the employers and no thought or cohesiveness among the workers. All of this I learned on the morning of my first quest for work. I began to think that my exalted idea of man's equality in the American republic was rather mythical. To work under a republican form of government was no more advantageous than it was under an aristocratic form. Its commercialism and competitive methods being allowed free rein made it decidedly disadvantageous to the worker, and unlike monarchical countries there was no restraining influence.

In New York, however, I had not yet seen any of the hardships or distress so glaringly prevalent in the large English and Irish towns that I had been in. It was many years afterwards when I visited New York that I realized the existence of a condition of things as bad as had ever existed in the worst portions of Europe under the most oppressive governments. In the meantime I had also, as I think, learned what caused poverty and how it could be abolished if men could divest themselves of selfishness and the ambition of being better off than their neighbor at the neighbor's cost.

Jersey City—

My quest for work took me to Jersey City. One foreman told me that work was slack but that he expected it to pick up and to call again. I bore the unmistakable marks of a recent arrival although I had been three months in the country. But the cut of my clothes marked me, and as he was an Englishman and I spoke that language he inquired where I came from. When I told him he became most friendly, asking about several of the older and most respected moulders in Belfast. It was the first town he had worked in as a young journeyman when he left his home in London and he had been so well treated by Belfast men that he entertained the kindest regard for them all. He concluded by telling me to begin work the next morning.

Mr. Carey proved to be an excellent man, as fair and considerate a foreman as one could wish. None of the wrecking and oppressive sordidness of the New York stove-plate moulders was visible in this foundry. It was a place for competent mechanics and not for slaves, voluntary or involuntary. There was nothing cringing or servile about the men who worked there nor was there anything domineering or exacting about the foreman.

It occurred to me that a man's environment and his domestic and corporeal needs often make him the thing he is yet does not want to be. Constant association with men similarly situated confirms him in the hopelessness of any effort for relief, and he stays put without energy or ambition, to rot and die a slave.

William Hampson, of Celbridge, County Kildare, wrote to me from St. Louis enclosing a ticket to carry me to that city. So many of our men, forced to leave Ireland, arrived in New York wretchedly poverty stricken that he concluded that I was in that condition. Knowing New York as he did he believed that the West was a much better place for me. Mr. Carey advised me to remain where I was and offered several inducements to detain me, but I decided to go farther west.

Extinguished hopes—

My experiences with my countrymen in New York had extinguished the hope of anything of an immediate practical benefit for Ireland. Already some of them had formed an organization to invade Canada as a preliminary to the liberation of Ireland.[1] The home organization did not favor that

[1] An invasion of Canada by several armed divisions of the American Fenians had actually taken place in May, 1866, but with disastrous results for the invaders. Another invasion was attempted in April, 1870, but a spy was active in the ranks, and in his capacity as commander of one of the divisions did much to bring failure to the invading army. Cf. Henri Le Caron (T. M. Beach), *Twenty-five Years in the Secret Service*, 26–36, 73–99.

project, nor did I. Others had an overweening desire for public office and strove to make their prominence as Irish patriots and as members of Irish societies important factors to that end. Many of the recent arrivals had lost all hope of further success and went aimlessly among their friends posing as suffering exiles and living in a precarious way on that reputation without making any effort at living independent of charity. I had befriended several of these dispirited men who had become suffering professional exiles and patriots until it became apparent that I must leave New York to save myself or become one of them, neither to be useful to myself nor to any cause. For these reasons I went to St. Louis.

St. Louis—

Hampson was the superintendent of the city fire-alarm system of St. Louis, a position for which he was quite competent. How he obtained it I never inquired. He was the son of English parents, born and educated in Ireland, and was as intensely Irish as if he had had a thousand generations of Irish ancestors behind him. He was a natural mechanic. Beginning as a watch and clockmaker he became a skilled engine constructor and developed as an expert in all matters relating to electricity. Electricity was then in its infancy. The telephone and the uses of electricity as a motive power were undiscovered and perhaps undreamed of. He had identified himself with our organization as a worker among the soldiers stationed at the Curragh, a large military camp, and in Dublin, where he became one of the most successful organizers. It was in Dublin that I first knew him and I came to like him as a fearless and courageous rebel. He was glad to leave Mountjoy Prison many months before my liberation so as to avoid the result of an investigation then going on regarding the death of a man who had been filling the rôle of a spy and informer. This information came direct from one of our own spies at Dublin Castle.

Exiles—

Quite a galaxy of talented exiles were living in St. Louis at that time, including Ed. Coyne and his brothers, Jim Rice of Monaghan, Dr. Cleary, and Joe Flaherty. The latter was a native of Philadelphia and was formerly sergeant major in Colonel Sam Spires' Pennsylvania Cavalry regiment, on which account he was appointed on the St. Louis police force.

Proposed invasion of Canada—

During my stay in St. Louis Colonel John O'Neill and a Mr. Brophy came to raise subscriptions and to get men to aid in a contemplated raid on Canada. My opinion on the latter proposition was quite well-known and all our ex-patriots were of the same mind. It was proposed by them at a meeting of the local branch of the secret organization of which I had become a member in New York that, being the latest arrival in St. Louis from Ireland, I should speak at O'Neill's meeting. I had no fancy for the task, but I accepted it as a duty, and accordingly was in attendance.

It was an immense assemblage that gathered in the rotunda of the Court House. After the Colonel and Brophy had spoken in earnest appeal for funds, I was introduced by the chairman. I told the audience in substance that the proposed expedition was not approved by the members of the Supreme Council which represented the Irish people in Ireland and which expected the Irish everywhere to heed their advice. The people in Ireland had no quarrel with the people of Canada; besides it was too far off for a base of operations as it was proposed to make it, and even if this could be done successfully, with the British fleet patroling the Atlantic Ocean on the look-out for contraband in man and munitions, the scheme was sure to be a failure. Besides a raid or expedition of the proposed sort was likely to embroil the United States in a war with England. To some who did not view the matter in all its detailed consequences this might appear to be the correct thing to do, but to men of Irish birth, who had sworn allegiance to the United States and who realized their conscientious duty to the country of their adoption, it looked like perjury if it did not amount to treason. No true American citizen of

Irish birth could in my opinion take part in or encourage in any manner such an enterprise. The amazement of the Colonel and his friend Brophy was overwhelming, for it seemed from the applause given me that I had the audience with me. It may also be mentioned that the contributions were extremely light and few.

Labor conditions—

I found conditions in the foundries in St. Louis to be much the same as in the stove foundry in New York. There was no piece work outside of the stove foundries. Men worked at breakneck pace in competition with each other. The only limit to their efforts was the shortness of the day and this was extended by lick-spittle foremen anxious to prove their worth by neglecting to put the blast on in time to finish at six P.M. Such humble, docile, dirt-eating fellows I had never seen before. I quit my job intending to go to Chicago.

A silly escapade—

The night before my departure Hampson, who regretted my leaving, proposed that we spend an hour or two with Joe Flaherty on his beat as a policeman. We had fraternized very much and were really very good friends. Accordingly we met Joe. Policemen in St. Louis in those days were privileged to visit saloons, with the further privilege of treating friends without its costing anything. There were quite a number of saloons on Joe's beat, many of which we visited and the hours passed rapidly.

I did not notice that Hampson had been drinking too freely. Because of the lateness of the hour, I concluded that it was time for me to retire for an early start in the morning. Coming towards us were a number of Germans singing "Wacht am Rhein," and otherwise jovially and peacefully behaving themselves. Singing made Hampson intensely nervous and pugnacious when under the influence of liquor, a trait neither Joe nor I was aware of. When the Germans met us, without a word of warning Hampson knocked one of them down and ran. I like a fool ran too. Hampson knew the neighborhood, and Joe was not anxious to overtake us. I felt that we were free from further trouble when to my surprise Hampson landed us in the midst of the crowd, who valiantly and properly enough seized us and insisted upon Joe's taking us to the police station. This was a predicament which I had not bargained for when I left the hotel earlier in the evening, and I saw that it was going to interfere with my departure as I had made all arrangements to leave except purchasing the ticket.

Joe assured us that he would not bring us to the station if we would handle ourselves as he indicated and go home, which Hampson promised to do, for he realized his job as a municipal employe was now imperiled. At the right moment, as I thought, when our escort was off guard, I made a violent blow at

Joe, who dropped apparently senseless to the ground and then we ran, this time to the hotel, which we reached in safety. While Hampson and I were still talking over the silly and needless adventure Joe entered the room and sat down silently and solemnly. Then as a climax he told us that he got into an altercation with the crowd, who charged him with conniving at our escape and threatened to have him removed from the force. This and the previous excitement exasperated Joe, who drew his pistol and fired, hitting one of the Germans. It was a woebegone ending to what I had hoped would be a pleasant parting. Joe decided that he would leave the city, preferring to do so rather than to undergo arrest and ultimate dismissal, which he was sure would follow.

Flaherty was without means and was perplexed how to secure money on which to make the trip. I offered to abandon going by rail. I believed that I had enough money to defray our expenses until we reached Chicago. He had an uncle somewhere in Iowa, a prosperous farmer, who held some sort of official position, to whom he wished to go. No other more feasible plan suggesting itself, this was agreed to and we began our preparations to cross the Mississippi to East St. Louis upon the first boat leaving in the morning. Hampson promised to forward our belongings by express to one of my men from Belfast then living in Chicago. Arriving in Illinois early in the morning, we struck into the country from the railroad to keep clear of any intercepting messages that might be sent out for Joe's apprehension. At the time we were not aware that extradition proceeding were necessary to take a prisoner from one state to another. We lodged in a village each night and had a fairly good time of it in spite of the fact that we were constantly under the fear of a disagreeable interruption.

Rural intelligence—

Illustrative of the intelligence of men residing in the country, we dropped into what appeared to be a grocery and found it a typical country store with everything on hand that anyone might want, including liquids. We asked for crackers, cheese, and beer, which were duly supplied. Our appearance interrupted a discussion between a couple of the village solons, which was resumed when it was seen that we were industriously employed in supplying the wants of the inner man without regard to those present, who were quite numerous, considering the size of the place.

The subject under discussion related to the Constitution of the United States of which neither of the disputants seemed to know very much. The most emphatic orator delivered himself with great magnificence in despite of the feeble protests of his opponent, and the audience with open mouths were absorbing with delight the words of wisdom which demolished the argument of the other. The scene was entertaining in the extreme and I enjoyed it. But the interpretation of the Constitution was so absurb that I injected myself into the discussion with the remark that the gentleman was decidedly in error. My interruption caused a complete silence as if it was not welcome. Nothing daunted I went on to explain my position on the matter and I believe that I convinced him. The silence continued until the gentleman arose and left without speaking a word. One by one the crowd quietly departed, leaving the groceryman, Joe and me the only occupants of the battle ground. It was easy enough to recognize me as a foreigner and the only way to censure me most effectually for my uninvited interference was to treat me with silent contempt, which was done most effectively. This feature failed to destroy my sense of pleasure at the whole affair.

The groceryman could see no fun in the situation for no doubt he had been so long used to hearing the declamations of his customer and neighbor that he looked upon them as veritable gospel truths. To have them shattered, even if done politely, was too much for him to stand. To have it done by a young foreigner was intolerable. This incident gave me an insight into the intellectual attainments of the average rural inhabitant and an inkling into their small latent prejudices.

At another place in the same town the following morning, seeing a sign announcing the meal hours, we entered the sitting room and found ourselves in the midst of a large crowd of farmers and farm laborers awaiting breakfast. With the ringing of a bell the sliding doors leading to the dining room were drawn and a rush pell-mell was made for seats at the tables that stretched the length of the room. Before Joe or I had settled at the table, which we were doing leisurely, those who had been first in the room were rushing out of it. Presently, we were alone. With the departure of the diners the waitresses began clearing off the tables, leaving nothing in sight but what was actually in front of us. The girls were peeking from the kitchen wondering and doubtless disgusted at our want of speed in bolting our food. This also gave me an insight into the reasons for the extraordinary consumption of patent medicines for which at that time the United States was notorious.

Chicago—

Weary and footsore we arrived a week later in Chicago at night and stumbled along the uneven wooden sidewalks in the poorly lighted streets, making our way to the home of my friend, Connolly, on State Street. He soon procured us desirable lodgings which were a pleasure and a relief. Two days later Joe had procured employment as an attendant in a lunch room near the railroad depot. Within a week I had secured a job in the Phoenix Foundry owned by Thomas Holden, a Belfast man.

Holden's father owned the foundry of that name in Belfast. My father was a good customer of the foundry and when it became bankrupt and the sons of Holden, Sr., resolved to try their fortunes in far-off lands, he secured passage for Robert Holden to Australia, where he became Mayor of the City of Melbourne. Tom Holden, the other son, prospered in Chicago and employed several hundred men in his foundry and machine shop. He was an approved modern type of employer. His main endeavor was to squeeze every ounce of work out of his men with the least financial expenditure. His men were non-resistant, permitting the operation with a meekness not in harmony with my ideas of what the free American should be in justice to himself.

This foundry was typical of all the other foundries in Chicago at that time (1868). They were all operated on the breakneck principle, the men being governed by the exalted old adage of "Root hog or die," and "The devil take the hindmost." Their disintegration and individual selfishness were as perfectly complete as the most exacting taskmaster could desire without resorting to the use of the whip. Mr. Holden, as an enlightened up-to-date employer, availed himself of every advantage that the brutal stupidity of his workmen gave him, and profited by so doing.

My friend Flaherty had stipulated before we left St. Louis that when he had the means he would reimburse me for any expenditures that I made on his account. I did not want reimbursement. I was pleased to help him out of a bad situation and that was sufficient. It turned out that the man whom he had shot was only slightly injured, but at the time much would have been made of the affair. It is probable that Joe would have suffered more than he was entitled to had he remained in St. Louis.

On the second Sunday in Chicago Joe made his appearance at my lodging, radiant in new clothes, wearing a stunning white vest adorned with what appeared to be a gold chain, and altogether presenting the appearance of affluence. I was very much surprised at all this grandeur on a wage of two dollars per day. When he handed me twice as much as I had spent for him I was more astonished and wished to know how it all came about. Besides the two dollars which he received as his legitimate earnings he had "knocked down" double that amount on his twelve-hour watch. "Knocked down" was a new phrase to me in connection with employees' handling money and required explanation. He gave me the explanation very briefly and very clearly, and proceeded to justify the practice. I had been taught that this was stealing, and as I saw it, it was mean, sneaky thieving at that. Joe held that it was a national trait, well understood by employers, who themselves lost no opportunity of thieving off their customers when the chance came easily. I was not well pleased with Joe and told him so, with the result that I only saw him twice after that time.

Business in America!—

I was fast acquiring a knowledge of how all business was conducted in America. First, an organized system of decoying young female emigrants into a life of shame, which appeared to excite no wonder and which was not condemned as heartily as it should have been by those cognizant of its existence. Then, the desperation with which men worked in competition with each other to earn a pitiful living. Again, the cut-throat competition between employers striving to out-do each other through the blood and sweat of their workmen. And now, the dishonesty of employees purloining from their employers in compensation for inadequate wages for long exhausting hours of labor. But worst of all, the illegal manufacturing of emigrants into citizens while still ignorant of the duties and obligations that they were assuming. This in my opinion, the disregard for law, was the foundation and keynote of all the other wrongs.

My stay in Chicago was brief. I refused to work overtime for Holden without being paid for it. I was not one of those who were delighted with hard labor, nor was I specially disposed to give to a conscienceless employer the time which I might better spend at something else, simply to place in his hands the wealth that I produced to be used afterwards as a bludgeon to batter me and others to death.

Omaha—

Another of my Belfast men and a fellow-apprentice, John Quinn, invited me to come to Omaha. The Union Pacific Railroad was in course of construction and Omaha, its chief base of supplies, was, he informed me, a very busy place. Also, which was more important, he had secured a job for me. Omaha had at that time a reputed resident population of 15,000. It had been in existence for only a few years and possessed many of the characteristics of the typical western towns of which I had read and heard so much. It was certainly famous as a whiskey-drinking place, for the saloons were always crowded and kept up a rushing and profitable business to a late hour every night, or rather to an early morning hour. Most of their customers were men returning from the end of the road after having made a "stake" sufficiently large to enable them to return to their homes or friends in the East and engage in more congenial employment, free from the hardship, risks, and dangers of rough frontier life.

Very few of the streets of Omaha were paved or graded, the others were so many bogs and slush passages through which one plodded in top boots in the winter and early spring. A few substantial buildings had been erected, such as the railroad offices, hotels, and banks. A few fine residences, owned and occupied by the well-off and professional people, adorned the western part of the town. The houses occupied by the men employed in the shops and their families were fairly comfortable although many were no better than "shanties." It was undoubtedly a lively town and the people were of the happy, cheerful, "devil may care" order, characteristic of those satisfied with an abundance for all their material wants and who desired nothing more. I rather liked the free and easy style so universally prevalent, and readily adopted their ways.

Officer of a union—

It was immediately upon beginning work in the foundry that I became a member of Iron Moulders Union, No. 190, and in a remarkably short time I was elected its secretary. I preferred the conduct of this union to that of the Belfast union. Here all were anxious to do something, though none seemed to know just what should be done or how to do it. Oratory of a vague and sometimes florid description enlivened the meetings and was such a contrast to the cold, methodic business proceedings of the old country trade organization that the meetings charmed me. I somehow filled the office of secretary so satisfactorily that at the next election I was selected president, although I had solicited neither office. This was considered in the line of a promotion and an honor. I had looked upon presiding officers merely as persons temporarily engaged in directing meetings and maintaining order during the proceedings. To be president of an American labor union was much more than being a mere casual employee. The president was the director of the union and to a great extent also of its individual members, when the union was not in session. Metaphorically the union was a ship and the president was its captain. He was presumed to possess all the concentrated wisdom of the union and to be its administrator at all times. For one so green in the ways of the country and the rules governing the union it was a little irksome to have such a position thrust upon me, but I stood it fairly well.

National Labor Reform Party—

At one of our meetings a stranger sent in the request that he desired to address us upon a subject of vital interest to union men as well as to the people of the entire country. Upon his admission he informed us that he was the state executive, lately appointed, of an organization of national character, whose object was to place all the people upon a plane of independence and thereby remove poverty. It then had no existence in Nebraska, but, as the National President of the Moulders' Union, William H. Sylvis, was also the national president of the organization, he hoped that the local moulders would agree to become members, and it was to give the moulders' union the first opportunity of doing so that he had visited us. On behalf of the union I thanked Mr. William H. Jones for his visit and promised him the attendance of our membership when he held his first meeting. When the meeting was held I was grievously disappointed at the non-attendance of the moulders. The reason for their absence was that it was purely a meeting to organize a new political party and as most of them were loyal Democrats they would take no part in helping to form a party, no matter what its objects or however fair its prospects. They feared that it would hamper or retard the success of *their* party, which, with a sanguine and unparalleled hopefulness, they expected soon to see in power. They also claimed that it was only in the success of the Democratic Party that the working people of America could hope to improve their condition.

This sort of reasoning was to my way of thinking puerile in the extreme. I had identified myself already with the Republicans and was doing my best to prove to the Irish Democrats, who were many, that by supporting the Democratic Party they were indirectly aiding England and the Orange element in Ireland, both of which were their hereditary and venomous enemies. Nevertheless, I would abandon Republicanism and join any party which held out the hope of abolishing poverty.

Jones was a man well advanced in years, an Englishman, a former Democrat, and unusually well informed on the principles of the party whose cause he espoused. These he set forth and explained quite lucidly, and opened the roll for membership in the new party, the National Labor Reform Party of the

United States.[2] With several moulders who were present, mostly Republicans, I signed the roll and became a member. I was unanimously elected president.

American politics—

Prior to this I had written a few short articles, which had been published in the *Omaha Herald,* of which George L. Miller was editor and part owner, with a Mr. Richardson as his partner. I was a frequent visitor to the editor's sanctum and was well received notwithstanding the fact that the editor was an implacable Democrat, limiting his business relations and friendships to persons of that creed. He was intense in his hatred of Republicans and Republicanism. I was, I believe, the sole exception to this long established and ineradicable hatred. I admired Miller for his unflinching advocacy of a cause so hopeless and so foreign to my own conceptions. I esteemed him for his probity and the numerous fine traits of character which he possessed outside of his political beliefs. Whatever I wrote, however, the foreman printer had orders to insert in the paper whether Miller had seen it or not. I never transgressed by writing anything antagonistic to the fixed policy of the paper.

As president of the new organization, I hoped, with Miller's approval, to make the *Herald* the

[2] The National Labor Reform Party was organized as the political arm of the National Labor Union, the latter having been founded in 1866.—Ed.

medium of disseminating the principles of the new party. He saw in it the leaven of true Democracy and if it succeeded he felt that it would bring about the destruction of his hated enemy, the Republican Party.

Very soon we had well attended and enthusiastic meetings. Secretary of War Belknap's glaring malfeasance,[3] condoned by Grant, who was then President, and who accepted his resignation instead of impeaching or imprisoning him, afforded our orators a theme which they used to abuse the Republican Party with marked success. Our speakers also condemned the exploits of carpet baggers, who had gone South to reconstruct the Confederate states, ruined and in ashes by the Civil War, tales which excited the indignation of every man not shackled by the chains of party. Our party grew and flourished, attaining an importance quite surprising to me.

[3] W. W. Belknap, Secretary of War under President Grant, had a socially ambitious wife who, it was claimed without the knowledge of her husband, made arrangements with a holder of a trading post appointment to share in the proceeds of the latter's office. About $20,000 was received from that source. Belknap, however, declared that he thought the money came from his wife's own investments. The House of Representatives investigated the case. A few hours before it voted to impeach him, Belknap resigned and the President accepted his resignation. Belknap then claimed that legally he could not be impeached because he was no longer a government employee. The courts, however, held otherwise. The Senate failed to convict. Belknap later died in disgrace and poverty.—Ed.

St. Patrick's Day procession—

Upon coming to Omaha I had organized a branch of the secret Irish organization which I had joined in New York. Since Omaha had assumed the rank and habiliments of a city, some of my countrymen, who were residents before me, were accustomed to celebrate St. Patrick's Day by a procession and other marks of festivity. To formulate and make effective the plan of procedure for the celebration it was necessary to hold a convention. Being recently from Ireland, and knowing the sentiments of the home organization regarding processions and their perfect inutility and impracticability for benefit, and being aware that the newly organized American secret society was also opposed to such displays, also that my brief experience had shown me that they were mainly used to boost some of the prominent leaders into political office, I attended the gathering as a delegate.

An Irishman, engaged in the wholesale liquor business, had usually presided at such gatherings in the past and had acted as Grand Marshal of the procession. He was a very decent sort of man with the mistaken idea firmly fixed in his mind that these shows terrified England and would eventually terminate in his country's liberation when they became large enough. In addition to this his prominence as an Irish patriot on the occasion helped along his business.

Personally I disliked shams and subterfuges and proposed that no man should prostitute the cause of Ireland either to advance his political career or to benefit his business when it was apparent that either or both was his object. I succeeded at the very start in dissolving the convention by having it pass a resolution that there should be no procession. The worthy chairman was bewildered, then indignant, and at last furious, but the deed was done, final action was taken, and the glory of the Grand-Marshal-to-be was not his ever again. The same course was generally adopted that year all over the United States. St. Patrick's Day processions have ceased to be the contributing stock performances of men seeking public office or selling whiskey.

Clinton Briggs—

Clinton Briggs, a retired lawyer, in more than comfortable circumstances, and an early follower of the teachings of Wendell Phillips and Wm. Lloyd Garrison, was one of the earliest men outside the ranks of labor to become a member of our new political party. He was not an orator nor much of a speaker, but he was a man of profound thought, earnest and honest. He entertained and often expressed broader views of man's rights and status than I had thought of. He took a personal interest in my welfare and urged me time and again to throw up foundry work and become a lawyer. In suggesting the law business he believed that it would bring me directly in contact with the men most opposed to the principles of our party and afford me undreamed of opportunities to advance them by that means. My notions of lawyers were so crude that I believed all lawyers to be rogues and their practices to be dishonest. This was the generally accepted and popular belief at the time concerning lawyers. I have later learned that aside from having to possess ability, to be successful a lawyer must also be an honest man. Mr. Briggs tried to convince me of that fact, but I was immovable.

Sylvis, with whom I had had a limited correspondence both as a moulder and as a member of the National Labor Reform Party, died[4] and was succeeded by Richard Trevellick,[5] of Detroit, Michigan. Briggs succeeded me as president of our party and I became its secretary. In order to spread a knowledge of our principles I wrote and addressed not less than 250 letters, sending them to every man of prominence in the state. Nebraska was sparsely populated at the time. Most of my letters were not acknowledged. A number of replies came with assurances of belief in the principles and with promises of aid when needed.

[4] Sylvis died July 27, 1869.—Ed.

[5] Richard F. Trevellick, a ship carpenter and caulker, was a national figure in the American labor movement during 1860–1880.—Ed.

Morton and Roney discussion—

James Sterling Morton, afterwards President Cleveland's Secretary of Agriculture and the father of Mr. Paul Morton, Mr. Roosevelt's Secretary of the Navy, as editor of a Nebraska City paper wrote a reply to my letter, first publishing it in the *Omaha Herald*. Publicity of this sort was more than I expected or desired, because this letter of Mr. Morton's demanded a reply, and I was too uninformed on the subject of our principles to reply with credit. I was in a much worried state of mind to know what should be done under the circumstances. It would never do, if our party was to live, to permit this letter to go unchallenged or unreplied to. I decided that Jones was the best informed man that we had and that he must take up the battle and do the fighting, for I was most decidedly unequal to the task. When I saw Jones he peremptorily declined doing so, insisting that it was my duty to reply. I had invited the contest and he said that I was equal to the undertaking if I would only rid myself of the fear of meeting such a contestant. He took up Morton's letter and began its criticism, which he did very thoroughly. I went to my room, dismissed all thought of defeat, and wrote a reply, which appeared under large head lines in the *Herald* as the "Morton and Roney Discussion." Six letters from each of us appeared in that paper and attracted a great deal of attention.

Mr. Morton had been Territorial Secretary of State and enjoyed the reputation of being one of the ablest Democrats in Nebraska or in the then new Northwest. I was an obscure mechanic and not yet a citizen, which of course was not known. The law of Nebraska at that time permitted for political purposes all residents of six months, who had declared their intentions to become citizens, to exercise the franchise as if they were bona fide citizens. As the discussion progressed I received many compliments from prominent Republicans, who cheerfully urged me to give Mr. Morton a good thrashing, encouraging me with assurances that I had the best of the argument.

The quality of the greenback and its sustaining power during the Civil War was the chief feature of the controversy. Thaddeus Stevens in Congress had made the greenback his special subject for praise when Democrats and some Republicans were belittling it during the debates evoked by the scheme of George H. Pendleton, of Ohio, for repudiating the debt incurred on account of the war. I was an admirer of the stand taken by Mr. Stevens, and had read his speeches with much satisfaction before I was a National Labor Reform Party man, and, as the greenback was the salient subject of attack, I was fairly well instructed as to its value and potency. That was why Silas Strickland, John I. Redick, Judge Lake, and innumerable other Republican luminaries gave me their moral support. Mr. Morton's sympathies as a Southern-born man were with the Confederacy and that was another reason why they wished to see him beaten or at least silenced.

My sixth letter appeared on the morning when Judge Briggs appeared at the Court House in Nebraska City to wind up some law business left unfinished when he had retired. Meeting Mr. Morton, with whom he was upon very friendly terms, the latter inquired who I was and what was my profession. Briggs, who was my warmest friend, was delighted with the opportunity this gave him of extolling me and incidentally of hitting Morton in a vulnerable spot. He informed him that I was not a professional man but a mechanic who read his (Morton's) letters in the morning before going to work and wrote my replies after ten hours' hard labor. Mr. Morton, like many southerners of the period, looked upon a man who labored with his hands as a "mud sill" and unworthy of recognition in any other way. I do not know whether or not this was the reason, but the discussion ended. I only know that Morton wrote no more and that mine was the last letter that appeared.

The discussion did much to spread the principles of our party, for every little local paper in the state irrespective of its politics had something to say about it one way or the other. To push the ideas further ahead Richard Trevellick, National President of the party, was invited to make a tour of the state. Trevellick was a ship caulker, an eloquent and forcible speaker, and a splendid man in all respects. He and I toured Nebraska and sowed the seed which has fructified so well that Nebraska is today one of the foremost commonwealths in political progressive thought.

Impecunious visitors—

While I was engaged in this propaganda I did not neglect my Irish connections. I had visitors without number who thought that my prominence was a sure means of acquiring wealth. They were invariably hard up and seeking work of any kind, and in many instances were possessed of the finest education. Unfortunately, I was as poor as they were. I reprobated the taking of pay for such services as I rendered or for the doing of anything having the uplifting of the poor for its ultimate object. I paid my own way wherever I went and also bore all my own expenses incurred in furthering our Cause. I nearly always succeeded in finding some work for the poor fellows and in the meantime secured them a respectable place in which to live. This was often very burdensome, but my credit was good and I worked steadily at my trade as a moulder.

Mr. P. Murphy, afterwards Mayor of Omaha, and John Quinn, my townsman, proposed that in order to relieve me of the burden of supporting so many, a house be rented and fitted up in a rough way so as to accommodate the many impecunious visitors. We furnished a stove, dishes, and food, and suggested that they do their own cooking. This lightened my burden and divided the responsibility and worked charmingly. It was almost as good and in some ways better than having them in a boarding house costing six dollars per week per man.

Captain P. J. Condon, the surviving senior officer of General Thomas Francis Meagher's Irish Brigade, which was almost annihilated during one of the battles of the Civil War, was one of our star boarders. He had been tried for high treason in the city of Cork in 1867 and to the surprise of every one familiar with the circumstances was acquitted. The Captain was a civil engineer and not inclined to hard labor, so that it was a difficult matter to get desirable employment for him. We installed him as superintendent of our refuge home and afterwards started him in the saloon business. Under no circumstances would he serve behind the bar, and this compelled the employment of a barkeeper. It was amusing to see the Captain of a morning resplendent in spotless white vest and clothes to match, pace the saloon back and forth in all the dignity of proprietorship when he did not own a cent in it. If the Captain had been less dignified and had paid more attention to the business, the "Jolly Bacchus," as I named his saloon, would have proved a solvent concern. It was so wretchedly conducted, however, and had so much dignity to sustain that when its door closed, the Captain was again out of employment and my friends, Quinn and Murphy, and I had a number of unapid bills on our hands.

During the state campaign which was to determine, by the election of members of the legislature, the successor to John M. Thayer as United States Senator, I proposed that we help out the Captain by giving the Senator a send-off in the "Jolly Bacchus." About fifty gentlemen, all ex-officers in the late war, grading in rank from general down to captain, assembled at Captain Condon's and were ostentatiously received by that genial and dignified gentleman who was oblivious to the fact that he was to be the financial beneficiary of the entertainment. It was a hilarious, jovial, and amusing assemblage. Speeches, stories of personal adventure, recitations, songs, and good humor ruled that night, humor and wit being predominant. It was discovered, when the proceedings were well advanced, that I was the lone civilian in the party. I dared not flaunt my rank as a colonel in the Irish Republican Army, for that army had never been in the field and the Irish Republic had existed for a short time only in New York City and had never assumed the functions of a *de facto* government because 3,000 miles lay between it and the country it was presumed to govern. General Thayer remembered that there was a vacancy on his staff and immediately appointed me to the position of paymaster with the rank of colonel amid the plaudits of my new brother officers. Although the meeting was a success in every way, it neither resulted in General Thayer's election to the United States Senate nor stayed the approaching bankruptcy of my friend, Captain Condon.

More politics—

A lesson in political waste and extravagance, nearly approaching corruption, occurred on the day of the election of members of the legislature. Kountze Brothers were the principal bankers in Nebraska at the time. They were the chief financial factors in every large enterprise. Their bank was the United States depository and their relations with the National Treasury were of so much value as to excite the envy of the lesser banks of the state. As the advantages the Kountzes enjoyed were claimed to be attributable to General Thayer, the lesser banks united to defeat all candidates for the legislature favorable to him. The railroad shops closed on the day of the election because the Union Pacific Railroad was also involved in the outcome, and it was hoped by the local management that the workmen would vote for the railroad interests. None of those in power spoke to me about the matter for it was generally known that I was for General Thayer, and I presume it was considered unnecessary to speak to me. I did not know whether or not the General was for the railroad. I recognized him as a friend and that was my reason for supporting him, regardless of what interests he represented.

It was the first election that had occurred since I had come to America and in a general way I was interested in the way that it was to be conducted. Going to the business section of the town early on the morning of the election I observed a great crowd of shop workmen in the vicinity of the Nebraska State Bank, as I believe it was named. As I passed the bank, wondering what the crowd was there for, I met Mr. Paddock, afterwards United States Senator, proprietor of the Wyoming Hotel, who effusively hailed me and invited me into a side entrance of the bank. He hurriedly left me there asking me to remain where I was for a few minutes and presently returned with an envelope which he handed me, asking me to do what I could for him, and retired. I had gone but a short distance from the bank when I met ex-Governor Alvin Saunders, later United States Senator, father-in-law of Russell Harrison, President Harrison's son, who also was eager to see me. He also invited me into the bank, going through the same performance as Paddock and with the same injunction. Again I met a third man and went through an identical performance with the addition of an order on Captain Fury's livery stable for a buggy and team. I was curious to know what my three envelopes contained and was surprised to find that each held $250 worth of perfectly good United States greenbacks. This money was given to me without solicitation or contract, implied or otherwise. There were no conditions, but

I suppose in some inscrutable way the givers thought that I was opposed to General Thayer's candidates. I went to my room, placed the money in my trunk, proceeded to the livery stable, got the team, and took my future wife[6] on a day's excursion to Florence. Returning about the time the polls closed I dropped into a crowded saloon near the voting place and was in the midst of a jostling noisy crowd of partly drunken voters when Governor Saunders appeared at the door. He asked to speak with me and inquired how matters had gone. I said without the least consciousness of his meaning that everything was all right. He handed me a $50 bill telling me to treat the boys, that his standing as a church member and as an anti-liquor man prevented him from doing so. I did so and became immensely popular in consequence.

The day's proceedings gave Mr. Miller, editor of the *Herald,* ample grounds in his next issue to characterize the Republican Party as a base band of corruptionists who knew no limit to their despicable desire for power. It was charged that $30,000 was spent on that "black" day to corrupt the voters of Omaha. I knew of $800 of the money that was not so spent, if that was the intention of the bood-

[6] Roney married during his stay in Omaha. Two boys and a girl were born of this union. His wife died in San Francisco, January 24, 1904. Shortly thereafter he married a Mrs. Jones, of San Francisco, who died in 1912. Roney spent the last years of his life in Southern California, and while there married a third time. I have no information concerning his last matrimonial venture.—Ed.

lers. All the leaders concerned in the disgraceful affair were prominent in church doings, and, if they were to be taken at their word, exemplars and upholders of civic purity. To them the practices of the Democratic Party, its ignorance, and petty debaucheries, were outrages on intelligence and decency, but at the same time they were, with smug complacency and in sanctimonious garb, assailing the foundations of democratic government by the corrupt and lavish use of money.

To a young beginner and observing student, as I was, the spectacle was not enchanting. As a believer in Phillips, Garrison, and Lincoln, as one ardently believing in the untainted purity of the ballot as the ultimate determining, intelligently and freely expressed will of the people, the whole affair was a shock, teaching me how little reliance was to be placed upon the words of the politician, however smug he might be or how high his social standing.

Nominating convention—

The enthusiastic members of the National Labor Reform Party were of the opinion that we were numerically strong enough as a third party to stand a fair chance of electing our ticket should we put one in the field. I was willing that we should do so and at least try our strength. A call for a convention was issued and the basis of representation was set forth duly signed by the president and secretary. The Democrats issued a call for a convention to be held, singularly enough, on the same day. To unite with the Democrats and to vanquish the actors of that "black" election day were purposes agreeable to me. The Democrats agreed to allow the National Labor Reform Party one-half of the nominees on the county ticket.

Our convention chose me as its chairman. One of our delegates, who had just come from California where the feeling against the Chinese was intensely hostile, proposed a resolution that in the interest of Labor we should pledge ourselves against the continuance of Chinese immigration and should support the Californians in all the measures demanded. It looked to me as if the resolution, with which I did not agree, would be adopted. I left the chair and spoke against the resolution. I was too heartily a believer in the doctrine of the Brotherhood of Man to allow myself to be bound by so sweeping a proposition. Besides, I was too recently an immigrant to consent to a measure to bar from the country any people coming to it with the idea of improving their condition. My experience taught me that there was no improvement for the immigrant who came from the British Isles, although possibly other Europeans might be more favorably affected. I thought that I saw some chance of improvement for the Chinese. I believe that what I said defeated the resolution.

We were entitled to one state senator and two representatives or members of the Lower House, as it was termed. My friend Judge Briggs, in the kindness of his heart, nominated me for the state senatorship, and as I was chairman he was required to put the nomination to the meeting, which adopted it unanimously before I could enter a protest. I vigorously protested after the nomination, but my protest went unheeded, and as it was noon we immediately adjourned. The Democrats approved my nomination. If I had been a *bona fide* citizen I might have accepted the nomination. I was scarcely two years from Ireland and practically the leader of a political party and now their nominee for an important state office, which would seem to indicate that I was progressing rather rapidly.

At the next session of the legislature Nebraska was to vote upon the Fourteenth Amendment to the United States Constitution, and I was opposed to it, for I did not believe in forcing people into a situation for which they were not qualified. Much as I was opposed to Negro slavery, I was just as much opposed to the slavery that the proposed amendment would impose upon the white men. My desire was to be a legislator, but I was not a citizen, so I had to decline the nomination. Some important measure might have been adopted by my vote, and its legality therefore might have been questioned. Anyway, I had no legitimate right to the position. The excuse which I offered for declining was that to accept the nomination could be construed by some as remunerating me for my work as an officer of the party, which I claimed should never be done.

My declination was accepted, and I was accorded the privilege of naming my substitute. I named Mr. O'Leary, foreman carpenter in the Union Pacific shops, who was elected. I wrote a speech for O'Leary, against the Fourteenth Amendment. I had Mr. Miller put it in type with orders to hold it until O'Leary notified us by telegram that it had been delivered, whereupon it was to appear in the *Herald* the following morning. O'Leary voted against the amendment but failed to take the floor to read his speech, disgusting Mr. Miller, who had incurred the expense of paying his compositor for setting it up.

A new type of politics—

At this election I introduced some new features in American politics and I believe that it was the only election ever so conducted. In the convention the qualifications of candidates presented for the office were freely discussed. If it appeared that any candidate was anxious for the place and sought it by the least solicitation he was disqualified at once. It was strictly a case of the office seeking the man without the slightest approach to personal desire. Another feature was that, since we demanded the services of the individual it was our duty not to embarrass him by political assessments or to permit him to incur any expense whatever. In this way I hoped to have established and rigidly practised the principle that a poor man, penniless, but thoroughly qualified by education, of recognized honesty, industry, and capability, should have an equal chance for any public office with the most financially favored. No candidate paid for any publication necessary to set forth his claims and all seemed quite well satisfied with my program. Unfortunately the subscriptions were slower in coming in than I had hoped for. The expenses at the end of the campaign were greatly in excess of the receipts, and I personally settled for them, as the campaign had been carried out in accordance with my plans. As I gained experience I came to understand that in that campaign I figured as a political "boss." My will was never controverted and I had the pleasure of paying for its gratification.

Political bosses—

To my mind political "bosses" are as inevitable and as necessary as any other instrument in our political machinery. In all associations of men claiming continuous existence, one man will appear in each association whose will is recognized as the concentration of the wisdom of the whole. So long as he acts with the single purpose of benefitting all impartially and unselfishly, he is a benefit to the society or community which claims him. If, however, he obtrudes his personality by a display of self-interest in the outcome of any of his proposals he becomes justly an object of suspicion and his efficiency for good ceases. An honest political boss is, in the nature of his environment, a *rara avis*. In an ordinary and general way he may not be corrupt or have corrupt inclinations, but the interests of those for whom he is working are usually so varied and conflicting that it is impossible for him to move along free from distrust. A man exercising the functions of a boss who seeks office is properly entitled to be suspected. Where selfishness enters, unsullied purpose is at a discount. Our political system demands bosses and we will have them in some form regardless of our opposition to them. The office-seeking boss or the office-holding boss is the most dangerous of all bosses, and should be frequently changed if he cannot be eliminated.

The frontier West—

At one period of my employment in Omaha, soon after the railroad was completed, and for reasons best known to the local management, a large number of workmen were laid off indefinitely. At the same time reports from the West came to us of depredations by the Indians on the frontier settlers. The stealing of cattle, the burning of homes, and the killing of settlers and their families were of only too frequent occurrence. I was one of those laid off and being desirous of seeing something of rough western life I hired as a teamster for the United States Government. With about twenty others similarly engaged we were sent to Fort Sedgewick. Cheyenne was the nearest railroad station. Close by was what remained of the famous or infamous town of Julesburg, viz., a few dilapidated wooden shanties, one of which was the inevitable saloon. This town, which had had ten thousand inhabitants, had sprung up almost in a night, equipped as a municipality with a mayor, city council, marshal, and all the functionaries usually belonging to a well organized respectable community. The mayor was a wild young man named Roberts, who came from respectable and well-to-do parents residing in Illinois. He was well educated and of fine address, but addicted to the vice of gambling, which led him into associations of a riotous character. All the officials were gamblers and most of the tents were used by saloons and dance resorts. As a matter of fact there were no houses, all the residences and buildings were tents, large or small, as the business or needs and means of their occupants required.

Reports of the doings and the peculiar civilization of Julesburg were a constant thrill to us in Omaha. Julesburg was an intermediate supply depot used and considered necessary by the railroad contractors for renewing great quantities of supplies, which were forwarded to the front to prevent delay in track laying, construction of station houses, and other activities necessary to the operation of the road when completed. The town lasted three months, disappearing as suddenly as it had arisen. During its brief existence the coroner and undertaker were as profitably employed as the saloon keepers and gamblers. When the town disappeared it left behind as the memento of its existence a well filled graveyard on the hillside north of it, where at the head of each grave was a white painted wooden cross with the legend "unknown" on them all. It was a pathetic sight, this last lonely spot of record of the brief, wild, and frightful existence of a vanished town.

"Buffalo Bill"—

One night our party from Omaha with others from Cheyenne gathered in the railroad station for shelter, as it was exceedingly cold. We were composing ourselves for the night, a night in which we were to experience our first taste of "roughing" it, when "Buffalo Bill" Cody accompanied by Ned Buntline (Colonel Judson) entered.[7] The Colonel was upon his first trip west to gather material for his subsequent numerous prairie tales with Cody as the hero. The Colonel thought this a splendid opportunity to hear stories of the plainsmen, but "Buffalo Bill," better versed in affairs of the plains, knew that something more attractive than the presence of so distinguished a visitor was required to induce the crowd to talk. He suggested that at least one gallon of "red eye" would be necessary for the purpose, whereupon Judson handed "Buffalo Bill" $6 to purchase a gallon of real fire water. Cody also provided himself with a tin cup out of which

[7] Our author is referring to Edward Z. Judson, author of prairie and sea stories, who wrote under the *nom de plume* of Ned Buntline. —Ed.

he dispensed the villainous stuff, giving each of us what he considered his due allowance to allow it go around all the company. When it came my turn and I swallowed the portion given me, it seemed as if the upper portion of my head had parted from what remained, leaving me dazed and speechless. It was "tarantula juice" of the purest quality, as I was afterwards told. The experienced plainsmen relished it immensely for its strength and it immediately opened the flood gates of their memory, causing them to recite story after story to the Colonel's infinite pleasure and future profit.

Cody's expedition lasted about three months, traversing western Nebraska, part of Colorado, and a portion of Wyoming, led by Cody as the chief and a couple of assistant scouts. We did not come into direct contact with the Indians, who had fled to the Black Hills.

Horse thieves—

One fine morning we arose to be informed that a raid had been made on our horses during the night and that about 150 of them had been run off. How it was done seemed mysterious, for if Indians were the thieves no alarm had been given by the animals, which was invariably the case. It was decided that white men were the guilty ones and a pursuing party was sent after them led by the redoubtable "Buffalo Bill" as chief scout. At evening the pursuing party returned to camp without the horses. Our party could not move without the same number of animals, compelling us to remain in camp until the loss could be replaced. In a few days a couple of Colorado horse dealers visited the camp, readily agreeing to furnish the necessary number of animals within a week or less. Within the time specified they were back again with the complement required, getting an average of $150 for each one of the herd. From what I could pick up from one and another of the oldtimers I believe that the newly purchased animals were in the main the identical animals that had been run off a few nights previous. Such transactions were of common occurrence on the plains at that time and were charged up to the Government as losses sustained in fights with Indians, when it was simply a left-handed way of dipping into the National Treasury while Uncle Sam was a little off guard.

Losses of grain for feed purposes were becoming so frequent that the wagon boss, in whose charge the grain was placed and who, I believe, was an honest man, resolved to put a stop to it or discover the thieves. He selected several upon whom he believed he could depend as guards, myself being one of the crowd. I was directed to watch the wagons containing the grain and if I saw anyone or heard any suspicious noise I was to fire a rifle shot as a signal. The arrangements were to be kept a profound secret by those engaged in it so as to make sure that we could discover the thieves. I happened to be the first put on guard. About midnight I imagined that I saw the figures of several men in proximity to the wagons and immediately fired the signal, when just as quickly two shots in quick succession were fired in my direction. The camp was aroused and no grain was stolen that night nor for many nights thereafter. Nor were the thieves discovered.

I liked the adventure that the experience on the plains gave me. The associations were not inspiring. Many were among us who had forgotten their original patronymics. There were many who sought security from arrest for deeds of violence committed in places far off. Here, as servants of the Government under other names, they were lost to their pursuers until another deed of violence, usually the result of drink, revealed their identity. One thing was apparent, namely, these men herded together and seldom trespassed on the society of those not of their class, although all were engaged in the same line of work.

Pawnee Indians—

The most amusing thing to me was to see Major North's warriors, the Pawnee Indians, in the morning as they began their day's march. They were mounted upon small scraggy Indian ponies, many without halters or bridles, enveloped in blankets covering their heads, or when not so covered, decorated with all descriptions of head-gear, hats and caps of all sorts of shapes and material, with an odd one, occasionally, denoting its original owner to be a woman. Jogging along at an irregular gate, costumed as they were, they looked more like a troupe of performers in a Christmas extravaganza out to amuse children than a troop of cavalry with a well-earned reputation for bravery gained in many a fierce conflict with their implacable foes, the Sioux.

Frontier justice—

It was while I lived in Omaha after my return from the plains that I received a pressing invitation from Messrs. Charley Collins and John Brennan, afterwards Judge Brennan, to visit them in their new quarters in Sioux City, Iowa, where they had gone to establish a paper simultaneously with the beginning of the town. The paper office was a large tent, as most of the structures were at the time, and served for a printing office, editorial sanctum, bed-chamber, kitchen, dining and sitting apartments and general business office. It was the essence of primitiveness, but the boys were happy and hopeful. Collins was an erratic, clever newspaper genius of indomitable courage and possessed of a great big heart. As the honored guest I was treated to the best my hosts could afford, which, in the light of later entertainment by others, was limited in the extreme. It took about ten minutes to survey the town and more than as many hours to discuss its probabilities.

In order to get the latest and most startling news items it was necessary to make a tour of the saloons.

In one of them, much larger than the others, a green baize curtain ran the width of the room, making two compartments. In the rear a court was in session, a man being arraigned for the preliminary examination on the charge of murder. He had killed a desperado who for a long time had been the terror of every well disposed person in the community. The judge, not impressively prepossessing, occupied a raised seat at the end of the room. As a lawyer, he seemed to me deficient in the use of the plainest language. Ordinary court rules observed elsewhere were out of place in this learned chamber of justice. It was the funniest travesty on the law courts that I had ever seen, and I enjoyed the scene enacted with the keenest relish, notwithstanding the gravity of the charge being investigated. We had entered the court about noon and had heard only a little of the proceedings when one of the lawyers arose and said, "Your Honor, it's about lunch hour and I move that we take a recess to two o'clock." Another learned gentleman seconded the motion, whereupon his Honor arose, evidently taking his cue from the proceedings in a society or lodge, and with great solemnity announced that the motion to adjourn was regularly moved and seconded and as he heard no expressions of dissent he declared an adjournment to the hour named. The prisoner, with nonchalance as perfect as it was innocent, addressing the judge said, "Well, Judge, I guess the drinks are on me this time," and as no objection was raised we all, prosecutor, judge, sheriff, and a few others, drank at his expense. Western methods of justice were new to me and were so unlike those to which I had been accustomed that they were positively fascinating. For a prisoner on trial to treat the prosecuting lawyer and the judge trying him was so novel a proceeding that it rather charmed me. In the afternoon the prisoner was acquitted and discharged. The man whom he had killed was an all-round bad man and desperado of whom the community appeared to be well rid, and the man who accomplished the job without injury to himself or anyone else was looked upon as a public benefactor and treated accordingly.

Workingman's Advocate—

The *Workingman's Advocate,* printed in Chicago, was the able western exponent of the principles of the National Labor Reform Party. Its circulation was not in accordance with its merits and with the indefatigable industry and honesty of its owner, Mr. Andrew Cameron, a Scotchman. I never met Mr. Cameron but I read and occasionally contributed to his paper. I was a sincere admirer of his far-sightedness and sound good sense in discussing the future of the American workingman. As an able and unselfish pioneer in a Cause which has attained the proportions it now occupies in the public mind, Andy Cameron's memory deserves to be remembered with gratitude by the trades unionists of this country.

A lady interested in the future of the laboring class, and believing that improvement could be accomplished only through organization, offered a prize of $100 for the best plan of organization published in the columns of the *Workingman's Advocate.* I did not see the lady's offer until it was too late to become a competitor. I had given the subject of organization considerable thought, and I believed that I had the ideas for creating an organization that would, if established, prove most efficient in securing the solidarity of Labor, preserving the autonomy of its units, and effecting every advantage the workingmen needed.

American Labor organizations—

Labor organization at the time was neither appreciated as a true necessity nor valued for its possibilities. With the large number of wage-earners it was regarded as a foreign importation peculiarly British in character, and they considered themselves so truly American as to disdain the acceptance of any system coming from that source. Local unions were few and meagerly sustained, and their meetings were indifferently attended. It was usually before the political elections that the attendance became fairly large and regular and the receipts in excess of weekly disbursements. When the election was over the attendance dwindled to its normal state of lifelessness, owing not infrequently to the bitterness engendered by the rivalry of candidates and their backers during the campaign. Many aspirants for political office regarded unions as a cheap, sure, and easy method of advertising their claims and pretensions, while, if successful, with the gratitude characteristic of the average politician they forgot their pledges and the means employed for their advancement. The uses made of unions by politicians and the steadfastness of the small number of earnest men who kept them alive, though inactive, hoping good might come from the slumbering organization, retarded the growth of unionism.

Prior to the Civil War and for some years thereafter the prevalent opinion among working people, and that opinion was deep-seated, was that the workman of today might become the employer of tomorrow, or at least he might be his own employer. Individualism, carried to the extreme, pervaded every line of manual activity. Combination in industrial pursuits was deemed incompatible with the exalted status of American citizenship. Men of the Sylvis, Cameron, and Geo. McNeill stamp were eager to unite workingmen into a political organization through which it was hoped would come every benefit required or demanded and also by the same means to establish trade unionism.

Although I cooperated with them in every detail, I never could see the utility of building unionism by the aid of political association and of maintaining it by keeping alive an interest in politics. If political action could be confined within the limits of manual industry it might be possible to effect a degree of permanent good for those engaged in it. But politics was something in which the entire population was concerned, and the wage-earning portion of the community formed but a small part. The mere placing of a man in office conferred no benefit of a social or economic character upon those of the industrial world. It made the individual office-holder a little better off, but in requital he as often as not turned against the people who placed him there.

A plan for a Labor federation—

I conceived the idea that through the instrumentality of trade unionism alone workingmen could acquire every social and economic advantage that they desired. And their needs were above all else economic in character. I held that men should understand primarily what their needs were and then go about getting them most intelligently; that they must depend upon themselves absolutely for their success, and that at no time should they delegate to others outside their organizations the power to act or negotiate for them. The plan which I proposed and which was printed in the *Workingman's Advocate* in the latter part of 1869, was as follows:

First. The organization into local unions of all those engaged in a particular occupation or calling.

Second. The formation of all local unions of an industry into local councils, as, for instance, in the iron industry, the moulders, pattern-makers, blacksmiths, boiler-makers, machinists, and others locally organized should form a local council to be known as the "Iron Trades Council" of the city of its existence. The building trades local unions should similarly organize and be known as the "Building Trades Council" of the city of its existence. The unions of the printing, leather, transportation, culinary, and all industries in which several unions had been organized, each should have its local trades council.

THIRD. These councils should form by representation a central labor council at whose meetings an interchange of thought should be made on such matters originating in or affecting one union or council which in the course of events would be likely to involve or affect other unions or councils; and to act as a mediator in all trade or industrial disputes.

FOURTH. Locals composed of men not identified with any of the larger divisions of labor, and whose numbers were too small to entitle them to form a local trades council of a distinctive character, should organize a miscellaneous trades council, and be entitled to representation in the central labor council.

FIFTH. Every local union should be a bona fide branch of its national or international organization.

SIXTH. The national and international unions should organize into councils similar to the local trade councils and by limited representation form a supreme council.

SEVENTH. The duties of the supreme council should be confined to the supervision and direction of the entire organized labor element of the country.

EIGHTH. A small per capita tax should be levied on each local union to pay the necessary expenses of the local trades council, the central labor council, and the national organization. Each local union should be the custodian of its own funds, subject on order to transfer any portion thereof to places designated by their national or international unions. No moneys over a limited amount should ever be permanently in the hands or possession of a national or international union or its officers. As in a true democracy the people are the source of all power, so the local union should forever retain the rights of initiative and affirmation on all questions vital to the organization, particularly in the selection of its officers and the custody of its funds.

I felt that an organization formed on these lines would in a short time demonstrate its efficiency. The essential feature of the plan lay in the perfection of the local trades council. The supreme council should not be a semi-negative body existing through tolerance and incapable of exercising any authoritative function with the expectation of its observance. After due deliberation an order issued by the supreme council should be observed immediately by the smallest and most remote local in the country because that order would be the expression of the will of a decisive majority of the entire membership. Take, for instance, the question, "Shall eight hours constitute a day's labor in the United States?" A vote taken by unions through their national or international offices would then be transmitted to the supreme council. If a substantial majority were given to the proposal the supreme council would fix the date for its introduction and it would immediately thereupon become effective. The local trades councils would be equally potent in

Charles F. Burgman

Dennis Kearney

determining such matters as were vital to the interests of working men and women within the radius of their jurisdictions.

This is in outline the plan of organization which I proposed. I have attempted to carry it into effect on several occasions. Once in 1882, when the American Federation of Labor was called into existence, I had Mr. Charles F. Burgman, who represented the San Francisco Trades Assembly at the initial meeting of that organization, introduce it and ask for its adoption. It was commended by all present as good, but the organization was embryonic and an immediate demand was made for a national organization, for which, it was felt, this plan was not suited. Again in 1886, when the Federated Trades Council of San Francisco was formed, I tried to have my plan adopted, but failed in the effort because the local unions constituting that body would not and really could not comply with its requirements. I did succeed, however, in organizing the Iron Trades Council of San Francisco in accordance with my plan in 1885, and the following year saw it adopted by the local building trades unions. Had the national trade unions adopted it when they were in their infancy, the labor movement in the United States would now be in a solid impregnable position and not the mere frothing, impotent bubble that it is, the laughing stock of its enemies, and to its friends the mournful epitome of what it ought to be after over thirty years of experimentation.

Impending industrial changes—

At the time that I proposed this plan, I could see that great changes were imminent in the industrial world. An unprecedented impetus was being given to railroad construction, ostensibly to develop the millions of acres of arable land which land laws and homestead laws rendered feasible for occupancy by the poor man, but really to place these lands within easy access of the capitalists whose absorption of them by perjury and intimidation and the ready compliance of venal commissioners and land office agents has left the great West a crippled travesty of what it should have been. Congress was too interested in other things, being busy in reconstructing the South and in imposing servile conditions on the people of that section of the country in the interests of ruthless carpet-baggers, as though they were a conquered, instead of a mistaken, people. Our infant industries, such as coal and oil, tin plate plants, great steel producing concerns, the cotton and shoe industries of Massachusetts, sewing machine manufacturing and many other businesses, that have since become monsters of production and oppression, all could have been controlled by this system of labor organization.

In all walks of life people were mad, greedy, gasping mad for money—all but the laborer, and he was stupid and content. To have the privilege of voting a partisan ticket at elections, to be told that he was the most intelligent and best workman in the world and could produce more than any other, that he was a free-born, noble American citizen, although he had just enough to eat and a little surplus money to spend for beer so that he might be enabled to swagger and puff and pat his chest, that was sufficient for him.

The foundation for systematic legalized robbery was thus firmly laid, and then came a pause. With the momentary cessation came a new inspiration and the much denounced trust, conceived, born, and nurtured by our industrial system, was abroad in all its flaring, grinding, hideous monstrosity. Then the laborer began to pinch himself and upon waking up found, as he looked around, that he had been lulled into the rôle of a Rip Van Winkle. Then he began to do something that he should have done long before. The glamour of the idea of becoming an employer had faded into the reality of perpetual servitude and the boasted freedom of American citizenship had become as mythical as any fairy tale told in a nursery.

Advantages of suggested plan—

Had this proposed plan of organization been adopted and vigorously pushed, it would have produced men who would have stood as barriers against impositions inflicted upon all the people by venal legislators. These wrongs were all of an economic character and would properly have been within the scope of union activities. By this system of organization the unions might have wielded a power so deadly to the aspirations of the politicians as to deter them from their lavish distribution of franchises and the innumerable other bare-faced extravagances of which, in defiance of decency, they were guilty.

One of the chief reasons why this method of organization found little favor in the eyes of the presumptuous so-called labor leader was that no leadership was needed, or it was so attenuated as to be undesirable as a means of personal gratification. Changes in the personnel were inevitable and continuance in office improbable if its democratic character was to be preserved. Only those most competent could hope to serve for a lengthy period.

Another reason for objection by the same individuals was the economy of its management, which prohibited the payment of excessive salaries. Why workingmen should so far forget themselves as to deem it necessary by voluntary taxation to pay $4,000 or $5,000 per year to any man whose heart and brain are presumed to be in the Cause is more than I can understand. Decent compensation for faithful work is the right of any capable, honest servant as it is also the duty of every honest, appreciative employer to pay it. I could never see the equity of men earning by the hardest labor two or three dollars a day and having a family to maintain in some degree of decency and contributing toward the payment of a $5,000 salary to one of their number however talented he might be. Nor could I understand the conscience of a workingman who accepted that salary from that source. When laboring men are guilty of such folly and extravagance they have little cause to complain of the exploitations practised upon them by other harpies.

I consider the above mentioned plan of organization to be the true method of effecting the solidarity of the working class, free from the vagaries and uncertain assurances of Socialism as well as the foolish demonstrations of I. W. W. expounders, the dishonesty of the syndicalist, and the lethargy of the American Federation of Labor, which at present are and for many years past have been so regretfully and painfully apparent.

Testing an invention—

At the request of Mr. Fawcett, the foreman moulder of the Union Pacific Railroad foundry, I wrote an article which was published in the *Omaha Herald,* giving an account of his attempt to melt iron with Rock Springs coal. This coal deposit had just been discovered in Wyoming and its value was unknown. Fawcett saw some of it while en route east where it was to be tested, and he decided that, as it looked like anthracite, it must possess the heating power of that coal and therefore be capable of melting iron. He mentioned his opinion to Mr. Nichols, purchasing agent of the railroad, who only too cheerfully agreed to give him a few carloads with which to make the test. Fawcett, poor man, was profoundly honest in his opinion that he could do as he said with the coal, and as he was a practical foundryman his opinion was accepted without a doubt by the high officials of the road. He had also gained a dubious fame as the inventor of a furnace to reduce iron without the aid of a blast by either blower or fan. His invention called for the insertion of a steam jet into the neck of the furnace above the charging hole. The furnace, being like a bottle, the steam jet created a vacuum, causing the air to rush into the furnace through holes at the bottom.

All the officials of the road were present at the melting test and I was selected by Fawcett as the reporter. Sure enough, iron was melted by Rock Springs coal, but it was so thick that it was only fit to put in moulds to make car bumpers. Iron was melted beyond a doubt, and I so reported in the following morning's *Herald* to the delight of all concerned. My performance was considered as announcing a great stride in the development of the unknown West. Mr. Miller of the *Herald* was pleased to believe that his paper had been made the vehicle of this great announcement, and when it became necessary for him to dispense with the services of his city editor he offered me the position. I accepted the job to oblige him and remained until he secured another man. He was most anxious to make a newspaper man out of me. I now regret that I did not allow him to do so.

Real estate—

There was such a variety of things occurring in Omaha during my residence there that it is impossible to enumerate them all. One incident out of many may be mentioned to show how little dependable the people are even when personally affected. An Indian reservation in the southern part of the state, in proximity to the Republican River and adjoining Kansas, had recently reverted to the Government in the customary way when Indian reservations became valuable. It was opened for occupancy by homestead, preemption, or purchase. The local agent of the Burlington & Missouri Railroad, alive to future possibilities for his road and himself as well, issued a call requesting the attendance at a meeting, of those desiring land in this exceptionally fine section of the state. A large number of the Union Pacific employees responded and the meeting was held. Mr. Shaler, the agent, presided. Every one present signified how much land he desired and became a member of the association. I desired a quarter-section and became a member. An executive or managing committee of five was selected, of which I was one. Shaler explained to the committee how the business was to be managed, to which I took decided exceptions. The committee was to have the lands surveyed and staked into quarter-sections. The subdivisions were then to be numbered and as the land was identical in every respect as to its fertility it made little matter which parcel fell to any one person. This was to be determined by lot. Each quarter-section was to cost $200, payable at the land office at Beatrice. The cost of surveying and entering the claim at the land office was estimated to total $50 more, making $250 for each quarter-section. Land warrants acceptable at the land office at their face value were to be bought at the Kountze Brothers' bank at 10 per cent discount. Two sections were to be set apart for a town and divided into five equal parts, one for each member of the committee. The extra charge of $50 was to compensate the committee members for their time and all expenses incurred in surveying, visiting the land office, etc. After deducting all expenses, about $1,000 would accrue to each member of the committee to compensate for the time he had spent in the work. The time to be devoted to the enterprise was to be about six weeks, perhaps two months. This, with the fifth of the proposed townsite for each member of the committee, I thought was out of all reason and was downright swindling. Shaler laid his program before a full membership of the association, after which I gave my views. Shaler interrupted me by moving that my seat on the committee be declared vacant, which was promptly concurred in without a protest from a single member. I considered this the most unkind and stupid transaction with which I ever had any connection and resigned my membership in the association at once. I believe the enterprise was carried to a conclusion, and the location was named Franklin.

I believed that the time and labor of the committee should be paid for, together with the expenses incident to the work, and that a city lot should go to every owner of a quarter-section. I desired all to be upon a footing of equality and hoped to see a community established eliminating gouging, sharp practices, and dishonesty. I have found in all my experience but few disposed to put into practice the ideal of man's equality. I have also found men in associations of this kind who submit to impositions of the sort above described with the expectation of reaching a turn in the road landing them in the position of evening up on their losses by making others pay them.

Railroad director—

Another instance of neglected business opportunity offered me, and I will have ended the story of my stay in Omaha. Judge Briggs informed me that he would soon secure articles of incorporation for a railroad whose route would be to St. Louis, Missouri, and also to the new town of Denver, Colorado. He wished me to be one of five directors of the proposed railroad. I considered the proposition a huge joke and enjoyed it immensely. The bare thought of inviting me with my position and income to be a railroad director was so ridiculous a proposition that I believed the Judge to be crazy.

On the contrary he was very serious. The Judge explained the procedure to me in this way:

The river counties in Nebraska are settling rapidly; the land is good; taxation is light and there is no indebtedness. A railroad is needed now and will be in greater demand presently to haul the farm products to market. These counties will readily grant a right of way for a railroad and no doubt will vote bonds for its construction and afterwards pay freight and passenger charges without a whimper, the same as has been done on the other subsidized roads. It will be our business to build the road, own it and operate it for our mutual benefit. When we secure the county bonds we will also secure a fiduciary agent in New York to dispose of them, which will be an easy matter as the counties are solvent and growing. With the proceeds we will grade the road, lay tracks and switches, build depots, buy engines, cars and other equipment, and be in running order within a year. Building a railroad nowadays is simply a question of cheek, jaw-bone, energy, and perseverance. Look at the Union Pacific and the Central Pacific, and the Illinois Central and others, all built in the way that I have described. We can build this road as well as the others were built with the money advanced to the projectors. Your business will be to pit the counties in competition and the one giving the most liberal bonus with fewest strings is the county through which we will build the road.

I saw the Judge was in earnest, and began considering the proposition. But I was too recently from Ireland and my training was of a character that forced me to look upon the proposition as a swindle more than as a business proposal. To have men furnish the means to build and equip a railroad and make it a success by using it, without a word to say in its management or deriving a cent's worth of income from it, appeared to me a thoroughly dishonest affair. The Judge said it was purely a business transaction. My sensibilities and moral training had already received several severe jolts without being blunted or badly damaged, but this was the worst of any, and coming from a man whose probity I held in the highest esteem, and who I knew had a sincere regard for me—that was what pinched. I stuck to my first declaration of having nothing whatever to do with the project notwithstanding the Judge's assurance that I was rejecting the turning point of my life. The road was built and was soon afterwards sold to a larger corporation seeking an entrance into Omaha. I have been informed that each of the five original incorporators realized the sum of $500,000 on their investment of brains and energy. I have never regretted what I did in this matter although the man who took my place became a multimillionaire and has often thanked me for stepping aside.

Utah Territory—

After the completion of the Union Pacific Railroad, business in the shops began to decrease until less than one-half of the original force remained, and Omaha began to shrink to the proportions of a village through the loss of its population. It looked as if George Francis Train's dream of its being the future national capital would fade into oblivion.

Mr. Fawcett, on his reputation as a furnace man, was employed by a New Jersey corporation to smelt the ores taken from their mines situated in Ophir Canyon, Utah. He required a great number of castings in the constant changes that he was making with his patent furnaces. This led him to the Salt Lake Iron Works, the only place in Utah Territory where he could be supplied. The opening of Utah to the outside world by the completion of the Pacific railroads brought thousands of Gentiles into it, anxious to exploit the great mineral deposits scattered throughout the Territory. New works were put up in all directions to handle the ores, causing a daily increasing demand for the equipment with which to do it.

The men employed by the Salt Lake Iron Works were all English Mormons. They took little interest in the great influx to the sacred soil of Utah, acting as if they could discourage it. Fawcett suggested that the company get a man who understood the business, which Hawley, part owner of the foundry, agreed to do if Fawcett would recommend the right person. My name was mentioned and I was communicated with at once. A brief correspondence ensued, and soon I was in the land of Brigham Young and the Latter Day Saints.

My first experience in Utah was disconcerting. The men struck against me. I have known many causes and pretexts for strikes, but this was the first of its kind and the only one of the sort that I ever heard or knew of. I was not a Mormon. It was a novel pretext, but better than none, and reminded me of Orange bigotry in Ireland. Hawley was completely nonplussed. Next day he suggested that in order to get the work out I must leave. This I consented to do provided he complied with the terms upon which I had agreed to come to Utah and pay me six dollars for every working day for one year. The proposal was more than Hawley could stand for and he said so. I telegraphed to Omaha for two moulders and secured two other Gentiles in Salt Lake City, and by systematizing the work I produced about three times more output in the same hours than the ten men who had struck against me had done. I paid the men $4.50 per day. Hawley had been paying his men $3.00 per day. He was a cheap, narrow-visioned fellow, and believed that high wages were the wasting of money. I showed him how wrong he was and he admitted it.

I organized a moulders' union in Salt Lake City, all the Mormon moulders becoming members, and as I had defeated them in their strike against me they professed their regret at doing so, declaring that if they had known that I was the man I had proved to be they would not have done so. I readily forgave them.

The inrush of Gentiles brought the subject of polygamy prominently before the country as it had never been before. From the days of Nauvoo[8] it was well understood that polygamy was the cornerstone of the structure upon which Mormonism was built. Since that time it had not been brought face to face with so many whose public professions were against it. The miners and those in quest of work or attracted to Utah as prospectors by the reports of rich discoveries, paid little attention to polygamy or Mormonism: it was Mormon exclusiveness that they objected to. The Mormons held aloof from the Gentiles under all circumstances. They had dwelt so long in the Great Salt Lake Valley as an exclusive people, "Saints," as they termed themselves, that they did not seek the contaminating associations of those whom they were taught to regard as vile and immoral, treacherous and dishonest. The majority of Mormons were originally an extremely poor, uneducated class, recruited from the substrata of society in the larger cities of Europe. The itinerant elders, full of enthusiasm, inspired them with a belief in the material benefits and spiritual beauties of the new religion, setting it forth in such glowing terms as they had never heard and knew nothing of. The very poor in the large cities of England know no more about Christianity than the untutored savages for whose conversion thousands of pounds are spent annually.

[8] The Mormons had previously settled at Nauvoo, Ill.—Ed.

The "Avenging Angels"—

The most impressive doctrine taught by the Mormons was faith in the heads of the Church upon whom depended the future happiness and comfort of the members of the Church. Translation from a condition of penury to one of moderate comfort confirmed these people in their allegiance to their leaders, and inspired them with horror at the base thought of associating with the "unregenerate," as the Gentiles were said to be. The greatest number became fanatics, ready at all times to do the bidding of their leaders, even to the extent of committing murder. The stories told of the deeds done by bishops and elders in the days before the influx of Gentiles were picturesquely horrible. The Mountain Meadow Massacre was still fresh in the memories of a few of the inhabitants who remembered its sickening details.[9] Bill Hickman of the "Avenging Angels,"[10] who participated in that butchery and was tried and executed for it, frequently visited a daughter who was my neighbor.[11] He was a big,

9 The Mountain Meadow Massacre occurred in September, 1857. One hundred and twenty men, women, and children, emigrants from Missouri and Arkansas on their way to California, were butchered by a group of Mormons and Indians under the direction of J. D. Lee. Lee later claimed that he did it with the sanction and approval of the leaders of the Mormon Church. It was not until 1875 that he was arrestd for his participation in the crime, tried, and sentenced to be shot.—Ed.

10 This murderous band of Mormon followers was more commonly known as Brigham Young's "Destroying Angels."—Ed.

11 Roney is in error in making the statement that Hickman was connected with the Mountain Meadow Massacre. Hickman's pub-

strong, hulking fellow and a fanatic blinded to the enormity of the atrocity. I often spoke to him. To me he was a repulsive, ignorant brute.

I was on terms of intimacy with another "Avenging Angel," Porter Rockwell, also a participant in that massacre who was shot in the Utah penitentiary according to law for his part in that deed. Rockwell was at Nauvoo at the time Joseph Smith was murdered and the Mormons driven out and he swore never to cut his hair while he lived and a Gentile remained on the earth. He plaited his hair, wearing it as the Chinese do, but he did not succeed in killing all the Gentiles. When drunk, and that was at least once a week, he was wild and ferocious enough to be guilty of indiscriminate slaughter, but when at this stage he was usually arrested by a Mormon policeman and saved from the commission of such horrors. He was a human hyena when in the cups. I do not know how it came about that I became acquainted with him or why it was that he became so friendly with me. He mistook me for a Mormon, I presume, for had he known that I was a Gentile he would have given me the cold shoulder, and perhaps something worse.

Brigham Young and "Whiskey" Howard—

Brigham Young was a man of consummate ability. With but little technical education he became

lished confession makes no mention of that event. Hickman was arrested in 1871 with others for the murder of a man named Buck at Warm Springs, Utah.—Ed.

the head of the Mormon Church. With the power that that position gave him, and with the subserviency of the people, he ruled as a king might have done. His people looked upon him as God's prophet. It was seldom that he was the victim of sharp practice in trading, but if this happened, as president of the Church he found a speedy way of at least getting even with the offender. If a brother succeeded in getting the better of Brigham Young and was otherwise a faithful Mormon, he was apt to pass over the matter so long as it was not boasted about.

"Whiskey" Howard, as he was known, was an Irish Mormon who operated a distillery at Cottonwood, a few miles south of Salt Lake City. The Saints found added spirituality in the consumption of Howard's product, and consumed a great deal more of it than was consistent with their title of Saints. Howard was getting rich very fast and President Young decided that he would run the distillery as a church affair. He made a proposition to Howard, who absolutely declined to accept it at the price offered. "Brother" Howard fell into disfavor, but was able to sell his whiskey as readily as before and matters were highly satisfactory, when to his chagrin at the October Conference, he was called for a "mission" to go to Ireland. Howard could not decline the "mission" without jeopardizing his standing as a Saint and thereby losing the sale of his whiskey. Brigham Young secured the distillery on his own terms, and Howard left on his "mission" in no saintly humor. He was to be gone two years.

The October Conference is a sort of general meeting of the Saints at which the President announces the names of the missionaries that have been revealed to him. Every important law or affair of any sort necessary to be enforced was always the result of a revelation of the President, whose duty it was to announce it and see that it was carried out. To object to the terms of a revelation was simply an act of apostasy which brought upon the offender many evils, the least of which was financial ruin.

Howard got his money from Brigham Young with the understanding that when he returned he could regain possession of his distillery if he desired by simply returning the sum paid him. The men put in charge of the distillery knew nothing about the business, particularly the rectifying, and were obliged to cease operations soon after Howard's departure, and when the stock on hand was exhausted there was a famine among the Saints for whiskey.

Howard returned bringing with him one convert, a cousin of his wife, who became his second wife. He also brought at great expense for freightage, for this was before the days of railroads, a large quantity of machinery purchased in New York. He saw his distillery closed and knew the reason, but appeared uninterested, devoting himself to the establishment of a machine shop. The Saints were clamoring for whiskey and Brigham Young was anxious to part with the distillery and have the price which he had paid for it returned. Howard had no desire to return to whiskey making, no matter how much the demand for it might be. He was reminded of the contract, but as it was entirely optional with him he refused compliance. Finally, upon payment of about one-third what he had received for it he consented to take it back, and whiskey manufacture was resumed, to the great joy and satisfaction of the Saints. This was one of the very few transactions which proved disappointing to the head of the Church. It took an Irish Saint to do this.

In some unaccountable way the Mormons have acquired the reputation for being most abstemious. My experience with them led me to feel that if they were temperate in the consumption of alcoholic drink it was either because they could not get it or did not have the means to purchase it. In the southern portion of the Territory where the grape was grown, brandy also was made and used by the people most liberally. It was no unusual thing, in fact it was the custom, for young men and women to go on horseback a distance of twenty miles to be present at the orgies of a "harvest home" when the crops were gathered, and remain a week in imitation of the Spanish fiestas, but indulging in the lowest debaucheries. The domestic relations of their elders taught the young people lessons in no way conducive to a high standard of morality.

Brigham Young duped—

Mr. George Perry, a New Englander, obtained work in the Salt Lake Iron Works and in a very short time proved to be a thorough machinist as well as a most agreeable person. Mr. Perry permitted it to be known that he was an inventor and that it was his intention to make Salt Lake City the great manufacturing center for his invention for which he believed there would be a world-wide demand. The huge iron deposits in Utah led him to believe that blast furnaces would be established to supply the entire West with superior iron and also supply his own demand for that commodity, which he expected would be great as soon as he had his factories under way. Every intimation he gave of his project was enthusiastically believed in by those to whom he carefully communicated it. He was so extremely modest and so profoundly logical in all that he said that not the shadow of a doubt of his immediate success was entertained by any one. He was prevailed upon to give a demonstration of its efficiency, and I made the journal boxes to be used in running a circular saw in the pattern shop. The invention was an anti-lubricating journal or ball-bearing box. It worked splendidly.

President Young and his son, Brigham Jr., hearing of this great invention, came to the foundry to see it in operation. Neither of the Youngs knew anything about machinery, and when an enthusiastic "Brother," in whom they had implicit confidence, explained it to them they immediately became fascinated with its immense possibilities. The introduction of the very retiring inventor followed. Perry's great scheme of manufacturing was already known to them and believed in. Brigham, Sr., suggested to Mr. Perry the formation of a joint stock company, but it was so good and feasible an invention that Mr. Perry thought that he could interest several monied friends to advance the cash to go on with its manufacture in a moderate way and increase the works as the demand for the invention increased. He believed that he had a fortune within easy reach and saw no reason why he should divide it with anyone unless they were intimate personal friends. He was at length induced to adopt the suggestion of Brigham Young, Sr., with the proviso that he would hold a majority of the stock. The company was duly incorporated with Brigham, Sr. as President and Mr. Perry as General Manager. Young paid Perry $8,000 cash and gave his note endorsed by Mr. Mumford, part owner with Hawley in the Salt Lake Iron Works, for the same amount, payable in six months. The President named the directors.

Great excitement of a suppressed character took possession of all the well-to-do or monied Saints in Salt Lake City and Mr. Perry was shown the greatest attention by them all, which he received with modest grace. All wanted stock in the new enterprise of which the head of the Church was president. Perry quietly permitted himself to be interveiwed by these men one at a time and confidentially sold each of them a portion of his stock with the understanding that the transaction should be kept a profound secret as it was a special favor that he was conferring upon each purchaser. Having disposed of all of his stock at par Perry proposed that he be authorized by the directors to go to Washington, D. C. and there arrange to secure patent rights through the diplomatic representatives of those countries that had such laws. This was agreed to, and $2,000 was voted to pay his expenses. Meanwhile he was having a large number of patterns made in the shops of the Salt Lake Central Railroad Company, which before his departure for the East he committed to my care. Mr. Perry left Salt Lake on the highly momentous trip and nothing more was ever seen or heard of him.

When Brigham, Sr. realized that he was the victim of a clever confidence operator the only thing he did was to order that it should be kept quiet, and nothing would have been known about it if he had not attempted to force Mumford to bear the loss of the money advanced on his note which Mr. Perry had adroitly negotiated. Mumford, good Mormon that he was, demanded his money, which was refused. Then he talked about the deal and when too late to preserve secrecy he received the money, in order to prevent his filing a suit. Mumford and Hawley disposed of their interest in the Salt Lake Iron Works to a young inexperienced New Yorker, a Mr. Sutherland, whose father-in-law, General Roome, President of the Manhattan Gas Company, had sent him into temporary exile. I was informed later that General Roome or some one acting for him was so impressed with my article on Rock Springs coal, which was kept in circulation in the financial papers in the East for two years, that he purchased 100,000 tons of the coal to convert into gas. As it contained no gas of value it was sold for domestic use at a loss. Sutherland, the ostensible owner of the Iron Works, dying after a few months' residence in Salt Lake City, the shop passed into the hands of Major Wilkes, a brother of the celebrated Commodore Wilkes.[12]

Unemployed again—

Major Wilkes had been acting as one of the managers of the notorious Emma mine, but as that disreputable enterprise was nearing its finish he cast around for a lucrative business, which if not so prolific as the mine in its yield of cash, would at least be sufficiently remunerative to keep him financially in the limelight. The Major's knowledge of the business which he had undertaken was as lim-

[12] Charles Wilkes, the noted explorer, discovered the Antarctic Continent. He became a Commodore in the Northern Navy in July 1862.—Ed.

ited as his energy was untiring and his determination to make it a success was great. His reputation as a wealthy man, which he had gained while distributing the money of the English stockholders of the Emma mine, soon disappeared. He was unable to pay the wages of the men, which gave rise to ugly rumors of financial stress that upon inquiry proved to be too true. To determine what should be done the men met in my house. Two weeks' wages were owing them and they did not feel inclined to give the Major more of their labor without an assurance of compensation. I gave their ultimatum to the Major in the morning and he in turn gave me his, which was that all would be paid one week's wages, and if they wished to quit work they were to receive all money due them. My name was the first on the list. When asked, I said that I wished all that was coming to me, and every one else did the same. The Major was dumbfounded, for this action ended his career as a foundry owner. It also saved him from future financial trouble and possible disgrace, for when he undertook the management of the concern he had assumed obligations which it was impossible to fulfill.

It was in Utah that I received a letter from my father in which he urged me to return to Ireland if I could do no better than work as a foundry employee. He further informed me that if I had not the means to pay my way I should let him know and he would send sufficient to carry my wife and me and my two children back to Ireland. I was deeply offended at his letter and never replied to it.

Utah, like the rest of the country, was suffering from the effects of the panic precipitated by the failure of Jay Cooke & Company and the Northern Pacific Railroad, then almost completed. I could see but little ahead for me in Utah and resolved to try my luck in California.

Regrets—

From my experience in Utah I learned the seriousness of the mistake that I had made in leaving Omaha. I cast aside many good and valuable friends and a well established, if only a brief, career. I was short-sighted enough to believe that with the completion of the Union Pacific Railroad the future of Omaha was one of darkness. George Francis Train endeavored to impress me with some of the faith that he had in the future of the city. Ed. Rosewater, who became later a commanding figure in the new Northwest, advised me against going to Utah, but I thought that in the heart of the Rockies my practical knowledge of reducing ores and refining silver and gold, which I had learned in the Omaha Smelting Works, would lead me almost without effort into a position demanding that knowledge assisted with some deeply rooted notions of honor and honesty. I learned that skill, knowledge, and honesty were not assets of value at that time in Utah. The braggard and blundering swaggerer took precedence over the man who was modest in his pretensions. I was disgusted with what I saw and with what I came in contact in Utah. The Mormons were not blameless. They were exclusive, insincere, bigoted, and unreliable. The anti-Mormons, or political regenerators, were no more moral than those whom they denounced, and seemed to be seeking some method by which to effect wholesale confiscation. The miners and work-people outside the Church were only intent on good wages and steady employment. Bustle, excitement, and hurry were the common order of things. Utah was a large mining camp and Salt Lake City was its main street. It was a relief to leave the Territory.

IV

SAN FRANCISCO AND THE CHINESE

IV

SAN FRANCISCO AND THE CHINESE

Upon my arrival in San Francisco in April, 1875, my first experience was with a thieving hack driver who charged exorbitantly for carrying my family to a hotel.

At work by the Golden Gate—

W. H. Allen, to whom I had a letter of introduction from his partner, Jas. B. White, was the first person upon whom I called. He introduced me to Mr. Irving M. Scott, whose foreman moulder instructed me to be at work in the Union Iron Works the following morning. White and Allen were stamp-mill builders who purchased all their machinery and other material from the Union Iron Works. When Major Wilkes gave up his interest in the Salt Lake Iron Works, White was anxious to get hold of it and either operate it himself or convert it into a branch of the San Francisco firm. I did what I could for them in the matter, for which they were grateful, but the place fell into the hands of "Whiskey" Howard.

Curiosity led me into the Pacific Iron Works where I met Jim Wharburton, an Englishman whom

I had known in Belfast and who had worked with me in Omaha. Through him I made the acquaintance of the foreman, E. T. Jones, also an Englishman, who had been a London member of the executive committee of the English moulders' union when I appealed from the decision of the Belfast branch. Jones offered me a job which I accepted. At that time foundry work was very brisk in San Francisco. The Comstock mines in Nevada were yielding ore by the million dollars' worth. Stock was booming and the people in every walk of life were crazy to become millionaires through stock speculation. Upon beginning work I learned that there was a moulders' union in the city, a weak struggling affair, and requested its secretary to send to the Salt Lake City union for my card. For some unexplained reason he delayed doing so.

Characteristics of western workers—

The Pacific Iron Works job lasted only a few months. I then went to the Union Iron Works and secured a job, although I had been advised of the tyranous reputation of Mr. Dimmick, the foreman. I was a total stranger in the shop, which gave me a splendid opportunity to observe and study the men. The American style of working, which I had noticed in New York, St. Louis, and Chicago, consisted of competing to secure the favor of the foreman and through that means retain steady employment. It was carried to the limit in the Union Iron

Works. No foreman was needed to urge these men to work to the point of exhaustion. They labored hard of their own volition and displayed an eagerness most discouraging to one who wished to see each of them occupy the niche of a man.

It looked as if my stay would be brief in such a place working among men so utterly selfish and slavish. I did not and would not descend to their level if I never worked at moulding. When business did slacken somewhat I was surprised at my good fortune in being retained when many of the other workers were allowed to go. I never hurried and always suppressed any disposition that I might have had to take work away from others. Strangely enough I seemingly prospered although others, exhibiting the traits mentioned, were set aside.

I discovered in the foreman, Mr. Dimmick, something that others who had known him for years had not discovered, viz., that he was a thinking man and was strongly disposed to be fair. He was rough spoken and peremptory in his manner, but beneath the surface he had a big heart and a desire to play the game squarely. I became a steady worker in that plant and continued so until during the days of the Workingmen's Party agitation headed by Dennis Kearney.

An American citizen—

In the month of August, 1875, I became an American citizen in the Fourth District Court presided over by Judge Morrison. By that act I dissolved all future active participation in hostility to England and severed all connection with the Irish revolutionary organizations on American soil. My sentiments toward the British Government remained the same as they had been, but as a citizen of a country on terms of amity with England I believed it to be my duty to subordinate those sentiments to those in keeping with the policy of my adopted country. Ireland still held my love and I still hoped strongly for her redemption, but I was determined that no act of mine should ever in any way contribute to embroil my newly adopted country with the one whose citizen I had formerly been. I felt that I would be a perjurer if I acted otherwise. Such was my conception of my duties as a citizen of the United States of America.

After that time I persistently repudiated all connection with political clubs designated as "Irish-American." National distinctions of that character would indicate a preference for the original country to which those belonging to such clubs owed their nativity, the country of their adoption being but of secondary consideration to them. When anyone is guilty of such an attitude I consider him not to be a citizen of this nation but a person who should be denied the privileges of citizenship in this western republic.

At the elections in San Francisco I have noticed political clubs formed with national preferences and fostered by politicians in the interests of whose party they are organized, when as a proper thing they should be frowned upon and not allowed to exist. So long as clubs of this character are encouraged, so long will be retarded the effectiveness of the so called "melting pot," which aims at homogeneity and the obliteration of the distinguishing marks that keep people of various nationalities from associating as citizens of one nation. In order to perpetuate this obstacle to cohesion, the proceedings of these clubs are conducted in the language of the country after which they are named. Their managers are usually unprincipled "grafters," making use of the naturalized citizens for the double purpose of (1) exploiting the membership by a parade of their numbers, and (2) of extracting money from inexperienced aspirants for office by having them believe that the vote of the membership of such clubs will be cast for them on election day. The whole business of hyphenated clubs is fraudulent and an outrageous injustice to the uninformed voter who is apt to confuse affairs of the kind with the belief that this is Liberty.

The Chinese—

As a stranger in San Francisco and one disinclined to form extensive acquaintance I was content with the tenor of my existence, colorless and monotonous though it was. I was slightly interested in the newspaper reports of attacks upon the Chinese, which I considered unreasonable and antagonistic to the principles of American Liberty as I had understood them. I passed through Chinatown several times, lingering there to observe the Chinese as well as I could at close range, and except for their dress and pigtails I discovered little difference between them and those residing in certain districts in New York City. The restrictions, which many were at that time advocating should be placed upon the Chinese were, I thought, brutal and such as no self-respecting civilized people would dream of imposing upon the members of any race within their midst. The only objection to them that I felt had any validity was that they were cheap workers. In this respect they were no worse than the immigrants arriving upon the Atlantic side of the continent. It seemed to me that this objection would in a short time pass away, provided the Chinese were allowed the liberty, without molestation, that was accorded to other immigrants.

The Irish immigrant, driven to America by famine and landlord oppression, had at first worked as a cheap laborer on the railroads and wherever work was hardest and most menial. The native Americans regarded him as a menace, treating him with contempt, varied by assaults with rocks and brickbats. In a few years the Irishman became a citizen. No longer a cheap laborer, he became interested in politics, held office, conducted businesses of various kinds, entered the professions and developed into a good American with the vested right of jeering at the cheap laboring German who succeeded him, whom he in turn treated as he had been treated. This then continued until the German had asserted himself as a business man and politician. Then both pitched into the Italian for the same reasons that they had been assailed, and then all of them concentrated upon the Chinaman. To assail and assault and oppress one portion of humanity seems to be the delight, inherent right, and practice of another portion.

As a cheaper laborer than the others the Chinaman was hailed by the conscienceless exploiting employers as a veritable Godsend. Chinamen of education and wealth cooperated with the white men in the importation of their countrymen and just as cheerfully and ruthlessly robbed them. The difficulty of mastering the English language forced the Chinese to herd together, and thus placed them under the eye and management of their rapacious countrymen, the Six Companies.[1] If the energy and intelligence of the white man had been directed against herding and toward the creating of a picturesque Oriental section like Chinatown, they would have benefited themselves and also the Chinaman.

[1] "The Chinese Six Companies were really contractors and importers, although they attempted to pass themselves off as benevolent organizations. They governed and controlled with an iron hand all the Chinese in the country" (H. H. Bancroft, *History of California*, vol. 7, footnote p. 344).—Ed.

These were the views that I entertained during the period immediately following my arrival in San Francisco and during the early days of the Workingmen's Party in 1878. Later my views underwent a modification in some respects and an enlargement in others.

Sandlot meeting—

San Francisco was thrown into a whirlwind of excitement when the news came of the strike upon the Pennsylvania Central Railroad.[2] On that day[3] thousands of handbills were scattered and distributed in all parts of the city inviting the people to assemble upon the sandlots in front of the City Hall, which building was then being leisurely constructed. Thousands responded to the call. Improvised speakers' stands were erected on the space between Larkin and Leavenworth streets and Market and the City Hall grounds. All shades of political thought were expressed by a variety of orators. Some denounced the capitalists as rich men, attributing to them all the evils then existing in society. Others denounced the railroad, particularly the Southern Pacific and the Central Pacific railroads, as the cause of their

[2] On June 1, 1877, the Pennsylvania Central Railroad announced a wage reduction of 10 per cent. Similar reductions were made by other companies. The employees of the Baltimore & Ohio Railroad were the first to strike, which they did on July 17. The conflict soon spread to other lines and became of serious nature, being characterized by violence, riots, the use of militia, etc. The strike was lost. —Ed.

[3] July 23, 1877.—Ed.

woes. Those who were most vociferously applauded pointed to the Chinaman as the true source of all the trouble. Another and smaller gathering was told that the lack of organization and their ignorance as to their duties as citizens were at the base of every wrong. Resolutions were adopted at several of the platforms pledging support to the strikers and urging them to continue the fight.

When the meeting broke up the effect of the anti-Chinese oratory was at once demonstrated. A band of youngsters, unconsciously imitating the acts of their predecessors for over half a century, proceeded to wreck Chinese wash-houses in the same way that the Irish had been abused in former times. These hoodlums thought it intelligent and delightful sport to wreck the Chinese laundries and to maul any Chinese who happened to cross their paths. I have no record to remind me if it was at this time that the Pacific Mail Steamship Company's wharf and sheds were burned.[4] If so, several men were killed by the militia who were ordered under arms to protect life and property.

Kearney and the Workingmen's Party—

At this time a Public Safety Committee was formed which, armed with pick handles, paraded the streets in detachments to preserve order. One night's revelry in smashing seemed to satisfy the

[4] The docks of the Pacific Mail Steamship Company were not burned, but an adjoining lumber yard was set on fire by the mob on July 25, 1877.—Ed.

appetites of the incipient rioters. For some Sundays thereafter small crowds gathered upon the sandlots[5] to hear the oratory of the saviours of the country. Nothing practical was accomplished, nothing but denunciation and a fostering of hatred for the Chinese. A man eventually appeared on the sandlots who declared himself to be the president of the Workingmen's Party of California with W. H. Smith, a foreman plumber, as vice-president,[6] H. L. Knight, a Mexican War veteran and newspaper man, as secretary, and Thomas Donnelly, as treasurer. That man was Dennis Kearney, formerly a sailor, but at the time a drayman. Kearney had also been a member of the "Pick Handle Brigade," as the Public Safety Committee had been called. Before the adjournment of his first meeting he announced a series of gatherings to be held during the ensuing week in certain sections of the city. A collection was taken to defray the expenses of the forthcoming campaign, for which plans were announced by Kearney. H. L. Knight, in his speech, had said, "The Chinese must go," and that statement proved to be a rare expression which Kearney adopted and used as his own. It was later employed as the slogan and motto of the Workingmen's Party of California.

[5] The sandlots were the open, sandy spaces in front of the City Hall.—Ed.

[6] J. G. Day was announced by the local newspapers as vice-president of the new party.—Ed.

It was a customary thing, this holding of liberal meetings on Sunday afternoons in San Francisco. All manner of questions were presented for debate, and anyone who chose, whether called by name or not, had the right to take part in the discussion. Kearney had worked himself into the belief that he was a liberal and a free thinker on religious subjects, and embraced the opportunities afforded by these meetings to ventilate his views. As an extemporaneous orator he proved to be a complete failure, and usually after each of his efforts left the platform dissatisfied. When he began to speak on the sandlots as the self-appointed head of the Workingmen's Party of California, he took the precaution to memorize speeches prepared for him by Chester Hull, a newspaper man well known at Virginia City as the "Monumental Liar," who at that time was in the employ of the San Francisco *Morning Chronicle*. Kearney got off those speeches to the satisfaction and with the plaudits of the crowd. Hull wrote several speeches for him, making each one more incendiary than the previous effort, and, as Hull personally assured me, he never dreamed that Kearney would deliver them as they had been written. But this was what Kearney did, although he occasionally dovetailed a trifle of original matter into them.

Nightly speeches of this character delivered all over town soon attracted attention and brought increasingly large crowds to the sandlots on Sunday afternoons. Kearney and his meetings became the main subject of conversation, inasmuch as they were duly published in the San Francisco *Morning Chronicle,* whose editor and ostensible proprietor was Charles DeYoung. A few ward clubs were organized and other incendiary orators, unable to speak in the open air, held forth before their members.

Attempts at repression—

The Mayor of the city, Andrew Jackson Bryant, the District Attorney, Daniel J. Murphy, Chief of Police Kirkpatrick, and Isaiah N. Lees, head of detectives, the functionaries who ran the town, became alarmed at Kearney's apparent progress and resolved to nip it in the bud before it reached what they deemed to be dangerous dimensions. Kearney called a meeting for a Sunday afternoon in Agricultural Hall located at Stockton and Post Streets, which was largely attended. The meeting was, like its predecessors, enthusiastically incendiary and harmless. Without warning or cause for the act, unless it might have been the groundless fears of the officials mentioned, Captain Douglas and a detachment of police entered the hall and arrested Kearney, Knight, Bates, Day, and others and marched them to prison.[7] The expectations were

[7] Roney's statement in this connection is somewhat inaccurate. Kearney was arrested on November 3, 1877, while addressing an outdoor meeting. Day, Knight, Willey, and Kennedy were jailed the following day while conducting a protest meeting in Horticultural Hall. Bates was taken into custody a day later when he went to visit the prisoners.—Ed.

that resistance would be offered and thus justification given for a murderous onslaught by the police upon those present, which would consequently bring the agitation to an end. No resistance was offered by the agitators or by the audience, with the result that the effects of the arrest were contrary to the desires and hopes of its instigators. Instead of stopping the meetings it only increased the interest in them. That which had previously been an unorganized rabble was accordingly greatly strengthened by the addition of men who had little if any confidence in Kearney and who for the most part did not approve of his speeches. The latent spirit of fair play inherent in most people asserted itself, and instead of suppressing the agitation, this action of the city authorities only gave it new and vigorous life.

I had previously read the platform of the Workingmen's Party of the United States, and, feeling that it advocated the adoption of measures which were essential to the comfort and happiness of the whole people, I was seriously considering the advisability of applying for membership in that organization. The local organizer had published several letters in the local press setting forth its principles in a most forceful manner. I considered P. J. Healy, the organizer, to be the right man in the right place and was about to join with him when the above mentioned arrests were made. The actions of the city authorities in attempting to suppress free speech and free assembly so angered me that, instead of joining the Workingmen's Party of the United States, I applied for and was granted membership in the Eighth Ward Club of the Workingmen's Party of California, which met on Friday evenings in Charter Oak Hall, Market Street near Fourth.[8] On the night that I became a member of the Eighth Ward Club a large number of others also joined, principally as a protest at the high-handed arrests which had been made on the previous Sunday. Bryant and his associates had defeated their own ends.

Dictatorial tactics of Kearney—

Kearney upon being freed by the Court made even more violent speeches than before and also began to use the same tactics that had been used by those in league to silence him. At a meeting of the presidents of the ward clubs of the Workingmen's Party of California several of them had expressed themselves as opposed to Kearney's antics, which grievously offended him. He got together a howling, disorderly mob of young fellows led by George Whiteman, afterwards Chief of Police, and a little chap named Krause, later a stockbroker, and began a tour of the ward clubs with the intention of displacing those presidents who had dared to oppose him. With a howling mob at his heels the members of those clubs visited were intimidated so suc-

[8] There was no connection between these two Workingmen's parties.—Ed.

cessfully that he had no difficulty in removing the objectionable presidents.

The president of the Eighth Ward Club, Thomas Bates, was, without the knowledge of the members, listed by Kearney for decapitation. One evening as our club was decorously proceeding with its business we were suddenly interrupted by the entrance of Kearney and his mob yelling with all the strength of their powerful lungs. When order had been restored Bates, who had lost his nerve and who knew by the demonstration what was in store for him, pulled himself together and introduced Kearney to the meeting. Kearney promptly took the floor and began a tirade against Bates as vehement as it was unjustified, and wound up by moving that the president's chair be declared vacant. The audacity of the speaker and his proposition was superb. His earnestness and determination were also apparent. We were all momentarily speechless. Urged by an old Omaha friend, Frank Kauffman, I took the floor and asked if the mover of the motion was a member of the Eighth Ward Club. Bates perceived a ray of comfort in the question and informed me that he was not. Kearney, however, as president of the Workingmen's Party of California, claimed that he was ex-officio a member of every club. This I disputed and instructed the president to declare the motion out of order and to go on with the regular business. Bates with the courage of a victor saw the point and so decided. Kearney became furious and began to harangue his mob, who cheered him lustily.

The encounter warmed me up so that I asked permission to observe that the speaker having no rights in the club and not being invited to address us and as we had much business to transact, I hoped that the president would direct the gentleman to take his seat so that we might proceed. Bates, with perfect courage this time, so directed. Kearney again sputteringly attempted to talk, but I directed the president's attention to the fact that we had a sergeant-at-arms whose duty it was to remove disorderly persons, and that if Kearney persisted in his interruptions the president should order his removal. One of the gang yelled, "You can't do it." I immediately faced him and promptly informed him that we would throw the gang and their master down the stairs. Kearney left at once, and to my surprsie I found myself, according to the newspapers, the champion of decency and order and the conqueror of Kearney, who had been defeated for the first time on his own ground. Kearney stopped his irregular despotic course and harmony reigned for a time within the party.

Fight for free speech—

Kearney persisted in his foolish speech-making and the town was kept in a constant state of excitement. The course pursued by the city authorities was one of criminal folly, as bad in every respect as that of Kearney. In fact the former was most to blame for the turmoil and unrest which were so universal. Force was the only agency they could think of using in coping with the situation. Invested with authority they felt that the display of force was necessary to sustain it. Nothing was conceded to the intelligence and peaceable disposition of many of the leading men of the city. The century-old idea prevailed that workingmen, even in a republic, must be coerced in order to obtain the preservation of peace and a respect for order. The city authorities appeared to think that force was the one visible and always ready means to accomplish peaceful results. I considered Andy Bryant, Dan Murphy, and Detective Lees a triumvirate of cowardly incompetents, unworthy of respect or confidence. I believe that they were prompted to their folly by rich men trembling at the shadows of misdeeds and wrongs committed in their greed for wealth and who believed that they stood in deadly peril of the nemesis about to overwhelm them. As a climax to Bryant's folly he issued a proclamation[9] forbidding meetings in halls or upon the streets, hoping by this illegal and revolutionary course to suppress the anti-Chinese agitation.

The proclamation was published on Friday morning and on that evening the Eighth Ward Club, of which I was then president, held its usual weekly

[9] The proclamation of Mayor Bryant was issued on January 17, 1878.—Ed.

meeting. Our club enjoyed the reputation of being composed mainly of intelligent, conservative men, some of whom had taken an active interest in shaping the affairs of the State in its earlier days. Gen. A. M. Winn, first mayor of Sacramento, former adjutant general of the State Militia, and later president of the Mechanics State Council and also the chief advocate of the United States Eight-Hour Day Law, was one of them; John A. Steenbach, organizer of the Native Sons of the Golden West, was another. If Bryant and the fools operating with him had understood the situation they would not have issued a proclamation forbidding our meetings or any other meeting. It was left to me to decide whether we should meet in defiance of the Mayor's proclamation, and I so decided. Thousands assembled that night in the vicinity of the hall anxious to see the outcome. Our hall was crowded, and promptly at 8 o'clock I called the meeting to order and calmly proceeded with our regular order of business. At about 9 o'clock, Captain Douglas with a number of policemen entered the hall while Edward Fair was speaking upon the money question. Captain Douglas came in front of me and informed me that he and his men were present to enforce the Mayor's order. He requested me to dismiss the meeting. I informed him we were a club composed of American citizens assembled to discuss matters which we considered to be of vital importance to the country, a right conceded to every citizen by the Constitution and the laws of the nation and which we proposed to exercise so long as the peace of the city was not endangered. I told him that I considered the Mayor's proclamation to be illegal and unwarranted and that it was likely to precipitate a breach of the peace if it were enforced. I therefore declined to comply with the order that the meeting be dismissed.

I believe that my remarks caused the Captain to feel that he was about to take part in a proceeding of more serious consequences than merely the enforcement of the Mayor's orders. Perceiving this, I requested Mr. Fair to proceed with his address, and invited Captain Douglas to be seated. When Fair had finished I informed the Captain that the proceedings were at an end and requested him to keep in mind the sort of meeting that our club was accustomed to hold. I then declared the meeting adjourned to the following Friday night. I am under the impression that the Captain was disappointed and somewhat displeased with himself. He had been placed in an awkward position and he knew no way of extricating himself without resorting to force, which he feared to do because of the presence of members whose word had weight in the affairs of the city.

At all gatherings at this time the foolish custom prevailed of calling for cheers for Kearney. When the police who were at our meeting joined a larger body of their fellows awaiting them on the sidewalk the citizens outside the hall greeted the police with cheers for Kearney, which the police construed as a challenge, and they thereupon attacked the crowd with billy-clubs, which they used brutally and ferociously.

On the evening after our experience with Captain Douglas the Germans of San Francisco called a meeting[10] in Dashaway Hall in defiance of the Mayor's proclamation, and expecting that force would be used by the police to prevent it most of them went armed. The meeting, however, was not interfered with, but as the crowd left the hall the police belabored the people in their customary brutal way until the streets in the neighborhood were cleared of pedestrians.

The "Gag Law"—

Bryant, Murphy, and others had caused to be introduced in the Legislature a measure which became known as the "Gag Law." It was designed to break up all street assemblages by conferring arbitrary power upon police authorities to arrest all persons numbering from three upwards found together on the streets.[11] It was a most despotic

10 The meeting to which Roney refers occurred on January 19, 1878.—Ed.

11 The "Gag Law" provided that "Any person who, in the presence or hearing of twenty-five or more persons, shall utter any language with intent either to incite a riot at present or in the future, or any act or acts of criminal violence against any person or property, or who shall suggest or advise or encourage any act or acts of criminal violence against any person, or persons, or property, or shall

proposition. It passed the State Assembly, but still had to be adopted by the State Senate and be signed by the Governor, and it was hoped that if proper and timely representations were made to either or both of those parties we might succeed in preventing its enactment. Grove L. Johnson, a Republican, and John J. Tobin, a Democrat, had made eloquent and able appeals to the Assembly to kill the measure without avail.

After the above mentioned meeting of the Eighth Ward Club a confidential conference was called to determine what was best to be done to prevent the adoption of this outrageous piece of legislation. The result was that Thomas Johnson, John Lenahan, and myself were selected as a committee to visit Sacramento and to point out to the Senate and the Governor the offensive and despotic character of the proposed measure. Kearney was being tried in the City Criminal Court before Judge Robert Ferrell for an offense growing out of his intemperate speeches. A state convention of the Workingmen's Party of California was to be held in San Francisco in a few days. The proceedings of our conference were to be kept a profound secret. My surprise and indignation were great when on the following morn-

advise or encourage forcible resistance to any of the laws of this State, shall be deemed guilty of a felony, and on conviction thereof shall be punished by imprisonment in the State Prison, or in a County Jail, not exceeding two years, or by a fine not exceeding five thousand dollars or both."—*Amendments to Calif. Codes,* 1877–78, pp. 117–118. —Ed.

ing a full report of our secret meeting, its purpose, and our plans appeared in the San Francisco *Morning Chronicle.* The publicity given to our meeting killed whatever hope I had entertained for the success of our mission. My colleagues, however, thought that something might even yet be accomplished, so our committee went to Sacramento. Upon reaching the Capitol we learned that the Senate had been called hurriedly, the bill had been read three times, had been passed, and the Senate had adjourned. Upon meeting the Governor, Mr. Wm. Irwin, he informed us that he had just signed it.[12] At the request of Bryant, Murphy, and others, the Governor and the Adjutant General, P. F. Walsh, were going to San Francisco to look into the situation and to determine the necessity of ordering out the militia. I gave the Governor to understand that whatever violence had been committed in San Francisco had been provoked by and had been carried out at the instance of the Mayor and his associates. I assured him that the peace of the city was not endangered by Kearney's intemperate language. I also advised him that if the local authorities would only pay less heed to Kearney they would be better off for their own peace of mind and the general peace of the community. But the city's officials had been exasperating in the extreme and it seemed to me that they were inviting a crisis with a possible bloody ending. The result was that the

[12] Governor Irwin signed the bill on January 19, 1878.—Ed.

militia was not ordered out, although the night[13] of the Governor's visit to San Francisco was the most turbulent that we had had up to that time.

State investigation planned—

We considered it due to Assemblyman Grove L. Johnson to wait upon him and thank him for his able and voluntary defense of the rights of the working people of San Francisco, assailed as they had been so unjustifiably by cowardly and incompetent city officials seeking, under cover of a revolutionary legislative act, an excuse for the commission of future tyrannous acts. Mr. Johnson was found in bed suffering from serious prostration as a result of his efforts against the passage of the "Gag Law." I suggested to him the desirability of a legislative investigation to discover the authors of the turmoil in San Francisco and if possible to place the blame on the right parties. I had no hope that this could be successfully done through the instrumentality of a body which had shown its hostility by its speed in passing an outrageous law at the instance of those whom I knew to be the parties really culpable. The only thing that I hoped to accomplish from such an investigation was the publicity that it would give to each side of the controversy, leaving to the public at large the final word as to which was the guilty party. On all matters wherein working men were concerned, then and now, I have had unbounded con-

[13] January 19, 1878.—Ed.

fidence in the jury of Public Opinion as the court of last resort. Mr. Johnson thought that my suggestion was a good one, but did not think that he would be well enough to offer it in time. He also stated that he was a member of the minority and that consequently it might fail of adoption. He suggested Colonel John J. Tobin as the man to present the resolution, and as he had shown himself to be our friend and as he was a member of the majority, its chances of passage would therefore be more probable.

I wrote the resolution and interviewed Mr. Tobin when I returned to San Francisco. He very kindly undertook the task and was successful in having it adopted. I then began the collection of such evidence as I deemed necessary to prove the culpability of Bryant and his friends and the falsity of the charges made against the Workingmen's Party of California. I did not propose to justify or defend Kearney's utterances, but I intended to prove that his speeches were unheeded by the party members and that his violent harangues had in no way influenced their acts or opinions. While engaged in the collection of this evidence the time for holding the state convention of the Workingmen's Party was at hand. I was vitally interested in making it a success because I hoped by that means to be able to nullify the effects of the "Gag Law" and Mayor Bryant's proclamation, but I was forced to cease my efforts in connection with the proposed investigation.

Convention of Workingmen's Party—

In order to prevent an interruption of the proceedings of the convention of the Workingmen's Party of California, it was planned to hold it in one place while announcing that it would be held in another. We met in Humboldt Hall, corner of Mission and Erie streets, opposite the entrance to Woodward's Garden.[14] I was selected as temporary chairman. About 10:00 P.M. the sergeant-at-arms informed us that Captain Short with a number of policemen demanded admission. I instructed him to admit Captain Short with the understanding that no other officer was to accompany him. The Captain took a seat and quietly observed the proceedings. When we got through the Captain mounted a chair and said that at the order of the Mayor he had spent the evening hunting for us and that had he found us before the convention was organized he would have acted upon his orders and broken up our meeting, but finding us organized he decided to see what manner of meeting we were holding before he took action, and from what he had seen and heard he had decided that he would have committed a grave error to have interfered with our proceedings. He had seen many conventions and had been a member of a few of them, but none, to his mind, had equaled our convention in its conduct of business. If future proceedings were to be prohibited it would have to

[14] The convention of the Workingmen's Party of California assembled January 21, 1878.—Ed.

be done by some one else, for as an American citizen believing in peaceful assemblage he would be unjustified in interfering, and that he would so report to the Mayor, which he subsequently did. Captain Short's action and judgment were universally approved, and Bryant's orders were just as widely condemned.

The next day Kearney was acquitted in Judge Ferrell's Court and at the same time a Central Pacific Railroad employee, J. W. Bones, whom Kearney had vouched for as being a proper workingmen's representative, was elected State Senator from Alameda County. It had been agreed by the convention that in case Kearney should be acquitted he was to act as its permanent chairman. On the following evening, therefore, Kearney, accompanied by the newly elected Senator Bones of Oakland and escorted by a mob of enthusiastic yelling supporters, came to the convention hall. These events occurring simultaneously gave an immediate prestige to the Workingmen's Party, placing it prominently before the people as a political factor to be reckoned with in the future. Mayor Bryant's conduct and the action of the Legislature were ascribed to the Democratic Party and they could not be denied. This also gave to the new party a strength in numbers and a standing which it could not have attained except through years of effort and agitation.

I wrote the first platform or declaration of principles for the new party and generally took as active a part as I could during the convention to make the party as robust and as progressive as the times and circumstances permitted. It was essentially an anti-Chinese party as was indicated by its motto, "The Chinese must go." However, I never warmed to that feature of the agitation. I realized that that cry was superficial, but agreed to sail under the flag so emblazoned in order that I might in time have other and real subjects considered by the people, which I deemed to be of far greater importance to their permanent well-being. I recollect incorporating in the platform several propositions of greater value than that of antagonism to the Chinese. There was little that I proposed that was rejected and nothing that I disapproved that was adopted. I certainly stood in the way of becoming a political boss had my ambition led in that direction. I proposed the resolution which a few weeks later called into existence the Trades and Labor Assembly, which Kearney thoroughly disliked.[15] I opposed

[15] I have no reason to doubt the correctness of Roney's statement that he proposed the resolution which "called into existence the Trades and Labor Assembly," but I have been unable to find any supporting evidence in the newspapers of the time. Roney is so consistently accurate in his statements that I am willing to accept his claim in this connection.

The story of the founding of "The Representative Assembly of Trades and Labor Unions," which I have gathered from several of those who participated in the organization meetings, is briefly as follows:

During the meetings of the State Convention of the Workingmen's Party of California a number of delegates were present who were also members of local trade unions. Kearney and his closest associates were not advocates of Organized Labor and consequently gave

Kearney's proposition to make war on the *Morning Call* in the interest of the *Morning Chronicle* and defeated it.

Charles De Young and the Chronicle—

For years past the *Call* and the *Chronicle* had been bitter enemies. Charles De Young, the editor of the *Chronicle,* was envious of the circulation of the *Call* and hoped, through the instrumentality of Kearney as the leader of the Workingmen's Party, to increase the circulation of his paper to the detriment of the *Call.* I knew neither De Young nor his rival, Loring Pickering. Nor did I care about the causes of their enmity. As a matter of fact the *Call* had consistently given more complete and reliable reports of our meetings than had the *Chronicle,* although the latter had posed as the official organ of the Workingmen's Party. Fair play and the future of the party should have placed Kearney on my side, but for reasons best known to himself, which I never

no recognition to the unions in the proceedings of the convention. This angered the union men, and while the convention was in session several of them met to air their grievances. Fifteen or twenty persons were present and during the discussion that followed it was suggested that a federation of unions be organized. W. Clack, a printer, and C. W. Pope, a boot and shoe maker, were the leaders of the union group. After some delay ten unions sent delegates to a meeting on March 10, 1878, at which certain plans were discussed, and on March 31, "The Representative Assembly of Trades and Labor Unions" was formally organized with H. B. Warner, president, J. W. Jamison, vice-president, A. H. Morrison, secretary, and J. Robinson, treasurer.

The Trades Assembly, as it was popularly known, continued active until towards the close of 1884.—Ed.

inquired into, he took a different course. He felt badly chagrined at his defeat and wanted to have the matter reconsidered, but I opposed him in that also and was sustained by the assembled delegates.

It is remarkable with what unanimity a number of men act who come together with an honest purpose uninfluenced by the desire of personal gain or the gratification of some hidden ambition. The members of this convention were mostly strangers to each other. They had no clear conception of what they wanted. They knew the affairs of state were sadly out of joint, but how to untangle them or where to begin to do so was beyond their immediate comprehension. It was an easy matter for them to recognize that I had no ulterior purpose in mind, either personal or otherwise. They saw that my only aim was to devise some plan whereby the whole people would be benefitted. I did not even strive for a reputation. I have always followed that rule, and as is always the case with those who have no personal object in view and in consequence enter no cliques or combinations to forward their aims I am still alone, poor, and misunderstood while others have profited through my efforts.

At about this time Charles De Young sent a message to me asking me to call upon him. I had never seen him and wondered what he wanted. I was shown to the editorial rooms and upon knocking was invited to enter. A man in his shirt sleeves was writing at a great rate and looking up inquired as to what he could do for me. I asked for Mr. De Young. He said that he was that person. He never had seen me, and when I told him who I was he stopped writing and taking a good look at me said, "I want you to fall into line with Kearney upon the *Call* matter. He is going into the country to show that paper to be the enemy of your party and while he is gone you will do the same in the city." "If I have no inclination to do as you say," I replied, "what then do you suggest might be the outcome?" "Oh, you will do as I direct," he vigorously replied. "I know, because if you do not I will roast you so thoroughly in my paper that you will be glad to leave the State." "Well," said I, "I wish to tell you that I will not take orders from you or obey you in this or anything else, and, if you say one word of a derogatory character about me, you had better be prepared to die, for I will kill you or any other traducer that lies about me! So look out." With that I left him. After that day my name was never again mentioned in the *Chronicle*. If I presided at a meeting my name was always omitted. De Young was a small-minded, domineering fellow, incapable of anything unselfish, and when he was later shot to death by young Kalloch,[16] San Francisco did not suffer much from the loss.

[16] Charles De Young was shot by I. N. Kalloch on April 23, 1880. —Ed.

A party organizer—

I never took part in the sandlot meetings. They were largely attended and the contributions averaged about $125 each Sunday. Kearney regarded the contributions as personal donations, and when he wanted money for any purpose Treasurer Donnelly gave it to him. Donnelly was, I believe, an honest man, but as he kept no record of receipts or expenditures it was impossible to know with any degree of accuracy just what became of the funds. As was to be expected inquiries began to be made about the contributions. The amounts of each collection were grossly exaggerated. I insisted at the meetings of the executive committee of the party that some sort of an accounting should be made in order to allay the growing distrust. Kearney persisted in disregarding the request and considered it unworthy of attention. However, I persisted and finally succeeded in having it done. The accounting showed that he and vice-president William Wellock were the principal beneficiaries and that H. L. Knight, who did most of the work, was the recipient of $10 per week as secretary of the organization.

My duties as chairman of the organizing committee of the party caused me to absent myself from work more frequently than I should have liked, besides requiring me to spend some money in going about town from meeting to meeting, but no item of expense was charged to my name at any time. Clubs were organized all over the city, several of them in each ward. It was my business to settle disputes and as far as possible to allay jealousies and otherwise keep up the *esprit-de-corps* to the highest pitch. It was quite a job.

Workingmen's military organization—

I was also chairman of the committee on military organization. As the *"Chinese had to go,"* many of the younger elements in the party believed that the speediest and most effectual method of expelling the Chinese was by means of force. They therefore organized military companies with that laudable(?) object in view. I was unqualifiedly opposed to military organization within the party as being unnecessary, demoralizing, and the silent expression of a threat of violence. Some of the companies had uniforms and rifles.

Captain Montell, an employee of the Central Pacific Railroad and a member of the Tenth Ward Club, suggested to the members of the military company of that organization that if they would agree to protect the railroad's property in case of riot the railroad would equip them in fine shape, pay them while serving as guards, and give some if not all steady employment. This was an attractive proposition to many of the young men. Several members of the military company were opposed to the scheme and notified me that a meeting was to be held to decide what was to be done about Montell's proposal. As chairman of the committee on military organization I presided at the meeting. Mr. Montell made an elaborate statement. Wellock, who was aware of the proposal, endorsed it and urged its acceptance. I opposed it. I was opposed to placing any portion of the membership of the Workingmen's Party in the position of beneficiaries of the railroad or any other corporation or individual. Personally, I had no enmity to the railroad, nor did I seek any favors from it. If it should ever be necessary the military companies would guard the railroad property as they would any other property without being "bought off" by equipment or the promise of jobs. I denounced as a disgrace the acceptance of such a proposition and declared that I was sure that our military boys valued their individual and collective independence too highly to become the hirelings of any corporation. Entanglements of the sort proposed were dangerous to our future existence as a political party and I urged the club to reject Mr. Montell's proposal. And that was the decision arrived at. Wellock was simply furious because he had encouraged its acceptance and was present to back up whatever agreement he had previously made with Montell.

Lieutenant General Kearney—

At the next meeting of the executive committee of the party a most amusing performance took place. Wellock assumed that, as vice-president of the party and my superior officer, his attitude on Montell's proposal should have had my support. I maintained, however, that inasmuch as he was neither a member of the committee on military organization nor of the Tenth Ward Club or its military company, he had been treated with marked courtesy by being permitted to speak at all, and that his position as vice-president gave him no standing other than that which belonged to any other ordinary member. Kearney was inclined to favor Wellock but was afraid that the majority of the executive committee would side with me. He had already had two contests with me which had resulted disastrously and did not choose to risk a third. In order to settle the controversy I suggested that the military feature be eliminated, and also that, since it was a waste of time to bother about such matters, the committee on military organization ought to be abolished. Kearney and Wellock were pleased at the suggestion, but claimed that so long as the party sanctioned military companies among its members, some sort of plan should be devised to control them as long as they remained active. Wellock suggested that Kearney be made the chief of the military organizations, which was agreed to. His rank or title therefore had to be determined. Should it be "General" or "Commander" or "Commodore" or what? At last Wellock proposed that Kearney be called "Lieutenant General." I protested, but the other members of the executive committee considered it to be a huge joke. Kearney then put the following motion amidst the laughter of the committee, "All in favor of making me a Lieutenant General will say, aye," and it was almost unanimously passed. The aftermath of this absurdity was worse than the act itself. The cartoonist of the San Francisco *Wasp* pictured Kearney with the head of an ass in the uniform of a lieutenant general. Thus, through his egotism, Kearney brought ridicule upon the workingmen and their party.

Political action began to be demanded by the little fellows who ran their local clubs and made speeches at the various meetings. They considered their popularity established when their names appeared in the daily papers. Incipient politicians with towering ambitions were plentiful and irrepressible. Those seeking office and unable to gain recognition in the older parties flocked to the new party bringing nothing with them but the ideas acquired by previous and none too creditable association with the ward bosses of the older organizations.

Roney vs. Kearney—

A state constitutional convention was to be held and delegates were to be elected who were supposed to understand the present wants and future needs of the people of California. Aspirants were legion. From my contact with the men who were prominent in the ward clubs I had formed a very high regard for their ability. I felt that if the Workingmen's Party was to nominate a ticket of worth-while candidates these competent men ought to be selected.

The horde of incompetent aspirants knew of my previously expressed attitude and feared that, if it were made the rule of the party, I would insistently urge the claims of the competents, thus hurting the chances of the cheap politicians. At a meeting of the executive committee Kearney proposed that no officer of a ward club should be nominated by the party for any political office. Kearney expected that I would fall in with the proposition. I never imagined that he would father a plan so opposed to his old methods. A hot dispute resulted between us and became warmer as it continued, lasting until midnight and keeping relays of reporters busy to have it appear fully in the papers of the next morning. Personalities were freely indulged in by both of us. Kearney had the remembrance of several defeats to avenge and as he was this time on a higher plane than usual he proposed utilizing his position for all that it was worth. At the same time he was unwilling to let it go to a vote of the committee. Remembering his dubious conduct upon several occasions where corporations were concerned and the rumors of how he was controlled by them through their agents, who were his frequent companions, I used very strong language and reiterated my accusations. I was finally supported in my claims by a majority of the executive committee.[17]

[17] The occurred at a meeting of the executive committee on April 27, 1878. On May 4, 1878, Kearney held a meeting of his faction and received an endorsement for his radical proposal. A resolution was also passed calling for the resignation of those who had opposed

Next morning the citizens of San Francisco read a full report of the break in the Workingmen's Party. It was Sunday and on that morning I appeared before the county committee of the party and recounted the trouble and its causes. My action and that of the majority of the executive committee were approved and I was requested to appear in the afternoon on the sandlots and give a correct version of the affair.

Kearney branded a traitor—

There were a number of the frequenters of the sandlots who endorsed all that Kearney said or did whether it was right or wrong and who had the reputation of being not unwilling to resort to violence to attain their ends if violence was necessary. It was the first time that I had appeared on the sandlots and the situation was not especially inviting to me. However, I appeared at the open-air meeting, mounted the platform, and told Wellock that I was going to speak. He demurred at first, but agreed

his plan of action. Among those named as the enemies of the party was Frank Roney. The rebellious members of the executive committee then proceeded by vote to depose Kearney as the leader of the movement, and elected Roney as the chairman of the bolting faction.

This split in the Kearney forces led to the calling of two separate and antagonistic conventions of the Workingmen's Party on May 16, 1878, for the purpose of nominating delegates to the State Constitutional Convention. The anti-Kearney convention was presided over by Roney, and nominated delegates only for the First Congressional District. The Kearney convention nominated a full list of delegates. In the ensuing election, the anti-Kearney group was practically unheard of, but the Kearney faction elected fifty delegates.—Ed.

that I should follow Kearney. Kearney told the crowd that he had been assailed because he had wished to prevent office seekers from forcing themselves upon the party. He declared that it was necessary to guard against traitors and office seekers, as they were nearly always traitors. I followed and explained that a majority of the executive committee had differed from Kearney's opinion because it was deemed advisable to guard against a rising set of ignorant office seekers who were sure to be traitors. I then placed my hand on Kearney's shoulder and said, "If there be one traitor who is ahead of all the others it is this man. If you follow him you will rue that day and your party will accomplish nothing." Both addresses were received without mark of approval or dissent, and jumping from the platform into the midst of the crowd, which numbered about 10,000, I made my way to the street and never again visited the sandlots.

The county committee kept up its war against Kearney, but I had lost interest in the controversy. A fight against an individual was not to my liking. If the people were stupid or perverse enough to accept Kearney's utterances and actions the only thing to do under the circumstances was to let them continue to do so until they had become surfeited. The county committee nominated a list of delegates to the Constitutional Convention. One of those nominated was Henry George, the author of *Progress and Poverty*.

Kearney's spectacular tactics—

A daily paper was also projected, and to keep it going I was obliged to leave my work in the foundry in the endeavor to raise the necessary funds to keep it afloat. At one of the Sunday meetings, Kearney held a copy of it before the audience on the sandlots and said, "I hold before you a copy of a paper. Frank Roney got $3,000 from Peter Donahue to publish an attack on me and destroy our party. What will I do with it?" "Tear it up," cried one of the audience, and Kearney proceeded most dramatically to tear it to pieces. He was very fond of such little dramatic exhibitions. Bones, the Alameda County Senator, had not fulfilled his obligations as a Workingmen's legislator, and to impress the people with what should be done with him and to square himself with the people for having supported Bones, Kearney at one of the Sunday meetings flourished a piece of rope from which he declared the defaulting Senator and other backsliding officials should dangle as their just reward. Such actions and remarks charmed the audience immensely, and always produced riotous applause.

Delegates to State Constitutional Convention—

The election of many of the Kearney delegates to the Constitutional Convention[18] convinced me of the futility of attempting to bring about reforms

18 Out of 149 delegates elected by the voters to frame a new State Constitution, fifty were representatives of the Workingmen's Party of California.—Ed.

without the preliminary education of the voters. When I claimed that poverty, misery, distress, crime, and the innumerable other evils afflicting mankind were primarily due to the evil of land monopoly my good friends balked because they felt that the Chinese alone were to be blamed for the existing conditions. The members of the Workingmen's Party of California were interested solely in driving out the Mongolians. Antagonism to the Chinese was at no time relished by me. I could not feel that a mere war of race against race could be productive of permanent good to the working class which stood most in need of permanent benefit.

The staunchest members of the Workingmen's Party were the small property holders. And how lovingly that name was paraded! The party developed as being specially designed for their salvation. Real estate values were supposed to have been decreased because of the presence of the Chinese, when as a matter of fact they had actually increased and were increasing. The fellow without property was not considered, nor did he seem to want consideration. His hope was to be a small property holder at some time in the near future; consequently his sympathies were with the class to which he later hoped to belong. What the small property owners wanted was some method by means of which to secure higher rentals from the man who had no property but who was looking forward to the day when he would have it if high rents did not prevent him. And so it went.

The numerous and diverse interests, more or less at war with each other, precluded intelligent concentration upon any thought or idea other than that contained in Knight's slogan, "The Chinese must go," which Kearney had exploited and was still exploiting for all it was worth. Intelligent and beneficial measures were not to be considered, and they were not.

The Workingmen's delegates elected to the State Constitutional Convention were the poorest material that San Francisco could select to frame laws of any kind, much less to frame the basic law of the State. And a fine job they made of it! I was unqualifiedly opposed to the document which finally resulted from the deliberations of that body, but refused publicly to go out against it because of the combination of those who opposed it and also for other reasons. The San Francisco *Morning Chronicle* was the most able paper which fought for the new constitution. The subsequent adoption of the latter by the voters was considered a great victory for the Workingmen's Party, but it proved to be no victory at all.[19]

At the next election,[20] Wm. F. White, Kearney's choice, ran for governor on the Workingmen's ticket and received about 44,000 votes, enough to defeat Dr. H. G. Glenn, the Democratic candidate, and to elect Geo. C. Perkins, a Republican. In the San

19 At the election, May 7, 1879, the new constitution was adopted by a vote of 77,959 to 67,134.—Ed.

20 The election referred to occurred in September, 1879.—Ed.

Francisco city election,[21] Rev. I. S. Kalloch, a Baptist preacher, was elected Mayor on the Workingmen's Party ticket. All the city officials except the supervisors were also elected from the same party. The corporations did not want a Workingmen's Party Board of Supervisors, and the political bosses carried through their wishes most successfully.

San Francisco's political bosses—

It took from Tuesday night, the day of election, to the following Saturday to count the ballots cast for the supervisors of San Francisco. This state of affairs was brought about in this way: Bill Higgins, the Republican boss, controlled about one-half of the election boards in each of the precincts in San Francisco. The Workingmen's Party was supposed to control the remainder. Chris Buckley, who had for years been the Republican boss in Vallejo, dispensing the patronage at the Mare Island Navy Yard, noted that John Mannix and Owen Brady, the Democratic bosses in San Francisco, had lost their power, and concluded to try his chances for the Democratic boss-ship. At the party primary he found himself opposed by Captain Al Fritz. To beat Fritz it was necessary to draw into his (Buckley's) camp as many of the leading Workingmen as possible. Fritz had made himself obnoxious to the Workingmen by threatening on one occasion to direct his military company with their Gatling guns to fire upon them.

[21] This election occurred on September 3, 1879.—Ed.

The leading Workingmen were then and always had been Democrats, so that it was an easy matter for Buckley to secure their cooperation. Jim Flynn was the most powerful member of the local Democratic party. He was its secretary. Flynn willingly used every means at his command to defeat Fritz and to elect the Buckley delegates to the Democratic County Convention. Buckley, in addition to his own party quota on the precinct election boards, also largely controlled the make-believe Workingmen's representatives. Higgins and Buckley, thus controlling a clear majority of efficient workers in nearly all the precincts, directed the counting of the votes so that it was not possible to secure a majority for any Workingmen's candidate. So long as the offices with patronage went to the Workingmen's candidates the bosses of the Workingmen's Party were satisfied to let anybody have the supervisorial offices which had no patronage. The corporations, however, were not interested in patronage; their interests lay in controlling the supervisors. It was a glaringly disgraceful proceeding and so well executed that no attempt was made to rectify it. It is doubtful if sufficient evidence could have been obtained to prove the fraud. The citizens accepted the result without a murmur and all sides appeared pleased.

From that moment the decadence of the Workingmen's Party began. In two short years it had become a fast-fading memory. It left its impress for years afterwards in having produced during its brief existence an inferior and more numerous class of political bosses and blacklegs than had been produced in all the preceding history of the city.

De Young shot by Kalloch—

The shooting of Reverend I. S. Kalloch by Charles De Young contributed largely to the success of the Workingmen's candidates for city office in San Francisco. Kalloch was a fluent and forceful speaker, and early in the formation of the party devoted his Sunday evening addresses to its defense. Metropolitan Temple on Fifth Street, where he held his services, was both commodious and centrally located and proved to be the most popular resort in San Francisco at the time. It was usually crowded much beyond its seating capacity while the preacher thundered and the audience shook the building with applause. He became the most popular man in the party and was nominated for mayor.

Charles De Young of the *Morning Chronicle,* believing that his paper was still the official organ of the party, warned against Kalloch's election. De Young had a candidate for mayor whom he could control, and he knew that he could not control Kalloch. In order to make Kalloch's election impossible, De Young began to attack the former on grounds of morality, quoting certain episodes beginning in Boston, continuing in Kansas City, and winding up in San Francisco. Kalloch, who was a courageous man, warned De Young that if he continued his scandalous statements he (Kalloch) would reply and assail De Young's parentage. De Young, in no way daunted, went ahead with his exposé, which drew from Kalloch a terrifying history of the De Young family. De Young engaged a carriage one afternoon[22] and with the blinds drawn drove to the Metropolitan Temple at an hour when he knew that Kalloch would be there. He sent a messenger to the preacher with the statement that a lady in a carriage wished to see him. When Kalloch came out to the carriage De Young raised the blind and fired, seriously but not fatally wounding Kalloch. That shot made Kalloch mayor of San Francisco and aided in the election of other candidates of the Workingmen's Party. During Kalloch's term as mayor his son shot and killed De Young in the *Morning Chronicle* office.[23] Both were tried for their respective shootings and through the miscarriage of justice both were acquitted.

At about the time that young Kalloch killed De Young, Kearney was making a desperate effort to revive interest in the Workingmen's Party. The Socialist agitation was taking deep root among the workers and the mere agitation against the Chinese was yielding to something bigger and broader. The Representative Assembly of Trades and Labor Unions, which my resolution adopted by the State

[22] August 23, 1879.—Ed.

[23] De Young was killed on April 23, 1880.—Ed.

Convention of the Workingmen's Party had called into existence, was making fair headway in weaning trade unionists from Kearney's standard. In order to destroy the defection and to bring the discordant elements again under his banner, Kearney changed his tactics. In one of his speeches he denounced Claus Spreckels as a labor thief and was arrested. Because he did not know how to prove his charge he was convicted and sentenced to six months' imprisonment in the House of Correction.[24]

Exultation of the mob—

The socialists knew Kearney's object in reviving his agitation and how opposed he was to anything other than "The Chinese must go." Nevertheless, since he had made a blind stagger in their direction it was decided to hold a mass meeting to protest against his imprisonment. Accordingly a meeting in the interest of "Citizen Kearney" was announced to be held in Irish-American Hall. The hall was filled to suffocation and the crowd overflowed to the adjacent streets. As the meeting neared its close a messenger informed me of the De Young tragedy. When the chairman arose to dismiss the meeting I told him to make the announcement of De Young's death.

I hope never again to witness so fiendish an exhibition of exultation as I saw that night. It

[24] Kearney was arrested on March 11, 1880. The sentence of the lower court was appealed, and on May 27, 1880, the State Supreme Court reversed the decision and freed Kearney.—Ed.

paralyzed me beyond anything that I had ever experienced. Women waved their handkerchiefs, men yelled and cheered and yelled and cheered again as if some great, unexpected benefit had been conferred upon them. To rejoice as these people did at the sudden, untimely murder of a human being betokened a low grade of mentality and impressed me with the impossibility of the task of raising them to a full comprehension of their duty to their fellow-men and of the equities due to themselves. It seemed to me that any people who could exult at such a deed were little better than uncivilized. Christians they all considered themselves and they doubtless boasted of being civilized, yet they were without any instinct of charity and failed to show any characteristics denoting their superiority over the savage. The exhibition horrified and appalled me. Poor, ignorant, brutal, merciless human nature, and yet in all its cruelty the crowd had gathered to sympathize with Kearney over his imprisonment resulting from his ignorance. But they gave sympathy fully and freely to Kearney, whose only title to consideration was the memory of the hatred which he had instilled in them against another race. Only a short while before the man who lay murdered had been the inspirer of the man against whose imprisonment they had met to protest. De Young was practically their leader for he led the leader whom they acknowledged. Selfish, domineering, and ambitious, possessed of stupendous energy and great executive ability, but without scruples or a high ideal of public or private morality, the one aim of Charles De Young was to make his paper, the *Chronicle,* the arbiter and mouthpiece of California and thus permit him to shape the destiny and direct the policies of the state.

The Workingmen's Party evolved others like De Young and with like pretensions, but with possibly a finer sense of what was due to the people. These were the obstructionists in the way of De Young in his march toward his goal and he felt that they had to be put out of the way. De Young shot Kalloch in a cowardly, treacherous way, trusting to the grip that he had upon many of the leading men in the city and the influence of his paper to get out of the difficulty. Then came nemesis in bolder form than had been anticipated, and De Young's ambitions died with his body. It was unfortunate for San Francisco that she ever had a De Young or a Kalloch. Neither were citizens of the type needed to infuse the citizens of a growing city with the civic pride of accomplishing results by the slow, patient but enduring methods of unselfishness, fairness, and a recognition of the fundamental law of *meuum et tuum.* They were the children, the outcroppings of an earlier spirit of greed and semi-outlawry which to some extent still permeates California.

Discharged—

On the evening preceding the election of delegates to the Constitutional Convention[25] a mass meeting was held at the corner of First and Mission streets, the site of the Union Iron Works where I was employed. The chairman of the meeting was a man named Rooney. It was well-known that Irving M. Scott, the managing partner of the concern, was opposed to the idea of a new state constitution and had acquired the reputation of being an enemy of every measure tending to improve the social and economic condition of the working class. Rooney held the meeting to spite Scott and lost no opportunity to denounce him in most acrimonious terms. I had been absent from work for several days campaigning against the proposal to call a constitutional convention. Upon appearing for work the day after the balloting had taken place and the delegates to the constitutional convention had been chosen, Mr. Dimmick, the foreman, informed me that my services were no longer needed, giving as his reason the receipt of orders from the office because of the meeting held by Rooney. The discharge was followed up as I subsequently learned by a personal canvass of all the local foundries against my employment.

The situation was most embarrassing. Every business was depressed. The gates of all the foundries were closed and locked against me. With a

[25] The election took place on June. 19, 1878.—Ed.

small, young, helpless family and up to my neck in debt, owing to my frequent absences from work and to my having freely spent the little money that I had in carrying on the fight, all combined to make my situation decidedly unenviable. The irony of it was enhanced by the knowledge that although on the same side as Scott my opposition to the idea of a new state constitution was based on the belief that no constitution could be sweeping enough to benefit the poor man, while Scott's opposition was due to his belief that it would give the poor man too much. Inasmuch as no other person with my name or any name similar to it had taken part in the agitation of the Workingmen's Party, the holding of a meeting by a man with a name so similar to mine had led Scott to think that I was the party involved. I solicited no sympathy or aid from any one and tried to act as though I were a man free from pressing need.

Through the Odd Fellows' Employment Bureau, of which order I was then a member in good standing, I secured a temporary job for two weeks shovelling coal on one of the wharves. What made the job harder was that a small, physically weak member of the Order secured employment alongside of me at the same time. Through positive hunger he was unable to do his share of the work and would have been obliged, much as he needed the money, to give it up had I not braced him with the assurance that I would do the work for both of us or at least as much of it as I could. Fortunately, we had a very decent man, named Brady, for a foreman. When I told him of my partner's plight he immediately gave him a meal ticket and sent him off to a restaurant. Brady did this in such a whole-hearted, generous and inoffensive way that although I have never seen him since that day I have always remembered him as a gentleman of fine nature.

A job in Nevada—

Dimmick, the Union Iron Works foreman, learning that a man was needed at the foundry of the Meadow Valley Mill and Mining Company at Dry Valley near Pioche, Nevada, sent for me and asked if I would take the job. I promptly said that I would provided I could obtain the funds to get to the place, for the fare was $100. He gave me the money and two days later I was on my way to southern Nevada. To leave my family penniless was more than I wished to do, but in my straitened circumstances I called upon Henry Paulsen, a German grocer in the neighborhood, who assured me that during my absence they would not want for anything that money could buy. Mr. Paulsen and his wife fulfilled their voluntary obligation in a kind and generous manner.

When James Ryan, who had charge of the mechanical department of my new employers, saw that I was an experienced moulder he made my wages $6 per day instead of $5, the amount that I had agreed to accept. Cost of living was very high, yet in the three months that I was there I sent more than $300 to my wife. I regretted leaving Dry Valley and need not have done so but for my determination to be loyal to my fellow-workingmen. An order had come from the San Francisco office of the company to reduce the wages of all mechanics $1 per day. A meeting was held by the mechanics and all agreed to strike against the announced reduction. After I left I learned that they all resumed work at the lower wages.

Workingmen's delegates—

On my way back to San Francisco I stopped for two days at Sacramento to see how the Workingmen's representatives were getting along in shaping the new constitution. As members of the Convention they sat in their places and voted for the adoption or rejection of clauses as they were directed. Only two of their number, Clitus Barbour and Charles Beerstecher, both lawyers, were distinguished from the general dumbness prevalent among them. The first named was an able and honest man; the other had come to the State at an opportune time, found his place on the platform at the sandlots, had a good, loud, pleasant voice, and used it by uttering platitudes pleasing to his audience while expressing himself on the horrid Chinese incubus. Beerstecher was clearly a politician seeking office by any method, and as he was without legal practice he hoped to attain a fortune, which he later did.[26] The majority of the remainder of the Workingmen's delegates studied fundamental law and what was best for their constituents in near-by saloons and played cards with a nourishing glass of foam-topped beer near by.

And this was the result of so much honest effort on the part of the people hoping for reform! The worst brand of standpat, corporation-ridden politician would have made a better showing than this primitive band of fake reformers. But then they were as good in all respects as those who sent them there, a river being no higher than its source.

Upon reaching San Francisco I experienced no difficulty in getting work in the Union Iron Works. Business was brisk everywhere and Dimmick, my old foreman, appeared to have a kindly feeling toward me.

[26] Beerstecher was elected on the Workingmen's Party ticket to the State Railroad Commission. He had never been a man of wealth but in some unexplained manner, during his term as Railroad Commissioner, he acquired a fortune estimated by some at about $27,000. He announced that he had obtained it from the estate of his deceased parents. A few years later, however, the latter arrived from Germany and took up their residence with him. "The charge is made that the Central Pacific Railroad bought and paid for Beerstecher's services while a member of the Railroad Commission. . . . . The evidence in the case is purely circumstantial, but seems convincing."—Stuart Daggett, *Some Chapters on the History of the Southern Pacific Railway*, p. 194.—Ed.

V

A LEADER IN THE CAUSE OF LABOR

V

A LEADER IN THE CAUSE OF LABOR

The Socialist Party was struggling to be understood and as far as its members could do the work, being largely German, they were doing it very slowly. The area of their endeavor was limited to the space occupied by the Humboldt Saloon, located in a cellar at the corner of Morton and Kearney streets. At a convention held in Patterson, New Jersey, about two years previously, the name "Workingmen's Party of the United States" had been abandoned and that of "Socialist Party" had been adopted. The movement was peculiarly German. Socialism was presumed to be exclusively and especially German in character, having its origin in Germany where, in was thought, the only true and unadulterated Socialism could be found.

A member of the Socialist Party—

I was much taken with the principles of Socialism, believing them to be the means of abolishing poverty and bringing about the social and moral uplifting of humanity to the plane designed by the Creator. I never could believe that God's design was to have one portion of His creatures live in an atmosphere of luxury upon the sweat and blood and toil of another and larger portion of humanity. I never believed that it was His intention that widespread misery and want should stalk throughout the land, and that only a few, the wealthy, should be exempt. I felt that injustice should be abolished, that equity should prevail, that the incentives to crime should stop, and that men should live in harmony to fulfill God's will. Socialism appeared to hold open the door for this happy result, and I resolved to enter it and strive for that end. I joined the Socialist Party with the ardent determination of making it the most potent agency for at least the amelioration of our many evils, if not for their eradication. Other English-speaking citizens became members and a vigorous campaign was begun which lasted for several years.

I never had so much genuine pleasure in any enterprise as I had with my German and English associates in spreading the socialist propaganda. Most of them are gone and forgotten, but the memory of them and their work remains with me as clear as when they endeavored night after night to arouse the people to an appreciation of their condition and the means by which to better their lot. Among the many the following were the accepted leaders: Thomas F. Hagerty, a mechanical engineer of excellent ability and an uncompromising socialist; S. R. Wilson, originally an Irish school teacher, a profound thinker, an eloquent and forceful speaker, and

T. F. Hagerty

John P. Devereux

a man of unimpeachable integrity; Wm. Herbert, a cooper, a partner of John Vogel, and a good exponent of the Cause; C. F. Burgman, a tailor and the son-in-law of Helen Wilmans, a sincere and enthusiastic propagandist; Edward Fair, a bricklayer; A. J. Starkweather, John Klaus, and William Rottermund, all good Socialists of fine character.

Great as was the ability of each of these men, without election or appointment they invariably complied with every suggestion that I made both as to the manner of their speeches and where to deliver them. Their confidence in my judgment and direction was as unqualified as it was gratifying. I had no axe to grind or personal ambition to serve and I strove to do my part of the work with the same fidelity that they did theirs. Not one of us showed at any time a disposition to be in the least ahead of the others. We were, I must say, an exceptionally harmonious group of associates.

Prison reform convention—

It was customary to hold an annual state convention of officials concerned with jails and prisons to consider the best means of handling prisoners sentenced to long terms. The personnel of these conventions was made up of wardens and ex-wardens, sheriffs, chiefs of police, district attorneys, and all those engaged officially in the repression of crime or in the care and management of prisoners. The motive actuating the managers of these conventions was, I believe, a humane one, but when it came to an actual expression of the sentiment of the majority upon some resolution that might prove advantageous to the prisoners and of relative benefit to the public, it was invariably voted down. Nothing practical that I could see had ever resulted from those meetings.

One of the managers, for a reason not apparent, sent me an invitation to attend the annual convention to be held in San Francisco. I believed that Hagerty and Wilson both desired to attend, and I really thought them better qualified to do so. Accordingly I made out credentials for them and they attended every session and voted on every action of importance. On the last day of the convention a resolution was offered recommending that the Legislature modify, in some way that I do not recollect, the treatment of prisoners in the penitentiary. It met with a sturdy opposition from wardens and those who had had any official relations with those institutions at any time. Leniency to prisoners was considered so unorthodox by those in attendance at the convention that the resolution was sneered at most contemptuously. Hagerty, who up to that time had remained silent, took the floor and scored State prison officials as being worse than the criminals they had charge of. He made every member of the convention take special notice of his remarks which lasted about twenty minutes. When he resumed his seat he was applauded to the echo by the audience, but not by the delegates.

Wilson, more argumentative and philosophic than Hagerty, and possessed of ability and diction to which the delegates were not accustomed, reviewed the work of the convention as so much time wasted on absurdities and phantasies of no practical benefit to prisoners nor in the least elevating to the delegates. Prisoners were human beings, a fact so potent that he was surprised to find that officials could ignore it. If prisoners became refractory it was generally because their innate sense of justice had been outraged by the men whom the law had placed in charge. Society in the majority of instances made criminals out of men and women who under proper living conditions would have proved themselves superior to the majority of those whom he was addressing. He concluded with the statement that

> Once branded as a felon, you torture and persecute and punish him, goading him into a state of frenzied criminality that he concludes is his normal state. You turn him loose upon the expiration of his term, and rather than extend to him a helping hand you follow him relentlessly, depriving him of every opportunity to better himself, until driven at bay in sheer desperation he commits another crime and then you point to him as irreclaimable. Your convention is a farce and all here taking part in it are weak fools, pretending to benefit society and prisoners by bolstering up a rotten condition that we are too stupid or too criminal to understand.

Wilson's remarks also evoked thunderous applause. That was the last meeting of such annual conventions to be held in San Francisco or California.

Socialists and the detectives—

The Tenth Ward Workingmen's Club continued its meetings in the basement at the corner of Fourth and Mission streets. I proposed that our socialist speakers should, so far as they could do so without causing friction or unnecessary alarm, address the club, whose meetings were well attended. This proved a success. The word "socialist" was never used, nor did any of the socialists show an eagerness for office, which therefore made them unobjectionable to the politicians of the party who still hoped to land a "fat" job. The word "socialist" was synonymous with murder, arson, destruction, and the other delectable terms attributed to radical reformers. Consequently we were careful not to use a word which would deprive us of our audiences. The land for the people and the abolition of land monopoly, then so firmly rooted and protected in California, was our theme.

At our meetings we were usually favored by the attendance of two detectives, Messrs. Bee and Harper. Neither supposed that we were aware of their being detectives. So they mingled with the crowd and passed muster as good socialists. I nearly always presided at the public meetings, having become a sort of professional chairman. At a meeting called in a hall on New Montgomery Street all the seats were occupied when our two detectives arrived. Noticing them standing at the door and concluding that it was time to let the audience know who they were, I requested two men occupying front seats to vacate them so as to enable our friends, the detectives, to hear better as they had reports of the proceedings to make to their superior officers, which reports had to be as complete as possible. The men left the seats but I could not prevail upon Bee and Harper to take them, notwithstanding all my coaxing. I succeeded in pointing them out, however, thus destroying their usefulness as police agents, and that was the last of them.

A man named Maurice Carey, one of the earliest trainers of the Chinese in Buckingham & Hecht's boot and shoe factory, but who, upon his discharge, became their intense foe, suggested to me that something of a threatening character should be done to scare the employers into discharging the Chinese. I received the proposition as a joke and, knowing the man to be a rank physical and moral coward, asked him how it was to be done. Being a man of imagination he suggested the posting of a handwritten proclamation at the entrance of all the local churches, signed by "The Council of Thirteen." After a great deal of discussion with Carey, I at last consented to write the proclamation and also agreed to have them posted.

Every night following the murder of De Young by young Kalloch, the basement occupied by the Tenth Ward Club was packed. I was afraid police agents would be around to incite violence so as to redeem themselves for their many previous discomfitures, and sure enough they were there, happily at first without plans. I became acquainted at once with Charley Moore and George Morton, the two *mouchards* first to appear, and I pretended to take seriously all that they said and in turn gave them, as they thought, my confidence. When I had prepared the proclamation of "The Council of Thirteen" and had purchased the paste with which to stick them up, I had them brought to the basement headquarters of the Socialist Party. I then detailed Moore and Morton to the task of putting up the sheets, instructing them at what churches they were to be posted. They demurred to this, but I insisted that this was their job, and that if they did not do it they were no longer needed in our ranks. I further cautioned them that they would be watched to see that they did the work as ordered. Having sent them on their way I destroyed the remainder of the stuff so that they were the only persons to post the proclamation, and I had them watched by two reliable citizens. Moore later stuck to me like a leech, making various proposals to commit violence.

An organizer of the Knights of Labor—

The first Assembly of the Knights of Labor organized in California was established in Sacramento.[1] It was then a strictly secret society and so enveloped in mystery that it partook of a strong revolutionary aspect. One of the Sacramento members was commissioned to visit me, and in case I became a member to constitute me organizer for San Francisco. I met the gentleman on Market Street and under pledge of secrecy he explained to me the working of the order, its profound secrecy and its revolutionary aims.

All radical movements were necessarily supposed to be revolutionary. There are two kinds of revolution, physical and moral. If the movement is moral it means education. Since education concerning economic questions can be given only to a limited extent in schools, and since numbers are needed to effect a revolution, it is necessary to carry on the education of the masses through the agency of intelligent, open agitation which destroys the necessity of secrecy. If the revolution is to be a physical one, numbers are required to make it a success. In spending the time required to organize an army a good part of it must be devoted to explaining the whys and wherefores of the revolution. When the numbers needed for success have been gathered together and educated as to the reasons for the revolt, then to resort to force would be criminal

[1] This occurred sometime during 1878.—Ed.

because those numbers could accomplish the avowed purposes of their organization at the ballot box. Also during the period of organization traitors must be contended against and the enthusiastic must be held in check to prevent premature demonstrations. That was about the way I reasoned out the matter.

When I was told that the revolution was to be physical I resolved to join the Knights of Labor so as to prevent anyone else becoming the local organizer. I took the obligation of membership, was commissioned organizer for the San Francisco district, and for at least two years was able to prevent the introduction of the order into San Francisco. When the first local assembly of the organization was founded in San Francisco, it came about through the delegates of the Workingmen's Party who had joined it in Sacramento while in attendance at the constitutional convention. It was they who established Local Assembly 1390 of the Knights of Labor in San Francisco. In the meantime the character of the organization had changed, and it had ceased being so profoundly secret as well as so revolutionary.

Socialism and trade unionism—

Attending meetings every night in some part of the city enlarged my acquaintance, and gave me the opportunity of learning to what extent the people felt themselves aggrieved by the impositions of government and the manner of their relief. It was only on rare occasions that I met any one who had any conception of his position as a citizen or a consciousness of how his position could be improved. A universal chaos of ideas prevailed, and yet all desired something different from what existed. Some believed that force provided the only direct and speedy remedy, but the force needed must be the work of others, not of the proposers. Others were content with present conditions provided a little improvement could be obtained. All agreed that their environment did not permit the realization of their aspirations. A few believed in trying by propaganda to induce the workers to recognize as wrong many of those abuses which had existed for so long that they had become recognized legally and morally as the normal conditions. By remedying those wrongs a sympathy would be created among all the workers, thus eventually terminating in partial or permanent relief for all.

I was fairly well informed of the disabilities under which most working people labored, and I knew that if amelioration or improvement was desired it must come through the organization of the workers and the intelligent and determined presentation of the demand for the removal of abuses. It was evident that my association with the socialists was leading me back to my earlier ideas of the best means of obtaining improved conditions through trade union autonomy and later by concentration of the forces of Labor. Socialists did not approve of trade unions and many do not now approve of them. They regarded them as only pseudo agencies for the attainment of benefits for the workers. Socialists denounced them because by the limitation of their demands they obscured the view and retarded the progress that would otherwise be made in the realization of Universal Cooperation in the production and distribution of the products of Labor. Considering the educational deficiencies of the great bulk of the working people and their scanty opportunities for studying the problems of economic science involved in socialistic demonstrations, trades unionism is the best and most productive means of immediately gaining improved conditions and of educating the workers to the standard set by the socialists. These were my opinions then and they are still my opinions.

The English-speaking socialists accepted my definition of our relation to trade unionism and saw in it a greater opportunity for disseminating their views, inasmuch as each trade union was a permanent organization and always afforded a regular audience. The German socialists would have nothing to do with my plan, simply disapproving of it for the reasons which I have mentioned above.

Organizing the sailors—

A man named Devereux,[2] who had been a deep-water sailor for many years, kept telling me of the many injustices to which that class of toilers was

[2] John P. Devereux.—Ed.

subjected. The men in the coast-wise trade were also the victims of many abuses. So harrowing were his repeated recitals that I finally resolved to effect an organization of seafaring men and endeavor to mitigate and eventually and effectually to destroy every existing wrong. Accompanied by Devereux and two or three others I went to the water front of San Francisco and began a campaign of organization among all branches of the coast-wise seamen. I kept this up for several weeks assisted by some of my close friends, and succeeded in securing a membership of about 300 sailors, firemen, cooks, and waiters. Permanent organization was effected in a temporary building owned by the Democratic Party of the district and loaned to us for this purpose, situated at the corner of Third and Silver streets. We called our organization "The Seamen's Protective Association," and I became its president, Wilson its secretary, and McAvoy its treasurer. Hagerty, Starkweather, Pygeorge, Steinman, and Devereux, with the three officers mentioned, formed the executive committee.[3]

Between meetings for recruiting purposes I kept the agitation going upon the water front, varying

[3] The Seamen's Protective Association was the third attempt on the part of the sailors to organize a union. "The Seamen's Friendly Union and Protective Society" had been formed in January, 1866, and lasted for about four months. "The Seamen's Protective Union" resulted from a meeting of sailors held on January 31, 1879. In three months it had a membership of 600, but it passed away in about half a year. Roney gives to us the most complete story of the Seamen's Protective Association that has thus far appeared.—Ed.

the place of gathering according to the location of the ships in port. It was very tiring and an immense tax upon me physically, for I was working as a moulder frequently from 5 A.M. till at least 6 P.M.

Opposition of water front boarding-house keepers—

The boarding-house keepers on the water front began to discover that if the organization of the sailors and our agitation continued it meant death to most of their practices in enslaving the sailor. They thought that if they could stop it by scaring me some advantage would accrue to them. At a gathering on Stuart Street opposite the boarding house of a notorious shanghaier named Curtin, at which but few of our members were present, I was assaulted with a volley of antiquated eggs, one of which struck me squarely on the breast. I jumped off the hay wagon that I was using as a platform and dashed at the crowd before Curtin's, which immediately sought protection within the house, where they remained during the rest of our meeting. It was a cowardly act of contemptible cowards.[4]

[4] This incident occurred at a meeting held on September 28, 1880. The following statement taken from the minute book of the union, to which I had access several years ago through the courtesy of J. P. Devereux, is of interest in this connection:

"During the meeting there were continuous interruptions by the boarding-house sharks and their whiskey-bought bummers, going even so far as to throw valuable eggs, that did not have time to get the proper age and odor, at the agitators; but they made a bad failure, for the superior intelligence and calmness of the speakers entirely discomfited their enemies."—Ed.

The proceedings of all our meetings were published in the morning papers. I wrote the reports for each of the morning papers before going home, which was always at a late hour. The treatment accorded sailors on the high seas, which I always mentioned in my newspaper articles, began to draw the attention and condemnation of the public.

Commissioner O'Brien ousted—

A captain was arrested for some offense committed against his men and was brought before United States Shipping Commissioner O'Brien. Any person of ordinary mind, even though indifferent, would have pronounced him guilty. I was certain from the testimony given that he would be held for trial. To our astonishment he was discharged. I resolved to punish Commissioner O'Brien in the way that I knew would be most effective. I framed a resolution condemning him and his act in freeing the brutal captain, and as political clubs were running full speed because an election was at hand, I visited several of these organizations every night, presented the resolution, and said a few words asking its adoption, which was invariably complied with. The papers of the next day would then carry the story that United States Shipping Commissioner O'Brien, in flagrant violation of conclusive evidence of guilt and of every sentiment of justice and decency, had discharged a certain captain arraigned before him for offenses of a grave character committed against his men when upon the high seas. Morning after morning for several weeks this resolution appeared as part of the proceedings of both Democratic and Republican clubs. The result was that he was discharged from the position. Years afterwards when he had become the attorney for Senator Jerry Mahoney's detective agency I became acquainted with him. He attributed all of his subsequent misfortunes to that resolution and declared that he had discharged the captain out of pure good nature and because of the customary unreliability of seamen's testimony, and not from corrupt motives. I believe that he was truthful in that statement.

Shanghaiing of sailors—

Boarding-house crimps were ever on the lookout for unsuspecting young men along the water front in order to inveigle them into signing as sailors and shipping on a long voyage. One Sunday I read a lengthy and startling detailed account in the newspaper dealing with the entrapping of a young fellow named Flower, from Wheeling, West Virginia, who had never seen the sea or salt water until he arrived in San Francisco, and who was then in the County Jail by order of Justice of the Peace Ryan awaiting the order of the captain with whom he had signed for a voyage to England. Shanghaiing and tricks of that kind were regularly and frequently played upon the unwary especially when a scarcity of sailors existed. The boarding-house bosses always made handsomely out of this traffic, for in addition to the exorbitant charges for board and lodging and drinks, deducted from the man's pay in advance before the ship left port, they were paid a sum called "blood money" for each man secured and delivered on board the vessel.

I went to the County Jail to see the young man and to find out if I could be of any assistance to him. His story was that when wandering aimlessly along the water front he met a pleasantly spoken man to whom he said that he was a stranger in California without friends, relatives, or money and that he needed work immediately. The sympathetic stranger inquired if work in a hotel would suit, and if so stated that he thought he could get him a job. Any job at anything was to the young man a clear Godsend. He went happily along with his newly found friend who conducted him to a sailor boarding house. Soon he was escorted to the employment office, or rather the Shipping Commissioner's office, where he was introduced to the captain posing as the hotel keeper. He eagerly agreed to the proposed terms to await the hour when he would be taken to the boat, as the hotel was up the coast and only to be reached by water. Happy and confident he awaited the hour of his departure when luckily for him a man sitting beside him asked the name of the ship for which he had signed as a sailor. To his consternation he learned the exact situation, and walking to the door made a break for his liberty just at the time when the crimp, who had impressed him, made his appearance. The crimp followed calling upon him to stop, but the louder he was called the harder he ran. Then the crimp raised the cry of "Stop thief," and a policeman arrested him. The crimp charged that he was a deserting sailor, whereupon the policeman conducted him to Judge Ryan's court room and thence to the jail to be held pending the captain's order to be taken on board. I proposed to release Flower by habeas corpus proceedings. It took me all day to find a Superior Court Judge to issue the writ, and I was about to give up the effort when I ran against Judge Edmunds, who at once handed me the order to serve on the sheriff. I found the under-sheriff at 11:00 P.M. in a saloon and then at that late hour found an able lawyer in Mr. P. J. Morgan, who undertook the case without fee or the promise of fee or reward. In the morning after hearing Mr. Morgan's statement the Judge discharged the prisoner without waiting for the remarks of Senator Davis McClure, the attorney for the boarding house keeper.

The deputy sheriff being a friend of mine, and perhaps not knowing his duty, surrendered the prisoner to me without receiving the order of court, and I then turned Flower over to Simeon Stetson, whom I instructed to take him to my house. Mr. J. M. Days, clerk of the court, observing the irregularity of the young man's discharge, hurriedly made out the order which I handed to the deputy sheriff a moment before a United States Marshal entered the court with a warrant for his arrest. When asked what I had done with the prisoner I simply said that he had left the court a moment earlier and that I supposed that he had gone to his previous lodgings on Pacific Street, but where he was at that moment I did not know, which was all literally true.

I made arrangements with Mr. John Munroe on Brannan Street to keep the boy, fearing the issuance of a search warrant. No search was made; the only alarming thing that resulted was the threat of Colonel Stevenson, the shipping commissioner, who declared that he would later "fix" me for interfering with what he termed "his business." I kept Flower for three weeks closely hidden at Munroe's, and my wife bought him shirts, socks, and underclothes, of which he had not a vestige at that time. I gave him enough money to carry him to Stockton where he got work, also got drunk, and got into a fracas of some sort. He appealed to me to get him out of it, and I suppose that I would have tried to do so had I been near him. I should never have regretted the time sacrificed and the expense incurred if Flower had shown any appreciation for what I had done for him by simply behaving himself.

Evidences of sailors' gratitude—

I was urged repeatedly to give up my trade as a moulder and open a cigar store and news stand on the water front. It was most necessary that I do so if I desired to see the Seamen's Protective Association live and be of service to the men for whom it had been organized. On the other hand I had a decided repugnance to being dependent upon or a beneficiary of the sailors who earned such small wages at such great risks and so very laboriously. Consequently, I refused to open the store as suggested. I had no desire to be beholden to those whom I wished to serve. The sailors felt themselves indebted to me and wished to reciprocate in a measure by presenting me with a gold watch. One of the men engaged in collecting the fund for this purpose confidentially informed me what was afoot. I told him to have the money returned to the donors as I did not want them to give me the watch and furthermore that I would accept nothing from them.

Instead of going to the water front to sell cigars and tobacco and thus keep more closely in touch with the seamen's union I appointed one of the sailors, John P. Devereux, as agent of the union at the munificent salary of $5 per week. I also appointed two other agents, John Pygeorge and a friend by the name of Steinman, who alternated with Devereux, all honest, sincere, active, energetic men and wholly reliable in all things. I hoped by that means to keep in close touch with all that was going on along the water front and at the same time attend to my increasing duties arising out of my connection with other organizations. It was very hard exacting work, work that is entirely forgotten, not the shadow of a remembrance remains of it or of my connection with it. At the time it appeared to me to be very necessary and important, and it kept me under a high-pressure strain.

Aiding British sailors—

Shortly after the organization of the Seaman's Protective Association one of the agents brought a number of sailors to my house. They had left a British vessel at Wilmington, now Port of Los Angeles, because of the ill treatment which they had received at the hands of the captain on their voyage to San Francisco. I believe that they left the ship at Wilmington with the intention of making their complaint to the British Consul at Los Angeles. At the time there was either no Vice-Consul at Los Angeles or if there was they could not find him, and knowing that if their complaint was not filed before the expiration of the time permitting absence from ship without leave they would be in the position of deserters to be dealt with, if captured, according to British law as administered by the Consul, they came on to San Francisco to lay their case before the Consul at this port. They arrived within the time specified by law exempting them from desertion but the next day was a holiday, Thanksgiving Day if I remember correctly, and then they could be jailed as deserters and held pending the captain's orders to re-ship them on the homeward voyage without redress and possibly with loss of pay. To me they seemed to be above the average deep-sea sailor both in intelligence and outward appearance, and were, I thought, fully conscious of the dangers of their position.

I hardly knew what to do for the men. I had them sit down and calmly talk the matter over with me so that I could fully understand the situation and perhaps, during the conversation, discover a way out of the difficulty. I wrote out each man's complaint against the captain and the other officers of the ship and had them sign the statement. I agreed to meet them near the Consul's office the next morning. It seemed a hopeless case, but I was resolved to play a big bluff. We went to the Consul's office the next morning and had some difficulty in arousing a clerk who slept in the office. Keeping the door ajar he impatiently listened to my story and as the day was a holiday instructed me to appear the following morning. I believed that an American holiday was no cause for delaying the enforcement of British law, so I forced my way into the office and insisted that he should receive the complaints of the men. British officials, like all officials of every country, then looked upon sailors as creatures unworthy of consideration. British law requires that seamen in foreign ports are to be treated justly and with consideration, but the officials, assuming the men to be ignorant and accustomed to harsh treatment, both upon shore and sea, looked upon them superciliously and paid little heed to their complaints.

This clerk was about the most self-sufficient, arrogant, little monster of a British official that I had ever met. He refused, after a long parley, to receive the documents. "Well," said I, "this office is British territory and you are the only visible representative of the Queen of England that I can see around here. These men are British seamen, mistreated upon the ocean, who come to you for protection and justice. I won't take your refusal of this document. I will leave it here in the presence of these witnesses at this hour which is within the time limit when they would become deserters, and I will be here tomorrow morning at this hour and see what your masters think of your behavior and this case." Next morning I appeared with the men at the Consul's office and was told that the complaint had been filed within the time allowed and that as soon as the ship came into port a hearing would be held. The result was that the captain was fined and censured by the Consul, and all the sailors were exonerated.

Another shanghaiing case—

Steinman also brought to me a poor fellow who had shipped at Cardiff upon an American vessel. When the boat arrived in San Francisco, the sailor found himself in debt to the ship instead of having any pay coming to him. Not having an adequate supply of clothes when he had shipped he had drawn upon the "slop chest" for enough to wear, including a pair of boots so small that he could not wear them. He was compelled to keep the boots and was charged $10 for them. The captain told him that he was using him nicely when he only wanted him to sign clearance papers in lieu of his indebtedness, for which he could put him into jail. The unfortunate man, none too intelligent and a stranger, did not know what to do. He met Steinman, however, who brought him to me. I instructed Steinman to go with him to the Shipping Commisioner's Office and insist upon his being paid $20 before he signed the papers. Steinman was quite alert in preventing the poor stupid fellow from signing and was so much in evidence as to attract the attention of the Commissioner, who demanded his business and a statement as to whom he represented. Steinman with great fervor proclaimed that he represented "Frank Roney" and was present to see that a little justice was done a poor man. He finally secured the $20 for the sailor and again brought him to me. I advised him as to his future conduct and told him to take care of his money and not to spend it foolishly. On his rounds the following day Steineman learned that the unfortunate creature had spent his $20 and was then aboard a ship ready to sail, having been shanghaiied with little difficulty. Many months later I received a letter covered with the marks of many post offices through which it had passed in its transit from Calcutta to San Francisco. I could not read it. A young man, a native of Schleswig-Holstein, read it for me. It was from my $20 friend, who was also a native of Schleswig-Holstein, informing me that he was in trouble with a captain with whom he had shipped to Liverpool. He hoped that I would see him through his trouble when he reached that port for I was the only one who had ever done him justice. He may at some later time have remembered my advice, and he may have taken it to heart. At least I hope so.

Seamen's Protective Association disbands—

Later when I became so active in the affairs of the Trades Assembly and the League of Deliverance my duties were so onerous that I could not give the time necessary to the Seamen's Protective Association and disintegration set in. The agents, whom I had appointed to assist me, were unable to keep it up to anything like its former standard. The weekly meetings were so poorly attended that I concluded not to continue them because of the expense for hall rent, etc. Before this had occurred, however, a man named "Scotty" Donohue became treasurer of the union. After his election to the office he became irregular in his attendance at meetings and doubt was also expressed as to his integrity. The few remaining members of the union, looking upon the president of the union in the same manner as they did upon the captain of a ship, expected me to recover the funds of the union from Donohue. I had considerable difficulty in doing so, but finally succeeded. I deposited the amount, about $105, in the Hibernia Savings Bank, hoping to revive the union as soon as possible.

Devereux, who had been to sea while these occurrences were taking place, returned and insisted upon resuming the meetings. This I positively refused to do. Then he demanded that I turn the union's funds over to him. I also refused that request. He had been one of the first and also one of the most energetic members of the union, but I could see no reason for surrendering the funds to him. He then placed the matter before the Trades Assembly, to which I was at that time a delegate as a representative of the moulder's union. Devereux intimated that I had appropriated the funds to my own use. My explanation to the Trades Assembly satisfied the delegates as to the falsity of his insinuation. I further stated before that body that if a bona fide seamen's organization existed, as Devereux had said it did, and if the Trades Assembly upon inquiry believed it to exist and acknowledged it by accepting delegates from it, I was willing to hand the money, books, vouchers, and everything else over to the Trades Assembly to be disposed of as it thought best. I knew that there was no seamen's union, but a member of the Trades Assembly said that he had lately been to its meetings. Following that declaration I handed everything that I possessed relating to the Seamen's Protective Association to the treasurer of the Trades Assembly, who was instructed to give them to J. Judge, the supposed treasurer of the union. Judge, the treasurer, later claimed to have been waylaid on his way home that evening and robbed of the union's funds. Devereux had Judge arrested,[5] but the charge of misappropriation was dismissed by the court on the ground that as the union was not incorporated, Judge, the treasurer, had as much right to the money as any other member, and as he was not under bonds it could not be recovered. Queer law, I thought, but the decision of the court was final.

Devereux did me a grievous wrong by insinuating that I had appropriated the money of the union to my own ends. Later, however, he expressed his sincere regrets at having done so. Regrets are useless, however, in remedying a wrong already done. The first reports make lasting impressions which later retractions fail to amend. All that Devereux gained by his squabbling contention was to besmirch my character and good name after I had worked so earnestly and loyally for him and other seafaring men for nearly two years, which effort had cost me money as well as time and absence from work. The ingratitude of this act hurt me very keenly. I was well aware that it did not damage me with those who knew me and who were cognizant of the facts, but inuendoes of that character travel far and fast

5 Judge was arrested in the latter part of October, 1882.—Ed.

and can never be overtaken. So far as I was concerned that incident ended my connection with the sailors.

Efforts on behalf of sailors—

The long tedious battle which I made to secure the Sailor's Home as a headquarters for the union and for all seamen along lines similar to those of a like-named institution in Liverpool is long forgotten and my memory of it is too hazy to depend upon in writing its story. I wanted that building as a proper home for deep-water seamen, out of which I hoped would come a sailors' organization as beneficial as that which has lately come to pass through the efforts of Andrew Furuseth.[6] I was successful in having the interiors of ships remodeled so as to afford better sleeping quarters for the men. I was also mainly instrumental in bringing about the arrest and conviction of Captain Sparks of the "Gatherer" for the cruelties perpetrated by that wretch and his subordinates upon the poor men who sailed under them.

It has long been a question with me as to whether or not my services and sacrifices were of any practical, permanent benefit to the sailors. I know that I instructed them as to the necessity and value of organization. Without appearing to them as a preacher, I also impressed upon them the necessity

6 Roney is referring to the present Sailors' Union, in the affairs of which Andrew Furuseth has long played an active and important part.—Ed.

Sigmund Danielewicz

A. J. Starkweather

of honesty as between men, to have an honest purpose, to have confidence in each other, and always to be loyal and true. I know that my experiment taught others how to guard against future failure. The succeeding Coast Seamen's Union[7] took in as members only those who were actual seamen. Its organizers, Sigmund Danielewicz, Burnette G. Haskell, P. Ross Martin, and others, have long since been forgotten by the sailors, as I have been, but they indicated the course for the sailors to follow which was along the same lines as I did. Those who succeeded, being more practical than I and my associates, instituted paid office-holders, and to that I attribute the success and permanence of the present Sailors' Union, the successor of those earlier efforts.

A delegate to the Trades Assembly—

During my connection with the Seamen's Protective Association it grew in numbers, taking the lead in advancing trade union principles far ahead of the older unions in the city. The Trades Assembly sent one of its members to solicit our affiliation. Wilson, Hagerty, McAvoy, and Devereux, the last two being seafaring men, went as our delegates to that body. Our membership entitled us to a larger representation and I was urged to be a delegate. I had repeatedly requested the secretary of the local moulders' union to send to Salt Lake City for my card, but whatever his reason he as frequently neglected to

[7] Organized March 6, 1885.—Ed.

do so. The moulders were represented in the Trades Assembly and I did not care to go as a delegate from the sailors' organization when I was not a member of the local union of my own trade. I did not believe in that kind of representation. Wilson and Hagerty could go because there was no union of their occupations. The moulders' delegates insisted upon the secretary of their union sending for my card, which he finally did, after which I went as a sailors' delegate to the Trade Assembly.[8] Upon becoming a member of that body I soon perceived that it was practically no better than a mutual admiration club. Its practical usefulness as the center of trade unionism did not appeal to me. Its membership was excellent, but the grasp of its members on trade principles was negative. I had long been of the opinion that if any permanent benefit was ever to accrue to the working people of America it must be obtained through trade unionism. The program of the socialists was excellent but not capable of being realized except through a long period of education. Education must be extended through generation after generation in order to obtain effective results. Improvement of the condition of the working class was needed and must gradually continue in future years. Simply to ameliorate the lot of the workers was not the program of the socialists.

[8] Roney went to the Trades Assembly as a delegate from the Seamen's Protective Association on June 21, 1881. In April, 1882, he was sent as a delegate from the moulders' union.—Ed.

The complete revolution of society had to be accomplished.

I believed in the principle of progression, in gaining one thing before seeking another. Whatever was to be gained had to come through organization. I was also cognizant of the fact that beyond a small increase in their wages most workingmen were interested in nothing else. Organization was therefore the first step necessary to be taken for any improvement in the condition of the working class. I recognized that the socialists could fill an important rôle as instructors in carrying on the program of organization, and they consented to do so. Then we began a vigorous campaign in the Trades Assembly which had the effect of awakening the delegates to a full sense of their duty.

President of the Trades Assembly—

I was not long a member of the Assembly before I was elected its president.[9] I thereupon appointed an executive committee of five men, distinctively trade unionists, who I believed would carry out the program that I had outlined. This was to gather into our association many unions which had not affiliated and which were purely local in character. In many instances several visits were paid to these unions and every endeavor was made to impress upon them the importance of cooperative effort. I

9 Roney was elected president of the Trades Assembly in August, 1881.—Ed.

found the members of most of the unions ready and willing to join the Trades Assembly, but I also found the leaders of some of them to be inveterate obstructionists to every endeavor of that sort.

Organizing activities—

One noticeable instance of this type was with the locomotive engineers. After speaking to them for half an hour on the occasion of my first and only visit they unanimously adopted a resolution to send two representatives to the Trades Assembly. Just as the matter had been decided their district officer entered the room. When he understood what had been done he took the floor and told them that the policy of the national organization, as expressed by Grand Chief Engineer Arthur,[10] was against all association with other labor unions. Local unions were always involved in difficulties or troubles of some kind with their employers, frequently leading to strikes in which the locomotive engineers had no concern. They must keep themselves free from all entanglements of that description. They were different from other wage-earners inasmuch as they were part of the great railroad system of America. Their first duty was to the companies employing them which should never be embarrassed when it became necessary for them to serve patrons who might be involved in labor troubles. Immediately a

10 P. M. Arthur was for many years the national executive of the Brotherhood of Locomotive Engineers.—Ed.

resolution to rescind their previous action was put and carried unanimously, and I left the hall much exasperated.

The Riggers and Stevedores Union was another organization whose action disgusted me. Its membership included three employers. The initiation fee had been placed at $100. If the person seeking membership was favorably regarded the entrance fee could be paid in installments, and if he were not so regarded it had to be paid in a lump sum. During rush periods outsiders were employed at the same rates as members, i.e., $5 per day for eight hours' work. If business became slack the outsiders were laid off and members only were employed. This organization refused to send delegates to the Trades Assembly or to become a distinctive trade union by ousting the employer-members. The commerce of San Francisco was increasing at such a rate that about as many outsiders were as steadily employed as union members, but only a few members were admitted to the union from time to time. I finally got the outsiders to organize a union, and they took from the consignees the contract of loading and unloading the ships at a cheaper rate than was charged by the bosses in the older organization. As the men of the new union worked cooperatively their pay was always much more than that of those of the older organization. In addition, as the new union sent delegates to the Trades Assembly they were recognized as the representatives of the only body of union stevedores on the wharves. The hoisting engineers employed along the docks also organized and sent delegates to the Trades Assembly. They gave their support to the new stevedores' union because of the failure of the older union to affiliate with the Trades Assembly. A stiff, short fight ensued with the result that the bosses withdrew from the older union of stevedores, the entrance fee was reduced, and harmony prevailed. This also ended the attempt of the stevedores to establish an aristocracy of Labor.

Equality among the workers—

A certain aloofness or feeling of superiority exists even today among the members of certain trades, but not so markedly as was formerly the case. Mechanics thought themselves superior to the laborers who helped them and the latter tacitly admitted the superiority. I personally desired to destroy that sentiment. It was difficult of accomplishment because it was in a measure recognized by both sides. Talking of the folly of the claim of the mechanics on the one hand and on the other urging the laborers to assert their demand of equality and recognition was, I felt, the most direct method of bringing about a correct understanding.

The injustice of placing men upon a footing of inferiority because of their poverty was repugnant to my sense of justice and appeared to me to be destructive of the democracy which should prevail among laborers of every degree. The laborer was usually the son of poor parents whose necessities compelled him at an early age to seek such employment as afforded him a fair living. The mechanic was the son of parents in more favorable circumstances who could afford to board him during the whole period of his apprenticeship without feeling the pinch. There were and still are other contributing causes to this disparity, but this I considered the main one, and it was sufficient for me. There was another which appealed to the selfishness of the mechanic more forcibly than the first, and that was that in case of a strike the young intelligent helper might in his resentment take the place of the not always too skilful striker. I wanted every worker, skilled and unskilled, organized into a union of the craft or industry in which he was employed.

Plans for a Labor Temple—

As a member of the Trades Assembly I projected a scheme which has just come to fruition after lying dormant for thirty years,[11] but which was hailed with enthusiasm when first mentioned, i.e., a headquarters for all the unions of San Francisco, a Labor Temple.[12] We went so far as to have the articles of incorporation issued by the Secretary of State. The corpora-

[11] Roney is referring to the completion of the Labor Temple of San Francisco in 1912.—Ed.

[12] This proposal was made sometime during the latter part of May or the early part of June, 1882. Articles of incorporation were issued authorizing the sale of $100,000 capital stock.—Ed.

tion was formed by one representative from each union. These representatives also constituted the board of directors. I secured an option on two buildings, both situated on Mission Street. When it came to gathering in the money needed to make the first payment for the property I discovered that the enthusiasm of the members of the Trades Assembly had evaporated. As a consequence we had to abondon our plans of having a Labor Temple.

When I became president of the Trades Assembly I wrote an earnest appeal to the laboring people of San Francisco to organize unions, which appeal, I believe, from its wide and judicious circulation did much to help in that way. Like other documents of similar character nothing remains of it but a memory.[13] After I had completed my term as president, I wrote another appeal in the form of a report which was printed in the *Call*, the only local paper which gave the people accurate reports without exacting promises of reciprocal benefit.

A projected strike—

Notwithstanding the *Call's* fairness toward our movement the Typographical Union was much opposed to it as well as to its afternoon contemporary and associate, the *Evening Bulletin.* Both papers were jointly owned by Loring Pickering and George K. Fitch, although Pickering managed the

13 I have a copy of this document, given to me by Mr. Roney in 1907.—Ed.

Call and Fitch the *Evening Bulletin.* The *Call* was conducted as a regular and reliable family morning newspaper without yellow or sensational coloring or the parading in correct language of the immoralities of the divorce courts or the other crimes to which in the nature of things our large centers of population are unfortunately subject. The *Bulletin,* conducted by George K. Fitch, was an afternoon commercial paper as reliable and as clean in every respect as its morning contemporary.

Although both papers paid their compositors ten cents more per one thousand ems than required by the union scale or paid by the other newspapers, neither the *Call* nor the *Bulletin* was regarded with favor by the printers' union because several of the compositors consistently refused to become members of the union. Neither Pickering nor Fitch would do anything to compel them to join the union. Delegation after delegation had waited upon Pickering and Fitch demanding the complete unionization of the offices. The invariable reply which Fitch and Pickering gave was that they had no objection to the union, that they did not discriminate against union men, and that they left it optional with their employees to join or not to join the union as they chose. I served on one of those delegations and was so convinced by the reasoning of Mr. Pickering as to the correctness of his attitude that I declined to serve again in the same capacity when asked to do so.

The closed shop opposed—

My position on the matter of the closed shop differed and still differs fundamentally from that of the great majority of trade unionists. They believe in compulsion or force by strike or boycott to attain their object. I believe in solicitation and persuasion to reach the same end without the interference of foreman or employer. No union is perfect in its organization. Nor is it capable of accomplishing any great permanent social reform unless all who are engaged in the occupation which it represents are enrolled as members. If men do not see the importance of associations for mutual benefit and protection, then to compel them to belong to such organizations does not make them reliable or faithful members and trespasses upon their rights as individuals, which, I feel, should never be done by union organizations. No fair-minded men can with the least self-respect enjoy the benefits which accrue to him through the organized efforts of the union and not feel under obligations to it for those favors which as an individual under our industrial system he could not obtain for himself. Men of intelligence are never compelled to join a labor organization any more than they are compelled to become members of a religious body or of a beneficial order. They realize its utility and importance and readily become members as the surest and safest means of conserving their individual rights as well as of extending them as a result of cooperative effort. There are men of intelligence and sound character who object to belonging to unions because of the treachery and mistreatment which they have received from alleged union men in times past. Ignorant, domineering, and self-sufficient managers and officers of unions have done more harm by ostracizing this class of men than they have done good by enlisting a less intelligent class in greater numbers by means of coercion and duress. They have the numbers, it is true, but they lack the brains, and in all contests between Labor and Capital it is brains that count the most if permanent benefit is to result.

Some of the compositors in the *Call* office were former members of the union who, when involved in a strike, had been discriminated against by the union officials because of personal dislike and had also been betrayed by them for the same poor reason. The recollection of these injustices had estranged them from unionism; they dreaded a repetition thereof if they should again become members. I had several conversations with these workingmen and knew that had an earnest, intelligent, conciliatory effort been made by the union they would have become members without the necessity of resorting to compulsion.

Call-Bulletin strike—

Steady and hard continuous work in the foundry and late hours caused by my activities on behalf of Labor began to leave their mark upon me and I was laid up with an infection in one of my legs. A delegation of printers called upon me to advise me that they were about to begin a fight against the *Call* and the *Bulletin*. I was very sick and weak but my head was very clear and my consciousness of their inability to win was as conclusive as was their determination to engage in the fight. Everything that they proposed to do was explained to me in detail, and I must say that it all looked well enough except one feature. That was the question as to whether or not they could be assured of public sympathy. They thought that they could be sure of having it with them in the forthcoming struggle. I thought differently and told them so. And I also told them that unless the public was with them from the start defeat would surely follow. I was too weak to argue with them and thought that I had raised objections enough to cause them to think the matter over. So they left me and their fight began.[14] It lasted but a short time and ended in defeat. I was deeply disappointed and chagrined over the entire matter.

Employers join workers in opposing Chinese—

During my presidency of the Trades Assembly[15] the anti-Chinese agitation was kept going by the politicians. So long as the Chinese confined their competition to the laborer many regarded the agitation as due to race prejudice and mere sentiment, but

[14] The strike began on July 30, 1883.—Ed.

[15] Roney served two six-month terms as president of the Trades Assembly.—Ed.

when the Chinese became employers and invaded the territory so carefully guarded by our manufacturers then they became dangerous to the nation. The cigar business was largely controlled by the Chinese. Numerous Chinese-owned factories were running and prospering. Where factories were not entirely in the hands of Chinese, wealthy Americans employed them in large numbers to the exclusion of all white workers. Only 200 white men, including the men who were operating their own individual shops, were employed in that industry, although there were about 8,000 Chinese so employed. Chinese cigars were in successful competition with the New York tenement-house article and were really made under sanitary conditions superior to those that existed in the tenements of New York City. To keep alive the fact that white men made cigars in San Francisco a White Cigar Makers' Association with delegates in the Trades Assembly was kept in existence.

Chinese manufacturers of boots and shoes were lively and successful competitors of the white manufacturers operating exclusively with Chinese labor. All the large laundries owned by white men were operated with Chinese labor. The smaller ones, being owned by Chinese, competed successfully with the larger ones. The Chinese manufacturers of women's and children's underwear had absorbed that business. Chinese domestics were everywhere. In gardening and upon farms they were considered the ideal laborers because they worked cheaply for long hours, accepted any conditions, and never rebelled.

Statistical study of Chinese—

During the entire agitation an elaborate authentic statement had never been prepared dealing with the business and industries which the Chinese had absorbed or chiefly controlled. This omission was a serious one. Denunciation was of no value. Neither did results follow by charging the Chinese with being filthy, for the Chinese as a people are far more cleanly in all respects than many of those who were hostile to them. As president of the Trades Assembly I appointed Henry Marsden and Charles F. Burgman to investigate the Chinese from a purely industrial standpoint and gave them what personal assistance I could. Their labor resulted in the production of the most comprehensive and accurate report that had ever been made on the subject up to that time. With my customary carelessness I did not preserve a copy of the report which was sent to every member of Congress.[16]

16 Roney criticizes himself unjustly in this connection, for I find a copy of that report among the clippings and pamphlets which he gave me many years ago. The report was prepared by a committee composed of Henry Marsden, Charles F. Burgman, C. W. Schenck, M. McAvoy, and Louis Alexander. In a pencilled note on the copy which I have, Roney states that Burgman and Marsden did all of the work of compiling the information and writing the document. The report is addressed to "The Workingmen and Women of the United

Anti-Chinese convention—

On my suggestion the Trades Assembly issued a call for a Pacific Coast Labor Union Convention to devise the best plan to submit to Congress for the purpose of getting rid of the Chinese without injury or violence. The State had already taken a vote on the subject and had almost unanimously decided that they should be excluded.

The convention assembled in Eintracht Hall on Post Street and was attended by a large number of California delegates and by a creditable representation from Nevada.[17] The management and direction of the convention was left to me. Geo. H. Morrison, of Virginia City, was made chairman, and a most competent and brilliant chairman he made. Dennis Kearney, unwilling to admit his retirement from the Chinese agitation, now that it had taken a different shape to what he had launched, was present hoping that an accident of some sort might open the way for his reinstatement as a leader, from which position he had been retired for some time. Whatever hopes he might have had when he entered the hall were rudely blasted by Robert Morrison, representing the Miners' Union of Virginia City, Nevada. Morrison was a vigorous and fluent speaker and

States,'' and its four pages present a statistical study of the extent of Chinese competition in San Francisco.

Marsden succeeded Roney as president of the Trades Assembly in 1882.—Ed.

[17] The convention assembled in San Francisco on April 24, 1882. —Ed.

flayed Kearney most unmercifully, going through his entire connection with the Workingmen's Party. The applause given the speaker satisfied Kearney that there was no hope for his resurrection and he quietly retired. I would hardly be human if I did not admit that Morrison's scathing remarks and the applause given them afforded me some satisfaction for Kearney's having deliberately and falsely charged me with getting $3,000 from Peter Donohue to run a labor paper. The convention ended by appointing a committee on plan of action and an executive committee to carry out the plan. Senator Hoar, of Massachusetts, in his speech opposing the passage of the Chinese Exclusion Law, had stated that the people generally who demanded that law were almost to a man wage-earners and that wage-earners were almost exclusively the patrons of the Chinese, purchasing goods of every description manufactured by them. Since this was the case he was satisfied that the people *en masse* had no serious objection to the Chinese and that the agitation against the Orientals was merely a scheme of selfish ignorant persons to foster race prejudice. The speech was an able one and was true in every particular. This I considered was the test, for if the people were honest and sincere in their expressed desire to exclude the Chinese they would not buy their goods or patronize them in any way.

The Chinese boycott—

The people of Ireland had shown how restricted intercourse could be made effective by the treatment accorded Captain Boycott, a notorious rack-renting agent in the west of that island. Captain Boycott could get no one, male or female, to work for him in or about his house or on his land, and it was the harvest season. He could buy or sell nothing in the adjacent town, nor would anyone speak to him. Although living in a populated district he was as much isolated as Robinson Crusoe and feeling it far more because he had animals to care for and crops to harvest and not a soul to assist him or to say one word to him. The upshot was that Captain Boycott gave up the fight although supported by the British Government, and left the country with his family.

It was a cruel, tortuous proceeding, this manner of handling Boycott, but it was peaceful and legal. There was no law of England which compelled people to work, speak, or trade with him, and so long as no act of aggression was committed the people were strictly within their legal rights. I thought that if our working people were only one-quarter as sincere in their desire to be rid of Chinese cheap labor as the Irish had proved to be in getting rid of Captain Boycott the victory would be as substantial in one case as it was in the other.

Boycotting commended itself to me as the most effective way to work out the problem of Chinese cheap labor. The committee on plan of action was largely in favor of organizing a secret society, to which I was absolutely opposed. I pointed out the futility of an organization of that sort. The Chinese labor problem was a public question in which every citizen was interested. A secret society was necessarily limited in its membership and could be diverted from its original purpose by designing men having ulterior views. It could also be made the ready means of wreaking revenge upon well-meaning citizens not in accord with it for conscientious or other reasons. Its existence afforded a fruitful field for *agents provocateurs* and informers. I had been directed by the convention to carry out whatever plan might be formulated and I also had the privilege of resigning. I was resolved to do the latter if a secret organization were instituted. The committee reluctantly abandoned the notion of secrecy and adopted the plan which I had formulated, naming the organization "The League of Deliverance."

Discharged again—

My activities prior to the meeting of the convention demonstrated my determination to create a solid trade union movement in San Francisco. I had been getting men together and organizing them into unions with the intention of ultimately attempting the formation of a central body upon the plan published in 1869 in the Chicago *Workingmen's Advocate.* Irving M. Scott and the management of the Union Iron Works thought unfavorably of the part that I was taking in this movement, and to mark their hostility to it as well as to punish me directed Mr. Dimmick to discharge me. Work was plentiful at the time and Dimmick, who had come to understand my motives and had himself changed from being a most exacting foreman to one of absolute fairness to both employer and workmen refused to do so on the ground that he needed my services and that he had no cause for discharging me. If I was to be discharged and an injustice done it must be done by the management. My discharge was delayed in consequence of Dimmick's attitude. At length Geo. W. Prescott, a member of the firm and Dimmick's special friend, informed him that "Anarchist" Roney had to be discharged at once or his own discharge would follow. As there was nothing else for Dimmick to do he told me the story, and I quit the Union Iron Works. I secured employment at the Risdon Iron Works, which was then manufacturing the machinery for the Spreckels Sugar Refinery in the Potrero. It was an excellent job, and the foreman, Mr. Robert Rafael, was a fine, considerate gentleman. When I told Rafael that I was going to quit my job to manage the League of Deliverance he did his best to dissuade me. The Risdon job was, with easily earned overtime, worth $130 per month to me. The executive committee of the League of Deliverance fixed my salary and also that of W. F. Eastman, the secretary, at $75 a month without indicating the source thereof. The unions composing the convention had all promised a small per capita contribution to keep the League in efficient working order and then promptly forgot all about the League and its support.

The League of Deliverance—

To launch the League and to proclaim its purposes with becoming éclat was our first serious task. Accordingly a mass meeting was called to meet in Union Hall on Howard Street, the largest place of assemblage in the city. I selected the speakers and arranged the speeches in such a way that each speaker confined himself within certain limits to only a part of the subject, but all of the speeches together told a complete story. It was a new method of conducting a meeting and met the approval of all the participants. I took no active public part in the meeting.

A number of politicians who had gained the reputation of being friendly to Labor's interests were anxious to appear on the program for the reason that participation would enhance their value to their party and be of personal advantage to themselves. I declined to entertain the application of any of them, informing them that we had in our unions all the talent needed to give a clear exposition of our wants and desires, and that we depended absolutely upon ourselves for their attainment. Whatever outside aid we received would be duly appreciated, but for the present union men were determined to rely upon themselves. There was to be no coquetting with politicians or political parties if I could prevent it. I made some enemies among the politicians by my attitude in the matter, and I did not strengthen myself with those for whose sake I did it.

After paying the expenses of the mass meeting enough money remained to hire a cheap back room in the basement of the old St. Ignatius building on Market Street, the present site of the Emporium. We purchased a cheap second-hand desk and a few chairs, and thus equipped we began our campaign against Chinese cheap labor. The backwardness of the unions in contributing their per capita or even to pay current expenses was painfully apparent from the start. Auxiliary organizations were necessary to keep the movement alive, healthy, and effective. Eastman, seeing how remote was the salary upon which he was absolutely dependent, threw up the secretaryship and accepted a job in a printing office in Vancouver, British Columbia. He expressed the hope that enough would be contributed to give me a salary as I had a dependent family. He, being unmarried, could make out some way or other, and if necessary could go a considerable distance in search of employment. Neither his hope nor mine was ever realized, and the salary agreed upon remained unpaid.

Organizing activities—

I began the organization of branches all over town with decided success but without deriving any revenue from them. In fact they were a source of expense inasmuch as hall rent and all initial expenses of organization had to be defrayed out of the scanty and irregular contributions of the unions. As chairman, secretary, treasurer, and organizer of the League my hands were well filled, and my time, day and night, fully occupied. I have observed how gingerly men touch offices in organizations which occupy much of their time when there is no corresponding compensation. In my case, had there been any expectation of remuneration I am under the impression that so many offices would not have been thrust upon me.

I wished to test the disposition and sincerity of the people upon the Chinese question and to see how far collectively and individually they were prepared to go in a peaceful way, and how long they would continue their interest in such a campaign. In order to facilitate organization and to aid those who pledged themselves to sell nothing but goods made by white labor, I issued a handsome card to be placed in store windows in guaranty of the quality of the goods sold. I charged one dollar for its use.

Campaign to enlist retailers' support—

I began the campaign against the Chinese by canvassing all the retail shoe dealers doing business upon the principal down-town streets. They were all willing to take the pledge to dispose of their Chinese stock within 90 days and thereafter to handle nothing but white-labor goods, but each declined to head the list. Their refusal to sign, taken with their readiness to comply with the conditions, placed me in a rather awkward position. It was a case of "Now you have it and now you don't." To meet the emergency I sent to each retailer an invitation to meet me at the office of the League at a fixed hour. They all responded. They were also surprised to meet each other for each imagined that he was the only one invited.

> Gentlemen [I said to them] I have resorted to this pardonable subterfuge to get you here in a body to sign this pledge if you believe that you can honestly and faithfully comply with its requirements. If you cannot, that ends the matter, and I will seek some other method by which the people can be supplied with boots and shoes made by white labor. You each say that you can comply and will sign the pledge, but none of you wishes to head the list. If you are not agreeable to doing so in five minutes this meeting will stand adjourned and I will make another and different kind of effort to attain our end.

They were completely trapped and had to do something, but again none wished to take the lead. Finally Mr. Moore, of Moore & Murphy, whose store was located on Sixth Street, stepped forward and signed the pledge. All the others followed and I scored the first step towards ultimate victory. Each dealer upon signing the pledge received a card and paid his dollar.

While the meeting was in progress, it was whispered to me that two of the dealers, who had signed the agreement, could not be relied upon. I detailed two men to watch them, for if they went down-town it was surely to lay in a fresh stock of Chinese-manufactured goods. Sure enough, they went straight to a Chinese factory on Battery Street, showing how little they valued their pledged word. Next morning the cases of Chinese goods were delivered at both stores and I was notified by my amateur detectives. As soon as the boxes were opened to expose the goods I was alongside and charged the dealers with treachery. I withdrew their cards and left.

The Butterfield boycott—

A dealer on Market Street near Fourth Street, named Butterfield, absolutely refused to consider my proposition, and so I decided to boycott him. I procured three linen dusters, as they were then called, and had painted on the back of each the request not to patronize Butterfield. I sent my friend A. J. Starkweather out with one of the dusters and told him to parade back and forth before Butterfield's store. He did this during the afternoon of the first day without attracting any attention. In the evening a crowd collected and he was arrested. I had previously arranged with H. C. Kinne, a public school teacher, who at once put up $100 bail, and Starkweather was immediately released. No sooner had he been arrested than I put another man similarly dressed in front of the store. He was also arrested and met Starkweather as he was returning after being bailed out. Meantime I had the third man on the job.[18] Kinne put up the necessary bail for them as each was arrested and then found other bondsmen for them, thus releasing his money for ready use.

Our boycotting activities went on for several days, the news of which spread over town with great rapidity. Boycotting in a new form and application became an established thing in San Francisco, and besides being an attractive sport to the crowds which assembled, particularly in the evenings, it did its work satisfactorily as not one person entered Butterfield's store after the boycott started. The thermometer of enthusiasm was away above blood heat and no disorder had been occasioned except as the police made each arrest. Then, the crowd merely hooted the police for their acts.

I varied the program somewhat by getting a peddler's license, a handcart, and a basket of peaches for a little fellow who was a friend of mine. I also clothed him with one of our linen dusters. He sold his peaches from the street for the reason that the police

[18] John Monroe, who had taken Starkweather's place while the latter was at lunch, was the first to be arrested, then Starkweather, then Roney himself, and finally Isaac Coronson. All were immediately released on bail. This incident occurred on July 5, 1882.—Ed.

objected to my men parading on the sidewalk. The crowd continued interested in our demonstration. Captain Short then arrested my peddler, and refused bail for his liberation. I soon called into service Superior Court Judge Robert Ferrell, who, against the vehement protests of Captain Short, ordered his discharge on a bond of $50. My man was held so many hours in jail that when freed it was too late on that Saturday night to resume his boycotting activities. It was taken up the following Monday with unusual vigor on both sides, so much so that all three of my men were under arrest at the same time.

Believing that a good officer should never refuse to do the work he asks others to do I began parading back and forth in front of the store and was promptly arrested. Returning to the scene after my liberation on bail I found the store closed, from which I claimed a victory. Starkweather was arrested over 250 times and the others not less than 100 times each. I was arrested once.

As I was the chairman of the League I was the first to be tried. I had quite an array of legal talent to defend me. Charley Wolf was the lawyer in charge, assisted by Judge Maguire and Walter Gallagher. John Steenbach, a member of my old Eighth Ward Club, was foreman of the jury, which, after two minutes' deliberation, brought in a verdict of acquittal. The acting police judge, Judge Nicholsen, was a member of the League and approved of the verdict. The cases against my associates were dismissed, and Butterfield quit business. Afterwards I learned that Butterfield was simply employed by the local Chinese manufacturers and could not, even had he desired to do so, have agreed to our program. It was a common custom in many lines of trade to employ white persons, making them the ostensible owners of the business although it really belonged to Chinese capitalists.

The inauguration of boycotting was looked upon favorably by others than the shoemakers as an interesting, not to say hilarious, way of accomplishing its purpose. Applications began to come in to the League of Deliverance to boycott various persons or firms alleged to be enamored with the sale of Chinese manufactured goods. Behind some of the requests I discovered other motives than the good of the community. I was careful to investigate personally all suggestions to boycott, and only those firms that did not come up to our requirements were boycotted.

An attempted bribe—

Mr. M. J. Flavin, proprietor of the I.X.L. Store on Kearney Street, invited me to inspect his shirt factory and to say what I thought about it. I pronounced it in every respect a genuine white-labor concern. Shortly thereafter he favored me with a box of fine Key West cigars every day or two, which I passed around among my favored visitors. In a little while he sent a messenger to me with an invitation to dine. I accepted, and went with him to a "swell" French restaurant.

After partaking of all the good things mentioned on the menu, we began an interesting conversation about things in general and nothing in particular. Intuitively I felt that something already incubated was coming and held myself in readiness for the revelation. And it came without disturbing my equanimity a particle. My host drew my attention to a neighbor's store, known as the X.L.N.T. The names of both stores were so similar that one was frequently taken for the other by persons not knowing that the I.X.L. was the first and original one. It was because of Flavin's well-established reputation that his neighbor adopted a name so similar for the purpose of drawing from him a large share of the trade. Flavin considered it a great hardship and also felt that a personal wrong had been committed. If the League would boycott his competitor it would, so he thought, place matters in the proper light. Then the people generally would learn to know the difference between the stores and that his was the correct one to deal with. He further proposed to pay all expenses incurred by the League in levying the boycott, and as an evidence of his good faith offered me $100 to do with as I pleased. In other words, here was a preliminary bribe.

At first the feeling was strong within me to enter an indignant refusal and denounce him as a double-dealing, dishonest trickster, but I restrained myself, for I saw that no good would come from that course of action. As he seemed to regard his proposition as a business one I also feigned to look upon it in that light. I told him that we must have good grounds upon which to institute a boycott. Infringement upon his business was not sufficient cause to justify boycotting his rival. Further, I told him that I had already inspected his competitor's stock and had found it to be of as much white-labor make as his own. I also advised him that his competitor had one of our cards in his window as evidence of our inspection. It was simply impossible to do what he suggested so long as the X.L.N.T. conformed to our rules. My decision paralyzed him, but he saw that it was straight business and the subject was dropped. So also was my supply of cigars.

At about this time I resigned my management of the League. I had held the position for three months without receiving any salary and the pinch of poverty at home was getting unbearable. I had to quit. A week or so later I was astonished to see boycotters in front of the X.L.N.T. store. I, of course, knew that the new management of the League was not so exacting as I had been. Some one had received the $100 which I had refused, though I had needed it badly. Several other boycotts were conducted simultaneously in various parts of the city against different lines of business and this brought the League into contempt and final dissolution, the enactment of the Exclusion Law aiding most effectually in causing its demise.

The organization of the branches had given me plenty of occupation in the evenings and was generally well responded to. The well-to-do, or, as one might term them, the people who had the time and opportunity to think on questions of governmental policy, were those whose names filled the membership rolls. The only wrong of magnitude to which they objected as demanding immediate remedy was the Chinese question. Land monopoly, the source of political and economic evils, was wholly ignored. They claimed among other things that the Chinese were draining our country of its gold and that we would soon be confronted with its total absence. No account was taken of, nor credit given to, the equivalent in labor which the Chinese gave for the gold which they received as wages and sent home to China, nor did it occur to any but a few that the country could get along satisfactorily and prosper without gold.

The Ladies' Auxiliary—

A number of women formed an association ostensibly to assist the League in demonstrating its policy of displacing Chinese and Chinese-made goods by the substitution of competent white labor and white-made goods. They named their organization "The Ladies' Auxiliary to the League of Deliverance," and proposed to confine themselves to what was known as the servant girl or domestic feature of the problem. I hailed this effort as a healthy sign and a wholly unexpected development, and proposed to encourage it. It was soon apparent, however, that petty grafting was the true motive for its organization and not that of substituting competent white girls for the Chinese. I cut out all connection with it as soon as I made the discovery, and it fell to pieces without accomplishing the least bit of good.

While the Ladies' Auxiliary lasted I gained an insight into the employment of women as domestic servants, and also into the reasons behind the employment of Chinese in that capacity. A large number of the San Francisco women employing servants at that time had only a few years earlier been glad to obtain employment of any sort. Lucky speculation in mining stock and other adventitious circumstances had placed them in all their naked ignorance in positions for which their most sanguine expectations had never hoped. Ignorant parvenus are as a rule more exacting and domineering than parvenus with the shadow of an education. They were all exacting. White girls or women of some refinement and education, whose needs compelled them to accept employment, found the demands made upon them so strenuous as to be unendurable. Their feelings and wishes were ignored and their time night and day was always in demand. They were simply required to fill the rôle of docile slaves and they were abused in many ways if the least feature of rebellion cropped out. The white domestics could not endure for any length of time the treatment accorded them by their vulgar, pitiless mistresses. The Chinese could endure or ignore the treatment, and as for being docile they were *par excellence.* Before any success could be hoped for in the displacement of Chinese domestics, the women employing them would have to mend their manners. This the so-called Ladies' Auxiliary could not do, nor did it make any effort in that direction, perhaps because its members were unable to appreciate that such a state of affairs existed.

A white-labor shirt factory—

A young man, whose name I have forgotten, started a shirt factory on Valencia Street near Fourteenth, with the intention of employing only white women. I was anxious to see him succeed and gave him assurances of my support. He advertised for girls, and directed that they should apply through the League's office, thus giving me the opportunity of seeing the applicants. The first one to appear was a girl of uncertain age, clean and smart looking, with a jaunty little sailor hat perched on the side of her head. She had all the appearance of a typical girl of the street, and her vernacular did not belie her appearance. "Say," she said bursting in upon me, "are you the feller that wants girls to work on shirts against the Chinamen," I told her that I was not, but that I was acting for him. Then she told me that she could do every detail of the work and wanted that kind of a job as she had a sick mother and a young sister to provide for. I had serious doubts that she would be given the job which she coveted and I also doubted her ability to do the work, even though she were given employment. I gave her a note to my friend and thought no more about her. Her name was Mary Harrington. A few weeks later I was in the vicinity of the factory and casually dropped in to see how it was progressing. My friend said that he was doing splendidly and could hardly fill his orders. Altogether he was well satisfied with his venture. When I was about to leave he asked me to meet his forelady. He said, "If it had not been for her this business would have been a failure. She has almost from the first day managed this business so far as manufacturing is concerned and has proved herself simply invaluable." All this praise was for none other than Mary Harrington, who neatly attired was giving instructions to some of the workers who were making up a shipment. The transformation was so complete in so short a time as to be beyond belief. Not a vestige of her former appearance or language remained. She was wholly and completely a clever little business woman.

A white-labor laundry—

One day two young men entered the office of the League and informed me that they were about to start a white laundry. This was welcome news to me for there was only one such laundry on either side of San Francisco Bay, viz., the Contra Costa Laundry Company of Oakland. The new laundry was to be located in an uninhabited and not very inviting spot, a distance west of St. Luke's Hospital, now a densely populated section of San Francisco. Neither of the young men knew enough to write an advertisement or get up a circular and handbill to announce their enterprise. I had previously organized the Laundry Workers' Union and this enterprise I believed would add to the union's strength and possibly be of mutual advantage to both the workers and the laundry proprietors. I wrote what they required, for which they generously and without hint or solicitation subscribed $5 to the League. Ferguson and Biggy were the names of the young men. Both were later identified with the United States Laundry. Biggy became Chief of Police in San Francisco, and while so acting was drowned on his way to the city from Sausalito when passing Alcatraz Island in the police launch.[19]

[19] William L. Biggy was appointed Chief of Police of San Francisco by the reform administration which took over the reins of government following the conviction of Mayor E. E. Schmitz for participation in the grafting activities of the city's officials. Biggy necessarily played an important part in the graft prosecution. While returning in the police launch from Belvedere, where he had gone

The work rolled in upon Ferguson and Biggy in such volume that it was impossible for them to take care of it all in their new establishment. Instead of making an effort to obtain additional quarters they had the washing done by Chinamen and converted their own establishment into a finishing shop. This information was soon brought to me. I had been largely instrumental in causing the great increase in their business, guaranteeing it to be wholly a white-labor laundry. I visited them and hold them of what I had learned. They denied the charge, but the proof was too conclusive for me to accept their denial. I told them that their laundry must either be a white laundry or nothing and gave them time to make up their minds on the matter. They refused to change their plan of operating, whereupon I gave orders to cease patronizing them, and within two weeks they vacated their premises and were out of the laundry business.

to consult one of the Police Commissioners who lived at that place, he mysteriously disappeared (November 30, 1908). Two weeks later his body was found floating on the waters of San Francisco Bay. Whether he committed suicide or whether he was pushed overboard by someone acting for those concerned with the graft prosecution, who desired to get him out of the way, will never be known. It is said that he was too cheerful on the day of his death to have committed suicide. Yet so far as is known there was no other person on the launch other than Biggy and the engineer, and the latter, up to the time that he became a raving maniac in June, 1911, consistently maintained his innocence.—Ed.

Another opportunity scorned—

About this time the agent of the Troy Laundry Machinery Company called upon me exhibiting designs of their machinery, none of which or of any other firm was in use in the San Francisco laundries. He urged me to become their representative and pointed out the possibility of a successful future. I fully realized the importance of his suggestions, but refused to use my position for such a purpose. I suppose that I might have done as he requested without seriously violating the rules or principles of morality, but I had the notion that to embark in anything else while acting as manager of the League would be a breach of ethics. There was undoubtedly big money in it at the time, but I felt that I must either be loyal to what was expected of me or resign and become a laundry machinery agent. I chose not to resign at that time, although I did assist in putting the company's agent in touch with a man who with my aid stocked all the big city laundries with up-to-date machinery.

Chinese Exclusion Act—

President Hayes vetoed the first Chinese Exclusion Act because it infringed upon the treaty obligations existing between the United States and China. When the objectionable features were later eliminated and the measure passed by Congress, President Arthur signed it on May 6, 1882, and it became the law of the land. Its adoption sounded the death knell of the League of Deliverance.

Importation of white cigar-makers —

The tricks practised by white people who made money out of the Chinese were numerous and varied in character. In the cigar trade it was really nothing other than cheating of the worst sort. The White Cigar Makers' Association thought the time ripe to increase its membership. An energetic member of their organization was selected to visit the populous centers in the East and endeavor to secure as many cigar-makers as it was possible to guarantee permanent remunerative employment to.[20] I encouraged this step with all my influence. Jake Wolfe[21] visited all the large cigar factories in San Francisco to ascertain how many of them were willing to sign an agreement to employ for a given length of time (about six months) a given number of men at certain specified wages. Enough guaranties were given and signed to warrant the bringing of at least four hundred cigar-makers. When the eastern cigar-makers arrived, I organized an impromptu parade of welcome to the strangers, followed by a reception in Union Hall.[22] The men were distributed among the factories as had previously been agreed upon.

20 This plan of action was decided upon in November, 1885.—Ed.

21 Jake Wolfe was president of the local branch of the International Cigar Makers' Union.—Ed.

22 At the time that this occurred Mr. Roney was president of the Federated Trades Council of San Francisco. The League of Deliverance had ceased to exist. The first contingent of eastern cigar-makers arrived in San Francisco on or about December 22, 1885. During the next six months about 600 were imported for the purpose of displacing the Mongolians. The parade and mass meeting which Roney mentions occurred on January 3, 1886.—Ed.

The largest and wealthiest firm in the city, Koenigsberg, Falk & Meyer, had agreed to take twenty-six men for six months. In about a month complaint was made that the firm was not living up to its contract. Men were laid off for one day, then for two, and so on, resulting in the utmost dissatisfaction and causing many of them, while they yet had the means, to return to their former homes.

I was asked to investigate the situation and if possible to secure an observance of the contract. Mr. Solomon Falk, a partner and the general manager of the concern, assured me that it was the firm's desire to live up to its agreement, but that it had found that there was no sale for the cigars made by cheap white labor. He claimed that if the situation did not improve he would be unhappily obliged to discharge all the imported men and perhaps go out of business as the result of his endeavor to assist white labor. As proof of his statement he showed me an immense pile of cigars in boxes for which there was no demand. I was much exercised over Mr. Falk's statement. Why the white men, who smoked the cheap cigar, preferred the Chinese article when both were sold at the same retail price, was something that was not quite clear to me. I went back to the office to think over the situation and to see if I could not find a solution of some sort or other. Having arrived at a decision as to what was wrong I again visited Falk's factory and asked him for one of the unsalable cigars. He generously gave me a box of them. Charles M. Leavey, a friend of mine, was an extensive dealer in leaf tobacco. I went to him and asked his opinion of one of Falk's cigars. He opened it, and while admitting that it was well made, said that the material composing it was the poorest stuff that he had ever seen. I pretended that there was a bet on as to its quality and that I was required to decide the bet, but inasmuch as I was not an expert in tobacco leaf would he not make an affidavit as to its quality. He did so, and fortified with this document I returned to Mr. Falk and charged him with falsification. Without displaying my precious document or saying from whom I had received it I convinced him that I was right and that he was entirely in the wrong. The affair ended by the firm's removal to Key West.

It was practices of this sort and others far more reprehensible, supported by white men of large capital, that protracted the fight against Chinese cheap labor. The men of smaller capital were being steadily crowded out of business by the Chinese factories, secretly owned in many cases by white men. It was the small white employer who cooperated with us in the fight against Chinese competition.

Organization of coopers and can-makers—

During the time that I was managing the offices of the League of Deliverance I never overlooked the opportunity of organizing a union. In fact, I preferred organizing unions to organizing branches of the League of Deliverance for the reason that the unions were permanent or could be made so, while I knew that branches of the League were mere transitory affairs created for a passing purpose.

A cooper named Dalmas was a frequent lounger in the headquarters of the League. I urged him to get the men of his trade together and told him that I would help them form a union. Competition and piece-work had brought the business, so far as the workers were concerned, to the verge of ruin. Wages, even when earned by the piece-work system, were small and oh, how hardly earned! I visited several of the cooperage shops to see for myself. At length Dalmas issued a call for a meeting. I attended, but those present were so few in number that it was decided to postpone organization until a later date. In order to get a good-sized crowd together, and knowing something of the habits of the coopers, I suggested that they be invited to an entertainment. Accordingly some cigars and beer were purchased and with these attractions a successful meeting was held and the union organized.[23] I, being the prime mover in the affair, bore my share of the expense, a thing not now required from organizers, who are usually paid for such work. The union so organized is, I believe, still in existence.[24]

The organizing of the can-makers was also a difficult matter. They were a rough, untrained set,

[23] The Coopers' Union was organized on May 15, 1882.—Ed.

[24] It is still in existence.—Ed.

unused to the least approach to civilized methods. Individually they were all right, but when together they were almost irrepressible in their boisterous, uncouth horseplay. One of them, Jim Neal, developed into a successful Buckleyite and later into a horse racer and sport. He was the worst of them all when it came to conforming to the amenities incident to the holding of meetings. With the assistance of Joseph Gilbert, a foreman and part owner in the Red Cross Packing Company, I succeeded in getting them under a form of discipline. The union lasted only a few years because of the introduction of machinery. While it lasted it was a vigorous aggressive union and was often heard from.

The American Federation of Labor—

In 1881, the secretary of the Trades Assembly received word that a meeting was to be held at Pittsburg, at which an effort would be made to federate the labor organizations of the United States into a national body. The Trades Assembly was asked to send delegates. It was generally agreed that I should be the representative. I was most anxious to go, but unfortunately my frequent absences from work had left my funds in a depleted condition. As I would be obliged to defray my expenses it was impossible for me to avail myself of the opportunity presented. I presume that if I had made my circumstances known to my friends enough money would have been raised to pay my way, but I always disliked to solicit aid for such purposes. I never wished it to be known that my activities on behalf of my fellow-workers were keeping me in a state of chronic pauperization. I now think that it would have been better for me and more advantageous to the Cause, which I had so much at heart, had I let in a ray of light on my financial condition. At my suggestion Charles F. Burgman, a tailor, was chosen for the position. Burgman was a dreamer. He, of all of us, had the grandest and most utopian ideas regarding the immediate future of Labor. He was single-minded and honest to the core, always dependable, always ready for any detail, and always capable of doing it.

Prospects for a Labor paper—

A national organization, later known as the American Federation of Labor, was called into existence at that conference and John Jarrett became its first president. Burgman did his best to have my plan of trade organization, which I have earlier outlined in these pages,[25] adopted by the new federation, but the impatience of some for immediate organization, and the desire of others to turn it to political account, rendered his efforts abortive. The American Federation of Labor has now been in existence for over thirty years, and it is only lately that the principle of organization which I early advocated has received any recognition, and that in a way quite

[25] See pp. 230–233.

removed from my design.[26] On Burgman's return to San Francisco I called a public meeting to hear his report.[27] After the meeting, Burgman informed me that a young man of evident ability had offered the columns of a paper, which he had recently started, to be used in any way most advantageous to trade unionism and if desired even to make it our official organ. I had long felt the need of a labor paper which we might call our own. It was an enormous tax upon my enegry to write reports of meetings each night of their occurrence and then to visit the newspaper offices, before going home to sleep a few hours. It was even harder for me to see what I most desired to have published eliminated or so emasculated as to be of no value. The *Call* was, as usual, by far the fairest paper, giving our news more space with less mutilation than its rival, the *Chronicle*. I did not propose to stop using the morning papers to print the current reports of the meeting, because of the extensive circulation that they received, but I did want a paper that we might call our own which would print at length such matter as would be advantageous to our organizations.

[26] Roney is here referring to his plan for the departmental grouping of trades, which plan was partly adopted in 1908 by the American Federation of Labor when it established a Building Trades Department, followed subsequently by a Metal Trades Department and a Railway Employees Department.—Ed.

[27] The meeting to which Roney refers was held on January 24, 1882.—Ed.

Burnette G. Haskell—

Acting upon my advice Burgman invited the young man to a meeting of the Trades Assembly and at that time introduced him to us. He was Burnette G. Haskell. Haskell informed the Assembly that he was a native of California and that he had lived most of his life in San Francisco. He was a lawyer and was employed in the law office of the chairman of the Republican State Central Committee. He had never heard of trade unions or of the trade union movement until he attended the meeting held to hear Burgman's report. When the Legislature was in session his duties led him often to Sacramento to secure by corrupt means the passage of measures beneficial to corporations and antagonistic to the interests of the people. It was also his duty to visit members of the Board of Supervisors and by corrupt means to secure the adoption of ordinances which were favorable to local corporations. He did all these things in blissful ignorance of their propriety, believing them to be simply acts in the political game necessary for the success of the party to which he belonged.

Haskell's speech was a frank and uncolored admission of the way politics were run in California and San Francisco at that time. It shocked most of us and was a revelation that we little expected. The cold-blooded callousness and indifference to everything except to be "found out" was amazing. When Haskell retired, Wilson was upon his feet in

Burnette G. Haskell

Haskell's Paper, *Truth*

a second, boiling with indignation. He declared that to have such a dog even remotely associated with us after listening to his voluntary admissions would be a disgrace so everwhelming as to bury us all in profoundest oblivion with the execrations of every decent man sounding an everlasting requiem over our damned souls. Hagerty was equally emphatic in condemning Haskell, damning him as volubly and as venomously as Wilson had done. Poor Burgman was as indignant as either of them and felt the humiliation keenly when charged with bringing a viper like Haskell to address decent men. As a matter of fact Burgman knew no more of Haskell than the others did. He had simply seen in him a ready way, through his paper, of advancing our movement.

Unless something was done at once to take the sting out of the remarks of Hagerty and Wilson all of my hopes of having an official paper were bound to be scattered and gone. I saw what they did not see, namely, that Haskell was talented beyond the average and was willing to redeem himself. It was unfortunate, I said, that this young man had such a record. The redeeming feature of its recital was its utter frankness. He might have concealed it all or have told us less. He might have won our confidence and waited for time to obscure his past or to have it become known to us after he had become an invaluable ally. Then we would be obliged to condemn or defend him. The truest sign of atonement for the past and a guaranty for the future was just such explicit admissions. Haskell evidently did not wish to sail under false colors. He was like a majority of the young men, raised and educated in an environment where he breathed, saw, and knew of nothing but corruption in politics. Therefore, he was not to blame. For the present we could get along without a paper, and the hope that if Haskell's eyes were opened, as he said they were, he would show by his publication how sincere he was in his desire to undo his past. I believed in giving every one who is sincere a chance to redeem himself.

My project of having a labor paper was accordingly held up for a time. Haskell, however, showed a proper grasp of the situation in subsequent issues of his weekly paper, sufficient to satisfy the most exacting. Then Eastman and I, the standing committee in whose hands the matter had been placed, got busy and concluded arrangements by which his paper, called *Truth,* became the official organ of the Trades Assembly. Haskell thereafter was one of the busiest men in the labor movement, and in a short time became a leading exponent of Socialism and then of Anarchism.[28]

[28] Burnette G. Haskell was born in Sierra County, California, June 11, 1857. His parents had been among the earliest pioneers of the State. He was admitted to the Bar in 1879, and appeared to be destined to become an outstanding lawyer. In 1882, he was given the opportunity of taking charge of a weekly paper and did so, the result being the appearance of *Truth.* It suspended publication after a few years partly because of lack of support and partly because Haskell was called to Denver to edit Joseph R. Buchanan's *Labor Enquirer.*

Haskell, brilliant, resourceful, a pleasing and compelling speaker, soon became a powerful but unreliable factor in the labor movement

The competition of convict labor—

The exploiting of convict labor in the State prisons at San Quentin and Folsom by favored contractors was beginning to interest both workmen and employers in several important occupations.[29] One of the contractors was operating a foundry. It was not known to what extent this foundry, operated by convict labor, was damaging the foundry business in San Francisco, nor could it be known unless the situation was investigated by one who understood the business. Other trades affected by the convict labor products of San Quentin were those that manufactured sashes, doors, blinds, boots, shoes, furniture, clothing, horse collars, and harness. The State, at great expense, had fitted up the large workshops at San Quentin with the most up-to-date machinery so as to facilitate the operations of the prison contractors in the employment of convicts. At Folsom, the quarrying and dressing of granite were interfering with operative stonecutters in San Francisco and with that of the quarrymen at Rosslyn and elsewhere. The Trades Assembly, before which came the question of investigating the effect of convict labor upon free labor and its employers, selected a

of San Francisco. He rapidly ran the gamut of trade unionist, Knights of Labor advocate, socialist, anarchist, communist, nationalist, and at last, a failure, dying in poverty on November 15, 1907. He would have been buried in the Potter's Field of San Francisco had not the Sailors' Union, which he had helped to organize in 1885, taken charge of his funeral and interred his remains in its own burial plot in Mount Olivet Cemetery.—Ed.

29 The contracting out of convict labor was in direct violation of the State Constitution and also of a statute enacted in 1880.—Ed.

harness-maker and myself to make the investigation, while the moulders' union selected another moulder and myself to investigate particularly the effects of the prison foundry.

An attempted investigation—

Judge Ames, of Redwood City, was warden and Mr. Edgar, later warden, was his deputy. Our reception by the deputy, who seemed not to know the purpose of the visit, was quite cordial, particularly as the harness-maker, Andy Lyons, was, when very young, a favorite of Mr. Edgar. The assistant bookkeeper, a young man serving a term for forgery committed in Oakland, was detailed to escort us through the workshops and prison quarters and was instructed to give us all the information we wished regarding the internal workings of the prison. Acting, I presume, upon previous instructions given when escorting visitors through the prison, our guide attempted to rush us through more rapidly than I desired. I told him that we wished to go through the workshops a little more slowly, to which he acceded. At the same time he let me know that he was aware of the object of our visit and that he believed that Captain Edgar had also been advised as to our purpose.

All that we could discover was that the prisoners employed in every occupation worked as attentively and, where machinery was employed, as expeditiously and as accurately as men similarly employed outside of the prison. We were royally entertained at Captain Edgar's orders in the officers' dining room. After luncheon, when in the Captain's office I made known the object of our visit, the Captain flew into a rage, charging poor Lyons with trying to betray him, when I knew that he was well aware of the purpose of our visit. But when I demanded to look at the books as the source of accurate information he became almost apoplectic in his vehemence. I insisted upon my right as a citizen of the State to inspect the books of the prison. This he promptly ignored, and in the end refused point-blank. The regret which appeared to have most influence with him was that he could not lock us up and keep us until all thoughts of interfering with the industries of San Quentin had totally and forever left us.

So far as obtaining accurate information went our visit to San Quentin was a dead failure. I was much chagrined since it stopped all further hope of proving what common rumor alleged, i.e., that the contracting of convict labor was a huge fraud upon the State, an imposition upon the convicts, an injury to the free labor employed in the same line of work, and a detriment to those hiring free labor. There was little use in soliciting the aid of the politicians in carrying on our fight, for it was stated time and time again that every one of them, from the highest to the lowest, who could get a finger into the convict-labor pie, usually pulled it out richly covered with fat and juicy gravy.

Proposed solution of convict-labor problem—

As a solution of the convict-labor problem I suggested that all of the prisoners at Folsom, who were accustomed to stone work and some of those at San Quentin, should be employed in quarrying and dressing rock with which to build a permanent system of docks for San Francisco in place of those which were then being constructed in our customary American temporary fashion.[30] I made this suggestion because I remembered that the great docks of Liverpool, England, had been constructed by similar labor. Over a hundred years had passed and the Liverpool docks stood as solid and in as fine a condition as when they were constructed. Of course the proposal raised a storm of protests. I was asked if I wished to drive the stone-cutting business out of the State. As a matter of fact, there never had been many men employed in the business and there were few then, whereas had the work of building the sea wall of San Francisco been done as I suggested it would have been a lasting monument to the administration which projected it and a permanent benefit to the city. The present decrepit thing called a sea wall would never have been called into existence, an offense against engineering skill, which caused the defacement of Telegraph Hill, the destruction of many homes, the loss of life, and innumerable injuries to the workers engaged on its construction.

[30] Roney made this suggestion at a public meeting held by the Mechanics League on December 10, 1881.—Ed.

Assistance from an unexpected source—

As I was studying what course to adopt so as to get at the prison books and knowing that I was in a serious dilemma, a personal advertisement addressed to me appeared in the *Chronicle* inviting me to meet the party who had inserted it at any place that I might designate, as he had information of importance to communicate to me. I replied to the advertisement, appointing the place of meeting. My correspondent was none other than the former assistant bookkeeper at San Quentin, who had acted as our guide and whose term of imprisonment had expired a few days after our visit to that institution. He had been present when Captain Edgar had become so excited in refusing me access to the prison's books, and he knew or believed that I wanted the information, which I requested, for a purpose beneficial to the people of the State. From the moment that he had been placed in charge of the books he realized that there was systematic fraud going on of greater magnitude than the offense for which he was undergoing a term of imprisonment. Without any definite object in mind and not knowing what use or disposition he could ever make of them, he began making copies of transactions clearly fraudulent. His opportunities to do this were not numerous, but when they came he was always prepared. He had experienced some difficulty in getting them outside the prison, but had succeeded and now offered them to me. With these excerpts in my possession, a clear way was present to expose State prison management as far as it applied to the contract labor of the convicts. I could now prove, and I knew that no one dare challenge me, that the raw material was purchased from favored dealers at exorbitant prices, and when manufactured was sold at ridiculously low rates to favored dealers. The contractors were *supposed* to handle the labor because of their expert knowledge, and they derived their profits out of the low prices obtained for the finished product, leaving no margin of profit to compensate the State for the food of the men and the use of the machinery, buildings, etc. They did, however, give the prisoners a small bonus for good behaviour and steadiness at work.

Anti-convict labor mass meeting—

It was a very mixed and tangled arrangement which was disclosed by the excerpts with which I had been furnished. The case of the foundry, in which as a moulder I was personally interested, was more easily understood. A Mr. Judson, who kept the machinery in order and who operated the foundry, was the partner of Irving M. Scott, of the Union Iron Works, in an iron blast or smelting works at Clipper Gap, Placer County. Scott had many contracts on hand to build quartz reducing mills in various mining districts. Cast-iron washers of various sizes were needed in great quantities in the erection of the mills and Mr. Judson had the convicts make them. His partner, Scott, bought them. The iron used was produced at the Clipper Gap mine in which both partners were interested. I called a public meeting of trade unionists to hear the report.[31] The meeting was largely attended by citizens not in any way identified with the trades union movement. Mr. Loring Pickering, editor and proprietor of the *Call,* wrote and published a leading article in his paper drawing attention to the report and pointing out the evils of the convict-labor system as practiced at San Quentin, the gravity of which should not be minimized or lightly considered. He followed this up with still another leading article equally emphatic. Our labor organizations discussed the matter with their usual fervor, but did nothing. I could do nothing further than to keep the subject alive by having it mentioned in the daily papers.

Roberts and McGreal—

It was not until the Federated Trades Council was organized several years later[32] that effective work was done in abolishing contract convict labor. At one of the first meetings of the Council after its organization,[33] I appointed Peter Roberts and Patrick McGreal with myself as a committee on contract convict labor. Roberts represented the plasterers in the

[31] This meeting was held on December 6, 1881.—Ed.

[32] The Federated Trades Council was organized January 12, 1886, with Roney as president.—Ed.

[33] This occurred at the second meeting of the Federated Trades Council.—Ed.

Council. His observations upon subjects of vital importance to unionism were so well expressed and so thoroughly in accord with my own views that I hailed his presence with extreme pleasure, realizing that in him was a union man who required no pre-education to qualify him for a front place in our ranks. He had received his education at the University of Michigan and had qualified as a lawyer. Reversing the order of things when applied to the selection of a vocation he quit the law and, serving his apprenticeship in regular form, became a journeyman plasterer. As a member of the plasterers' union in Detroit he had taken an active part in its affairs, and as a consequence was thrown into association with my friend Dick Trevellick, one of the ablest, best, and purest exponents of trade unionism in America or anywhere else. Mr. McGreal was vice-president of the Council and a street paver by occupation. He possessed none of the natural or acquired gifts enjoyed by Roberts except one, and that was his unflinching integrity. He was mentally keen and decidedly of an inquiring mind as well as being an indefatigable worker. Both were unselfish in the most perfect sense.

Anti-convict labor agitation successful—

Shortly after their appointment, the Legislature convened in Sacramento. Armed with my report and such information as I could impart, both Roberts and McGreal went to the Capitol. At that time the labor organizations had no fund to defray the expenses of agents engaged in doing their work. The men undertaking any task on behalf of the unions always had to pay their own expenses. Roberts and McGreal devoted a month of their time to this duty in Sacramento and footed all expenses incurred, which in the aggregate amounted to quite a sum for the two men. I was unable to accompany them as my presence in San Francisco was required at that time. As the result of their work they interested Senators Ready and Del Valle in the abolition of the contract-labor system prevalent in San Quentin prison. Senator Ready was a lawyer of great ability and a man of irreproachable character. He caused an investigation to be made into prison labor conditions and fought those upholding the system so vigorously that he succeeded in having it abolished. In its place a jute bag mill was installed.[34]

[34] As a result of the agitation of the trade unions against the competition of convict labor and primarily as a consequence of the excellent work done by the above mentioned committee of the Federated Trades Council of San Francisco, the Attorney General of the State was induced to file charges against the prison directors as being guilty of violating Article X, Section 6 of the State Constitution, which forbade the letting out of convicts on contract to any person or party, and also of violating the provisions of a convict-labor law passed in 1880. An invesitgation was undertaken at the request of Governor Stoneman, and although the latter refused to remove the prison directors or to declare them guilty, he ordered all prison contractors to be notified that their agreements were to be terminated within thirty days. It was not until March 1, 1889, however, and then only as the result of the continued agitation of the trade unionists, that the last vestiges of contract convict labor were removed from California prisons.—Ed.

Temporary retirement—

With the passing of the League of Deliverance came the waning of enthusiasm in advancing the cause of trade unionism. I was in debt and could not continue my absence from work as I had been doing. Accordingly I went back to my job as a moulder and paid close attention to it, limiting my labor activities to attending meetings of the Moulders' Union and the Knights of Labor. I also occasionally attended socialist meetings, although I had long made up my mind that the program of Socialism was incapable of accomplishing the results hoped for. As a means of arousing working people from their lethargy Socialism was admirable, but as the socialists wanted no piece-meal improvements, desiring the full realization of all that they advocated, which was impossible, I kept myself aloof from their public meetings. They still, however, considered me a member of the Socialist Party.

Campaign among the moulders—

From the time that I began working in the foundries of San Francisco I had noticed how little of fraternal feeling existed among the moulders. The few union men among them were no better in that or in any other respect than those who were not members. As a cold fact, many non-members were less "hoggish" than those who belonged to the union, and on occasion exhibited far more of the spirit which I thought should actuate union men than did the union men themselves. To work as hard as they were physically able to do, appeared to be the only ambition that most of the moulders had in mind. Men who work as hacks and drudges are not those from whom to expect high thoughts or ideas of social improvement. The conception of Sylvis and those of his associates in forming the National Moulders' Union was that by association and an interchange of thought better notions of social improvement would be cultivated and something superior to a two-bit-a-day increase in wages would be firmly implanted in the minds of the members. It was also hoped that there would be developed a thorough and practical spirit of fraternity, making of the membership of each local union a harmonious and homogeneous whole. A generation had passed and no results of the kind hoped for had been brought about. Hard work, with all its mentally degrading effects, still flourished as if Sylvis had never lived and had not taught such high principles.

I considered the San Francisco moulders at the time as being at a very low intellectual depth. Their selfishness and lack of desire for cooperative effort was as fixed as their rivalry in the shop to hold the favor of the boss. Now, however, they are quite changed and to a large extent the antipodes of what they were then. I believe too that those of this generation do not know that a great change has taken place, nor are they conscious of how it was brought about. I am glad to have had a part in making that change possible. I am not, I think, an egotist and have never believed in parading my special views or in pretending to be any better than the least among my associates. My want of pretense leaves me now in the position of being unknown to the present generation of moulders. If I am remembered by a few contemporaries, it is, I fear because my continued talks at union meetings of what we should do and what we should become did not harmonize with current practices. Reminders of this sort bred a sense of hostility, because it made the moulders appear contemptible in their own eyes. When a half-tutored man's inward consciousness is aroused by constant allusions to his everyday acts he is apt to resent the arraignment, and if he does not impute unworthy motives to his mentor, in self-defense he loses no opportunity of assailing him if there arises the slightest cause for doing so. A slavish worker has a slavish mind which colors all things inharmonious with its low bent.

I began my campaign of reformation by first studying the salient characteristics of my shopmates, their weaknesses being especially interesting. Gaining their confidence to some extent, the next step was to encourage active, ungrudging help when from whatever cause a fellow-worker was behind in completing his day's task. To do this voluntarily and cheerfully was a decided step toward comradeship because it begat an obligation that was entitled to reciprocation. Harmony and an interchange of opinions upon any subject, if continued, end in better understanding between individuals even if they should not always and upon all points be in perfect accord. Only a little time was needed to break through the icy barriers which selfishness and competitive rivalry had solidly established. The men actually worked better because of the agreeability engendered.

In the union it was necessary to adopt another course. When the opportunity offered I invariably commented upon the evils of "rushing" and competition. I attempted to point out that such practices always engendered hard feeling and never brought to the successful ones any permanent benefit. The contrary was more often the result and invariably to the profit and advantage of the employer. Such contests were also degrading because they were mere exhibitions of physical endurance backed by brute force. An occasional well-timed remark, illustrative of this condition, was more effective than long-winded dissertations on the subject. An imperceptible change took place among the members of the union, apparently of unexplainable origin, with which there grew an ardent desire to increase the membership to the full strength of all those employed at the trade. Steadily and gradually the union began to grow in numbers and to assume in consequence a leading part in the local trade union movement.

Moulders demand the closed shop—

So much happened during the period between the death of the League of Deliverance and the organization of the Iron Trades Council that I find it impossible after the lapse of many years to remember every detail. As secretary of the moulders' union, I was continuing my sporadic educational course at every favorable opportunity. I was making considerable headway, although without any apparently just cause also making an enemy here and there among the members. The rushing, "hoggish" workers did not relish being reminded at almost every meeting of their shortcomings. No reminder could induce them to give up their old habits. They had made a reputation with the boss and resolved to keep it, and no talk of mine could cause them to change their ways. Nearly all the moulders in the city were members of the union, but it struck one of the active members, incapable of thinking correctly on matters concerning others, that it was about time to compel those who were not members to join the union immediately. It was stated that the union was strong enough to do so and that it ought to be done. This talk met with a hearty response, force being the recognized and apparently the only means by which desirable ends could be attained. No further action was taken and the worthy brother who introduced the subject no doubt went to sleep that night believing himself to be among the first and best of union men. He kindled the fire which

I saw would envelope us all in its flames if care were not taken to extinguish it or keep it under control. At the next meeting it was suggested that the shop committee-men interview the non-union men and ask them to become members. Several of the latter had been union men in days gone by, and like the non-union compositors on the *Call* and *Evening Bulletin,* had suffered at the hands of ignorant, selfish, and inconsiderate union officials. Consequently, they were loath to trust themselves again in a union where the same wrongs might be repeated. The shop committee now reported progress and asked for further time, which was granted. The request was repeated at several consecutive meetings and was also granted. As a matter of fact the shop committee-men, having failed in their first attempt at recruiting, saw that they were confronted with a serious obstacle and ceased their efforts, hoping by repeated requests for more time to have the matter die a quiet death. The fire was kindled, however, and could not be smothered by subterfuges.

After about three months of procrastinating by the committee the subject was finally brought to a head by the same active, eloquent brother who proposed that if in a given length of time the non-union men had not signified their intention to join, then after giving due notice the union should demand their discharge. That resolution would have been adopted and a serious struggle would have followed had I not interposed and offered an amendment calling for the appointment of a special committee, naming the members in my motion, authorized to call upon the men and ascertain what could be done to secure their admission. The amendment was adopted; the committee did its work satisfactorily; the men, with one exception, joined the union; harmony was again established and a serious situation was avoided.

The Coast Seamen's Union—

Sigmund Danielewicz, an ardent socialist who was interested in the lot of the sailors, finally succeeded in 1885 in bringing the seamen together for the third time.[35] Burnette G. Haskell, who had displayed unusual activity in the propagation of Socialism as a writer and speaker, with the aid of several abler and better balanced men, also assisted Danielewicz in the work of reorganization. This time only sailors became members. Wages were lower than they had ever been. Shipping being at a low ebb and jobs scarce in consequence had caused an unusual increase in the number of idle seafaring men. Notwithstanding these drawbacks the union grew in numbers and prospered. Instead of their meeting place being

[35] It was really the fourth time, instead of the third, that the sailors had been brought together into an organization. The Sailors' Union, which still exists, was organized as the Coast Seamen's Union by Danielewicz, Haskell and others following a meeting of striking sailors held on the water front on March 6, 1885. Haskell was chosen its first treasurer. For details concerning this and other efforts at organizing the sailors, see P. S. Taylor, *The Sailors' Union of the Pacific,* and I. B. Cross, *First Coast Seamen's Unions, Coast Seamen's Journal,* July 8, 1908.—Ed.

up-town, as I had had it, a large room was taken on the water front where the men met every day during the organization period and were addressed by Haskell or some of his associates.

A demand for higher wages for men in the coastwise trade was made and refused, thus bringing the impending conflict to an issue. Patrolmen were appointed to keep the union informed and to report what vessels were ready to put to sea and whether or not they had a full crew. If not, measures were then taken to prevent the completion of the crew. If delayed a day the vessel was hauled into the bay and lay there until supplied with a crew by the boarding-house keepers. The boarding-house keepers were intimidated by the union men and ceased to act as agents in providing crews. Several rows occurred, a few of the union sailors were jailed, but finally victory perched on the banners of the Coast Seamen's Union. With victory came an increase of membership and an extension of the union to all coast ports. Socialism was preached to the sailors by Haskell and others as the only sure, safe, and speedy means of their redemption from wage slavery and from dependence upon ship-owners and captains.

The Pacific Coast Central Labor Union—

The Coast Seamen's Union was not a trade union in the sense that trade unionists understand that term. It was an organization willing to accept any plan, however remote, that promised better social conditions, and Socialism promised that. Haskell knew the necessity of being identified with the trade union movement upon which he relied for moral and financial support. Inasmuch as the Trades Assembly had gone out of existence Haskell proposed to create a central body by means of a convention which he decided to call. An invitation was extended to the unions to participate but was not responded to except by two or three of them. To make it appear that he had got together a large representative gathering Haskell divided the Coast Seamen's Union into a boatmen's union, a mates' union, and about a dozen other unions, all the members of which were, of course, part and parcel of the Coast Seamen's Union. The convention was held in Irish American Hall on Howard Street near Third[36] and was presided over by James B. Johnson, a pattern-maker. E. G. Anderson, of the Coast Seamen's Union, was secretary. I suggested to the moulders' union that it send delegates, but my associates were not inclined to do so because they had no faith in the men who were behind the movement. However, I was sent simply to act as an observer. My instructions were to observe the proceedings and report back to the union. Upon my appearance at the second session of the convention I was elected vice-president over my protest.[37] The delegates pro-

[36] The convention met on March 16–19, 1885.—Ed.

[37] Roney was also appointed a member of the organizing committee.—Ed.

ceeded to form what was to be known as the "Pacific Coast Central Labor Union." After adopting various resolutions the convention adjourned. Haskell undoubtedly felt that his new organization was doomed to failure, for after adjournment he made no further efforts in that direction, limiting his activities to the Coast Seamen's Union, and later to the propagation of Socialism under the guise of Nationalism, the product of Bellamy's *Looking Backward.*[38]

Nationalism—

Nationalism was a mild form of hysteria evoked by Bellamy's inspiring book. Its membership was composed largely of that neurotic crowd that invades all new catchy movements and abandons them when the novelty has passed or when practical work has to be done. While it lasted it created quite a furore in the United States. In California, its followers went so far as to hold a state convention which was largely attended. Unfortunately as a consequence of certain actions taken by the convention, enough ill feeling was engendered to weaken and ultimately to destroy the Nationalist movement in California.

38 Haskell and his associates were so much impressed with the ideas contained in Laurence Gronlund's *Cooperative Commonwealth* and Edward Bellamy's *Looking Backward,* that they organized the Kaweah Cooperative Colony, a communist colony, in the foothills of the Sierra Nevada near Visalia. It lasted for about six years, failing in 1891 after a rather tempestuous and precarious existence.

The iron trades strike—

The moulders' union in time became so powerful and some of its members so swaggering in their behaviour as to cause friction with a few employers who were as ignorant as the men and far more domineering. Business was wretchedly bad, and upon the pretense that a cut in wages would revive and stimulate business the foundry owners proposed a reduction of wages. A notification was also posted in the foundries to the effect that on and after the date given no attention would be paid to any rules or orders issued by the moulders' union. The wage reduction was to apply to all classes of workers engaged in the foundries. The moulders happened to be the only men in the iron trade that were really organized. The boiler-makers had a semblance of a union, but none of the other trades had any organization whatever. The necessity of organization was too plainly obvious to all of the men and they proceeded to organize for the contest with the employers. The struggle was brief and the men won.[39]

Formation of Iron Trades Council—

The necessity of bringing all the unions of the industry into one central body, patterned along the lines of the plan which I had published in the Chicago *Workingmen's Advocate* in 1869, was forcibly brought to my attention by this strike, and

39 The notice announcing a 25 per cent reduction in wages was posted February 7, 1885. The strike lasted from February 8 to February 20, 1885.—Ed.

I accordingly requested the moulders to call a conference of representatives of the unions in the iron trade to consider its practicability. Sam McKee, a level-headed, conservative member of the union, P. J. McBride a light-headed, frothy member, and myself were chosen to represent the moulders. I submitted my plan of organization to the assembled delegates, and it was at once adopted. The first meeting of the Federated Iron Trades Council was held on the evening of May 11, 1885. Representatives were present from the pattern-makers, moulders, machinists, blacksmiths, boiler-makers, and foundry laborers.[40] I had organized the laborers at the time of the above mentioned strike so that they as well as the moulders might mutually assist in maintaining what few rights they had. At the meeting at which the Iron Trades Council was formed, James B. Johnson was elected president, Thomas Roebuck, vice-president, Thomas Watson, treasurer, and myself, secretary.[41] An executive committee was composed of the foregoing officers with the addition of Arthur Wilson. Johnson was made chairman and I, secretary, of the committee.

The basis of representation in the new Iron Trades Council was three delegates from each union

[40] Representatives of the Amalgamated Society of Engineers were also present.—Ed.

[41] The newspaper reports of the meeting at which the Iron Trades Council was organized state that S. Gunn was chosen vice-president, Joseph Valentine, financial secretary, John Mahoney, recording secretary, and J. Turner, treasurer. Roney was placed on the executive committee, but later became secretary of the organization.—Ed.

regardless of the number of members. All questions of importance brought before the Council, affecting or likely to affect more than one union and requiring the cooperative action of the whole body, had first to be submitted to the unions separately and by their action, after proper deliberation, the Council was to be governed. If a majority of the unions decided action was necessary in any case the Council henceforth was required to take charge of the matter. It was thoroughly a democratic body recognizing the responsibility of the individual union as the source of all power and authority. A great deal of work was necessary to train the new unions in trade union ideals.

A union proclamation—

In order to facilitate organization and if possible increase the number of unions, it was suggested that I write an address setting forth the reasons for the organization of working people, its necessity, and the benefits to be derived from it. Although it was a direct appeal to the workers it was also an appeal to all humanitarians to aid in lightening the heavy burdens of the laborers. In my address I attempted to show that the progress in inventions and in the development of labor-saving machinery had only added to the burdens of the laborer. Hours of labor had remained the same, idle people had been multiplied, work was as arduous as ever, and under the factory system our labor had become brutalizing, degenerating, and exacting. I sent a copy of the address to every clergyman in San Francisco, believing that some of them might take the subject into consideration and discuss it publicly. Not one of them considered it worth his while to do so, although several of them subsequently developed into ultra-socialists when it became popular and profitable for them to do so. I look upon all clergymen doubtingly. The modern preacher fashions himself after the yellow newspaper. The preacher, to be a successful saver of souls and, as he imagines, to enlarge his usefulness, must be sensational in just the same way as the newspaper, which with less pretense seeks to increase its circulation and add to its profits by numerous, well paying, but questionable advertisements. The modern up-to-date preacher is no more regarded as the man of God that he was less than a century ago than the modern up-to-date newspaper is considered a reliable purveyor of Truth.

The shipwrights' union—

The shipwrights' union sought admission into the Iron Trades Council for the reason that some of its members were employed in iron shipbuilding. They made the templates used in shaping the plates that form the hull of the vessel under construction. The local boiler-makers' union had not yet changed its name or rules so as to take in the men working at iron shipbuilding, and so it was thought entirely proper to accept the shipwrights because a portion of them were employed in the iron shipbuilding business. They were accordingly admitted. Later they were also admitted to membership in the Federated Trades Council.

San Francisco Building Trades Council—

A man named Campbell who held an honorary card of membership in the moulders' union, but who had given up that trade and had become a member of Carpenters' Union No. 22, requested a copy of the constitution of the Iron Trades Council with the object of forming a like council in the building trades. I was pleased to furnish him with all the information that I could impart and assured him that I would urge the building trades unions in the Federated Trades Council to cooperate in the proposed organization. I spoke to P. Roberts, and Jim O'Sullivan, of the bricklayers, to the delegates of the painters', lathers', sheet-metal and cornice workers' unions, all of whom consented to take part in the new organization, and the "Building Trades Council of San Francisco" came into existence about a year after the formation of the Iron Trades Council.[42]

[42] The "Representative Council of the Building Trades of San Francisco" was formally organized on May 17, 1886, by the adoption of a constitution and the election of the following officers: president, J. D. Campbell; vice-president, G. Nicholson; recording secretary, J. D. DeGrear; treasurer, P. H. Kebrigan; financial secretary, B. Daggett. Delegates were in attendance from the following unions: carpenters, painters, roofers, lathers, plumbers, and gas fitters. It did not long play a part in the local labor world. The present Building Trades Council of San Francisco was organized in February, 1896.—Ed.

Again discharged—

The report that I had made on prison labor and the attention that it had received proved disastrous to me. As already related, Mr. McAfee, Judson's manager, demanded my discharge from the Union Iron Works. Dimmick, the foreman, refused to discharge me upon the ground that he needed me to handle the rush of work that he then had on hand. He also maintained that my outside activities in no way interfered with my work in the shop. When he told me of the situation, he said that if he did not discharge me he himself would be discharged. Of course, there was nothing else for me to do but to leave. He felt the humiliation of the order given him much more keenly than I felt my discharge. Sometime later, Dimmick himself was replaced by Daniel O'Neill, with whom I had worked as a partner on many a big moulding job in the Union Iron Works. He understood my motives better than any one in the foundry and felt that I had been shabbily treated. Consequently, in a short time I was again back on the job in the Union Iron Works and for a while things went along smoothly.

Ingratitude of fellow-unionists—

The Sunday after my discharge by Dimmick a number of moulders were discussing the matter and the reason for it, which Dimmick did not conceal, and it was decided by several of the moulders that I had got what was rightly coming to me for not having attended to "my own business," as they termed it. Their attitude hurt me more than twenty discharges would have done. I had been selected by the union of which they were members, to do a certain task presumably beneficial to the union, and had lost my job because I had done the task to the best of my ability. Had I attended to "my own business" my discharge would not have happened. If I had reported my discharge to the union I could have been put upon the list entitling me to weekly benefits and at the same time could have posed as a martyr to the cause. I asked for neither benefit nor sympathy, and none was offered me. If another man had been in my position I would have moved heaven and earth to credit and applaud him. I felt that I had done my simple duty which merited a slight recognition, but as I did not receive it I let it pass, satisfied in my conscience that I had done the right thing by everyone except my family.

For sake of a principle—

As the new shops of the Union Iron Works were nearing completion in the Potrero District its management applied to the Board of Supervisors for the passage of an ordinance to close the streets leading to it. The Board took the matter under consideration for two weeks, I think. Taking matters of this sort under advisement was a trick of the supervisors to discover in the interim how much of a corruption fund was in sight.

Colonel Richard Savage, a novelist of repute, connected with his father in the management of the Empire Foundry, thought that the Union Iron Works should be granted the concession asked for. He made the suggestion to Sam McKee and to J. F. Valentine, later National President of the Iron Moulders' Union of North America. Both agreed to call a special meeting of the local moulders' union to hear what the Colonel had to say upon the subject. Valentine and McKee were employees of the two Savages. I refused to sign the call for the meeting because I considered the proposal to close the street to the an affair apart from unionism. At noon of the day of the meeting a half-drunken moulder met me at First and Mission streets and loudly proclaimed me to be the originator of the meeting in the interest and at the instigation of the Union Iron Works. I had not intended going to the meeting, but this charge implied cowardice provided I were absent. I had not proposed to take part in the proceedings because I knew of no principle of unionism involved or at stake.

Colonel Savage made an excellent plea for the cause of the Union Iron Works and urged the union to go on record as favorable to the proposition to close the streets as requested. McKee, Valentine, and a man named Little, all employees of the two Savages, followed in similar vein. The prospect for the adoption of the resolution looked quite favorable when it occurred to one of the members that I should say something. I declined, but some of the members of the union were insistent, and finally I took the floor. I told them that I did not think that the matter was a subject for their consideration. It was outside of unionism and purely political in character. I did not think that the citizens of San Francisco would lose anything by closing the street to general traffic, for in the nature of things there never would be any general traffic upon it. The street ended with an entrance into the Pacific Rolling Mill on the one side and the Atlas Iron Works on the other, and led straight into the bay. In my opinion it made no difference what was done, because the people could lose nothing. The Union Iron Works wanted the street closed perhaps for some ulterior ultimate object not then apparent and like all corporations, which in the past had received public favors, trampled upon those from whom they were obtained. I would grant no favor to the Union Iron Works or to any other corporation without including a provision calling for reversion if the grant were abused. Inasmuch as such a condition had not been embodied in the request made to the supervisors, I claimed that the moulders' union should oppose the request of the Union Iron Works.

When I arose to speak I knew that I was about to jeopardize my job. As I never said anything before a union that I did not believe, I could not depart from that policy no matter what the cost might be. The resolution failed of adoption and I was congratulated for having defeated it. The next morning, before eight o'clock, O'Neill, my foreman at the Union Iron Works, informed me that a member of the union had reported my talk of the previous evening to Mr. Scott and had attributed the defeat of the resolution to my opposition. O'Neill denied that I was responsible and shook Scott's confidence in his informer. I boldly asked to be confronted with my accuser, which was not conceded for obvious reasons. I believed that I knew the traitor, but could not make an open charge against him. He was then and is now a prominent union man and has profited largely by his professions. I was not discharged at the time, owing chiefly to O'Neill's voluntary protestation of my innocence of which he was thoroughly convinced without a word of explanation by me. When the Union Iron Works finally moved to the Potrero, however, he informed me that the management had instructed him not to employ me under any circumstances.

In politics—

In the meantime I had been drawn into the campaign to further the election of James Gilleran as supervisor. He was a very incompetent workman but an excellent member of the moulders' union. For a number of years he had filled the position of treasurer of our union with commendable honesty. He was a pleasant fellow of no ability, good looking, and, as I believed, of strict integrity. He had embarked in the lodging-house business and was steeped in debt. He had been a Democrat, but as the Republicans were in power he sought to be nominated by the Republicans.

Phil Crimmins, afterwards associated with Martin Kelly as a "boss," was at the moment struggling to the front as a ward "boss" through the instrumentality of the Howard Club, a semi-social political organization. In reciprocation Crimmins proposed to get jobs for a number of the members of the club. Each supervisor was entitled to a certain portion of the patronage, always of course with the approval of the big "boss," Bill Higgins, who dominated all the patronage. Gilleran had agreed to give his patronage to Crimmins. The nomination had to be secured before the distribution of patronage could be discussed. Higgins was the man who named the nominees. He styled himself the Republican Party, as in fact he was, since the party convention met merely to ratify what he proposed. His selection of candidates for all the offices was generally made with the object of "strengthening" the ticket by the assured popularity of the individual candidates.

Higgins on the Republican side and Buckley on the Democratic side were the visible agents of the corporations. Behind them stood W. W. Stow, who instructed both of them as to what candidates should be nominated and as to what measures should be put through to benefit the corporations. The people, who did the voting, voted generally as partisans, while a large number, who were better informed and more venal, voted for immediate payment, usually cash or a guaranteed office. It struck me as most remarkable that American citizens, men of intelligence and wealth in many instances, could so meekly submit to a system fraught with so much danger to the perpetuity of free institutions and so utterly degrading to every instinct of decent manhood.

Crimmins introduced Gilleran to Higgins as his candidate for supervisor from the tenth ward. Higgins was a man of superior education and an excellent judge of men. It took him but a short time to discover that Gilleran would make an excellent tool, for which he was in search, but he also wanted a man with intelligence enough to defend himself when he acted contrary to the latent sentiment of decency that always existed. So Higgins rejected Gilleran because of his pronounced ignorance.

Gilleran lamented to me about his disappointment. When I came to comprehend the situation in all its bearings I assured Gilleran that we would compel Higgins to give him the nomination. Accordingly I visited several influential Democratic political friends and had them call upon Higgins to urge Gilleran's nomination. Not one of these men knew Gilleran and what they did was done to oblige me. Republican "bosses" preferred the recommendations of Democrats of influence, as Democratic "bosses" preferred Republican recommendations for their candidates. Higgins was convinced of

Gilleran's great strength as a vote getter and finally gave him the nomination. From the morning after his nomination until the evening before the election I was with Gilleran every day.

A city employee—

It was about the time that Gilleran was elected that O'Neill informed me that the Union Iron Works management had ordered that I be discharged. Times were dull with the foundries and my prospects for employment were not brilliant. I naturally supposed that Gilleran would be only too anxious to serve me by getting me a position with the city government. It was then that I learned that his patronage had been given to Crimmins with the consent of Higgins. Higgins had a thorough, not to say implacable, dislike for me. I never had sought him, and except in Gilleran's case I had never had anything in common with him. He considered me wholly unreliable, and from his standpoint I knew that I was such a person. Gilleran urged me to see him, but I absolutely refused to do so.

As the time approached when the supervisors were to take their places Gilleran informed me that I could have the fireman's job in the City Hall which paid $80 per month. I was in need of work, in debt, and the possessor of a reputation that foundry owners and slavish foremen did not esteem. Consequently I was forced to accept the job offered. McAvoy, a former member of the Seamen's Protective Association, was the City Engineer under whom I was to serve. He was a decent man in every respect and intensely earnest in his desire to see the condition of the working people improved. He knew that I was also equally earnest and proposed to help me in every way he could. For this purpose he had a writing desk brought into the fireroom, and I began my work as a labor organizer in real earnest, unencumbered with strenuous labor, possessed of a steady job for at least two years and assured of $80 each month without deductions for loss of time. McAvoy undertook to do as much of the work as he could consistent with his position as engineer.

I was continuously busy with the task of organizing the workers and continued to write reports of the meetings as a means of keeping steadily before non-unionists and the public just what was being done in that direction. The Iron Trades Council increased its membership by the addition of the stationary engineers, the San Francisco Branch of the Amalgamated Society of Engineers, an English society, and the brass moulders and finishers. I believe that the core-makers were also admitted.

Pacific Union Club building—

The contract for making the steel girders for the Pacific Union Club, a large building partly on the site of Agricultural Hall, corner of Post and Stockton Streets, was let to Rix & Firth. The girders were the heaviest of their kind yet used in any building in the city. Some of them were ponderous and weighed many tons. There were four competitors for the contract, three of whom had shops in the city in which the work could have been done. Rix & Firth did not have a shop, nor did they have the equipment for any part of the work. They sent the drawings to Chicago and had the order filled in that city. It was a large job and would have given many of our men employment, a great many of whom were at that time unemployed. When the girders began to arrive I had a most competent man, Tom Roebuck, look them over and report if they complied in all essentials with the requirements prescribed in the ordinances adopted by the Board of Fire Commissioners. Roebuck had formerly been in business and understood blue-prints and every requirement of the ordinances. He went over every piece of work with the result that he reported all of them to be defective. Upon the strength of his report to the Iron Trades Council I waited upon Fire Chief David Scannel and asked him what he was going to do about it. He told me that they were good enough and were going into the building whether they were perfect or not. He also expressed himself most discourteously by reminding me that it would pay me better if I attended to my own business, just as my moulder friends had said a short time before.

I would not accept Mr. Scannel's fiat as conclusive, and appeared before the Fire Commissioners, stated my case and demanded that a thorough examination be made of these imported girders. They directed their architect, Mr. O'Connor, to make the examination and report his findings. With Roebuck, I associated Arthur Wilson and Joseph Turner, who met Mr. O'Connor at his suggestion and examined each girder. None of them was found to be in accordance with the specifications, and Mr. O'Connor so reported. The Fire Commissioners at once condemned them, notwithstanding the sputtering protests of Dave Scannel, and all of the girders underwent a thorough overhauling. For several months thereafter Post Street from Stockton to Powell looked like a huge boiler shop. After the changes had been made Roebuck and O'Connor again examined and approved them. Rix & Firth took no more contracts for they became bankrupt.

Boiler-makers' strike—

The Risdon Iron Works undertook the contract for making and laying a line of huge water pipe from Crystal Springs in San Mateo County to San Francisco for the Spring Valley Water Company. A great number of men were required in the shop to make the pipe and many more to fit and lay it. Outside men were guaranteed a bonus of so much per day if they remained on the job until its completion or until their services were dispensed with. Mr. Robert Moore, the superintendent of the Risdon Iron Works, placed his brother, Mr. Andrew Moore, in charge of the outside work. The latter selected as his assistant a very competent machinist. This selection did not please the boiler-makers, who thought that only a boiler-maker was fitted for the job. A strike against the machinist foreman was contemplated, but they were warned that if they struck they would receive no support from the other unions and that any union man would be permitted to take the places of those who quit. It would be considered an unauthorized strike. That order had the effect of cooling their striking ardor, and they remained at work.

The job lasted about a year. When within a month of its completion, and with only about twenty men employed, the worthy boiler-makers decided to strike against the machinist foreman under whom they had worked so long, thus forfeiting their accumulated bonus, which for some of the men amounted to $200. When they struck they came to the city and began their swaggering. They demanded the summoning of a special meeting of the union to consider their case, and it was called. They soon began to realize that they had made fools of themselves and were sorry for their ill-advised action. Roebuck, Denis McCarthy, and Vaughan Morgan, the wisest members of the union, came to me to see what I could to to adjust the difficulty. I certainly felt disinclined to have any part in an effort to adjust it. There was not the semblance of reason on the part of the strikers and I suggested that the union condemn their action and permit other men to take the places of the strikers and finish the job. This I considered to be the proper course. Then it was suggested that if that course were adopted it would go far in dismembering the union, which was by no means strong, and that at a time when the national officers were endeavoring to consolidate with men employed on iron shipbuilding.

I did not care about taking a hand in this affair; the strike was so contrary to all my ideas as to what the conduct of workingmen should be in their relations with employers. I desired the personal conduct of workingmen to be as nearly as possible always one of dignity. I felt that they should always have a perfect understanding of every wrong complained of and the manhood and intelligence to assert their rights with the determination to uphold them. To become an apologist for a group of union men was to me a most distasteful proposition. However, I agree to see what could be done in the matter, and took Joe Turner along as a shrewd and wise adviser. Failing to meet Mr. Andrew Moore at the Third and Townsend Street Depot we went to his house on Leavenworth Street, where we met both Andrew and Robert Moore. They received us very cordially, but expressed their indignation very forcibly and declared their unwillingness to consider the case or any feature of it. I very plainly told Mr. Robert Moore that I was quite in accord with him in condemning the action of the men. I did not offer to excuse them and I would offer no apology.

I stated, however, that the strikers were sorry for their conduct, especially because of the delay it had caused in completing the work. I saw that I had made an impression on Mr. Moore, who appeared very willing to continue the conversation. We spent an hour in this way, Moore's anger visibly decreasing in the meantime. In the end it was agreed that if I would guarantee that the men would resume work in the morning and would pledge themselves to continue to the end Moore would overlook the unexpected interruption and would hold no grudge against the participants. I agreed to this with pleasure. In the matter of the bonus, however, he was firmly convinced that the strikers were not entitled to it. I convinced him that to concede this to them would be a magnanimous act. The bonus was a big thing to the men, while it was a small matter to the Risdon Iron Works Company. He at length consented to pay it, and I left to report my success to the union which was meeting in special session. I laid the matter briefly before the assembled boiler-makers, telling them that I had guaranteed in their name prompt compliance with the conditions agreed upon. Boiler-makers, as is well known, are more or less deaf because of the nature of their employment. As I was speaking I noticed one of them with his hand to his ear straining with evident distress to catch what I had to say. As I neared the conclusion of my remarks he was unable to restrain himself any longer in his effort to hear and understand me. He knew that I was not a member of the union and burst forth with the inquiry: "Mr. President, what is this damned fellow doing here, and what is he saying?" His questions made me gasp. I had been working under high pressure for four hours, without dinner, doing my best to adjust a discreditable difficulty, and here was the kind of appreciation given. Worse was yet to come. When I had finished my report a vote was taken upon its acceptance, and it was overwhelmingly rejected. I left the room, intending to see Mr. Moore again and tell him that my guarantee was not valid, and to express my regret at the outcome of the negotiations. Morgan and McCarthy called me back and told me that it was all a mistake and that it would be corrected at once. They asked me to wait a few minutes. I did so, and was amazed at the emphatic reversal of the previous vote by a two to one majority. To me the way of the boilermaker was mysterious and, to say the least, uncertain. I resolved to be careful in the future in engaging in anything involving or affecting boilermakers.

City's neglect of building inspection—

Several accidents of a minor character occurred in the wholesale section of the city because of the incompetency of those having charge of elevator machinery. The Hartford Insurance Company, through its boiler inspector, Mr. Warner, gave me a clear insight into the dangers that beset the unconscious public doing business in that district because of the ignorance of the employees in charge of the elevator machinery and the stupidity of the owners of the plants. Boys of no judgment or experience and Chinamen with no knowledge of the uses or of the fatal power of steam were largely placed in charge of steam boilers which were usually built under the sidewalks and invariably located in the basements of the buildings. Low wages were the inducement for the employment of that class of attendants. So long as the boilers did not explode, and the machinery of the elevators ran smoothly, all was well, and cheap labor was as good as any for the work, in fact, rather better in the estimation of many who should have known better.

The stationary engineers' union adopted a practical and unique test for those seeking admission to their union. The candidate was required to take all the parts of a steam engine and put each in its proper place. If he could do so he was admitted to the union, otherwise not. He was then examined upon the construction of boilers, the value and importance of the steam and water guages, the formation of scale, the use of check valves and escape valves, how to set the latter in accordance with the dimensions of the boiler, the amount of steam demanded, etc. A member of this organization could thus be trusted with boilers and engines with the certainty of their being well and intelligently cared for as well as the assurance of safety to the public.

Haskell had turned his weekly paper, *Truth,* into a monthly magazine and was advocating the teachings of the International Workingmen's Association, a blend between Socialism and Anarchism. No longer interested in trade unionism he mentioned its affairs only occasionally. Therefore I made arrangements with Mr. Sutherland, editor of the *Daily Report,* then emerging from its former title, *The Stock Report,* to publish all news relating to trade unionism. Through the columns of that paper I then began a discussion of the dangers of boiler management resulting from the employment of incompetent workmen, and lost no opportunity in exploiting the subject, which propaganda I considered would prove useful in securing the adoption of a boiler inspection law.

Mr. W. W. Hanson and myself as outsiders were invited to cooperate with Messrs. John Oswald, Owen Pegg, and M. McAvoy, of the stationary engineers' union, in framing a boiler inspection bill for presentation to the Legislature, which we did, committing it to Mr. Frank French, a member of the Assembly, who duly introduced it. He was laughed at by his colleagues for doing so. Mr. Hanson was a mechanical engineer and the owner of the Hope Iron Works situated in the Potrero. He was a remarkably able man and was profoundly sincere in all that he suggested in framing this act. The stationary engineers' union was also earnest in devising protection for the people as well as to benefit themselves. I engaged in the work to help as best I could. When the bill failed of passage by the Legislature we endeavored to have it become a city ordinance, but this too failed owing to the opposition of men of wealth, like Claus Spreckels and Geo. W. Gibbs. What reason on earth these men had to interfere in an affair so important to public safety I could never clearly understand. Why the supervisors of San Francisco should have heeded those who knew nothing of the dangers and risks of mismanagement of boilers was to be accounted for solely by the habitual slavish deference of politicians to ignorant wealth in preference to the intelligence of well-informed men who understood all about it.

Inattention, carelessness, or ignorance caused the explosion of one of the boilers used by the Spring Valley Water Company at its pumping station located at Lake Merced and resulted in the death of several men. I had two of the most competent members of the stationary engineers' union go to the scene of the disaster and make a thorough examination of the causes leading to it. I wished this done before any concealment could be attempted, which I knew would be the case. John McDermott and Owen Pegg hurried out as fast as horse and buggy could carry them and made a thorough examination, bringing to town with them a portion of the boiler plate which had been located at the point of the explosion. Enough evidence was gathered to prove the culpability of those in charge of the works and the fact that the men came to their death through the wilful negligence of the person in charge. Therefore the water company was responsible. The families of the deceased were miserably poor and dependent and I wished them compensated and relieved from beggary. It was a poor alternative, but the only one possible under the circumstances.

Blinded justice—

Dr. C. C. O'Donnell was then coroner. He had been bragging for years of his devotion to the interests of the working people and had been accustomed to use all the anti-Chinese catchpenny buncombe indulged in by politicians and office seekers. O'Donnell set the day for the inquest and agreed with our men to set the hour at two o'clock in the afternoon. Convincing evidence in addition to what we already had was to be procured and McDermott was to go out again to Lake Merced to secure it. Instead of keeping his promise O'Donnell held the inquest in the morning when no representative of the deceased or of the stationary engineers' union was present. It was entirely a perfunctory proceeding and, when the seriousness of the calamity was considered, a very hasty one. The jury gave a verdict of accidental death, exonerating every one responsible from blame. I wanted the blame and responsibility fixed as a preliminary step toward recovering damages for the unfortunate families doomed to penury. O'Donnell had been guilty of a most cowardly, treacherous, and base act. We then started a movement to put O'Donnell out of office and preferred charges of incompetency against him. I wrote all of the questions which were to be asked him in order that, out of his own mouth or by his refusal to answer, the charges might be proved. Gilleran was unable to fill the rôle of examiner, so I divided the questions, giving some to Supervisor Sam Vallon and some to Willard Farwell. In some unaccountable manner the political bosses interposed and the investigation ended abruptly with nothing accomplished.

The whole business, inquest and investigation, was a glaring, burning scandal and outrage. The Trades Assembly having disbanded there was no central labor body in existence to take up the matter and burn it into the brains of the corporation-ridden people of San Francisco. The District Assembly of the Knights of Labor was completely absorbed in petty contentions and petty politics among its members and had neither time nor inclination to handle affairs of this sort. I had often been urged to become a member of the District Assembly as delegate from the Local Assembly 1390, to which I belonged, but I had always declined. I could never learn that that body ever did anything or that it proposed to do anything of tangible benefit to the workers. I did know, however, that its proceedings consisted mostly of personal encounters originating in the political aspirations and ambitions of its members. I talked to the members of Assembly 1390 of the injustice done the families of the men who had lost their lives in the explosion at the Spring Valley pumping plant and asked them what should be done to vindicate the wrong. There was no response! It was a deplorable situation, and that was where the matter had to be dropped.

Call for a Labor convention—

The results of the Chinese Exclusion Act were unsatisfactory and an agitation was started by the newspapers to have the Act amended. The Chinese question had been a fruitful source of profit to the politicians, so I decided that if possible I would turn that sentiment to the advantage of Organized Labor. I suggested that the District Assembly of the Knights of Labor call a convention of the labor unions to consider and recommend to Congress such amendments to the Exclusion Act as would insure its successful operation in the future. The suggestion was taken kindly by my friends in that body and was immediately acted upon. John Payne, the District Master Workman, showed me the call for the meeting before its publication and I amended it in certain particulars.

The call created quite a stir among the unions as well as outside of them. Unionism was again taking quite a strong hold upon the working people.

I believe that this was due to the reports and articles concerning such matters which I wrote and which were being published in the daily papers. Every worker appeared to be eager to join some kind of organization. As typical of what was occurring, I may cite one instance out of many.

Organizing the upholsterers—

I received a letter from the upholsterers inviting me to visit their organization, which had recently formed. I did so, and found a small number of sickly looking young fellows in attendance. I made inquiries about their work, their wages, and their hours. The wages struck me as being ridiculously low for the work performed. The men worked ten hours a day and the maximum wage received was nine and ten dollars a week. It was to improve their condition that they had organized their union. They also wished to associate with a central body like the Iron Trades Council so as to be assisted in bettering their status. They were insistent upon associating with the Iron Trades Council. I explained to them how impossible it was to consider their proposal because the upholsterers were not engaged in the iron trades field, but assured them of my hope that a central labor body would soon be in existence with which they could associate. I do not remember meeting any group of union men so pitifully earnest as these poor fellows were and how deeply they felt their disappointment! I assured them that I would come often to their meetings and by that means keep them in touch with the other unions until something better could be devised.

Politicians vs. the radicals—

The politicians in the District Assembly of the Knights of Labor began making arrangements to control and direct the convention of the union delegates when it assembled and to exclude organizations whose delegates might be tinctured with Socialism as well as those which might be entirely socialistic. I knew of what great value the socialists had been and how valuable they were in enthusing men to join the unions. I knew how earnest they were in the work and how ably and disinterestedly they had performed it. W. C. Owen, Peter Ross Martin, J. J. Martin, and Burnette G. Haskell had all done excellent work in that connection, in fact much better work than the trade unionists had, and I knew that without such men in the convention the gathering would prove to be a flat and unprofitable affair. Haskell was the main cause of the opposition of the Knights of Labor politicians because of his intense aggressiveness and his outspoken denunciations of wrongs affecting the workers. It made no difference to me how he had offended; I did not propose that he and the others named should be sacrificed by a few political aspirants who could not and would not uphold the cause of Labor in the hour of stress if to do so conflicted with their personal aims and desires. I passed the word along among the bona fide trade unionists, who agreed with me that we must have Owen, the two Martins, and Haskell in the convention.

I was requested by John Payne to attend a conference or caucus to cooperate with the Knights of Labor. Roberts, Valentine,[43] and Haskell likewise held a much larger caucus for the purpose of laying plans to control the convention. I declined to attend either gathering. Thus, before it had convened the convention was split in two hostile camps. My sympathies were entirely with the Valentine-Haskell contingent because it was composed of men who were of importance to the future labor movement and who had proven themselves of great benefit to it.

On the night of the first meeting[44] the program of each side was disclosed. According to the plans of the Knights of Labor group Payne was to call the meeting to order, become the temporary chairman, and read from a prepared list the names of the members of the various committees. When permanent organization had been effected he was to be the permanent president. The other side had decided that I was to act as both temporary and permanent presiding officer without any prearranged program. They knew how familiar I was with the men in the movement and trusted to my record for fair play and to my desire to see the convention a success.

[43] Joseph F. Valentine later became President of the International Moulders' Union. He died in San Francisco in February, 1930.—Ed.

[44] November 30, 1885.—Ed.

The radicals control—

The convention assembled on November 30, 1885, in Bnai Brith Hall. Payne would not entertain a motion to nominate me for the chairmanship. A dozen others were nominated, but they all declined in my favor. Still Payne refused to accept my nomination. Calvin Ewing, one of the politicians of the District Assembly, appealed to me to withdraw in favor of Payne so as to restore harmony, because the meeting was becoming tumultous. I refused to do so. Thereupon, Valentine of the moulders' union arose and said, "Since the chairman has refused to put Roney's name before the convention, I shall do so." He then asked how many were in favor of John Payne acting in that capacity, and a weak response was given. When my name was mentioned the convention arose in a body and amidst cheers proclaimed for me. Valentine then announced that I had been elected temporary chairman. Payne was completely paralyzed at the decisive action of the meeting and stood at the table, gavel in hand, speechless and inert. I immediately went to the table, took the gavel out of his hand, directed him to take a seat, put the program he had before him into my pocket, and called the meeting to order. I did this in less time than it takes to write it. I made a short talk inviting all groups interested in the redemption of the toiler, to do their best by indicating the course that the forces of Labor should follow to improve the condition of the working class. To relieve the delegates of the trouble and loss of time necessary to elect a temporary secretary I appointed E. G. Anderson, a socialist.[45] Then I appointed committees and took up most of the time of the first night by inviting old-time workers in the Cause to tell us what should be done. By doing this I impressed those present with the belief that whatever the result might be the convention was beginning in a broad and healthy manner.

Harmonizing conflicting interests—

It was the first time that so many hitherto conflicting elements had assembled as one body. To preserve for each its undoubted rights and to keep the body a harmonious whole was the task that I cut out for myself if I were to become the permanent chairman.[46] We had the conservative trade unionist who favored an aristocracy or upper-class division of Labor; we had the democratic trade unionist who believed that all laborers were on a common level; we had the mild socialist who believed in party discipline when not too rigidly enforced; we had the socialist who demanded nothing less than the whole socialistic program; we had the internationalist who was an advocate of expedient methods designed to bring about the social revolution, and finally, we had

[45] E. G. Anderson, a sailor, was especially prominent in the local labor movement during the later eighties and the early nineties. He remained active for many years as treasurer of the Sailors' Union and of several other water front organizations in San Francisco. He died at his home in Berkeley, California, in 1929.—Ed.

[46] Roney was chosen permanent chairman at the second meeting of the convention.—Ed.

the anarchist, an exponent of individualism and a relentless foe of government in every form. It was a queer combination of heterogeneous elements that I had set myself to control and for the moment, at least, to harmonize. The leaders of every faction appeared to have confidence in my desire to give fair play to them all. I recognized every man as being sincere in his beliefs and was determined that no man should question the other's sincerity.

The radicals gave me less trouble than the conservatives. When not in session the conservatives would ask why I had permitted a certain radical to express himself so freely when the rights of private property were assailed or some fantastic theory was advanced. I always assured them that it was for the purpose of giving the conservatives an opportunity to combat the radical ideas which had been presented. Furthermore, if what the radicals advocated was not in accord with natural and true principles it would die anyway and never more be heard of. I claimed that we were all broad and liberal enough to hear our pet ideas abused without wincing and that the expression of opposing views could do no harm. If any idea was right it would live as it ought to, and if it was wrong it would die and be forgotten.

Politicians withdraw—

The second and subsequent meetings of the convention were held in Metropolitan Hall on Fifth Street, the scene of Rev. Kalloch's triumphs. It accommodated about 3,000 people, and was crowded at every meeting by an attentive and interested assemblage.

Calvin Ewing, a Republican, and W. W. Stone, a Democrat, both members of the District Assembly of the Knights of Labor, were united in their determination to turn the convention into political channels and were much disappointed at the turn of affairs. I had no confidence in either of them and believed that they would avail themselves of the first opportunity to direct its course away from the goal which I had in mind. I was resolved that in spite of all things the gathering was to be a clear-cut labor convention and should end by establishing the trade union movement solidly and permanently in San Francisco. There were about seventy members of the Knights of Labor present either as representatives of unions or of local assemblies of the Knights of Labor. Twenty of them stuck solidly with Ewing and Stone, believing those two men to be the exponents of true Knights of Labor principles; the others I knew I could depend upon.

At the second meeting in Metropolitan Hall, Joseph Kelly, of the Coast Seamen's Union, proposed a resolution demanding the complete removal within sixty days of the Chinese from all parts of the Pacific Coast. As it implied a threat of violence against the Chinese without indicating the manner of its execution I permitted its discussion at considerable length. Ewing and Stone vehemently protested against it as being incendiary and revolutionary. Those on the affirmative side claimed that it was only by extreme measures that we could hope to realize the object sought. Intense excitement pervaded the great throng. The conservative trade unionists were silent, their attention being concentrated upon my next move. A roll call was demanded by ayes and nays. When my name was called the profoundest silence reigned, because it was felt that as I went so would go the convention. I voted "Aye." Then a storm of applause burst from every part of the house delaying the voting for several minutes. When it subsided and order was restored the voting proceeded with the result showing an overwhelming majority for the resolution.

Immediately upon the result of the vote being declared, Ewing arose and stated that as a law-abiding citizen he and the Knights of Labor delegates could take no further part in such a convention and would withdraw. Hisses greeted his announcement, but I suppressed the demonstration, declaring that Ewing had a right to express himself without the necessity of the audience showing signs of disapproval. I told Ewing that I thought that he claimed too much when he included all the Knights of Labor representatives in his valedictory. I asked him if he knew how many Knights were members of the convention and he replied that he did not. I then requested the secretary to give us the needed information, and he said seventy. I again asked Mr.

Ewing how many would accompany him, and he replied, "About twenty." I courteously bade them farewell and they silently retired. The convention then adjourned for the evening.

I had a busy time in the interval of four days till the next meeting in holding the conservatives in line. The newspapers were unusually liberal in their criticism and condemnation, which in fact were a little precipitate. At the next meeting of the convention the resolution to expel the Chinese was reconsidered. It was amended by removing the 60-day clause. This met with the approval of the conservatives, and passed almost unanimously. The resolution had accomplished in an unexpected way what I thought was inevitable. It averted a breaking up of the convention by eliminating the Knights of Labor politicians obviously bent upon its ruin, and thus restored harmony and confidence. When Ewing and Stone saw that they had been outwitted[47] they asked to be readmitted, which was peremptorily refused.

Drafting a constitution—

A committee to formulate a plan for a central labor body and to make rules for its guidance was the last work of the convention and was really the

[47] The introduction of the resolution to remove the Chinese in 60 days was part of a prearranged program devised by the radicals for the purpose of getting rid of the Knights of Labor politicians. Having accomplished their object they were then free to proceed with the adoption of a program which called for a more thorough organization of the forces of Labor than had previously existed in San Francisco. —Ed.

Calvin Ewing

W. C. Owen

only object that I had in mind. I was anxious to have my plan of organization adopted, i.e., my idea which had found expression in the Iron Trades Council, and it was approved in a general way by the committee, but the demand for a central organization was so great and pressing that I abandoned it temporarily, hoping at a not too distant date to see it in perfect operation. The most active cooperator I had in the framing of a constitution of the new organization was W. C. Owen, an able and convincing speaker and an indefatigable worker.[48] I have forgotten the names of the other participants, all of whom I had appointed because of their possessing some individual characteristics necessary to the organization of a central labor body upon a broad and comprehensive plan.

Trades and Labor Federation of the Pacific Coast—

I believe that it was toward the latter part of 1885, that the Federated Trades and Labor Council was finally launched and I was elected its first presi-

[48] Owen was a graduate of an English university who came to San Francisco as a representative of a concern interested in providing credit ratings for business firms. He allied himself with the Federated Trades Council, became its statistical secretary, later adopted the tenets of Socialism, and in association with Haskell took an active part in the agitation for the International Workingmen's Association. As a lover of freedom, he later assisted the Magon brothers in their efforts to bring about a revolt in Mexico. Both he and they were arrested in Los Angeles by federal authorities. The Magons were sentenced to imprisonment, but I never learned what happened to Owen.—Ed.

dent for a term of six months.[49] Unions sprang up in all directions with great rapidity, increasing the original membership of the body over 100 per cent. At every meeting of the Federated Trades Council after its organization applications were received from new unions for admission. For the first time in the history of San Francisco every evidence was given of the widespread and deeply rooted spirit of organization. A stream of visitors was constantly flowing down to my fireroom headquarters in the City Hall. I was so tired at night when I left the City Hall that I would have given almost anything for one hour of peaceful rest. Listening to complaints, harmonizing difficulties between unions and between ambitious members of unions, and frequently censuring and privately lecturing well-meaning but ignorant and often impetuous union men without giving offense, was an arduous and in the end a thankless task.

Organizing the shoemakers—

From the days of the Workingmen's Party the boot and shoe workers' organization kept up a fitful existence under a variety of names, but at no time as a trade union. Before that period the name of their organization was the St. Crispins.[50] At all

[49] The organization meeting of the "Representative Council of Trades and Labor Federation of the Pacific Coast" was held on January 12, 1886. A year later the title of the new organization was changed to "The Federated Trades of the Pacific Coast." It remained the central labor body of San Francisco until 1892.—Ed.

[50] The Knights of St. Crispin was a national union of boot and shoe makers organized in 1867 which survived until about 1873. It had two lodges in San Francisco in 1870 and three in 1871.—Ed.

times the object of the organization was to combat the steady absorption of the trade by the Chinese. So far as obstructing the Chinese in gaining a firm hold upon the business was concerned the white-labor movement proved to be a decided failure. It was found that a Chinaman could operate the machinery used in the manufacture of boots and shoes as well as the white man or boy. Even though the product of the Chinese lacked some slight finishing touches it sold as well if not better than the product of white labor. Like the cigar-makers, the only result the shoe workers expected to derive from organization was that they might still retain a portion of the trade by stamping or labeling the articles made by white men and boys. To issue and advertise the label or stamp was therefore their chief reason for organization.

No organization of shoe workers had been in existence for some time. P. B. Gallagher, an active and aggressive member of former organizations and one of the first to introduce the union stamp, came to consult me as to the best way to revive the shoe workers' organization. I had taken part in their reorganization on previous occasions and was familiar with the personnel of its anticipated members, their frequent jealousies and quarrels, and had little faith in seeing a permanent organization established. At the same time I believed that on the basis of repeated failures and past experiences, there might be a permanent association built up.

Gallagher assured me that if a mass meeting were called no association could be formed because of certain heartburnings which had resulted from the last smash-up. He gave me the names of men not associated with the former quarrels and I arranged them as the officers of the new union. I wrote what purported to be a meeting of the Boot and Shoe Workers' Union, at which I was supposed to be present, and at the conclusion of the article I urged all those workers engaged in the business to be present at the next meeting, mentioning the date and place of meeting. The invitation was responded to by a greater number than we had expected and the authenticity of the article dealing with the supposed first meeting and the selection of officers was never questioned. I understand that the organization called into existence by this surreptitious method has been maintained ever since without a break in its ranks.

As this way of getting men together proved so successful with the shoe workers I tried it in bringing others together with equally satisfactory results. I also discovered that reports of bogus meetings when well written were read with the same interest as if they had been genuine. I have never charged myself with serious wrongdoing by indulging in that form of mild duplicity. It injured no one, not even the newspapers, and in the end always accomplished the good it was intended to accomplish.

The cooks and waiters—

The Cooks' and Waiters' White Labor League was another body called into existence during the period of the Workingmen's Party, which survived long after that party had passed away. It was not because of the fear that the Chinese might displace them that the members of this organization kept together. As white men actuated by race prejudice they believed in a distinctive organization to assist in the furtherance of the general anti-Chinese movement, in which the majority of the people of California were at the time greatly involved. To the most intelligent among them it was apparent that organization was necessary to obtain an improvement in their everyday working conditions if they proposed to continue as waiters. It was the waiters who were most affected by the exactions of the restaurant keepers, although the cooks also worked long and unreasonable hours, but the latter were partly compensated by the pay which they received and therefore did not seek to reduce their working time.

A recalcitrant employer—

Little troubles were constantly arising between the waiters and the restaurant owners calling for the frequent intervention of an outside party to adjust them and preserve harmony. I was frequently required to act as the outsider in such matters. I had more trouble with an employer named Johnson, whose restaurant was located on Market

Street near Fourth, than with all of the other employers in that line of work. Johnson was the harshest and most exacting man I ever met. He expected service from his waiters for as many hours and for as little compensation as possible. He had no feeling whatever for his men. He was a born tyrant. He scornfully rejected some of the mildest proposals that I offered. Occasionally, however, he accepted my propositions. I was so frequently in contact with him that I got to know him thoroughly. I never threatened him, but always appealed to his sense of justice and humanity, and I gained concessions when it appeared to him to be most profitable. His patrons were principally workingmen.

One day I told Johnson that he had to run his business more satisfactorily and harmoniously with his men for I was tired of the constant petty squabbles which he precipitated and I had something more important to attend to than to bother continuously with him. He laughed at my warning, but the next complaint brought Johnson to his knees.

Now [said I] I won't parley any longer with you. I have here an agreement between you and your men which I want you to sign and thus stop all future squabbling, and if you don't sign it I will call out all the people you have employed and place the men on the sidewalk to boycott you. If you persist in not signing I shall drive you out of business. I have all the arrangements made and will put them into operation at once. I will give you ten minutes to decide.

The restaurant was well filled at the time. When the time expired and the agreement was unsigned, I immediately passed the word to the waiters to put on their coats and to notify the kitchen help. Johnson saw that I was in earnest and demanded a modification of some of the terms, which I would not agree to. He surrendered. One of the conditions which I imposed forbade him to swear at the men. He kept the agreement for the time specified, later getting into further trouble, and eventually quitting the business.

A Labor reporter—

I continued writing the reports of our meetings for the *Daily Report,* making extensive comments on the proceedings of the Iron Trades Council and the Federated Trades Council. The *Daily Report* thus was regarded as the official organ of the local labor movement. I believe that I contributed not less than twelve columns of material a week. Sutherland, the editor, finally detailed a reporter to attend to labor matters, which proved to be a great relief to me. With a little training I broke him in so well into reporting union meetings that he did it most satisfactorily. George Tailor proved to be an apt and industrious reporter as well as a faithful recorder of trade union news written in the way to do unionism the most good.

Andrew Furuseth—

Among the delegates representing the Coast Seamen's Union was Andrew Furuseth. Because of his Scandinavian nationality and the evident influence that he exercised among his countrymen, he was made secretary of that organization. He had formerly been a member of the Lake Seamen's Union, whose headquarters were in Chicago, with branches in all the cities located on Lake Michigan. The president of the Lake Seamen's Union was Richard Powers, with whom I had maintained a correspondence beginning when I was president of the Seamen's Protective Association. During the time that I was associated with the Federated Trades Council, Furuseth took no part in its proceedings, giving no evidence whatever of the capacity for leadership which he has subsequently shown. I was continually on the lookout for talented, capable, and sincere exponents of trade unionism, but my attention was never by any chance directed to Furuseth.[51]

51 Andrew Furuseth was born in Norway in 1854. As a youth he followed the sea, arriving in San Francisco in 1880. He joined the Coast Seamen's Union, later known as the Sailors' Union, shortly after its organization in 1885. In 1886, he became its secretary, which position he has held almost continuously since that time. He has long been a prominent figure in the local, national, and international labor movement, fighting especially for the welfare of the sailors and against the use of the injunction in labor disputes. No man in the ranks of Labor in San Francisco has been so constant in his loyalty to the working class. His life in all its phases has been an outstanding example of sincere devotion to a Cause without hope or expectation of reward other than the economic well-being and happiness of those for whose benefit he has unceasingly struggled.—Ed.

Need for restraint—

The newly admitted delegates of nearly every new union entered the Federated Trades Council with their credentials in one hand and a bill of grievances demanding a boycott or strike in the other. Boycotts were being authorized by the inexperienced and enthusiastic members of the Council by the wholesale. I knew that if the order of things was to be continued, I could only see a long line of abortive effort piled up against us with resulting disaster at the end of a short inglorious career. I therefore wrote a resolution calling a halt to the too generous and ill-considered action of the Council, giving it to H. W. Hutton to introduce. I spoke from the chair in support of it and told the assembled delegates plainly that their actions, if continued, would bring the Council to an end. I had a sincere dislike for boycotts and strikes, believing that in most cases if the trouble were properly handled by men of brains on Labor's side the contention would end favorably for Labor, thus making boycotts and strikes unnecessary. Strikes should never be resorted to until every known means for amicable adjustment had been exhausted, and even then they should be undertaken with caution only after deliberate and careful consideration. If the cause or demand were just, if the resources were ample so as to sustain a protracted battle, and if there were a reasonable hope that victory could be attained by the strikers, then there was a proper basis afforded for entering into contentions of that sort. I held that the wrongs that men had endured for years prior to organizing their present unions could be borne a little longer with patience until their organizations had been perfected and the other accessories to success were almost within reach.

As a consequence of my attack upon the policy of the Council in so freely sanctioning strikes and boycotts, the delegates passed my resolution providing that no union should strike or boycott until it had been a member of the Council for six months. They also changed the constitution so as to require that strike benefits should not be paid unless the Council had approved a strike before it was called.

Attitude toward strikes—

As to the matter of strikes, may I say that I have no objections to them when they are forced upon men by the imposition of cruel and exacting rules or interdictions, or by the brutal wrongs which some employers adopt to enforce their despotic power. Strikes in such cases are justifiable even if there is not a dollar in the treasury of the union and aid is far off and uncertain. Workmen are not justified in submitting to any wrong, however slight, that trenches upon their individual rights or tends toward their degradation. Manhood must be upheld every time in preference to a fight for more wages. Wages are, in the long run, of less importance to every worker than subservience to rules that humiliate him. The soul in the individual must ever remain unshackled. It is through the inspirations of the soul that higher aims are conceived and the best methods devised for their attainment. Economic progress can never be surely advanced by the compulsory or voluntary imposition or acceptance of conditions stultifying to man's psychic nature.

The indifferent advancement of Socialism is due to its persistent advocacy of material benefits and its denial of man's sublime belief in a spiritual existence or immediate spiritual consolation. The workingman's fight against the hard, grinding exploitation of his physical nature is no more to redeem him from that thralldom than it is to find expansion for his spiritual wants and desires. To weaken or destroy the soul's aspirations and limit man's existence to his mere physical wants is to dominate unworthily the best that is in him. A movement, however laudable and externally worthy, is bound to fail if it has no soul. Advocates of reform without spiritual impulse never last long, however eloquent and argumentative they may be. And, the want of that innate feeling is soon recognized by the most illiterate followers although they are unable to say clearly what affects them. If trade unionism should ever reach that stage where it becomes a mere scrambling herd with a single demand for higher pay, it will inevitably decay and pass out of existence. So far, its work has given evidence of its higher aims in spite of the large number of its prominent leaders who are continually appealing to the sordidness of their fellows, with all its defective and debasing limitations.

An appeal for a boycott—

George Bayless, a most energetic representative of the local typographical union and a most unselfish man, came to me one evening after the adjournment of the Federated Trades Council and informed me that he had forgotten to bring a very important matter before the meeting. He had been instructed by his union to ask for the appointment of a conference committee to visit Messrs. Pickering of the *Call* and Fitch of the *Bulletin* with a view to unionizing those offices and thus avoiding a boycott being levied against both of them. The union had made every preparation to begin the boycott at once and his neglect would put him "in bad" with his union unless I should rectify it by immediately appointing the committee. I told him that such an act would be irregular and impossible, but I was finally prevailed upon to do so owing to his persistence. I appointed W. C. Owen, Peter Ross Martin, and myself.

Owen and Martin interviewed the two newspaper proprietors the next morning and taking their cue from Bayless' assurances of the union's preparedness gave them the choice of complying with the union's demand or standing a boycott. The publishers declined to comply with what seemed a mandate. Before noon of that day Mr. John White, business manager of the *Call,* called upon me to learn all the details preceding the ultimatum. He bluntly told me that he had been assured by a printer's delegate, who was present throughout the proceedings of the Federated Trades Council, that no such action had been taken, and that the whole affair was a concoction of Bayless and the committee.

I regretted having yielded to Bayless' representations of the night before and I was disappointed in the hasty action of the committee. I thought that Owen and Martin should have consulted me as the third member of the committee before delivering their final message. At the same time it was evident that the printers' union had a traitor in its camp, and to uphold him by declaring the exact truth would be to place him high in the confidence of the newspapermen to the great detriment of the union upon whose actions he would be a spy. I also knew that to tell the full facts of the situation would also set back indefinitely the union's preparations for the boycott and do much to injure the cause of unionism generally by showing up the trickery of the proceeding. I knew the *Call* and *Bulletin* would exploit my statement of the actual facts of the case to the discredit of the Typographical Union, which just then enjoyed popular confidence. All this I thought of instantly and so decided quickly to advise Mr. White that his informant was wrong and that a committee had been appointed.

Loring Pickering—

Personally I regarded Mr. Pickering as the cleanest, most truthful, fairest, and most honest newspaper editor and publisher in San Francisco. There were few newspaper men in any part of the country who could lay claim to the qualities of uprightness and lack of fanaticism that Loring Pickering could. And yet with all my admiration for him I was forced into the attitude of becoming an active boycotter of his paper.

I believe that had Pickering known what the outcome was to be he would have acted differently. His rival contemporaries gave every aid in their power to the boycotting activities of the printers' union. The death of Charley De Young did not mitigate the hatred of the *Chronicle* management against Pickering and the *Call*. The *Chronicle* became more sedate in its public utterances but equally bitter in its private conduct against its old-time and superior rival, the *Call*. The *Examiner* was a new fledgling and eager to obtain popular favor. It had lately become the property of W. R. Hearst and its subscription list was greatly in need of more names. Hearst became the personal champion of everything desired by the workingmen. His apparent sincerity caused workingmen to become voluntary solicitors for his paper, resulting in the rapid increase in its circulation. There was no favor that Hearst could bestow upon Organized Labor that he did not grant willingly and promptly.

The Call-Bulletin boycott—

Anything and everything was done to beat the *Call* and the *Bulletin* and the boycott succeeded.[52] Both the *Call* and the *Bulletin* suffered for many years from the results of the boycott. Mr. Pickering, before his death, which occurred a few years later, told me that the Southern Pacific Railroad Company had offered him $400,000 for the *Call* with $5,000 a year added if he would, after the sale, permit his name to appear as the ostensible owner. When the paper passed to John D. Spreckels it brought less than half that amount.

Ingratitude of trade unionists—

Bayless, the man mainly responsible for the boycott and its success, was later treated with scornful contempt by his union, which had failed several times in attempting to accomplish that which he was successful in securing. If there are any of its then active members alive now I believe that they would deny Bayless the slightest credit for winning the most gigantic fight that their union ever engaged in. And yet I know that he was the man who won it.

The ingratitude of trade unionists and their forgetfulness of voluntary services rendered them without pretense or solicitation of recognition is only equaled by their toadyism when they inscribe upon their rolls of honorary membership the names

[52] The boycott began March 4, 1886 and ended about April 15, 1886.—Ed.

of men who never did the union any practical service, whose claim to that distinction is due generally to service given in the glare of the limelight to one or several members and by them reciprocated with the sentimental honor of honorary membership. In the bestowal of such honors the rank and file of the union membership care but very little. They vote to confer the honor as much out of regard for the mover of the proposal as for the receiver of the honor. If the latter enjoys a fair reputation and is ordinarily well known and popular it is given him without a dissenting vote or protest. Fictitious service or a little service magnified is enough to warrant the motion going through with éclat.

Boycotts and proffered bribes—

A secret anti-Chinese Society was organized in Sacramento as the result of a convention that had been held there to further drastic legislation against those people. The operations of this society were precisely along the lines of the League of Deliverance, except that there was to be no publicity given to the actions of this later organization unless it could not be avoided. A committee from this society, composed of James H. Barry, W. M. Hinton, Volney Hoffmeier, and others whom I do not now remember, visited the Federated Trades Council and requested that a boycott be placed upon all strawberries sold in the San Francisco market except those grown by a farmer in Santa Clara County, whose name I have also forgotten. I considered the request so impossible that I protested strenuously against the adoption of a resolution offered to carry it into effect. The Council was young at the time and eager to do anything to display its activity, and my protest went unheeded. The boycott was declared and proved to be a miserable failure long before the strawberry season had passed.

On another occasion the fruit can-makers asked for a boycott upon the canned goods of the firm of Wm. T. Coleman & Co. This firm had quite a number of canneries running in various parts of the State outside of San Francisco as well as several within the city. Its goods were disposed of far and wide. I could not see how we could boycott this concern successfully with the limited information that we possessed regarding the localities of their sales and the labels and qualities of the goods, etc. I asked the Federated Trades Council to pause and consider well from all angles its proposed action, but it would not, and consequently declared the boycott. The Council wanted to fight someone, win or lose, and the bigger the antagonist the more it was to its liking. I did not want the Council to engage in a fight involving the expenditure of time, enegry, and money without a reasonable hope of success. I could see only waste and defeat ahead in the proposed boycott, and defeat meant a further weakening of our strength and the consequent discouragement to future organization. Notwithstanding all my protests the Council ordered the boycott.

Next day Mr. W. M. Bunker, one of the proprietors of the *Daily Report,* called upon me and requested to see me in some secluded place free from eavesdroppers as he had a confidential communication to make which was for my ears and mine only. I suggested that the fireroom of the City Hall was satisfactory, showing him how, when the gates were locked, no safer place could be found for his purpose. He then left and returned at closing time, 4 P.M. When I had made everything secure so far as listeners were concerned he stated his business. He had been delegated by W. T. Coleman & Co. to see me, as that firm had heard from a reliable source of my opposition to the boycott declared the night before by the Council. He was satisfied that I could have the boycott raised at the next meeting if I would take the trouble to do so simply by interviewing the members of the Council individually. Of course, it would take time and I would probably have to absent myself from work, but as compensation I would receive $1,000, and to show his good faith in the matter he planked $250 under my nose. The smaller sum was to defray current expenses, the larger sum was for the accomplishment of the job.

I never was so astonished. I was in need of money at the time. I was also, I might say, in a chronic condition of impecuniosity. Here was a clear $1,000 within my reach to be given to me for doing what I actually believed was the right thing to do. Were I to take it no one would ever suspect that I had accepted a bribe, for I was not required to change front or alter my position in the least, and I was quite sure that I could have brought about the change for which W. T. Coleman & Co. was so anxious. But to accept the money would have been to accept a bribe, to belie myself, and to be untrue to the Cause which I had so much at heart. I believed myself right in the position that I had taken on the boycott, but the acceptance of money to sustain that position would have been as much a bribe as if I had contended for the other side and had changed my attitude because of the influence of money. My astonishment was very great and I was unable to say a word in reply to Bunker for several minutes. He was certain that he had me sure and fast because he had, from some source or other, learned of my financial condition. I was disappointed that any person knowing me even remotely could believe that I placed a money value on my services for any cause that I espoused.

At first I was inclined to break up the meeting and indignantly spurn his offer, but I changed my mind and decided to act with discretion and coolness. I told him that his principal appeared to place a high value upon the damage that the boycott would do to him, and he assured me that such was the case. I then told him that since such was the case his offer had altered my views regarding the matter and now instead of opposing the boycott I would do all within my power to make it effective. My decision astonished him, and we soon parted. The Federated Trades Council never knew the reason why I became active in pushing that boycott and none of its members ever asked me. After six months it proved a failure, although it must have been a matter of great expense to W. T. Coleman & Co.

An arbitration plan—

The ferment in which Organized Labor found itself during these days of the movement (1883–86) and the desire so universally manifested to engage in strikes caused me to address a letter to the local Manufacturers' Association inviting it to consider some method by which industrial peace might be obtained.[53] I submitted at the same time a plan to carry so desirable a measure into effect. I proposed the organization of a permanent arbitration board to consist equally of members of the Manufacturers' Association and of the Federated Trades Council. My letter and proposition were well received. George C. Hickox, the secretary of the Manufacturers' Association, and his wife, came to my home to discuss the subject with me. He was so impressed with the possibility of the suggested plan that he reported in favor of it and his report was unanimously adopted. The plan was never put into execution. Wm. T. Garrett, the president of the Manufacturers' Association, who had been out of town when the report had been adopted, turned up at an inoppor-

[53] This communication was sent to the Manufacturers' Association of California on September 1, 1885.—Ed.

tune moment and vigorously protested against the action taken. He was ably supported by Irving M. Scott, who had also been out of the city when the proposed plan of arbitration was under consideration. Both took the ground that arbitration meant an acknowledgment of the right on the part of workingmen to organize and bargain collectively with their employers. Whatever rights workingmen claimed as individuals would always be considered by their employer. The worker alone should settle all controversies with his employer without consultation or interference by an outside body. To recognize arbitration was equivalent to acknowledging the unions, which no employer, who understood his position, could afford to do. There were many other arguments advanced in the same strain. A few of the members mildly protested against reconsidering the action which had been taken, but without avail. It was reconsidered and the plan was killed.

I deeply regretted the outcome of what would have saved San Francisco from many tumultous strikes, much distress, great financial loss, vast inconveniences, numerous violent deaths, and the disgrace of being unable to settle disputes in a sane and satisfactory manner. I had planned to place the clearest and ablest minds of the Federated Trades Council upon the arbitration board, and I was sure that in the contest of brains the laboring element could and would assert its superiority. Both Garrett and Scott lived to rue the day that they defeated this plan of arbitration and conciliation, for within a few years they became embroiled with the moulders' union in a strike that lasted nearly two years. San Francisco business interests lost heavily in that struggle, which greatly crippled the development of its iron and steel industry for many years thereafter.

An agent provocateur—

Busy as I was, my sleuth friend, Charley Moore, found opportunity to keep up his intimacy with me. He never suspected that I was aware of his real character. At his request I had him admitted to membership in the Socialist Party. He was sure that he was on the straight path to the discovery of important developments. The socialists were set down as a secret band of blood-thirsty cut-throats, always prepared to commit a heinous crime in order to vindicate their assertions about social inequality. Moore was disgusted when he realized that they were an inoffensive band of enthusiastic doctrinaires who proposed to revolutionize the world by consuming beer in Humboldt Hall and talking Socialism to each other. His interest in them evaporated when he discovered that they were anything else but conspirators.

The Knights of Labor, being a secret organization, presented a better field for an *agent provocateur* than the dawdling, visionary socialists, so Moore suggested that he would like to become a member. I accepted the suggestion and had him made a Knight. It took him but a short time to find how barren that field was for a man of his stripe and he did not know that already we were honored with the membership of several detectives, one of whom later rose to a position of consequence in the San Francisco police force.

A secret society—

As a last effort, Moore committed to my perusal a constitution for a real secret society written in red ink. I suppose to indicate its mission this society was to be known as "The Church," the presiding officer of each section or lodge to be styled a "Pope." Moore had the idea that those designations would become immensely popular with Catholics, particularly those of Irish parentage or birth. I did nothing to discourage his belief. Had he only known the Irish and the Catholics as well as I did his dream of inveigling them with such terms would have soon disappeared. He modestly suggested that I undertake the pleasant task as organizer and assume, at least temporarily, the exalted title of "Grand Pope." He thought that that title would fit me exactly and he was decidedly serious about it. As my time was too much occupied already I declined the honor and suggested that he go ahead himself with the organization.

Dirty work—

Moore abandoned the idea, and in turning to another scheme got together a little group of dupes to steal the body of W. S. O'Brien, then lying in a vault in Calvary Cemetery. The body of A. T. Stewart, of New York, had been stolen and a large reward had been offered by his widow for its recovery. A large reward would therefore be offered by the relatives of O'Brien for the return of the latter's body, which sum when divided would put all engaged in the job in fairly comfortable circumstances. The plot had almost reached its culminating point when one of the conspirators, not quite sure of its satisfactory ending, consulted me upon the matter. I learned from him the names of his fellow-conspirators and how far they had proceeded with the plot. Moore was the originator of the scheme, aided by Tom Bates, formerly of the Eighth Ward Workingmen's Party Club, who for want of honest employment had become a police agent.

This fellow Bates, with an associate, had been employed to rob the trunks of Mrs. Amelia Smallman Maginnis, in the Palace Hotel, and deprive her of certain evidence necessary to convict ex-United States Senator Wm. Sharon of certain acts with which she charged him. Her evidence having been stolen, she could not substantiate her previously sworn statement concerning Sharon's guilt, and she and her husband were tried and convicted of conspiracy and perjury and sentenced to four years' imprisonment each in San Quentin. Bates and his assistant were to receive $2,000 each for their work, if successful, but to encourage them, as a preliminary they were given $500 each. That was all they ever did receive. Bates, feeling himself outraged, began to harangue crowds upon the streets on Sunday afternoons to elicit sympathy for himself and at the same time to expose the rottenness of the police "upper office." He was quietly told to stop his speech-making or he would go to San Quentin with Mr. and Mrs. Maginnis. He did so and became a fit tool in the hands of a vile "upper office" for the performance of any dirty work.

Pygeorge, Steinman, Tom Allen, Moore, and Bates formed the group that was to steal O'Brien's body. I cautioned Pygeorge, who had mentioned the matter to me, under no circumstances to let Moore or Bates suspect that I knew about the plot. Nor was he or the other two to do anything but attend the meetings and agree to every proposition made. Moore was to have the tools on hand to open the vault and to have the wagon handy to carry off the body. He was also to secure a hiding place for it. The final meeting of the group was held in a room on Market Street opposite Grant Avenue to arrange for the part that each was to play in the drama. They then separated, Moore heading for Chinatown and Bates going toward the Ferry. Pygeorge shadowed Moore as I had advised him to do, and Allen kept Bates in sight. Moore passed through Chinatown as far as Washington, down which he went to the alley back of the old City Hall, and then into police headquarters. Bates turned down Montgomery and went as far as Merchant Street, entering police headquarters from that side. The dupes, Allen, Pygeorge, and Steinman, were thus convinced that a scheme to "job" them had been planned, and they decided that they had better leave the stealing of O'Brien's body to the leaders of the conspiracy.

Moore's labors as an *agent provocateur* not resulting in the success anticipated, he ceased all further effort. The only notable case in which he figured was when he was employed with another to rob the home of Louis Holtz, former Assessor of San Francisco, for evidence necessary to prove the latter's partnership with John Fogarty, former Deputy Surveyor of the Port, and Patrick Connolly, a former Sheriff, in the ownership of the yacht "Halcyon" engaged in opium smuggling. The *Examiner* made the charge against Fogarty, who sued the paper for $25,000 damages for defamation of character. Moore was engaged on the case by the paper for almost a year without success. His assistant was more daring and more successful in securing the evidence and placing it in the hands of Mr. Alexander Henderson, the managing editor of the *Examiner*. Fogarty did not press his suit.

I visited Moore at the City Hall when I was certain that he had thrown off all disguise and quietly informed him that I had known his real character from his first appearance, as did all the principal men in the labor movement. He was prevented from doing us any damage because of this knowledge and it also saved a few dupes from being entangled in the O'Brien body-snatching plot. Both Bates and Moore disappeared from San Francisco soon afterward, the former becoming a real estate dealer in Oregon.

Haskell and the International—

The penchant of Burnette G. Haskell for intrigue coupled with his amazing versatility led him into the ranks of the International Workingmen's Association.[54] In a very short time, after becoming associated with the local labor movement, Haskell announced himself a pronounced follower of, or believer in, the doctrines of Bakounin, the Russian anarchist. These doctrines are, for sake of brevity, summarized into two phrases: the denial of all authority and the denial of the State and of the Deity as the representatives of authority. The anarchism of Proudhon and Herbert Spencer was eclipsed by Bakounin's philosophy.

[54] In the summer of 1882 Haskell and a few radical associates organized "The Pacific Coast Division of the International Workingmen's Association." Although patterned after the Marxian International Workingmen's Association, it had no connection with it as the former had been disbanded some years prior to the formation of the Haskell group. The Pacific Coast Division of the International Workingmen's Association was a secret revolutionary body whose members carried "red cards," "white cards," and "blue cards" and who were known within the organization by number and not by name. The renewed life which came into the San Francisco labor movement during 1883–1886 was due to a great extent to the activity and enthusiasm of the local Internationalists. The International Workingmen's Association of Haskell spread throughout the United States, although its main strength and following were confined to California.—Ed.

A certain air of mystery and secrecy hung over the affairs of the International Workingmen's Association, its members being very reticent as to its projects and activities. The impression was given that something stupendous was about to occur to instantly emancipate the downtrodden worker. What it was to be was left to one's imagination. I carefully noted its membership as well as the number of aspirants to that questionable distinction. It was an easy thing to do inasmuch as they made the Federation headquarters on McAllister Street their rendezvous. The applicants for admission to membership all knew me and had no hesitancy in speaking with me about the affairs of the International. From them I gleaned some information, but it was from closely observing Haskell and from an occasional talk with him that I gleaned more. I saw that it was the usual glamour which attaches to secret societies that enhanced the importance of the International, which Haskell sedulously exaggerated. The membership consisted of less than one hundred persons and most of them were members of the Coast Seamen's Union. These were the men whose little knowledge might prove dangerous and I was careful to watch them so as to be on guard in case there was danger. This feature depended upon Haskell, whom I believed I could take care of.

A dynamiting plot—

A convention of the International Workingmen's Association was held in the Federation headquarters, the most notable visitors being Joseph R. Buchanan, of the Denver *Labor Enquirer,*[55] and Dr. Schillians, of Fresno. A scheme of some importance and as I believe of danger, was to be determined upon which alarmed Owen and Martin, who thought that I must become a member in order to head it off or defeat it. Haskell would not have me a member, for the reason that I was notoriously wedded to the principle of authority. Later on I learned what the scheme was and did my best to defeat it. The project was the far-fetched and insane proposal to blow up and destroy the County Hall of Records.[56]

[55] Buchanan arrived in San Francisco in April, 1886. For an interesting account of his connection with the International Workingmen's Association, see Chapter VII of his volume, *The Story of a Labor Agitator.*—Ed.

[56] In 1906–7, while investigating certain phases of the labor history of San Francisco, I consulted freely with Haskell and other former members of the International as to the validity of the rumor, which I had frequently heard, that he and others had planned to blow up the Hall of Records. I was assured that such was the case. A building was to be rented across the street, a tunnel was to be dug, and enough dynamite planted to destroy the Hall of Records. Then the conspirators were to squat on valuable pieces of property and defy eviction. With all records of property titles destroyed, the squatters hoped to experience no difficulty in maintaining their claims to the property in question. I have in my possession many of the official records of the Pacific Coast Division of the International Workingmen's Association, and although frequent allusions are made to the "proper use of dynamite" and how it should be used "in bringing about the Revolution," I find no mention of the plot described above. It was to have been carried out by the members of an "inside ring." —Ed.

How the laborer's condition was to be improved permanently or at all by the execution of this delectable enterprise was beyond my power of discovery. I knew that it would help the lawyers if only one volume of records were destroyed or injured by defacement, but the laborers would not benefit at all. When the night came for the execution of the outrage Haskell, the projector and leader, was absent.[57] The men to do the work were on hand and apparently willing. When I pointed out the absurdity of the enterprise so far as benefitting the working people was concerned they began to realize its utter folly and their own stupidity. Haskell's prestige as a revolutionary leader went into eclipse upon the bursting of that bubble.

The Kaweah Cooperative Colony—

Time and again Haskell had urged me to become a member of the Kaweah Cooperative Colony, volunteering to pay for me all dues and assessments up to date. It had then been over a year in existence. It was a scheme on the part of Haskell and some of his associates to take up what was supposed to be a large tract of government timber land as individual preemptors, pool it all when title had been acquired,

[57] The *Weekly Star* of San Francisco in an editorial appearing on May 3, 1890, under the caption "Dynamiter Haskell," refers to Haskell's connection with the plot to dynamite the Hall of Records in the following words: "Or he might arrange to set a little band of daring simpletons to blow up the Hall of Records, while he himself should skip away to San José to have a safe alibi during the day when the explosion was to be."—Ed.

and go into the saw mill and lumber business on an extensive scale.[58] The members of the Coast Seamen's Union were profitably utilized to forward this scheme. When there was no demand for sailors at San Francisco and there was a likelihood of wages being reduced, the members of the union were sent to Kaweah, where rude shelters were constructed for their accommodation and food supplied for their subsistence. There they worked, felling trees and building a twenty-six mile corduroy road to the site of the future saw mill, until there was a demand for sailors, whereupon they returned to San Francisco. No wages were paid for their labor, the men being satisfied that they were upholding the union. So long as they lived healthily and had all the food they needed they were satisfied.

Unfortunately for the success of the Kaweah scheme, it was discovered that the colonists were trespassers on government land inasmuch as it had not been opened for entry. They were accordingly notified to vacate and a detachment of soldiers was sent to enforce the order. It was claimed at the time that the government's action was taken at the instigation of wealthy lumber men who wished no rivalry with a cooperative company that could compete with them in the market to the point of ruin.

I was really sorry for the failure of the Kaweah Colony.[59] It might have proven beneficial in a small

[58] The land was filed upon by Haskell and associates on October 5, 1885.—Ed.

[59] It failed in 1891.—Ed.

way to a number of earnest cooperators, although I felt that to make it so, there would have to be a radical change in the management. Several years later I induced Charles N. Felton, then United States Senator from California, to do what he could to induce the federal government to reimburse the colonists for the construction of the twenty-six miles of road. He took quite an interest in the matter and had a Senate Committee appointed, which, after inspecting the work, recommended the payment of $200,000. This recommendation would have been adopted if another set of claimants had not turned up. A number of the colonists located in Los Angeles formed a company claiming to be the original members and demanding the payment of the money to them, with the result that the recommendation of the Senate Committee was withdrawn and neither they nor the Haskell group got anything.

Secret labor organizations condemned—

Secret societies as a means of hastening what is termed by a few light-headed enthusiasts, "The Social Revolution," are not so attractive to the ordinary workingman as they were when I was actively engaged in propagating trade unionism during the eighties. The fascination attaching to secret societies in the ranks of Labor has not wholly disappeared. Ignorant, earnest men, aroused to the sense of having been victimized by equally ignorant but brutal employers, readily become the too willing dupes and tools of characters like Moore, who invariably appear in every crisis arising through oppression and fomented by their agency. The hopelessness of their condition is in itself often stimulation enough to lead many well-meaning men to believe that they are in a state of war which justifies a resort to force and reprisal in vindication of their wrongs.

Secret labor societies founded in hate, having revenge as their object, always produce traitors who nullify every attempt that may be made even peacefully to secure a moiety of justice. Secret societies are not and never have been necessary for the accomplishment of great reforms. They are an appeal to the love of the mysterious, but they lend no vitality to the action nor strength to the power of the organization. If men are well informed as to their wants publicity is a surer, safer, and more successful method of gaining them than are secret underground ways. In the hands of unscrupulous vindictive men secret societies become agencies for the exercise of private malice and individual vengeance. Their members are always at the mercy of the spy informer and *agent provocateur.*

Labor spies—

Our trade unions are not strictly secret in their conduct or in their methods of procedure. Their internal business transactions, which concern no one but the members and, if published would be of no value to the public, are properly enough not advertised or publicly spoken of. Whatever else is done might as well be published and scattered broadcast as mere news for everyone's information. If this is not done it affords profitable employment for the spies and informers who infest our unions. There is not a trade union or labor organization in America today but has at least one of these reptiles. It would be difficult to prove that assertion although from my own experience I am well convinced of its correctness. As proof of their existence, we have the word of Mr. Earl Rogers, a Los Angeles attorney, who stated that when acting as attorney for the Merchants' and Manufacturers' Association of that city he received weekly reports from informers posing as loyal members of every union in that city. Los Angeles is not an exception to the rule. Every city and town in the country, boasting of its trade unions, has its quota of informers.

With this statement authenticated by so good an authority as Mr. Rogers, it behooves members of labor organizations to conduct themselves with becoming circumspection. There is no reason in the world why such knowledge should be intimidating or why it should influence in the least the progress of trade unionism. It should rather be a stimulant to rapid and more perfect organization. Its effect should be to restrain wild and incendiary speech and to encourage the wise, dispassionate, far-sighted, and practical member whose careful judgment in all matters concerning the future stability of the union outweighs the torrid effusions of the hasty and thoughtless agitator. The latter type of man, when it comes to the pinch, is usually the weak-kneed and unreliable member.

The dispassionately careful man is often misunderstood because he will not yield to what is most catchy and popular. His apparent conservatism makes him the target of the ever vigilant informer who sees in such a person the most dangerous enemy to the foul interests which he represents. It is an easy matter to stir up doubts about a wise man in the uneducated brains of a thoughtless multitude carried away by the fantastic and frequent vehement utterances of those opposed to him. This is the point where wise discrimination must be exercised by the union, both as a matter of even-handed justice and for its future stability. The real solid, thoughtful union man has more to contend against in the evanescent waywardness of his fellow-members than in devising the best means of ameliorating their economic condition.

The fight of unionism for its ultimate rights is a slow progressive and evolutionary one. It is a question of the superiority of brains backed by well disciplined, concentrated numbers and the undeniable justice of their cause against which is arrayed the traditional despotism of centuries protected by entrenched authority supported by bayonets, prejudice, and self-interest. In the long run brains, if well directed, will conquer prejudice and despotism.

The Haymarket Riot—

The tragedy of the Haymarket Riot in Chicago sent a shudder of horror through the labor movement of the entire country.[60] It also impressed the monied classes as much as it affected the working people. The speakers at the meeting where the explosion occurred that killed the policeman, were immediately arrested. Others known as prominent anarchists, but who did not speak at the meeting, were also arrested. The trades unionists and Knights of Labor in Chicago seemed united in their desire to convict the men arrested without the formality of a trial. They wished Organized Labor throughout the country to follow their cowardly example.

In San Francisco, the news of the calamity was received by the vast majority of the laboring people with mingled feelings of sorrow and condemnation. The condemnation was for the miscreant who threw the bomb, not for the men who led or spoke at the

[60] A mass meeting of about 3,000 workers gathered in Haymarket Square, Chicago, on May 4, 1886, to protest against the killing of four strikers and the wounding of many others who had taken part in a demonstration against strike breakers employed by the McCormick Harvester Works in Chicago. During the meeting the police attempted to disperse the crowd. A bomb was thrown, killing a policeman and throwing about sixty others to the ground. Eight of the leaders of the mass meeting were arrested, seven were subsequently sentenced to death and one was given fifteen years' imprisonment. Of those receiving the death sentence four were hanged, one committed suicide, and two had their sentence commuted to life imprisonment. The three that were imprisoned were pardoned by Governor Altgeld in 1893.—Ed.

meeting. The men of San Francisco refused to accept or endorse the course adopted by the Chicago trades unionists. They believed that the men who had been arrested were entitled to a fair and impartial trial, and that if guilty of the atrocious outrage they should merit condign punishment.

The men arrested were idealists, every one of them—not assassins or murderers.[61] They taught the doctrine of individualism, with the hope of soon seeing established on earth the millenium where each individual would have reached such a degree of perfection and acquired such a sense of equity as to be a government unto himself. The abolition of all government and every evidence of authority was to them the true and only means of placing workingmen and all people upon their true and natural basis and of giving them their God-given rights, with the proviso that God be eliminated from the fantastic scheme as the most potential symbol of authority.

Repression makes converts—

To my mind their whole propaganda was absurd and illogical if the advantages of the individual, which inventions in machinery through cooperative effort had made it possible for him to enjoy, were to be continued. Primitiveness and progress are antithetical. If either was to survive the other must succumb. There was no danger to the permanency

[61] Spies, Schwab, Fielden, Parsons, Fischer, Engel, Neebe, and Lingg, who had been arrested and sentenced, were all members of the revolutionary Black International.—Ed.

of society to be feared by the advocacy of such vagaries. It was only when they were opposed by and confronted with hostile forces that they received the recognition which their exponents sought. But the soulless exploiters of Labor, whose wealth had accumulated by grinding oppression, perjury, cheating, and the innumerable methods to which Capital so acquired resorts, thought that they saw danger to themselves in such expressions of radical views, and therefore the advocates of such ideas must be crushed by force. This exploiting class in reality is the dangerous class so far as the perpetuity of the Republic is concerned. It is they who are the true anarchists, and not Parsons, Spies, and their associates. It is they who as exploiters brutally rob and brutally maintain their right to do so because they are legally sustained by force, custom, and prejudice. No harm can ever result from according orators of the type of Parsons full liberty to express themselves in public. If this be granted, their audiences will remain small and their votaries few. Antagonize them and you not only increase the number of their followers but you also stir up in the minds of a still larger number the latent feeling that free speech is assailed. Sympathizers arise in all quarters, and people who never thought of their doctrines or in many instances never heard of them become interested and favor them.

Labor parade—

When the Haymarket catastrophe happened in Chicago, the San Francisco Federated Trades Council was engaged in arranging a huge Labor demonstration to celebrate the anniversary of the establishment of the Iron Trades Council. It also had in view a display of its numerical strength. Action was taken for both purposes at my suggestion. I was selected as chairman of all arrangements and was appointed Grand Marshal of the procession, which was to be a torchlight parade. I was also chosen to decide upon the mottoes which the various unions were to display so that a uniform idea of our purposes might be given to those who did not understand the objects of trade unionism. Many mottoes were submitted to me which I rejected, some because of their antiquity and others on account of their too radical statements.

The display projected by Haskell for the Coast Seamen's Union was the most objectionable of all. Haskell proposed that a large float should be a feature of the sailors' contribution, upon which should be constructed a replica of the French Bastile, typifying Authority. A number of men were to be attacking it with rifles and bayonets. Mottoes of a most incendiary character were to surround the float. The marching sailors were also to be armed. I at once told Haskell that neither the float nor the mottoes submitted would be permitted in the parade, that the parade was strictly of a trade union, and not of a revolutionary, character. He was highly indignant at what he termed my high-handed censorship which amounted to tyranny, which neither he nor the sailors would accept. He informed me that the float as described would appear in the parade in defiance of me or any one else.

In making my plans for the formation of the procession I had decided to have at the head of it a group of the uniformed sailors, without their guns, instead of the customary detachment of policemen which usually led all civic processions. Chief of Police Crowley sent Sergeant Tom Bethel to me offering the use of the police. When I declined Bethel urged their acceptance upon me. I absolutely and firmly declined.

Our demonstration was not looked upon with the favor it was entitled to by the *Chronicle,* which intimated that something disastrous would happen to the city upon the night of our celebration, set for May 11, 1886. Many robberies of more or less magnitude had taken place and the disposition was evident on the part of that paper to get up a scare of some sort. I told Mr. Bethel to let the Chief of Police know from me that I considered that he would be doing his full duty to the people of San Francisco if he would detail his force to guard the people in the outlying districts instead of having the police head our procession and guard it along the line from the eager crowd which usually witnessed such affairs. I further told him that I had perfected every arrangement for an orderly display without the Chief's aid and hoped that the Chief would take as good care of the portion of the city not traversed by the procession as I would take of that part traversed by the trade unionists. Mr. Bethel was much disappointed and predicted trouble for us.

On the heels of this came Haskell and his desire to demonstrate anarchy. I issued the order to Haskell that if at least three full days before the date set for the procession I were not notified that he would agree to my plans, I would then dispense with his sailors as our guard of honor and forbid the sailors' union to take part in the procession. The situation created by Haskell to force Anarchism upon our trade union movement caused me considerable anxiety. I was determined that no expression of Anarchy should appear in the entire procession and that the citizens should get a comprehensive, pure, and unadulterated view of the aims of trade unionism.

I made all arrangements to detach the sailors from the line of the procession if they appeared with arms and their objectionable float. And I was also determined to follow this up by excluding them from the Federated Trades Council and of confronting them with the active opposition of the several waterfront organizations. Before the expiration of the three days' notice which I had required of Haskell, I read on the blackboard in our headquarters the following notification addressed to me, "Your orders shall be obeyed, my Lord," signed "B. G. Haskell." Very few of the members understood the significance and importance of the message, and I made no explanation. It was a great relief to me for I was extremely desirous of having this, the first real Labor demonstration held in San Francisco, pass off harmoniously and successfully.

A legal Labor holiday—

To make our first Labor Day a legal holiday was to add to its success. Accordingly I wrote to Governor Stoneman asking him to proclaim it a legal holiday, which he did without hesitation. I also wrote between two and three hundred letters to firms, large and small, requesting them to give their employees the day off to celebrate. In every instance I got a courteous reply.

Labor politicians—

When it became an established fact that the procession was going to be a large and successful one, the politicians who had some slight connection with labor unions, began a siege upon me for appointment as aides to the Grand Marshal. The first of these was Gilleran, whom I had practically made supervisor and treasurer of the moulders' union. He was aspiring to the shrievality of the County and desired to advertise himself. I informed him that neither he nor any other prominent office-holder or aspirant would figure in the procession in any capacity. I held my job as fireman at his pleasure and could be removed at any moment if he chose, which was the risk that I took in refusing him a place in the procession.

No office-seeking or office-holding politicians up to that time had been permitted to use trade unionism to boost themselves along so as to continue in office or to gain a more lucrative one. If trade unionists could not perform their own work in handling their affairs with employers and in properly placing their claims, whatever they might be, before the public when such a course was needed, then they must go without such aid until they could learn to do it themselves. Nowadays, it is quite otherwise—only politicians transact the public work of unionism. It is true that they may be union men, but they are politicians first and always. Perpetuity in office is the incentive to their union work.

The Labor Day parade—

An intimation was given me that Governor Stoneman and his staff would take part in the procession if an invitation were extended them. I gave the Governor an invitation in recognition of the favor which he had bestowed upon us by making the day a legal holiday, and he accepted it. On the night of the parade the Governor and his staff were escorted to the starting point at the corner of Third and Brannan streets, and we were introduced by George Bayless, my chief aide, who had escorted them. I then gave the order to my old helper, Mike

Sexton, who was an ex-army bugler, to sound "The Advance."

The *Chronicle* credited the procession with being 8,000 strong, the *Call* with 10,000, and the *Examiner* set the number at between 12,000 and 15,000. My estimate, based on my knowledge of the membership of the unions, agreed with that of the *Call*. When the head of the line was at Lotta's Fountain, the rear at Third and Brannan had not yet started. It stretched from that point to Market, down Market to Montgomery, down Montgomery to Cogswell's Fountain at the junction of Montgomery Avenue, now Columbus Avenue, and Kearney, and along Kearney to Lotta's fountain.[62]

San Francisco has had many labor processions since that day, some of them numerically larger, but none of them so distinctively trade union in the personnel of those directing it and its every detail. Subsequent processions have been tinctured with more or less of a political bias and all with the tendency to favor the ambition of one or more individuals at their head. No man having anything to do with the first big Labor parade in San Francisco on May 11, 1886, had a political ax to grind or any other ambition to serve except the advancement of trade unionism and the hope by organization and cooperative effort to improve the worker's economic status without the aid of politicians.

[62] For a more detailed description of this, the first Labor Day parade in San Francisco, see I. B. Cross, "Early Labor Day Parades in the Metropolis," *Labor Clarion*, September 2, 1910.—Ed.

George Bayless

Reproduced from a tattered copy of *The Illustrated Open Letter*

SAN FRANCISCO'S FIRST LABOR DAY PARADE, MAY 11, 1886

Defeated for union presidency—

Some of the members of the moulders' union wished to transfer me from the secretaryship to the presidency of the union and nominated me for that office. I never sought an office or asked a man to vote for me at any time, anywhere. If I were elected to a position I accepted it and did my best to fill it impartially and as satisfactorily as I was able. I confess that I felt fairly certain of my election to the office and saw no cause to be disturbed when informed that a young man, named Spring, had been selected to run against me. For several years past I had been pointing out in a mild way the errors too frequently committed by members in the shops and in the union, but at no time had I been personal in my remarks. I never dreamed that my talks could lay the foundation for personal antagonism or that they could or would engender bitterness.

The opposition to me was conducted with unusual virulence. It was successful, however, for Spring was elected. He was not even a good member of the union, being seldom at the meetings, whereas I was constant in my attendance and always strove to do what I considered to be best for the benefit of the organization. The men who pushed Spring forward lived to rue their action if they were really actuated by trade union ideals, which I very much doubted.

Elected delegate to international convention—

An election of four delegates to represent the local moulders' union in the international convention of moulders' unions to be held in London, Ontario, on July 5, 1886, was called, and I was placed in nomination. Under the constitution of our union one of the candidates was entitled to go to the convention by virtue of the office which he held as corresponding secretary. On the first ballot two of the others who had been nominated were chosen, one of whom had had a little experience as an officer of the union, while the other had had none whatsoever. A second ballot was necessory to determine whether the man opposed to me or I should be selected as the remaining delegate. The man opposing me was a decent, quiet fellow with no pretensions of being a trade unionist. His desire was to visit friends in New Jersey at the expense of the union. He had never held office or served the local union in any capacity whatever and had come to California to take the place of moulders who were on strike. My record as a trade unionist was daily before the members and it could not be challenged, and yet I was hard run by a person with no qualifications whatever. It was a hard contest; the first voting showed more votes in the ballot box than there were persons present at the meeting. Another ballot was necessary and ordered, and I was finally chosen as the fourth delegate.

Punishing the Daily Report—

The morning after the election George Tailor of the *Daily Report* came to see me and informed me that he had been instructed by the proprietors of that paper to ask if I would accept free transportation to and from the convention. I accepted the offer very gratefully. At the same time I took the offer to be a recognition of the service which I had for two years given the paper gratuitously. During that time, as I stated earlier in these pages, I had written about twelve columns weekly for the paper and had made the *Daily Report* the exclusive medium of furnishing the public with other reliable trade union news. I did not consider that I was under the slightest obligation to the paper for the offer. In fact the obligation was really on the other side.

I heard no more about transportation until about ten days before the day upon which I was to leave for the East. I asked Tailor if it had been forgotten. He said that I would know all about it in a day or so. Mr. Heister, one of the partners in the concern, came to me the same day in a hurry and asked me to go with him to get my railroad ticket. We had gone as far as Harrison Street on a Fifth Street car when upon leaving it we met Bunker, the other partner. From him I learned that he had been to the Southern Pacific Railroad Company's office, and that he had been told that the company could not or would not issue a ticket for my use unless I would pledge my word to stand by that corporation in a political scheme then being hatched. Bunker knew me already and could not guarantee the company what I would do or whether I would do anything.

I was indignant that a pair of tricksters of that type should be interested in me in that manner. They evidently had never had the slightest intention of incurring the expense of a ticket on their own account. They expected to get it upon the strength of my own reputation. I was never so angry in my life as at those two rascals who seemed to consider such transactions to be perfectly legitimate. I told them what I thought of them in most emphatic language and left them to their reflections. It had been my intention to send two letters a week for publication in their paper, but after this treatment I decided to send them none and furthermore I arranged that their paper should receive no more exclusive trade union news in the future. As a consequence the *Daily Report* ceased being a sort of semi-official organ of the labor movement. It lost its standing with the workers, who ceased subscribing for it, and within a year it went out of existence. During my absence from San Francisco while at the convention I sent four letters to the *Examiner* for which, without hint or solicitation, Mr. Alexander Henderson insisted that I should receive remuneration. I considered the publication of the articles sufficient compensation, for I was punishing the *Daily Report* owners in the way to do them permanent injury, but Henderson insisted that I should accept pay for them and I finally did so.

Shipwrights vs. Union Iron Works—

The shipwrights requested the appointment of a committee by the Iron Trades Council to interview Mr. George W. Dickie, superintendent of the shipbuilding department of the Union Iron Works, and inform him that the members of the union, who were employed in that shop, worked longer hours and received less pay than men similarly employed by other firms. The request was also to be made that that state of affairs should be remedied by granting the working hours and wages paid elsewhere in the city. Arthur Wilson is the only member of the committee whose name I remember. He was spokesman for the committee and had a strenuous hour's argument with Mr. Dickie without arriving at a satisfactory result. Another committee, of which I was the spokesman, was appointed at a subsequent meeting of the Iron Trades Council for the same purpose. This second committee accomplished nothing in its interview with Mr. Dickie. I was then instructed to send him a written statement of what was requested, which I did, but received no reply. It was evident that the Union Iron Works management did not propose to concede any of our demands. As an offset several of the foremen and leading men met members of the shipwrights union and members of the Iron Trades Council, but without coming to an understanding.

The Union Iron Works absolutely refused to make any concession whatever. This naturally exasperated the shipwrights, who were demanding no more than other members of their union were receiving from other employers. All through the preliminary correspondence and interviews I could see that the end would be a strike unless something were done to avoid it. I was strongly opposed to having a strike declared and did everything within my power to prevent it. The rule of the Iron Trades Council was that when any question involved a strike or the united action of all the unions represented in the Council, the matter had to be submitted to each union separately and the action of the union bound it to the future course pursued by the Council. A majority of the unions determined the course to be adopted. I hoped the delay caused by submitting the shipwrights' controversy to the individual unions would bring about some kind of understanding which would make it possible for us to avoid a clash. Johnson, the chairman of the Iron Trades Council, was as eager for a strike as I was opposed to it. The unions debated the question and unanimously decided in favor of a strike. I had done my best to prevent it and I therefore either had to resign my office and membership in the Council or agree to take part in the strike. I chose the latter course.

Imagine my surprise when I found Johnson, for unexplained reasons, opposed to the strike.

It was a tremendously grave moment to me when I issued the order to strike.[63] I felt all the responsibility for the act resting on my shoulders. The unions, with the single exception of the moulders, were not financially prepared for a protracted contest. I did not want all the burden of the struggle to fall upon my union, as I feared would be the case and as it subsequently was. The shipwrights boasted of their ample treasury and of the freedom and liberality which they would show in sustaining weaker unions. This they never did. In fact, almost as soon as the strike was called they disclaimed all responsibility. Not only that, but when the strike had proved to be a dismal failure, they withdrew from both the Iron Trades Council and the Federated Trades Council. They had used both bodies and the unions represented in them to further their own ends without in any way harming themselves financially or otherwise. I considered the action of the shipwrights to be most treacherous and selfish and knew that it would take strong evidence and sound guaranties to make me believe in their sincerity of purpose in the future.

It was at the time that the strike was declared that I was required to leave San Francisco to attend the International Moulders' Convention in Canada.

[63] The strike began June 19, 1886, and affected about 400 employes.—Ed.

It was a most inopportune time to leave. I felt that I should remain and take an active part in the strike. I consulted my colleagues who were unanimous in stating that I must go with them to London, Ontario. My associates felt that the strike did not need or require the personal management or supervision of any particular individual, that many of the men involved in it were capable and willing to lead, and that they should be given the chance to prove themselves. Their arguments and representations failed to convince me. I still believed that I should stay at my post. I was run down physically and was nearing the point of collapse. I consulted my friend, Dr. W. Botsford, who insisted that I should take the vacation offered, for if I did not I would be sorry for it later. This decided me to go on to the convention. Besides, I had always been a stickler for the principle that no movement, which was entitled to live and flourish, was ever dependent upon any one man for its success. Every man was the equal of every other and only the opportunity was lacking for the least pretentious to prove his ability and capacity.

Labor policies—

Another thing influenced me in making my decision. For months before my selection as a delegate I had been sending a monthly letter for publication in the *Moulders' Journal.* These articles were intended to shape the future policy of the organization by attracting the attention of the delegates to the convention, where I hoped my ideas would receive favorable consideration. I was anxious to be present to urge the adoption of those ideas. In these articles I had limited myself to the themes, "The scab," and "Organization." The officers of the national organization claimed for it a membership of 25,000. How many moulders were not affiliated was never stated. I desired approximate figures on both points and believed that I could only secure them at the convention. I was aware that the "scab" was recruited in the majority of instances from those districts in which unionism did not exist. I was also aware that the "scab" was frequently the product of harsh and unfair treatment by presumptuous, silly-minded young men clothed for a time with power and acting as officials for local unions in centers of population. The production of the "scab" must be stopped or in some way mitigated if organization was to be extended. No one else could initiate the methods of forwarding the plans to carry out the ideas that I had on those points. After their inauguration any sincere man of energy could make them effective. I was going to the moulders' convention with the serious purpose of remodeling the national organization or putting it upon a better footing than it had yet occupied.

A gift—

On the morning of my departure I was surprised to find at the train the president and some other members of the cooks' and waiters' union present with a large basket filled with all sorts of edibles and drinkables as a "lunch," they called it, to keep me alive on my journey. The union had voted $25 to purchase it in recognition of what I had done for its members. I never accepted favors from any union no matter what I did for it, and did not want to accept this present, but there it was, composed largely of perishable stuff, and it appealed strongly to me and my colleagues, so I took it along. It proved a fine thing for our fellow-passengers, who were sumptuously taken care of by our large supply of drinkables as far as Omaha, where it was finally exhausted.

A Chicago episode—

Mr. Richard Powers, president of the Lake Seamen's Union, with whom I had been corresponding from the period of my presidency of the Seamen's Protective Association, learning of my trip eastward, invited me to attend a picnic to be held by the District Council of the Knights of Labor of Chicago on the day of my arrival in that city. He also informed me that I would be met at the depot of the Chicago & Northwestern Railroad upon my arrival. The leaders of the labor organization of Chicago were in a bad state of mind at that time.

The memory of the Haymarket Riot was still fresh and seemed to impose a seriousness upon them out of all proportion, dreadful as that deed was. It looked as if they imagined themselves suspected of the deed and were duly cautious and discreet in their speech. This was the impression made upon me at the picnic, for although no one met me as agreed upon, I made my way to the park and sauntered around for an hour before making myself known.

I had expressed myself in one of my letters to Powers in a manner which led him to believe that I was friendly to the men charged with the outrage. His misconstruction of my letter was the reason why no one had met me at the depot. I also learned that I was not wanted as a speaker at the picnic. My position on the issue was this: A dastardly outrage had been committed at an out-of-door public gathering mainly composed of working people, most of whom had attended primarily out of curiosity because the speakers had been hounded by the public on account of their incendiary utterances. It was the intention of the police to break up and disperse the meeting and arrest the speakers, for the policemen were there in force.[64] A bomb was thrown amongst the police killing several and creating consternation among the crowd.[65] None of the speakers had thrown the bomb and as far as is known neither did any of those managing or interested in the meet-

[64] One hundred and eighty policemen attempted to disperse the meeting.—Ed.

[65] One policeman was killed.—Ed.

ing do so. The speakers were well-known anarchists who frequently on previous occasions had used indiscreet or rather intemperate language. On this occasion their language was construed as inciting to the commission of the deed, and upon those grounds they were charged as accessories before the fact.

In the first place, it was well known days before the unfortunate occurrence that the heads of the Chicago Police Department, instigated by wealthy men, proposed to suppress these anarchistic meetings by force, and in consequence a large crowd was attracted to the place of meeting.[66] Nothing of an extra-incendiary character occurred at the meeting, and the inference has been made that the bomb throwing was the work of the police to justify them in subsequent acts of repression. But it was overdone, killing their own men.

Victims were needed to appease public clamor. Every one in authority lost his head. Reason fled, and the demands of savagery had to be gratified. Parsons and his comrades had to be immolated, and not a voice was raised from the ranks of Labor in protest. All that was wanted by the already condemned men was fair play. They were the enthusiastic but mistaken friends of Labor, and for that reason Organized Labor should have come to the front and protested against their vindictive treatment. And, if the accused men had never been identified with the cause of outraged and exploited Labor, it was still the duty of those claiming to be

[66] About 3,000 were present.—Ed.

leaders to insist that a fair and impartial trial was due them.

To me it was a most humiliating spectacle to see these so-called labor leaders moving around with bated breath, afraid to say one word on behalf of Justice. I had read of the peace that reigned in Warsaw and knew the means of repression adopted by the Russian soldiery to bring it about. I saw the fear inspired by the dread of imprisonment if sympathy was expressed for the Irish revolutionists, or hostility breathed against England's domination in Ireland. The reasons for those conditions were obvious, inevitable, and possibly excusable. But in the United States of America, where every citizen was a sovereign, where the right of free speech was inherent, to see men crawling around like poltroons, fearful to express a charitable thought in favor of fair play, was more than I expected or could stand.

The *mouchards* of the Chicago police force were untiringly vigilant and swarmed everywhere, thus offering an excuse for the cowardly behaviour of those whose instincts were those of the slave without his hope of freedom by opportune rebellion. In no country in the world could there be found so universal an expression of abject slavery as I found among the men who were presumably instructing their fellows in the higher duties of citizenship and lighting the way to a fuller realization of economic liberty. The mark of slavery was firmly implanted in their souls.

The International Moulders' Convention—

National and international gatherings at conventions seem to be mainly assemblages of delegates bent on having a good time. The men who do the actual work of the convention are usually very few. The majority are there to rest and enjoy themselves. Most of them are entirely unfitted by education and experience to initiate or accomplish anything of permanent benefit to the organization as a whole. Except the corresponding representative of each union, who by virtue of his office is a member of the convention, the greatest number owed their presence at the Canadian convention of the iron moulders' union to certain personal qualities that they possessed other than fitness for the task.

Why working men should waste $30,000 or more on their conventions, which accomplish so little, is beyond my comprehension. I attribute these meetings to the homogeneous gregariousness of the average American who, although strongly individualistic, delights in the display which large assemblages afford him. Large bodies are supposed to generate a higher degree of enthusiasm than do smaller bodies. The work for good or ill of the organization generally depends upon the enthusiasm developed. Solid, far-reaching, deeply considered, and matured thought is not always the result of the deliberations of such bodies. The "wild and woolly" fellow is there with fantastic theories and glib tongue, duly primed to capture the convention by sentimental appeals to its known horror of injustice when depicted with fervid eloquence. Other impracticables are there who find the convention the arena to invite disputes, often dangerous to the perpetuity of the organization. All who have the desire, regard the convention as the proper place to acquire cheap glory regardless of practicability or sense. Only a few fundamental laws are needed for any organization, and they could be abrogated, amended, or added to at any time by referendum. Thus, conventions could be dispensed with and the entire membership could participate in making new or in repealing old laws without a waste of time or funds.

Convention duties—

I became secretary of the committee on constitution and by-laws. About three meetings of the committee were held and all matters to be cared for were left in my hands. I worked upon the constitution diligently, denying myself ordinary recreation, and incorporated in it many new features in harmony with my preconceived notions of what was most desirable and what I believed would be acceptable to the committee. The majority of the committee were averse to all radical changes and I governed myself accordingly.

At my suggestion I was appointed a committee of one to ascertain the approximate number of moulders in every branch of the trade in the United States and Canada. This was a bigger undertaking than I at first supposed, owing to the marked indifference of the delegates. However, I repeatedly called the attention of the convention to the subject and succeeded in getting returns of fair authenticity from the delegates. When I tabulated the returns I found that there were nearly 80,000 moulders in all branches of the trade in the two countries. In many states there were many unions containing only a small percentage of the moulders eligible for membership. In other states there were large areas with hundreds of moulders and not a union. The executive officers of the union claimed for it an aggregate membership of 25,000, yet the figures given me by the delegates showed only a total of 18,000 members. I questioned Mr. Fitzpatrick, the president, and Martin Fox, the secretary, and they finally admitted the accuracy of my figures, a discrepancy of about 7,000. I thought it unfair to the members and also misleading, to claim a greater membership than we actually had.

I proposed that we call off as many strikes then prevailing as was possible without injury to the locals involved and devote the money so saved to the work of further organization among the members of our craft. The national officers were of the opinion that it would be inadvisable to announce my figures to the convention. I knew that the announcement would weaken confidence in them and perhaps do some momentary injury, but I also thought that if the figures were made known, it would restrain the unions from striking and make them understand that the building up of their local organizations was their just, greatest, and most imperative duty.

Fitzpatrick and Fox did not relish the exposure that my report would make of their duplicity and appealed to me most earnestly not to make it, promising if again elected to see that the official organizers should take the field and build up the membership. I finally abandoned the idea of presenting my report and became a party to the system of misinformation so long and so successfully practised upon the organization. My only excuse for doing this was to preserve confidence in the union's officials, which if once destroyed would lead to the general disintegration of the organization.

A man named Penton, of Detroit, Michigan, was at that very time making extraordinary efforts to separate the machinery moulders from the stove plate and other special classes of moulders. I was extremely desirous of keeping all moulders united and also of including the core makers and brass moulders in the union. I was opposed to segregation and in favor of still further concentration. My threatened exposé of the exact membership of the International Iron Moulders' Union would have defeated my object and would have ended in disaster by aiding the separationists.

Proposed for presidency—

Quite a number of the delegates suggested that I allow my name to be placed before the convention as a candidate for the presidency to displace Fitzpatrick. This I absolutely refused to do. Fitzpatrick had been president for so many years that it would have been impossible for him to return to the foundry and hold down a job, for he was well along in years. In addition he was paying by installment upon a house and lot in the belief that he would be reelected. The salary was $100 per month and therefore inadequate for me to maintain myself in the East where I would have been obliged to reside, and to keep my wife and family in California which they would not leave. I was elected vice-president, the only time in the history of the organization when there was only one vice-president. I was also elected with Messrs. Fitzpatrick and Fox as a delegate to the American Federation of Labor convention, which was to meet in December of that year.

Fitzpatrick and Fox assured me that if I wished to assume the duties of general organizer for the union they would see to it that I was appointed to that position by the executive committee. As this position would keep me on the road all the time and my living and traveling expenses would be defrayed, I would be enabled to send most of my salary of $4 per day to my family. I also declined that offer. Then as a further inducement to have me reside in the East they offered to work for my election as president of the American Federation of Labor. This I also declined.

O'Donovan Rossa—

Upon the adjournment of the convention I went to New York City. After much difficulty I met my old friend O'Donovan Rossa, whom I had not seen for about a year prior to his arrest, conviction, and imprisonment at Pentonville. Poor Jerry was much changed, and notwithstanding the opportunities that he had had of realizing how great were the military power and prestige of England, he was still convinced that Ireland could successfully cope with her. How a man of intelligence and capable of close observation in other respects could delude himself with such a hopeless chimera was beyond me.

Justus Schwab—

I also visited Justus Schwab, the man who carried the red flag in a procession headed for Union Square in New York City, where an immense meeting was to be held, which was broken up by the police. The newspapers made terrible statements regarding the bloodthirsty character of this man. No leader of banditti in Europe enjoyed the frightful character bestowed upon Schwab. It was a hot sultry morning when I finally made my way into the basement which he occupied as a saloonkeeper. I found a fine, open-faced, clear-eyed, utterly frank, and intelligent German, who answered to the name without a moment's hesitation. He had heard of me and we became friends at once. I seldom have met any one who had so clear a conception of the causes of the poverty and sufferings of the workers or one more charitable of their shortcomings. He found excuses for many of the abuses inflicted upon working people by their employers by charging them to their lack of education and proper environment. The incessant rushing at break-neck pace to acquire the fugitive dollar precluded all study of the economic question, leaving the employer and moneyed man as ignorant upon the subject as the victims who toiled for him. Schwab was as mild and humane a man as I ever met and the very antithesis of the brutal character assigned to him. The papers lied about him, deliberately, wilfully, and maliciously. He was an honest and good man whom God had endowed with a fine physique, a clear, sound brain, unimpeachable integrity, sterling firmness of purpose, and a charity as great as the love of God. I spent an hour with him and never met him afterwards.

Samuel Gompers—

That morning I also visited another prominent man identified with the cause of Labor, i.e., Samuel Gompers. Samuel Gompers was the first vice-president of the Cigar Makers' International Union. He had charge of the New York district and devoted all of his time to the duties of that position. He was assisted by a secretary, also a paid officer, and jointly they issued a paper devoted to the interests of the cigar-makers. Mr. Gompers, somehow, had learned that I was a delegate to the convention of the American Federation of Labor and also that I had been mentioned as a possible candidate for the presidency of that organization. He looked upon my candidacy for the office with deep concern as he informed me that he was also a candidate. To him the position was a most desirable one as the pay amounted to $100 per month. Situated as he was, his pay was that of a cigar-maker and was quite too small to keep a growing family in New York City. The salary of $100 would put him "on Easy Street." I assured him that I was not a candidate and did not expect to be present at the convention. My assurances relieved him very much.

The day of my visit to Mr. Gompers happened to be the one upon which he had to get his paper to the press, which duties kept him busy until noon. As we left the office he inquired as to whether or not I indulged in a glass of beer and I responded in the affirmative. He then led the way to a saloon having the Ehret Brewery Company sign on each side of the door. I was aware of the fact that the New York Central Labor Council a little while before this had issued a boycott order against the Ehret Brewery and I knew that Gompers was a member of that Council. I asked him if the boycott had been raised on Ehret's Brewery and he said that it had not and that he had forgotten about the matter. He thanked me for reminding him. We went to another and had two glasses of delightfully cool union beer. I invited Mr. Gompers and his secretary to have a cigar, which they each did without a moment's hesitation. I scrutinized the cigar box for the label of the International Cigar Makers' Union and not finding it pushed the box back to the barkeeper. Gompers asked if I did not smoke. I told him that I did, but that the box must have the union label upon it. It was only by that means that we had managed to keep two hundred white cigar-makers at work in San Francisco. Neither Gompers nor his secretary relished this reminder. They were the paid heads of the organization in New York City, whose duty it was to push the sale of union-made cigars and by so doing lessen the consumption of the tenement-house made goods and thus enlarge and extend their union. My reproof was keenly felt by both gentlemen and we soon parted.

Mr. Gompers' opinion of Schwab was in sad contrast to Schwab's opinion of Gompers. He considered Schwab as an obstructionist and peace disturber, one whose demands were extravagant and impossible of realization. Schwab regarded Gompers as a man whose personal necessities took precedence over principle. His necessities dominated his conduct. In another environment he believed that Gompers would prove to be a good and useful man. He conceded that Gompers had the unquestioned right to act as he was doing and hoped that in time he would adopt a different course. Gompers at that time professed to be a socialist. Schwab lies buried in an obscure grave near New York and no mention of his name is ever made. Gompers is *ex cathedra* the presumed spokesman of American trade unionism and will have a monument of great architectural dimensions to proclaim his great civic virtues to future generations. And yet I prefer Schwab's obscurity.

Omaha—

On my way back to San Francisco I stopped at Omaha and at Denver. I was met at Omaha by my friend John Groves, deputy county treasurer, with whom I remained for two days. Groves was one of the many who came to me when I lived in that city, who needed help. He was a young non-Catholic Irishman who had mixed up in the revolutionary movement in London and had been obliged to flee from that city on account of his being charged with the killing of an informer. I secured him employment in an humble capacity, which he improved upon and steadily rose till he became the head time-keeper for all the Union Pacific shops. He then became deputy county treasurer with the prospect of becoming treasurer.

The morning after my arrival Groves took me to the finest residence section of the city and told me that there lay the land which I had refused to take from James McArdle, five acres of it, for the $250 which I had loaned him. By owning that small parcel of land the man who did not refuse it became a very rich man.

While in Omaha I failed to meet Mr. Edward Rosewater, proprietor of the *Omaha Bee,* the most influential newspaper in developing that section of the nation. Rosewater had taken a small newspaper plant off my hands, which I had planned to purchase from the Redfield Brothers for the purpose of issuing a daily paper devoted to progressive ideas of all kinds. My friends failed to furnish the money that they had promised to subscribe, and I was glad that Mr. Rosewater relieved me by taking it off my hands.

Denver—

At Denver I was received by the moulders with much adoo. I was the first national officer to visit them and my reception was in proportion to the importance of the office. I disliked the reception and the flattery which was so large a part of it. It conveyed the impression that a high officer is wiser by virtue of his office than if he were not such an officer. This is a prevailing weakness not only among trade unionists but also among fraternal organizations. It smacks so much of toadyism, and toadyism is at least so much a half-brother to servility and slavery that American citizens should purge themselves of it as disgraceful and humiliating. To be polite, respectful, and dignified is the attitude that trade unionists and every one else should assume toward all men occupying temporarily an office above the common people.

Failure of shipwrights—

Upon arriving in San Francisco[67] I found that the strike inaugurated by the shipwrights had dwindled to a contest between the moulders and the Union Iron Works. The instigators of the trouble, the shipwrights, had crawled back to their original nothingness, unconscious that they were guilty of any wrong-doing. The moulders, as I had feared would be the case, had borne the brunt of the struggle and were still fighting, although the struggle had been abandoned by all the other unions. The latter were all financially weak and should never have voted to engage in it. They were promised such ultimate support by the shipwrights that they had no hesitancy in believing that those promises would be fulfilled to the letter. It was a woeful piece of deception and treachery that the shipwrights had played on their associates in the Iron Trades Council. The contest ended after a three months' struggle by a compromise in which the moulders had the best of it.[68]

A street car strike—

The carmen on the Geary and Sutter Street lines had been on a strike for about two months when I

[67] Roney returned to San Francisco on August 5, 1886.—Ed.
[68] The strike was called off on September 3, 1886.—Ed.

arrived.[69] Neither side had made any headway. I called at the headquarters of the union to enquire how things were going along. Two members of the executive committee managing the strike were emphatic in their declarations that something startling had to be done to arouse the people and break the monotony. In answer to my inquiry as to what could and should be done they asked me to accompany them to the Geary Street tracks and they would show me. They pointed out how easy it would be to put a stick of dynamite into one of the small oblong boxes distributed along the track of that cable road, placing it so that the bumper which gripped the cable would strike it and cause an explosion which

[69] The strike of the carmen began about July 13, 1886, and was called by the employees of the North Beach and Mission Street Car Company and the City Railroads Street Car Company as a protest against an order issued by their employers that the men must give up their membership in the Knights of Labor. The Geary, California, and Sutter Street car lines were not affected. During the strike there were two instances of explosives being used on the street car tracks, but no damage was done. The strike was declared off on July 18, when the employers rescinded their previous order. This was the only street car strike declared during Roney's absence from San Francisco, and inasmuch as it was settled before he returned from the moulders' convention he could have taken no part in it.

Roney is writing from memory, approximately thirty years after the incident took place, and consequently it is not surprising that he should become somewhat confused as to certain detailed happenings. I have carefully checked his manuscript against all possible sources of information, and have found it to be amazingly accurate in practically all respects. I surmise that Roney is here referring to certain occurrences which took place in connection with the strike on the California, Sutter and Geary street car lines in December of that year.—Ed.

would lift the dummy off of the track, and, I suggested, perhaps kill someone. They cheerfully admitted that that result was very possible. They further informed me that a man had already been detailed to purchase the explosive, and as he knew how to handle it something would happen within a couple of days.

My acquaintance with these men was very limited. They had every appearance of being honest and sincere, viewing the strike as war under which every weapon of offense could be used with impunity, and justifiably so. They offered the same argument that Mr. Lincoln Steffens later offered to palliate and excuse, if not to exonerate, the McNamaras for their murderous doings as the war lords of the structural iron workers.

When I had gained sufficient knowledge of their intentions I warned them to proceed no further in their design and told them that if an explosion occurred on either of the two street car lines during the strike and any person was injured, I would hold them personally responsible for the injuries which resulted. This declaration rather surprised them because I had listened to their proposals so attentively and apparently so approvingly. I told them that I would not stand for any lives being imperiled or sacrificed in this or any other strike occurring in San Francisco while I was president of the Federated Trades Council and could prevent it. If a strike could only be won by the sacrifice of human life, then the strike must be abandoned until a more favorable opportunity presented itself. If a strike meant war we must abstain from injuring innocent noncombatants, the only ones likely to be injured if their proposals were carried out. "You may," I told them, "scuffle as much as you please with scab motormen and conductors and tussle with the police, but you must leave passengers alone, and above all you must not resort to the cowardly method of using dynamite to accomplish your purpose."

While I was lecturing them I felt that I was putting myself in a dangerous situation if they were as murderous as they claimed to be. As a further warning I told them that I would write a full statement of our interview and give it to my wife to be opened immediately in case an accident befell me. This last statement clinched the interview and no dynamiting was done on either the Geary or the Sutter street railroads during that strike. On another occasion dynamiting was resorted to in a small way without any fatalities, but these men were not responsible, for they had left the city. I believe that the men gained their demands at this time.

Another street railroad strike occurred on the same lines,[70] the precise nature of which I do not now

70 Roney is here referring to the strike of the employees of the Geary and Sutter Street railroads, which was declared on December 8, 1886. The carmen demanded an increase in wages and a twelve-hour day with ample time for meals. The strike lasted 86 days and failed. It was accompanied by much violence and some dynamiting. John E. Stites and Chas. A. Dean were arrested and tried for dynamiting, the former being found guilty on March 17, 1887.—Ed.

remember. It was fought with customary bitterness and with no seeming disposition evinced on either side to yield or compromise. I was absent from one on the meetings of the Federated Trades Council when a delegate named Thurman,[71] a printer, proposed that in order to show their sympathy for the car men the trade unions should parade the following Sunday up the Geary Street line and down that of Sutter Street. When I read the report as published in the following morning's paper it became clear to me that the Federated Trades Council was retrograding. It still seemed to need a nurse to coddle it into doing what was sensible or a boss to dragoon its members in the direction of what was right. I knew that the unions would not parade because they did not have the chance to consider the proposition. At the same time I was aware that a mob of enthusiastic believers in the justice of the car men's demands might form a line and in the name of unionists parade the streets at the time named. I knew the projectors of the demonstration and I also knew their purposes. I was also alive to the fact that if trouble ensued they would in preservation of their anatomy be judiciously absent. The folly of the proposal worried me exceedingly.

An appeal from the police—

In the evening my wife and the children went out to see the sights of a Saturday night, she to do a

[71] E. W. Thurman at that time was a prominent member of the Typographical Union.—Ed.

little marketing. The door bell rang, revealing Captain Healey, secretary to the Chief of Police, who desired to speak with me. The Captain informed me that he had been sent by the Chief to notify me that the parade announced for the next day would not take place as it was a direct challenge to create a riot, which, he hoped, I would use my best effort to prevent. He was determined to prevent it by force if it was attempted. I assured Captain Healey that I was as desirous as the Chief to see the peace preserved, and further that I had had nothing whatever to do with calling the parade, which was not and could not be a trade union affair. Nevertheless, Healey still insisted that the Chief held me responsible for it and that I must devise some means of preventing it so as to preserve the good name of the city, which was being affected by the frequency of such occurrences. After a long discussion of the matter it was finally agreed that the Chief was to address me in a letter to appear in the Sunday issue of each of the morning papers notifying me of his purposes and demanding that I prevent the parade. The letter appeared, creating considerable flurry.[72] The police also appeared upon the streets armed with their riot batons.

Thurman, the man responsible for the trouble and folly, came to me in the morning in great excitement and urged me to go to the United States Mint,

[72] The original letter addressed to Roney by Chief of Police Crowley is in my possession and bears the date of December 18, 1886. —Ed.

RICHARD POWERS

E. W. Thurman

the starting point of the projected parade, and disperse the crowd which was then gathering. I told him that as he had raised the storm it was his duty, and not mine, to allay it. He said that if he made the attempt to do so he would surely be killed, and that the only man who could disperse the crowd was myself. I ordered him out of my house and said some strong things to him which I believe he remembered many years afterwards. Geo. Bayless and Jake Groosman also came to me and urged me to go to the Mint steps and forbid the parade.

It was a very grave moment for me. The parade was, I learned, instigated by Haskell and a number of his thoughtless, mentally overheated adherents, who thought that they saw in this the opportunity of beginning the Revolution which was to bring about the death of Capitalism and the extinction of class lines. I knew that these "warriors" would not risk their hides in the first effort or conflict with the police. I knew that if I acted in the matter they would brand me as a coward and probably as the tool of the capitalists whom we were all endeavoring to dethrone. I was fully conscious of their malignity and their capability of giving expression to it. I also knew what the consequences would be to them and to many other poor men inadvertently dragged into the tumult. I also appreciated the disgrace which would attach to the labor movement and all the dire results to participants and non-participants.

When I reached the Mint at a little before noon[73] I found the adjacent streets packed with people, some of whom were there out of curiosity and some from sympathy with the cause of the strikers. From Market to Howard and from Fourth to Sixth streets the crowd was densest. The carmen's union headed by a band drew up in front of the Mint and awaited orders. A profound silence prevailed as I came down the steps to address them. I briefly and simply told them that the affair was not a trade union demonstration, that the unions had not been consulted, and were not present. As president of the Federated Trades Council I advised the car men to return to their headquarters and requested the assembled people to disperse. Both requests were complied with and the threatened "revolution" was thus postponed.

As I anticipated, the projectors of the demonstration were dissatisfied and grievously disappointed at the miscarriage of their plans, and they began a crusade to undermine me. They did their work quietly, insidiously, and effectively. Haskell, the prime mover in the matter, studiously absented himself from the meetings of the Federated Trades Council, leaving to his followers the working out of later schemes.

[73] This event took place on December 19, 1886.—Ed.

Politics and trade unionism—

To engage in politics was always the object of a number of the delegates to the Federated Trades Council. Unionism and the advantages to be gained by thorough organization were secondary considerations with many and were frequently lost sight of for the allurements which participation in political combats offered. Some of the delegates were actually members of the Council at the instance of the political bosses of the city. The aparent strength which the Council had with the working class and the influence which it exercised among the fair-minded and unbiased citizenship created an anxiety among the professional politicians that could be allayed only by accurate information gained by contact from the inside. Buckley had several trusty men in the Council to head off any steps that might seem inimical to him and his party. Higgins had others in the Council for the same purpose, and both groups were always ready to unite if anything loomed on the horizon that was likely to prove detrimental to partyism.

I never could understand by what mental process a man could become a slave to party fetishes. Right or wrong "the party" must be upheld and kept intact. Trade unionism and social improvement could go to the dogs if "the party" were assailed. I succeeded measurably in convincing many of our unionists that this was all wrong, that politics was a profession, and that the "professors" were the hirelings of the corporations which owned and dictated to both Democrats and Republicans. Notwithstanding this, the desire for political action as unionists remained strong.

My experiences with reformers and trade unionists who concern themselves with politics gave me ample reason for believing that such ventures should not be indulged in. The desire for office overshadows every consideration for the improvement of the people *en masse.* A cry must be raised and a platform of principles promulgated wherein the woes of the unfortunate toilers are elaborated upon and promises made that the wrongs shall cease if the individuals selected are placed in office. Some of the men so chosen are sincere in their promises, but when elected they find themselves in a new situation. They never dreamed of breathing a different atmosphere amid strange environments. They begin to realize that the office is the thing of first consideration. The Cause which put them there becomes merely an incident to be remembered when its use will further aid in the retention of their office.

Union Labor Party politicians—

So far as the great bulk of the working people is concerned the trade union politician is no better than the politician of the regular parties. Frequently he is not so good. The disgrace attached to the trade union supervisors of San Francisco with

Eugene Schmitz as Mayor will long be remembered as the most pitiful and pathetic exhibition of human weakness and folly that has ever been exposed. At a time when San Francisco was stricken in the dust,[74] powerless and inert, our boasting champions of the poor man's redemption were wallowing in the filth of their own degradation with an impudent effrontery that no political hack had yet essayed. It was long known or suspected that preceding boards of supervisors had fared well at the hands of corporations but they had never been caught. Neither had they made professions of undying public virtue as our Labor representatives had done. I knew myself that Gilleran, when elected supervisor, was several thousands of dollars in debt, but when he retired at the expiration of his term he had a fine hotel free from debt, with property in the Mission valued at many thousands of dollars. I knew this intimately, and I also knew of others who became wealthy in the same questionable manner. But it remained for a clear-cut Union Labor mayor and a majority of Union Labor supervisors to reveal their own pollution and by inference the pollution of their predecessors. What has happened since the Schmitz régime, I do not know, but I do know that an active and alert politician has assured me that the union leaders are all right.

The political trade unionist is never guilty of an act likely to place him in opposition to an appre-

[74] Roney is referring to the earthquake and fire of April 18, 1906. —Ed.

ciable number of his fellows. If his opinion is invited and insisted upon he is sure to straddle the question and by evasion or subterfuge of some sort wriggle out of a direct reply. It is his business to keep his fellows interested by concentrating their minds upon matters of no special benefit to them but of such a character as to aid him and his clique when politics are booming. The party politician does not resort to such methods because he knows nothing of unionism and generally makes no pretense of doing so. His way is to tickle the bright American. Whether the politician is of the trade union stripe or simply a member of one of the regular political parties, his aim is the same, i.e., to befog and bamboozle the citizen to his own advantage. Of the two the unionist is the most despicably dishonest because he flourishes under the flag of reform, while the other does not.

Selfishness is the predominant characteristic of every politician. Every movement, every speech is made for the sole purpose of adding to his strength as a vote getter and successful candidate for office.

Retirement from San Francisco Labor movement—

I was so utterly exhausted, mentally and physically, at the end of 1886 that I declined to be a candidate for reelection to the office of president of the Federated Trades Council.[75] A number of the unions had withdrawn chiefly because of the partici-

[75] Roney was succeeded by W. A. Bushnell.—Ed.

pation of the unions and the union leaders in politics and the switching off from the straight course of unionism by so many who claimed to be union men before everything else. If I had exerted myself I could have prevented this and reestablished confidence. But I had myself lost confidence in most of the men when I discovered their duplicity and their disregard of all their vaunted professions. With the beginning of 1887 I was relieved of my job in the City Hall and also of my membership in the Federated Trades Council. Foundry employment was not plentiful, nor was I looked upon with favor by the employers. I had made enemies of the politicians and practically stood alone without work and with no immediate prospects of having any. I was also without any funds or material resources. I felt conscious, however, of having pursued a straight and undeviating course in every situation that I had faced, and at no time did I even think of dickering for favors from anyone or of using my position to my own advantage. I stood alone, almost forgotten. However, I felt some satisfaction in knowing that whether I was or was not given credit for it I had done much to infuse union men with the ideals and purposes of unionism.

The Federated Trades Council had dwindled to the point of insignificance. Only a few organizations were represented in it that had national or international affiliations. The local unions, with the exception of that of the sailors, were all numerically and financially weak, and their representatives were uneducated in the ways and traditions of unionism.

The brewery workers—

There were between seven and eight hundred men employed in the local breweries of San Francisco in 1886, and their living and working conditions were extremely bad. The majority of the brewery employees were Germans, many of whom had been taught the business of brewer and malster in the old country, and had thus become accustomed to the living and working conditions which prevailed there. The brewery workmen of San Francisco were the most degraded set of workers in the city with the possible exception of the German and French bakers, whose hours of labor, sanitary conditions, and pay were worse. In May, 1886, a committee from the brewery employees appeared before the Federated Trades Council and asked that someone be designated to organize the workers of that craft. Alfred Fuhrman, a German and an outstanding member of the sailors' union, was assigned to the task and succeeded in getting some of the men together in a local union.[76] The peculiar feature of the situation was that most of the men professed to be socialists,

[76] Alfred Fuhrman was born in Solingen, Germany, October 12, 1863. As a young man he went to sea, arriving in San Francisco in 1881. He then returned to Germany, where he entered the University of Bonn, but did not remain to graduate. He again went to sea. He arrived in San Francisco during the period when the Cost Seamen's Union was being formed, became a member of that organization, and soon was chosen one of its officers. From that time until 1893, he

German socialists. They imagined Socialism to be a German institution, unknown and not understood anywhere else or by any other people. It was thought to be exclusively and distinctively German and nothing else. Trade unionism had not yet obtained a firm footing in Germany and its establishment was opposed in that country, as elsewhere, as being unnecessary and obstructive to the socialistic program. The socialists held that trade unionism at its best was simply ameliorative in all its aims and could never be anything else, for it recognized wages as the compensation for labor performed and acknowledged the rights of employers to extract from the workers all that they could obtain. Trade unionism was therefore a new feature in the economic life of the German brewery workmen inasmuch as it proposed an immediate improvement in their mode of working and living by reducing and regulating their hours of labor and by fixing a higher compensation for their efforts.

Alfred Fuhrman—

A certain amount of clannishness pervaded the German workers as a whole to the exclusion of every other people. They traded exclusively with each

was one of the most prominent and active leaders in the labor movement of the Pacific Coast. He organized the Brewers and Malsters Union of San Francisco, was chosen its secretary, and retained that office until his withdrawal from the labor field in 1893 to engage in the practice of law. In 1890, he was elected president of the Federated Trades Council. He also became a national figure in the organized brewery workers' movement.—Ed.

other, herded together, and eschewed every association that was not purely and distinctively German in character. Clannishness was carried still further by the development and acknowledgment of factions which grew up among the natives of individual German provinces and principalities. Because of his nationality Fuhrman exercised a potent influence among a certain portion of the German brewery workers. His versatility aided in making him a person to be regarded as the fittest to undertake the organization of these men. He was also a man of great energy, possessed of considerable mental ability and was not too scrupulous about the methods employed in obtaining his ends.

Fuhrman was successful in a short time in forming a union among the brewery workers. When a hundred and twenty-four men composed that body he declared a boycott on the Philadelphia Brewery.[77] A demand was made upon Wieland Bros., who were then operating that establishment, that their workmen must join the union. The union was a new thing to the brewery owners as well as to the workmen, and so the demand was refused. The Philadelphia Brewery was the largest in the city, employing over a hundred and fifty men. If this brewery could be compelled to force its men into the union it was

[77] The strike of the brewery employees was declared on May 7, 1887, but owing to the fact that the union realized the impossibility of carrying on the strike against all the local breweries at the same time, it was decided to levy a boycott against only the Philadelphia Brewery.—Ed.

thought that it would be an easy matter to compel the others in succession to do likewise. The immense business done by this brewery was the cause of a deep-seated business jealousy on the part of the smaller concerns. As the boycott progressed, and as the saloon-keepers refused to sell the Wieland beer, the product of other breweries was immediately substituted. Thus, the smaller breweries aided most actively in the boycotting of the Wieland brewery, at the same time professing the utmost hostility to the boycott.

I opposed the boycott because I did not believe that the small membership represented in the union as compared to the greater number of workers not members[78] had the strength to carry through the strike successfully; also because I felt that the failure of the boycott would prove disastrous to unionism, and again, because the local unions generally were not consulted before the boycott had been declared. I also opposed it because the brewery union wished to compel the brewery employers to become the organizers of their association. This has now, however, become a recognized principle in unionism to which I have never subscribed and to which I was then bitterly opposed.

The closed shop policy—

My idea of unionism has never been to force membership upon anyone. I recognize every man's

[78] Roney claimed that only 124 out of 800 brewery employees were organized at the time.—Ed.

right to believe in that which he thinks is best for his own welfare. If he is an intelligent man he will perceive under industrial conditions, existing and developing, the imperative necessity of cooperating with his fellows for the protection of his social status and his future attainment of rights wrongly withheld from him by a system of legalized exploitation. To compel men to belong to a union weakens rather than strengthens it. A chain is no stronger than its weakest link. A union is only strong when all its members by voluntary act become associated and are all animated with the same hopes and fears, differently expressed but are a unit in all things for their social advancement. When men are forced into a union they become members grudgingly and seldom warm up to its true aims. When the moment of trial comes and all are required to stand unflinchingly the men who have been impressed are sure to waver, if they do not absolutely become blacklegs, spies, and scabs.

Unionism is like all civic organizations in its primary makeup as well as in the performance of all its subsequent functions and operations. To urge the men of a vocation or trade to become members is the duty, the incessant task of every member of a union. Its immediate aims as well as its remote aspirations must be clearly set forth to the workers. The strength that comes from cohesion and solidarity must be dwelt upon as well as the forces arrayed against them to restrain and hold them in the galling bondage which they should as men combat and subdue.

To ask employers to act as organizers for a union by compelling their employees, whether willing or not, to join a union is not unionism as I understand it. It is because employers resort to these very methods for other purposes when they have the will and power to do so that necessitates the formation of trade unions. If the members of the employing class were as just to their employees as they demand their employees be just to them, there would be no necessity for the existence of trade unions. It is the injustice arising from and fostered by greed, together with the rivalry of competitors in the same field of business, that compels the helpless individual worker to form associations to resist the impositions and aggressions of the employing class.

I have ever been opposed to force in all situations growing out of or due to industrial disputes. Sound reasoning, plain facts fairly demonstrated, and discriminating justice can always be depended upon as the surest, safest and most economical means by which amicably and satisfactorily to settle all labor disputes. At the same time I would have every man a member of the union of his occupation, and when justice is not done either to the individual or to the group complaining I would have the whole membership as one man stand firmly forth and subdue the ruthless tyrant by every civilized means at their command. Men of great or little wealth, titled gentry or potentates large or small, are only men and are no greater or better or wiser or worse than other people except as their minds, habits, training, and inclination makes them better or worse. The fair and just man is in the sight of God superior to any king, however powerful.

Involved in brewery boycott—

I became involved in the brewery boycott in a very simple and inadvertent way. I was with a couple of friends in a restaurant a few days after the boycotting began when a part owner in one of the breweries entered and began a conversation upon the subject with one of my friends. He stated the case very clearly and it seemed to me very fairly. I took little part in the conversation, but was an attentive and interested listener. The employer concerned was a young German reared in San Francisco and supremely ignorant of the working conditions of men in any other than the brewing business. The conditions prevailing in that industry, being imported from Germany, were considered in every way correct, for they had existed there for generations without protest. He was not opposed to organization, to the shortening and regulation of the working time, or to an increase of pay. He believed, since his attention had been called to it, in wiping out the wholesale consumption of beer by brewery workmen and in improving their social condition. He did not believe in being forced to act as organizer for the union by compelling his men to become members.

If they wished to be members they had the right to do so, but to compel them to join was one thing that he would not do.

His statement was so much in accord with my own views that I volunteered to address a letter to the public asking them to withhold support of the boycott, declaring it to be unjust and unnecessary.[79] I had previously done the same thing with other unions without publicity and I had called down individual members of unions repeatedly for acts analogous to those of the brewery men, but I had at that time been invested with authority. On this occasion I did not have authority, but I was the same person who had organized, and, as I believe, had guarded and directed unions in the true channels of unionism, and therefore felt entitled to protest against this brazen piece of arrogance instigated by Fuhrman.

[79] This letter appeared in the San Francisco papers on May 14, 1887, and reacted most disastrously against Roney. The *Daily Report* of July 16, 1887 stated that, "This of course turned against him nearly all of his old friends and he was left between two stools, flat on the ground. There were those who said he was paid to write the letter. But those who know him best do not believe anything of the kind, and ascribe a very different reason to his action. Certain it is that he had no money then or afterwards, and he is not thought to have had a dollar when he left home last Monday." The reference to his having left home had to do with his mysterious absence from San Francisco for a week without letting his friends know where he was. The *Daily Report* of the above date stated that some of his friends "fear he may have become involved in a quarrel over his recent course in labor matters and met with foul play." He had merely gone to Vallejo to seek employment after having searched in vain in San Francisco for about six months for some sort of job.—Ed.

My protest would have defeated the boycott if the smaller brewery owners had been honest and loyal in their professions. The opportunity given them to substitute their beer for the Wieland product was too good for them to let go easily, and in a surreptitious way they did all they could to keep the boycott going until the Wieland brothers saw where their friends were steering them. When they realized what was happening they yielded to the union and all their employees became members.[80] It was a repetition of the old adage, "Save me from my friends." Their friends would have absorbed their business if the boycott had continued much longer.

While the boycott was in progress I visited Fuhrman several times, showing him how opposite his organization scheme was to trade unionism. My representations fell upon deaf ears. He looked upon my interferences as unwarranted and appeared to believe that a union had the right, whether or not numerically and financially strong, to take any action in any way that it thought best to adopt for the attainment of its ends.

A feeling of personal antagonism was engendered by this contest which was not allayed when Fuhrman declared a boycott against the United States Brewery.[81] This was a repetition of the former fight in every particular. The brewers began to see that Fuhrman's plan was to attack them in detail and

80 The strike ended July 24, 1887.—Ed.

81 This boycott was declared in July, 1888.—Ed.

by subjugating one at a time to gain greater strength for the next contest. They also perceived that their treachery to the Wielands did not profit them. I reminded them of their conduct in that particular, which was not received very cordially by them. As it was practically a continuation of the former fight and the same good reasons existed to oppose the boycott I heartily aided in every way possible to accomplish its defeat. Several months of struggle followed. Then the brewers hauled down their colors and decided to order their men to join the union.

Branded a traitor to Labor—

As success is the important feature in disputes of this sort, no matter how obtained, the victory over the employing brewers gave Fuhrman an immediate position of prominence among the organizations represented in the Federated Trades Council. Nearly all of its members were involved in politics and had been active in the late State and municipal elections. I was always opposed to participation in politics as unionists and had censured some of the delegates for their very questionable methods. It was an easy matter for Fuhrman to get men with the feelings that they had toward me to pass a resolution denouncing me as an enemy of Organized Labor.[82] I

82 The resolution passed by the Federated Trades Council of San Francisco was as follows:

"Whereas, One Frank Roney has on previous occasions and notably during the just fights of the brewery workmen against the oppres-

replied to their resolution quite strongly and gave the public to understand who they were and what their practices and aims were. I am sorry that I have neither the resolution nor my letter. The Federation later became a pitiful skeleton of what it had been.

At the same time the rumor gained currency and was passed along with admirable promptitude by the pseudo union men that I was subsidized by the brewers in their contest with Fuhrman. I could never trace these rumors to their source nor combat them because they were never publicly made. They were simply put in circulation in the devious, snake-like, treacherous, cowardly way that all reports are circulated when character must be destroyed to serve the purposes of creatures untrue to every principle of truth and honor.

Ingratitude of Haskell—

One of the slyest and most industrious mediums and circulators, as I afterwards learned, was B. G.

sions of their employers, worked strenuously against the interests of organized labor; therefore be it

"Resolved, That we, the Representative Council of the Federated Trades and Labor Oraganizations of the Pacific Coast, in meeting assembled, brand the said Frank Roney as a traitor to the labor cause, and we warn all workingmen not to place any trust or confidence in him.

"Resolved, That these resolutions be forwarded to the daily and labor press and that a copy, with all necessary information, be sent to the American Federation of Labor, with the request that it make the record of this man known throughout the United States."

Roney was also condemned in resolutions passed by his associates in the iron moulders' union.—Ed.

Haskell. Gratitude, if nothing else, should have placed him in the front rank of my defenders if I needed defense. I had sponsored and defended him and became literally his protector from the moment he set foot in the Trades Assembly, and through all his vagaries and changes I stood by him until I left San Francisco. And even then after a number of years, knowing of his conduct toward me, when he appealed to me to secure for him a certain commissionership I began the letter which I hoped would gain it for him, but the disaster in San Francisco next day rendered my effort abortive and the letter was never finished.[83]

A marked man—

My activities and prominence as a trade union organizer and exponent had made me a marked man to my pecuniary disadvantage. Still, however, I had only the kindliest feelings toward every one and at all times was in full sympathy with the endeavors of those aiming to do the right thing by their associates even though I considered them, according to my standards, to be mistaken. I had never fraternized with the politicians, and consequently could not

[83] Under date of April 15, 1906, Haskell wrote asking Roney to address a communication to Mayor E. E. Schmitz of San Francisco, urging his (Haskell's) appointment as one of the election commissioners of that city. The earthquake and fire of April 18, 1906, put an end to Haskell's political aspirations. I met him a few months later. For years previous to my visit he had been living in poverty, friendless and forgotten by those in whose behalf he had labored during the eighties.—Ed.

expect any favors from them. My standing was exceedingly low with foundry foremen. My conception of my position as a trade union leader taught me that I must ever remain free from all outside entanglements and that at no time ought I to permit my personal needs to interfere with whatever future conditions might arise requiring unbiased and untrammeled action.

Notwithstanding the rigidity with which I followed this rule I found myself at the end of many years of anxious, arduous labor maligned and traduced by unscrupulous men bent chiefly on their own advancement. I was the obstacle, and my opposition to the brewery boycott, designedly misconstrued, was the means which they took to lessen my prestige. Conscious of my rectitude in this as in all matters concerning unionism I refused to acknowledge that I was at fault in the part I took against the brewery boycott. If the same conditions existed now I would do precisely the same thing again.

Appointed Immigration Inspector—

After nearly two years' delay and considerable jugglery I was appointed Immigration Inspector at the Port of San Francisco at a compensation of $5 per day. It was a new office with no well defined duties. I had been assured of a superior place as Deputy Surveyor of the Port, but the practical politicians were too much for me and the place was given to another.

The only thing of moment that transpired during my year's activity as Immigration Inspector was when two German tramp steamers came into port loaded with Japanese immigrants. Anti-Chinese legislation was telling on the farmers of the State by steadily reducing the number of Mongolians available for agricultural labor. Cheap labor being the desideratum of the California farmer, as it is in fact of all employers in every industry, the Japanese were sought as the best substitutes for the depleted ranks of the Chinese. As substitutes for the Chinese the Japanese did not strike me very favorably. They were inferior in physique and deficient in cleanliness and showed no evidences of the alertness which they have later exhibited. Altogether I considered them a most undesirable lot of immigrants, but no worse than many who came from some portions of Europe. In my judgment the Chinese were at least 50 per cent superior to them in every respect.

My duty was to see that no immigrants were landed in violation of the contract labor laws. I found this a hard matter to do. I neither understood their language, nor did they understand mine. I was totally dependent upon a vicious-looking Japanese who had been recommended to me as an interpreter. I held thirteen as coming in violation of the contract labor law, and the marine surgeon held one. I conscientiously believe that all of them should have been held and returned to Japan, but in the absence of the required evidence I could not do so. I was several days in making the examination. On the last day I remained on the ship until 7:00 P.M. to finish up, rather than take another day at it. When about to leave, the consignee invited me to the quarter-deck for a consultation. He began by asking me what he was to do with the fourteen men held. The ship was not returning to Japan but was going into the coasting trade, and besides he had broken up the temporary fireplace constructed upon the deck where the Japanese had done their cooking on the way across the Pacific. In addition the contract labor law had been enacted after the vessel had left Yokohama, and he thought for that reason the men should not be held.

I told him that the responsibility was entirely his. He would have to keep them until he could return them to Japan, and for every one of them missing he would pay $300 into the United States Treasury. He tried a different method by saying that he understood that I could discharge every man held without a question and that if I would do so he would pay me $50 for each person. I hotly asked him if he knew the danger and consequences of attempting to bribe a United States officer. He replied by saying that under the circumstances his word was as good as mine. I told him that I was not going to make any parade of superior virtue and that all he would be obliged to do was to conform to every requirement of the law.

Upon leaving the ship I gave strict orders to the Custom House Night Inspector and upon reaching home wrote and mailed my report to the Secretary of the Treasury. Next morning when I arrived at the Collector's office I found the consignee present with a strong protest. The Collector was a strictly honest man and informed him that he could not, even if disposed to do so, reverse my action. The only person to do so was the Secretary of the Treasury. He applied to the Secretary by a lengthy telegram which I anticipated by asking the Secretary to withhold his decision until he had received my report which was then on the way to him. In a few days the consignee received notification by telegraph that my action had been approved. The vessel went north soon after this and a curious thing happened. Every man whom I had held was landed through *habeas corpus* proceedings, and as I learned was later liberated. Curious!

Unemployed and forgotten—

I lost my position as Immigration Inspector after serving in that capacity for a year. My employment from that time on to the declaration of war against Spain was sporadic and precarious. I had no desire to trade upon my reputation as a trade unionist and kept aloof from all contact with those who would soon have learned about my straightened pecuniary circumstances. I had sacrificed much in the Cause and felt that if aid of any sort should come to me through that source it would lessen, at least in my own estimation, the value of my labors on behalf of the working class. So I kept away from them and when called to work at my trade in the Mare Island Navy Yard,[84] I left San Francisco without a regret, practically forgotten by those for whose welfare I had fought and sacrificed.

The illusion of popularity as well as the phantasy of recognition for continuous faithful service to people struggling to better themselves socially and economically was deeply impressed upon me. If I had utilized my position for my own advantage, and had been less earnest in my endeavors on their behalf, this would not have happened to me. But with it all I had no regrets and would most likely do precisely the same thing again under the same circumstances.

Mare Island Navy Yard—

In 1898, just as the war with Spain began, I obtained employment in the Construction and Repair Department of the Mare Island Navy Yard at Vallejo. Several years earlier I had been urged by Congressman Morrow to accept the foremanship of the foundry of the Steam Engineering Department of the Yard, but my old friend, Dimmick, formerly of the Union Iron Works, was seeking the job and actually needed it a great deal more than I did, so I withdrew in his favor.

[84] Roney left San Francisco for Vallejo lin 1898.—Ed.

Dimmick—

Dimmick in his day was an excellent foundry manager. For years he had served the Union Iron Works' management far too faithfully, to the damage of his reputation. His employer's interests were his only consideration at all times. He believed sincerely that such was the duty expected of him as a foreman. He had little consideration for the men except to secure from them the greatest amount of work with the least expenditure of money and in the quickest time. This was his reputation when I first knew him. I soon discovered that he was a different man from what he wished to be considered and was held to be by the majority of moulders in San Francisco. From the first we became the best of friends. Our intimacy became so close as time passed that I ventured some objections to his style of speaking to the men. He showed surprise at my first comments and slightly resented the criticism. I passed his resentment without remark, but kept on tactfully with my criticisms. Gradually I made an impression upon him. Being a man of large and generous nature he perceived my object to be the creation of permanent harmony between workmen, foremen, and employers, the first step toward which was to recognize workmen as intelligent, responsible human beings with feelings and aspirations as good and as high as those of foremen and employers and with the same right to live and enjoy life as the very best of them. Men were not dogs to be kicked, nor slaves to be whipped even if conditions compelled them to labor for others. Corporations were soulless and foremen were used as their tools to exact at a minimum of cost all that workmen had to give, without their also being insulted by opprobious epithets or ugly and threatening looks. It was because of the great change in his treatment of the men that he was finally discharged by Irving M. Scott and his partner, Geo. W. Prescott. After his discharge he attempted to work as a journeyman, but failed completely. As a workman he was completely deficient, but as a manager he was a decided success. When I found that he was seeking the foremanship at Mare Island I refused to consider it.

Navy Department efficiency—

From the establishment of the Navy Yard up to a few years before the Spanish War employment was entirely subject to the changes and mutations incident to politics. Foremen and workmen alike owed their employment and retention to their political activity or the political influence back of them. Efficiency as workmen or a thorough knowledge of the details of an occupation was not considered a qualification for employment. Neither was the want of knowledge a cause for debasement. Political "pull," as it is called, was the all-essential thing. Every tool or mechanical device used was antiquated. Slowness and dilatoriness were the supreme order of the day in everything. Men had been discharged for being ordinarily fair-minded and speedy.

Mare Island Navy Yard, the government workshop, was a huge and expensive joke as an industrial institution. For years a bull team was employed in hauling between the powder magazine and the shops at the north end of the yard, a distance of about two miles, and usually made the round trip in a day. A small monitor was constructed and reconstructed four times before its final completion. The machinery and general style of the latter were antiquated before its completion, necessitating a general overhauling, to be repeated when again it became obsolete. And so it went along with the air and pretense of work, fooling everyone but the politicians, and they did not care. The management of the Mare Island Navy Yard for many years was a disgrace, a scandal, and a robbery. Not a feature of its methods had a single redeeming characteristic.

It was against this reputation, so justly acquired, that it had most to contend when it entered the field to compete for the Government's building of its own ships. Then all was changed, but it was a hard matter to convince the level-headed but not too practical men at Washington that the old style was wholly eradicated. It is, however, wholly and completely changed, and Mare Island of late years has done much to redeem itself by its estimates on new ships, reducing their cost of construction by many hundreds of thousands of dollars.

The misfortune with Mare Island now is that it has drifted to the other extreme in its quest for efficiency. A horde of poorly trained, inefficient, pompous, and inexperienced young naval officers are inflicted upon it to its material detriment and to the infinite disgust of the men employed. Efficiency is their aim. To obtain efficient results two conditions must take precedence, and in these the young naval officers are sadly lacking. The first is to understand in detail the nature of the work they are required to superintend and the next is to know how to handle the men who perform the work. If these qualifications are not in evidence efficiency will be slow in developing and may never reach its zenith. If a young man trained at Annapolis as a constructor were obliged to work for a given time at each of the many mechanical branches involved in ship construction, and if his graduation depended upon the quality of his work, he would better comprehend the difficulties and obstacles the workingman is up against when efficiency is demanded. He would thereby learn more of a practical nature about the worker than he can ever hope to obtain as a mere poorly tutored superintendent.

Efficiency to be efficient must begin at the top. Steam engineering officers educated at Annapolis need the same accurate technical training in their pursuit that constructors do. If this course had been pursued in the past, fewer explosions and less loss of life and property would have resulted. When in San Diego a few years ago I met some of the crews of several of the torpedo boat destroyers from whom

I learned the deplorable condition of the boilers on several of the boats. Every day that steam was raised on these boats was as likely as not to be the last day on earth for the sailors. The foremen, oilers, and water tenders all knew and repeatedly called the attention of the officers to the defects without avail. They could not quit the service unless branded as deserters, nor could they go upon strike unless as mutineers. If they made statements to the papers properly authenticated it would be considered insubordination and subject them to court martial and punishment. Knowing all this the men went through their duties with death or torture staring them in the face, and all because of the inefficiency of their superior officers. Newspapers will print no complaints of this character unless vouched for by one whose reputation is established as a marine engineer or unless he is otherwise in a commanding position. The Navy Department ignores all complaints made by outsiders, priding itself upon its superiority.

A few weeks after I left San Diego an explosion occurred on one of those boats in which several men were killed and others were maimed for life. An investigation followed resulting in the disaster being attributed to an accident. An accident never happens with the use of steam. Fatalities are due to carelessness, ignorance, or wilful neglect. Every so-called accident could be avoided if the knowledge and care necessary to operate steam boilers were duly observed. Engineer officers and steam engineers in every industry should be held to a strict accountability for every mishap or fatality that happens with the boilers under their supervision. In the Navy a rule of this kind should be most rigidly enforced. Imprisonment and degradation should be the least of the punishments inflicted. The word "accident" and the excuse it conveys for the injury done should be eliminated from the maritime vocabulary, because an accident cannot happen with steam boilers. It is criminal carelessness that causes the disasters.

Navy Department economy—

Economy in operation, another of the hackneyed expressions used by naval officers to cover up their deficiencies at the expense of the workmen, is called into service to show their superiors how vigilant they are to save for the Government and incidentally to lighten the burdens of the taxpayer. Economy as understood and expressed by these young officers, and frequently by their elders in the service, is not economy in the strict sense when applied to government shipbuilding and repairing. A war vessel cannot be constructed too perfectly. There should be no economy in the composition of the material used in the construction of a warship. It should be exact in every particular of quality according to the best standardization in vogue obtained by careful scientific experiment.

Conscientious first-class mechanics in government or other employment are never wasteful of either their time or the materials handled by them. Being intelligent as well as conscientious they know the value of their labor, and while they regard the profit system of exploitation as legal they are also fully alive to its injustice, especially when by speeding up methods or wage reductions employers endeavor to extract from them every ounce of vitality. Naval officers are less careful in dealing with men in government employment than the average civilian employer. The latter will be confronted with a strike if he becomes too oppressive. The naval officer does not care and looks upon his fellow-citizen in civil life as the meanest part of the machine in which he was educated at public expense to be a cog, without regard to the man's feelings or his worth. In the opinion of these inexperienced young officers low wages are the speediest, safest, and surest way to economize for the government.

Vallejo Labor Council—

The threat of a universal reduction of the wages of the men employed at Mare Island and its actual enforcement in a few instances aroused them to a full sense of the danger imminent. The result was the organization of the Vallejo Labor Council.[85] What an organization of this character would hope

[85] The Trades and Labor Council of Vallejo was organized in 1899. —Ed.

to accomplish for Labor was not at first apparent. The Navy Yard was the only place where the men could obtain employment and labor organizations exercised but little influence with the Yard officials who received their orders from Washington.

A labor council is composed invariably of representatives of unions. Vallejo was a relatively small town in 1898. There was only one bona fide union in existence in Vallejo, i.e., the machinists. Later the ship-joiners formed a union as did the store clerks, and an effort was made to organize the few carpenters employed in the city. The boiler-makers and iron shipbuilders organized, but with the exception of the machinists none was of any importance numerically. The unions of San Francisco gave permission to their members employed on the yard to select a representative, and I was chosen by the moulders, and also selected as president of the new organization.

If this local labor council was to live and thrive and be of any value to the men employed at the Yard, I felt that it was necessary for it to accomplish something to invite the confidence and commendation of the community. My experience taught me the value of regular newspaper reports in impressing a community with the purposes of an organization. Without consultation with members of the Council or requesting their approval I began furnishing reports of the meetings to one of the local papers. I endeavored to make the reports interesting by touching upon matters of local interest affecting the citizens of Vallejo apart from those employed upon Mare Island. These reports made a favorable impression both upon the permanent residents as well as those employed at the Yard. If this had not been done, the Labor Council would have lasted only a few weeks. The reports gave the Council a permanency it never otherwise would have attained. The establishment of a permanent headquarters and reading room was the first step taken to demonstrate its usefulness. The reading room was popular with the thinking workers though it proved a failure because of lack of attendance and interest that should have been shown by those for whom it was established.

Federal compensation—

The most important thing done by the Council during my presidency was the framing of an act to indemnify government employees for injuries received during the hours of employment. A committee consisting of Wm. Brownlee, Richard Caverly, and myself was appointed to draft the law. We met once and decided that I should prepare the act. As I was unfamiliar with legal phraseology, when I completed my task I sent it to Mr. Tirey L. Ford, then Attorney General for California, who without hesitation generously and promptly put it into proper legal shape. Mr. Ford, as a State officer, could have declined doing so without giving offense as many officials of lesser consequence had done in the past, and as I was an utter stranger to him, it would have conveyed a merited rebuke. Instead of this he showed an eagerness for the task as commendable as the talent displayed by him in its execution.

I assumed the duty of secretary in the correspondence necessary to have this indemnity bill presented to Congress. The young man who was secretary of the Labor Council was wholly inexperienced and quite formal in his letter writing and as brief as it was possible to be. He had unbounded ambition but little tact and on that account I feared entrusting the correspondence to him. I had no trouble in getting Mr. G. C. Perkins, United States Senator from California, to introduce the measure in the Senate. Mr. Victor H. Metcalf presented it in the House of Representatives. I followed this with letters to the members of the committees of each house giving reasons why it should become law. I also endeavored to interest the men employed in the Brooklyn Navy Yard and those at the Arsenal at Washington, but without success. At the beginning of each session of Congress for several years the bill was introduced by Messrs. Perkins and Metcalf in their respective houses, but beyond that no further notice was taken of it. It was not until President Roosevelt in one of his messages to Congress urged the adoption of the measure that definite action was taken upon it. It was then also that the men in the

Washington Arsenal began to evince an interest in it. It finally became a law, but very much reduced from its original form. I was then no longer in the employ of the Government, and its enactment was taken as a matter of course with surprising stolidity. No attempt has been subsequently taken to restore it to its original form or to improve it in any way, although that is greatly needed.

The eight hour day—

The ship keepers of Vallejo had been agitating for twenty years or more for the privilege of enjoying the benefits of the eight-hour law without a reduction of pay. They had interested both State and national politicians for years in their demand, but without success. They at length formed an organization and were admitted to membership in the Council. Upon familiarizing myself with every detail of their demand I began a correspondence with the Navy Department at Washington, which ended with the demand being granted by Secretary Noble. The reward I received for my work in this matter was to learn that some of the men who had been benefited, did what they could to cloud and belittle my efforts, although at the beginning they offered to pay for my services, which offer I promptly refused. Neither for this, nor for the correspondence concerning the indemnity bill, did I ever put in a demand to the Council or to anyone else for even so much as a postage stamp.

The Atlantic Gulf & Pacific Company, a dredging and contracting corporation, secured from the Government a large share of the work to be done upon a new drydock at the Mare Island Navy Yard. It was reported that this corporation was persistently violating the United States eight-hour law, which, having been amended, rendered contractors and subcontractors upon Government work amenable to the same rules and conditions as were observed upon work directly performed under Government supervision. The State Labor Commissioner was advised of that fact and asked me to act as special deputy without pay to assist in obtaining the evidence necessary to secure a conviction. I agreed to do so, and with the deputy commissioner visited Admiral Millar, then in command of the Yard. The deputy commissioner proved himself lamentably deficient in tact and left the Admiral in his office in high dudgeon without accomplishing anything satisfactory. The deputy made such an outrageous blunder at the commencement of the interview that anything that I might have said would have been entirely useless. So I said nothing and with the deputy retired with the best grace possible. I resolved to have nothing further to do with Mr. Meyers, the Labor Commissioner, or with his deputy, and set about and did procure the evidence necessary to secure an indictment. I obtained still more conclusive evidence which I forwarded to United States District Attorney Frank Coombes, upon the strength of which the corporation was duly convicted and fined. This was an important victory at the time as it guaranteed to the large number of men employed in the construction of the drydock a strict observance of the eight-hour law, which all government contractors looked upon as a dead letter. The men for whose benefit I made the fight seemed totally indifferent about it and looked at it as one of the things that would have come to them anyway.

Early closing for store clerks—

The clerks in the retail stores in Vallejo were required to be at their posts during any and all hours that the proprietors felt like keeping the stores open, which was until ten o'clock every night during the week except on Saturdays and on Yard pay-days when they worked somewhat longer hours. On Sundays, the stores were kept open until noon. A decided opposition was developed to the proposition to limit the working hours of the clerks, directed by what was called a "Merchants' Association." Upon inquiry I found that the latter body consisted of four persons, the other dealers having abandoned it by consenting to a new and reduced time schedule. A very interesting but brief controversy took place between the president of the "Merchants' Association" and myself. The gentleman assailed me as a stranger who, he claimed, had no right to interfere in affairs concerning the citizens of Vallejo. He also charged that I was a "sandlotter'' and a follower of Dennis Kearney. I made the town laugh at the gentleman and I believe that he regretted beginning the fight, for he failed to continue it, and we afterwards became the best of friends. The closing of the stores on Sundays and at regular hours in the evenings did much to improve the condition of the clerks in Vallejo.

Labor Council politics—

All sorts of schemes were presented from time to time in the Labor Council of Vallejo, intended by the authors to benefit in some manner either the people or the city and often both. Trade unionism was a new thing to most of those who composed the Council and they felt it to be their duty to regulate everything needing regulation whether they had the power to do it or not. Besides being a trade union body they considered themselves a central improvement club. To inexperienced men this was natural enough. It compelled me to be on the lookout for the many new and often impracticable proposals presented and have them put aside.

San Francisco had made great progress in the way of organization, which the victories of several great strikes had aided substantially. The prominent labor unionists of that city, like their predecessors of that and other cities in days long past, felt that their numbers were sufficiently great to warrant entering the political arena. These men believed that it was only through politics that they could hope to receive the reward which they believed themselves entitled to as compensation for their work as unionists, notwithstanding the fact that many of them were then and had been for years in receipt of comfortable salaries as union secretaries, union business agents, etc. The disposition to subordinate trade unionism to politics has been a favorite method at all times with the men who care only to attain prominence by their connection with unionism and who seek their individual personal advancement. There was not a prominent member of any trade union in San Francisco who had the courage or disposition to protest against this method of prostituting the labor movement.[86]

The spirit rampant in San Francisco soon took possession of the politically ambitious in Vallejo. The secretary of the Council, John Davidson, developed a desire to become a member of the School Board of Vallejo and if possible to become its president. I was always opposed to such amalgamations and pretensions and opposed every endeavor to make him a labor union candidate. He and his supporters regarded my opposition as purely personal. I had no feeling of the sort, but why he wanted the position was unfathomable to me, for it carried no salary and entailed a great amount of labor. My opposition engendered considerable ill

[86] Roney is in error in making such a statement, for a number of the more conservative labor leaders of San Francisco bitterly and vigorously opposed the efforts of the local unions in supporting the Union Labor Party.—Ed.

feeling, although I had none of it myself. As time passed this feeling became intensified, Davidson's supporters because of his election being unusually militant. There was nothing that I proposed but what was rejected. Men who actually approved of some of my proposals voted against them as a demonstration of Davidson's strength.

Father Yorke—

One instance of this opposition I wish particularly to record. In order to add to the strike fund[87] of the teamsters' union in San Francisco it was proposed to have the Reverend Father Yorke deliver a lecture in Vallejo under the auspices of the Labor Council. This proposition was made by a member who had been notoriously opposed to Father Yorke when he was so ably and successfully combatting the aggressions of religious intolerance which infected San Francisco in the nineties. The annihilation of religious bigotry by the liberal-minded voters of San Francisco was so overwhelming that much of the credit for its success was attributed to Father Yorke. A keen, farsighted labor union politician, who subsequently became inordinately wealthy, began the exploitation of the priest as a champion of Labor with marked success.

I considered the Father's entrance into the strife of unionism an encroachment to be resented by every well meaning trade unionist. I had no objection to his advocacy of our Cause at such times and where

[87] This strike occurred in 1901.—Ed.

it needed defending, but I did not want him or any other preacher to assume the rôle of and be heralded as our champion. I believed that we had as good brains and as clear minds in the labor movement as there were out of it, and I wished Labor to be redeemed by laborers. I had no objection to Father Yorke's exposing the ignorance and deficiencies of blatant clerical bigots. That was within the line of his duty as a liberal, profound thinker and speaker. But as a trade union advocate, I proposed that we should do our own advocating. My reasons did not weigh with the majority of the Council, particularly with the reformed bigots, and it was voted down. The morning after Father Yorke's lecture I offered to introduce him to one of those who had voted for his coming, but the latter declined by informing me that he never spoke to a Catholic priest and would never do so willingly. I reminded him that he voted for Father Yorke's coming, when he amazed me by saying that he had done so merely to vote against me. The same man voted against a proposition I made in favor of government ship building for the sole reason that I made it. An organization originating from hate or held together by that motive has little to commend it whatever its pretensions.

Farewell to unionism—

The disputes continuously arising and their ending were amusing and ridiculous. I wrote several fictitious reports of the meetings of the Council in a way to make the members supremely ridiculous. They bore it complacently enough for a while, but finally preferred charges against me on the grounds of bringing them into contempt and of destroying what they termed their usefulness. Upon a flimsy technicality I was ruled out of order by the chairman, and so bade adieu to the Labor Council of Vallejo and the trade union movement forever.

FINIS

VI

FINIS

It has been a matter of much concern to me to know if the years that I have spent chiefly in the labor movement have been productive of any real benefit to those whom I hoped to benefit when I began. Every man who contributes in any way by thought or deed becomes a factor of more or less account in whatever enterprise he engages in. If his labors are misdirected or aimless then his work is clearly useless, no matter how busy he may have been. The accomplishment of a given purpose demands concentration and the expenditure of all his energy, mental and physical, to that end.

I began my career as a boy, weighed down with the horrors and suffering of the abject poor. I was taught to believe that that was the normal condition of humanity, one portion in a state bordering on permanent starvation and the other reveling in luxuries and extravagance. This belief sat very hard upon me, but I could see no way out of it that commended itself to my untutored Christian mind. The poor were called "God's poor" and were told that their reward would be in Heaven if they endured poverty and its accompanying degradation. Ignorance is conducive to the inspiring of high religious ideals in any one. Nor do I believe that they are God sent. Men may voluntarily suffer hardship and penury and all the evils arising from poverty if they believe such sufferings will advance them in some line of endeavor, spiritual or material, toward the attainment of a great end or object. To doom the helpless and innocent to such a fate and tell them that it is God's will is a blasphemy repugnant to the ordinances of God and every instinct of compassionate humanity. The poor, starving abject creature, shivering in his rags in his filthy hovel, is just as dear to the Merciful Providence of Him who redeemed us as the most exalted potentate directing armies or dictating policies.

I still retain the fundamentals of my earliest experiences and education. I sometimes think that my father did me wrong when he launched me into the midst of the poverty so widely prevalent in the commercial and manufacturing metropolis of Ireland. To mitigate that poverty made me a rebel in Ireland. When I discovered that the land of so-called Liberty in the Western Seas held as much poverty and destitution as Ireland, I became an active trade union propagandist. The fallacy of believing that there is less abject heart-rending poverty in America in proportion to population than there is in Europe is, I believe, being demonstrated very conclusively. For my own part the illusion of America's freedom from degrading destitution was dissipated before I was three months in the United States. A wider experience and more concrete knowledge of prevailing conditions only too painfully confirmed my first conclusions.

INDEX

INDEX

www.ingramcontent.com/pod-product-compliance
Ingram Content Group UK Ltd.
Pitfield, Milton Keynes, MK11 3LW, UK
UKHW040231290926
15471UKWH00002B/129

9 780520 349476